PRAISE FOR *EMBEDDING SUSTAINABILITY*

'I very much enjoyed reading this book. It teaches you that no matter your job, you play a role in the transition to a more sustainable future. Filled with useful tips, real-world examples, and advice on leading by example, it's inspiring and actionable for everyone, regardless of whether 'sustainability' is in your job title or not!'

Kirsten van Zandwijk, Senior Director of Sustainability & Partnerships for ASEAN & South Pacific, The Coca-Cola Company

'*Embedding Sustainability* is a vital resource for leaders dedicated to shaping a just world where children can thrive. This book inspires us to act responsibly and innovatively, reminding us that every decision we make impacts the future of our children. It's a call to reduce our footprint and make mindful choices in how we travel and consume, aligning our actions with the urgent need to safeguard our planet for future generations.'

Pim Kraan, Chief Executive, Save the Children Netherlands

'Every job is a climate job. The climate crisis is all-encompassing, and our approach to addressing it needs to be the same. Every trade, every skill set, every job function needs to be brought to bear, and this book is a groundbreaking and essential guide to doing just that. You don't need to find a new job to work on climate change – you can do the work from right where you are. This book will show you how.'

Jamie Alexander, Former Founding Director, Drawdown Labs

'Pia Heidenmark Cook and Lisen Wirén have given every senior business executive a most timely gift – a clear, compelling and comprehensive playbook for operationalizing sustainability in ways that drive real impact for business, for people and the planet. They provide practical guidance for leaders but do so without pulling punches on the urgency to drive more change in the way business

operates, given the existential threats of climate change, nature loss and inequality. An indispensable read for current and future Chief Sustainability Officers.'
Chris Coulter, CEO, GlobeScan

'Grounded in both practical wisdom and profound insights, *Embedding Sustainability* offers a compass for leaders embarking on the transformative journey toward sustainability. From fostering collaboration to nurturing personal resilience, it empowers leaders to navigate challenges with purpose, and drive meaningful change within their organizations and beyond. An indispensable resource for anyone committed to creating a more sustainable and equitable world.'
Barbara Martin Coppola, CEO, Decathlon

'*Embedding Sustainability* is an essential guide that clearly delineates the complex interconnections between environmental degradation and social issues such as how climate change contributes to forced migration. This book provides practical strategies for organizations aiming to integrate sustainability and social impact deeply into their core operations, effectively navigating and addressing these multifaceted challenges.'
Olga Dimytrow, Digital Transformation Officer, UNHCR

'This is a very timely and practical book. Businesses are under growing pressure to transform to become sustainable, resilient and remain relevant. This book is a practical guide for leaders that draws on both theory and lots of invaluable experience.'
Ben Kellard, Director of Business Strategy, Cambridge Institute for Sustainability Leadership (CISL)

'Pia Heidenmark Cook and Lisen Wirén have written the go-to handbook for sustainability professionals. A key book for anyone who wants to help steer their organization to be people and planet positive.'
Steve Howard, Vice Chair, Sustainability, Temasek

'Implementing a sustainable business transformation is the challenge of our time. *Embedding Sustainability* is as thoughtful as it is practical in aiding sustainability champions to increase their impact. A must read! Lisen Wirén and Pia Heidenmark Cook's new book is a treasure trove of practical advice on how to make a difference on one of today's biggest challenges.'
Florian Hoffmann, CEO, The DO Group

'*Embedding Sustainability* is a vital read for anyone eager to weave together personal and collective transformations for a sustainable future. It has become increasingly clear that individual actions and mindsets need to evolve. Drawing on behavioral change, this book illuminates the many roles each individual can use to co-create a more resilient planet. This book not only guides readers through the complexity of these changes but also inspires the necessary courage and innovation to embed them into our daily lives.'
Per Espen Stoknes, Psychologist & Associate Professor, BI Norwegian Business School

'This is an exceptional book with clear guidance on how to embed sustainability and examples that should get CSOs and all leaders to think about their current and future business models. It's a roadmap for a successful journey! The world needs you to read this book and get inspired to leave a significant positive mark.'
Helle Bank Jørgensen, CEO, Competent Boards

'*Embedding Sustainability* is a crucial guide for any leader determined to intertwine social and environmental objectives within their organizational fabric. This book not only illuminates the interconnectedness of our global challenges but also showcases the transformative power of partnerships between corporates and social businesses. With urgency and clarity, it provides actionable insights and tools that empower businesses to lead with purpose and accountability in today's complex world.'
Saskia Bruysten, Co-founder, Yunus Social Business

Embedding Sustainability

How to drive organizational transformation

Pia Heidenmark Cook and Lisen Wirén

KoganPage

First published in Great Britain and the United States in 2024 by Kogan Page Limited

2nd Floor, 45 Gee Street
London
EC1V 3RS
United Kingdom
www.koganpage.com

8 W 38th Street, Suite 902
New York, NY 10018
USA

Kogan Page books are printed on paper from sustainable forests.

ISBNs
Hardback 978 1 3986 1627 1
Paperback 978 1 3986 1580 9
Ebook 978 1 3986 1626 4

British Library Cataloguing-in-Publication Data
A CIP record for this book is available from the British Library.

Library of Congress Cataloging-in-Publication Data
A CIP record for this book is available from the Library of Congress.

Typeset by Hong Kong FIVE Workshop, Hong Kong
Print production managed by Jellyfish
Printed and bound by CPI Group (UK) Ltd, Croydon CR0 4YY

CONTENTS

LIST OF FIGURES AND TABLES

Figures

Tables

ACKNOWLEDGEMENTS

Lisen

To my dear children, Maja and Otto, this book is infused with hopes and actionable insights towards creating a brighter, more sustainable and inclusive world for you and your generation.

My deepest thanks go to my life partner, Niels. From the moment I shared the idea of this book with you on a Monday evening, your encouragement and support have been unwavering. Thank you for everything since that pivotal moment. To my family – my parents, Pia and Tojje, and my brothers, Jakob and Johannes – thank you for your foundational support and love. Elin, my dearest friend, your presence and encouragement have been indispensable. To all my friends and loved ones, your enduring support and belief in me – thank you.

Pia

Heartful thanks to my family, Kristofer, Hannah and Emma, for supporting me throughout my career as well as during the book writing process. You three are the most important people in my life. Hannah and Emma, this one is for you – I hope that the world you will inherit will be fair, sustainable and full of exciting opportunities to grow and develop! Thanks to family and close friends for your support and encouragement throughout the years. And to my mum, who always supported and believed in me, wish you were still here.

Together

Embedding Sustainability draws upon learnings accumulated from 15 years (and over 25 years respectively) of working with sustainability, enabled by meeting and working with many fantastic people – colleagues, peers, managers – who have shaped us into who we are today. Appreciate both good and challenging times as you learn from both.

Our heartfelt thanks go to Jens Andersson, Hannah Loake, Chris Williams, Ana Gastélum Dourritzague, Ben Kellard, Kirsten van Zandvik, Leonor Gonzales Valencia, Anouk Seuren and Ann-Sofie Gunnarsson for thoroughly reading through drafts and providing invaluable feedback that greatly enhanced this book. Your contributions made the book what it is today!

We are profoundly grateful to each expert who took the time to share their knowledge and perspectives through interviews, enriching our pages with depth and diversity. Our thanks to Per Espen Stoknes, Jonathan Foley, Maria Wolodarsky, Jakob Trollbäck, Lama Abdulrahman, Sophia Palmes, Ben Kellard, Hilde Jorgensen, Eva Iveroth, Chris Coulter, Laura Betancour, Julika Riegler, Chelsea Tschoerner-Budde, Sarah Garcia, Kresse Wessling, Kali Andersson, Kirsten van Zandvik, Therese Noorlander, Peter Lange, Filip Lundin, Mireille Geisen, Jakob König, Frida Berry Eklund, Kristina Zumpolle, and Fredrik Moberg. Your contributions are not merely names on a page but pivotal voices that have shaped this narrative towards action and transformation in sustainability.

We would like to thank Maria Mendiluce and Ryan Gellert for the insightful forewords, which set the perfect tone for our discussions on sustainability. And thank you to everyone for your kind words about the book. Your endorsements are not only deeply appreciated but also bolster the impact and reach of our work, encouraging broader dialogue and action on these critical issues.

Finally, we thank our publisher for believing in us as authors and in the vision of our book, and for their support throughout this journey.

Together, we share this journey of integrating sustainability into the core of our global community, fuelled by the shared vision of a sustainable tomorrow. Thank you all for being such an integral part of *Embedding Sustainability*.

FOREWORD

As we navigate the impacts of the climate and ecological crisis, it's easy to feel helpless. However, as Patagonia founder Yvon Chouinard often says, 'The cure for depression is action.' At Patagonia, we've long believed that the responsibility for minimizing our footprint and scaling solutions is shared by every employee around the globe. Much like quality and innovation, this commitment must be deeply embedded throughout our culture – a shared philosophy not a function.

Since our founding in 1973, we've experimented with numerous ways to minimize our product footprint through the materials we use and the services we scale to keep product in use as long as possible. We've supported grassroots organizations globally working on the frontlines of the climate and ecological crisis with funding, campaign support and via Patagonia Action Works. And we've done this in partnership with our employees via grants councils, activism hours, and environmental internships. Recognizing that we're running out of time, Yvon and his family restructured the ownership of the company in 2022 so that we now permanently donate 100% of our annual profits to the planet.

I provide this info, not to boast about the work we've done, but as context for the experimental, iterative, imperfect and whole-of-business approach we've tried to model and to scale. And while I recognize that each company is different – industry, ownership, size and reason for being – every company shares a responsibility to minimize their footprint and help clean up the mess that we as humans have made of our natural world. As conservationist David Brower was fond of saying, 'There is no business to be done on a dead planet.'

If you're reading *Embedding Sustainability*, then I will assume you need no convincing of what's at stake and why driving change within the business sector is so critical. What I enjoyed most about Pia and Lisen's framework is that it rests on two core principles. First, minimizing a company's footprint and scaling solutions must be integrated into the roles and responsibilities of every employee across the business. Second, the importance of active listening, clear communication and deep engagement in driving impact.

The book goes beyond theoretical discussions, providing practical tools and solutions – some of which can be implemented quickly. And yet it is clear-eyed on the complexity of the challenges and the reality that there is no finish line in the work to credibly reduce a company's environmental impact. *Embedding Sustainability* also makes clear that to solve the biggest problems we face will take businesses working in partnership with other businesses, with government and with civil society.

Businesses need to understand their supply chains – both those that directly help them bring their products and services to market – and those that provide services to their business. This includes financial institutions, trade organizations and others they spend money with. Gone are the days that taking responsibility solely for your own operations is good enough. We need full-scale systems change. Without that level of collective action, we will be unable to solve the problems that we as humans have created.

Whatever series of events conspired to put this book in front of you, I'm glad they did. While the work required to reverse the climate and ecological crisis can feel daunting, it is also filled with opportunities to learn, lead and impact the world far beyond our short time here. The lessons included in *Embedding Sustainability* provide a framework for the creativity, commitment, collaboration and joy needed to find and scale solutions while allowing us to embrace the reality that often in life the reward for solving a problem is an invitation to a bigger problem. Onward...

Ryan Gellert
CEO, Patagonia

Companies everywhere are on a journey to become more sustainable.

For many, implementing policies to cut emissions and become more resource efficient can be a daunting journey. Yet, like all good adventures, this journey should also be fun, exciting and rewarding for everyone concerned – employees, the board and directors, shareholders and customers alike. To ensure this is the case, businesses must put people at the heart of all sustainability measures. Everyone has a part to play in this journey and the benefits from steps taken to reduce a company's environmental footprint.

Sustainability is not a box-ticking exercise being imposed from on-high. It is not simply a legal requirement demanded by politicians. Sustainability is a business opportunity. Putting your operations on a net-zero trajectory is a chance to show real corporate leadership and make your company stand out from the crowd. Sustainability frontrunners will reap first mover rewards. And these facts stand for companies big and small.

Every day in my CEO role of the We Mean Business Coalition I see businesses striving to do their best to move the needle on sustainability and to introduce change that benefits people and the planet. These are the companies that will thrive today and tomorrow. At We Mean Business, we work with partners and over 15,000 businesses to advance climate leadership. Our goal is to halve emissions by 2030 and to accelerate an inclusive transition to a global net zero economy by 2050.

We define climate leadership through the 4As, namely ambition, action, advocacy and accountability. Ambition means companies setting science-based net zero targets with near-term and long-term goals, in line with the 1.5°C pathway set down in the 2015 Paris Agreement. Action means embedding change within and at all levels of a business. This is a process of innovation and transformation. Done right, climate action unlocks opportunities for business and protects them against risks.

Advocacy means speaking out. Advocacy is essential to bring policy that unlocks investment and delivers action at scale. Corporate climate leaders should use their powerful voices, activities and associations to call for strong policy ambition. All employees should be empowered to speak about the milestones of their company's net zero transition and to share solutions and best practice with others.

Finally, accountability. The climate emergency demands results. It demands that businesses clearly and consistently disclose plans, progress, risks and opportunities to build trust among stakeholders, to direct capital to where it is most needed and to inform strategy. Accountability shows resilience and a company's readiness for the net zero world.

We are also clear that sustainability means an end to fossil fuels. Over 200 businesses representing more than $1.5 trillion in global annual revenue have signed our open letter urging national governments to address the primary cause of climate change: burning fossil fuels. We want to see targets and timelines for phasing out unabated fossil fuels, and an end to all fossil fuel subsidies by 2025. The massive sums of public and private money that continue to be spent on supporting oil, coal and gas must be repurposed towards energy efficiency, renewable energy and other measures to support a people-centered and equitable clean energy transition.

The need for the transition to be fair is also another cornerstone of our approach to climate action. Sustainability plans and policies must ensure a just transition for affected workers and communities, and, on a global level, wealthier countries as historic emitters have the responsibility to be first movers.

This book provides many more examples that illustrate how companies are putting the climate emergency at the heart of their business operations. These companies see climate action for what it really is, a business opportunity that attracts talent and investments and reduces costs.

When companies take a long-term view on climate action they tend to win.

Companies in Europe that had invested heavily in renewables were able to manage the energy crisis, provoked by Russia's invasion of Ukraine, more smoothly than those that had remained dependent on fossil fuels. Consumers increasingly value companies that stand up for human rights, climate change or nature and become loyal purchasers of brands they trust. Investors are decarbonizing their portfolios and will prefer companies that have set a science-based path to net zero over businesses that make vague noises about going green. And governments everywhere are introducing tougher regulations that require companies to do more to reduce their emissions, and protect people and nature.

Companies that have anticipated these changes are best placed to have a competitive advantage. Anticipation is key. Feet dragging and procrastination cannot and will not bring solutions to the climate or the biodiversity crisis, nor will it make businesses successful or ready and able to deal with the challenges the twenty-first century is ready to throw at them. Becoming more sustainable means greater resilience to environmental shocks and to geopolitical risks.

Reliance on local renewable energy sources to power production is a much safer bet than depending on gas imports from far-flung countries. Likewise, having a thorough understanding of suppliers and supply chains will help companies make better decisions when trade routes become congested or impassable because of war or extreme weather events.

The best way to embed sustainability in a company is to bring everyone onboard and to get everyone to feed into net zero plans and proposals. Empowering your team, your employees and your families to unite behind a good purpose is fulfilling and will make the implementation of change easier. Address any backlash and challenges with an open mind. Don't be afraid to try new approaches and to admit if something doesn't work as planned.

Most importantly, make climate action interesting and fun. This is what this book is all about. In the hands of Pia and Lisen, sustainability is anything but boring.

They have done something very special, translating a complex subject into actionable and inspiring ideas.

This book is the perfect place to start or to continue your sustainability journey. Pia and Lisen are highly experienced guides whose words are a pleasure to read and whose ideas and enthusiasm will leave you ready for action. Grounded in real life, this book will enable you to become a sustainability leader at work and at home and empower you to be an engine of change. How you decide to read this book is, of course, up to you. You can choose to read it from cover to cover, but I would recommend you keep it with you as a handbook, as a guide to change, and whenever you need inspiration, some friendly words or some hard business advice, sit down and read the relevant section to lead you forward.

María Mendiluce
CEO, We Mean Business Coalition

PREFACE: GREETINGS FROM THE AUTHORS

'When Lisen approached me about joining her on this project, I was thrilled. Lisen and I worked together at IKEA many years ago, and I've always appreciated her energy, drive and get-it-done attitude. To put this book together, while working full-time with social entrepreneur programmes at IKEA and raising two small children, is just a testament of Lisen's determination and drive, and her wish to share her learnings to inspire others to also find ways to have a positive impact through work.'

'I was absolutely delighted when Pia agreed to join this project. Pia is a senior leader who has dedicated her entire professional life to sustainability. Her commitment and comprehensive understanding of sustainability practices have been an inspiration to me. She has been a guiding light not only as a professional but also in her role as a mother, managing to balance it all with grace.'

The project started with the idea to demonstrate that sustainability transcends job functions and sectors, highlighting a universal responsibility to address pressing social and environmental crises. The focus was on the untapped potential within all professional roles to drive substantial, equitable changes in sustainability practices. When Pia came on board we decided to broaden our approach, leveraging our combined strengths and experiences to enhance the scope and depth of this book. Rather than taking it from the individual work approach, we have adopted an organizational transformation lens for the book. We have collaborated seamlessly, bringing together our unique qualities to create a resource that we believe will energize and inspire you to transform your organization.

We hope you enjoy this book, find inspiration in its pages, and are moved to take action towards embedding sustainability in your own professional context.

Introduction

If you're reading this book, chances are you're deeply invested in sustainability and eager to make a positive social and environmental impact. Your motivations may vary – perhaps you're looking for a career in this growing field; maybe you've just been appointed as a sustainability manager and are seeking to familiarize yourself with the complexities of the role. But more than likely, your commitment transcends the professional sphere; you have probably also been exploring avenues to champion sustainability through other ways of life.

The call to action is clear. It is no longer a question of 'if', but 'how' and 'when'. The world needs your leadership, your ideas, your energy and your commitment. Together, with a unified vision and unyielding resolve, we can and will surmount the challenges that lie ahead. Each one of us and every organization has a significant role to play in this global endeavour. Let's courageously embrace this responsibility, leading change and sculpting a future where sustainability isn't merely an aspiration, but an integral part of our existence.

Through the corridors of time, our actions today will echo as testament to our courage, foresight and collective resolve. Let us seize this opportunity and make every moment count, embedding sustainability at the heart of all that we do. Because a sustainable future isn't just a destination – it's the journey we undertake together. The decisions and actions we take today determine tomorrow's outcomes.

Who this book is for

We firmly believe that in the face of unprecedented challenges, the pursuit of sustainability requires a collective effort. It is not the work of certain sectors; all types of sectors and organizations must contribute. And, it's not just about individuals or specific functions within an organization: we need entire organizations to engage. Thus, every person – no matter which role and function they hold – needs to take part for the sustainability transformation to succeed.

Having said that, this book targets sustainability leaders, especially chief sustainability officers (CSOs), who have the critical task of leading sustainability initiatives across their organizations. The book explores the evolving landscape of sustainability, providing insights into how sustainability can be integrated and transformed into a core element of an organization's business strategy. It also addresses the personal journey of sustainability leaders, offering advice on self-care and resilience. Sustainability is as much about management – managing the implementation process – as it is about leadership, both individual and organizational. And it is as much about change management, resilience and endurance as actual technical skills and competence. To successfully embed sustainability in the organization, all these elements are needed. This book thus aims to equip you with the knowledge and tools to effectively fulfil your role and drive sustainable change within your organization.

However, we've written this book with a broader audience in mind. We, as authors, are passionate about the necessity of inclusive participation in sustainability efforts. While specifically designed for CSOs, the principles and strategies detailed in this book are applicable across a variety of levels and roles within an organization, all aiming towards the common goal of instigating change and starting a sustainability transformation. We are dedicated to embedding sustainability at the heart of organizational operations, and we believe that everyone, in every role and sector, has a crucial part to play in this mission. We hope that this book will offer a practical guide for business leaders who are aiming to achieve a systemic and transformational change in their organization and beyond.

Therefore, whether you are an experienced sustainability leader or just beginning to explore this field, this book has something to offer. Hereafter we will address the reader as the sustainability leader. This encompasses both types of audiences – those who are in a CSO (or similar) role and a wider group of (sustainability) leaders across the organization.

The world needs your leadership

Welcome to one of the most transformative and impactful roles you could ever aspire to: being a CSO[1] or a business leader with the determination to make a positive impact and drive sustainability. We both truly enjoyed holding these roles, where dynamic tasks, collaborative work environments and meaningful external partnerships converge to form an unparalleled experience. Picture it: you're at the crossroads of strategy and execution, shaping the long-term vision of your organization while ensuring the granular details align with your sustainability goals. You're not just ticking boxes; you're painting the big picture and then colouring it, one sustainable choice at a time. You're tasked with the invigorating challenge of not only setting those sustainability goals but also tracking, measuring and reporting on their progress. It's strategy and accountability rolled into one incredible package.

The essence of your role lies in its human element – you're a leader working through people. Whether you're forging internal alliances, or expanding your network at high-profile conferences, your leadership serves as a linchpin for transformative change. Above all, your role holds a promise that few others do: the opportunity to leave a lasting, positive imprint on the world. Imagine heading an organization that isn't just commercially successful, but also socially responsible, environmentally friendly and a catalyst for a greener, more inclusive economy. This isn't just a job; it's a calling – one worth rising for each day and dedicating your best efforts to.

Yet, this is not a journey without its challenges. The growing demands of customers and tightening legislative landscapes make this a tough, yet timely, role. Let's be honest, the urgency of global challenges may at times feel overwhelming. The enormity of these concerns, ranging from climate change to overconsumption, the alarming loss of biodiversity, deeply entrenched inequality and the persistent specter of conflict and social divide, are issues that no longer afford us the luxury of procrastination or indifference. You're at the frontline, grappling with problems that the world is running out of time to solve. In those challenging moments, we recommend taking a step back to recharge, before returning to the fray revitalized and more focused than ever.

Yet, within this immense sea of challenges lies an equally impressive opportunity to galvanize global leadership and promote a transformative shift towards sustainability. Your leadership, indeed, is not just required – it is urgently needed. Today's world does not call for passive observers, but for engaged change agents who are unafraid to confront these global challenges head-on. You, along with every individual and organization that shares this planet, are a crucial part of the solution. We can no longer afford to act in isolation, pursuing disparate goals. Our shared future urges us to act collectively, aligning our efforts towards universally beneficial objectives. So, welcome aboard this incredible journey. Our aim with this book is to empower you to rise to the occasion, providing you with the insights and tools needed to guide and work with your organization towards a sustainable future.

Who are we? Our stories

We got to know each other while working together at IKEA. Pia held the position of CSO for Ingka, the largest IKEA franchisor, between 2017 and 2021. She guided a multinational team comprising regional sustainability managers and topic leaders. She led and steered the efforts of national sustainability managers in each of the markets in which IKEA operated, while also working closely with the global functional leaders across the business. Meanwhile, Lisen wore the mantle of sustainability manager for IKEA's retail operations in the Netherlands. Her role entailed crafting the country-specific sustainability strategy and ensuring its successful implementation across all operations. This role worked through every customer touchpoint, embedding sustainability within the overall customer experience.

We are both originally from Sweden. And in Sweden, or more broadly in Scandinavia, there's a tendency to value flat organizational structures and involve everyone in decision making, reflecting a cultural emphasis on equality. A commitment to sustainability is also deeply ingrained, both as a shared responsibility and a point of community pride. We've had the opportunity to live and work in and travel to many different countries, and we realize that not everyone shares these specific values, particularly the close connection to nature. Scandinavia is by no means perfect, but we do think there are elements worth reflecting on. The focus on open dialogue and broad participation in decision making and equality can create a more inclusive work atmosphere. And the commitment to sustainability is about more than being eco-friendly; it's built into how we think about economics, public policy and even design.

Thanks to more than 20 years of working in sustainability, at IKEA and elsewhere, we bring a diverse range of experiences spanning the energy sector, hospitality, food and beverage, apparel, supply chain, social entrepreneurship, compliance, product design and retail. We've operated at various levels, including project management, country leadership, headquarters and board membership. In this book, we share good examples, insights and case studies, gained from our own experience as well as through our network and the literature. We understand the complexities and challenges of navigating sustainability change journeys and crises, and we place great emphasis on collective effort.

Our motivation for writing this book

We're passionate about people and the planet and are driven to make the world a better place for ourselves, our children and future generations. This book was inspired by the knowledge that it's not enough for just one kind of job, organization or sector to tackle big challenges – everyone needs to chip in. With this book, we hope to contribute to the necessary shift in our approach to the biggest global challenges of our time. It's not just a handbook; it's a strong call to action for everyone to engage in sustainability. We want to inspire as many people as possible to join this journey, to make a collective effort towards a sustainable future. We believe that through shared knowledge, stories and insights, this book can motivate and guide people to make a positive impact on our world. Let's not just read about change; let's be the change.

Pia sits on boards of companies that are on a sustainability (and digital) transformation journey, works as advisor to companies and gives speeches to companies across the world. The realization that many people share the same struggles to become effective and truly have a transformative impact across their organizations led us to meet and discuss if there was a good way to share our learnings beyond what we were already doing. As much as we see tremendous progress across many sectors and geographies, we believe we still need to move faster and at bigger scale. More companies and organizations need to transform what they do and how they do business to fit within planetary boundaries, and this transformation depends on people making a change. We believe that as much as we can change as individuals in isolation, we need to make this change while also influencing others and our organizations to change. We need systemic change, which is about individuals changing and bringing other people with them.

Although this book is aimed at CSOs/heads of sustainability, our firm belief is that anyone can make a difference and contribute to sustainability, regardless of their function and organization. Not only can everyone make a difference, but the objective is to empower each individual, everywhere, to champion change. The sustainability leader's role is to guide and enable this shift, acting as the orchestrating maestro behind the transformation. In this book we focus on the corporate sector, but most non-corporate roles also have a critical role to play in the sustainability transformation. So, in essence, everyone has a role to play.

As authors deeply invested in the sustainability leadership journey, we advocate two foundational principles:

1 The comprehensive integration of sustainability into everything a company does
2 Using a human-centred approach.

We believe that in sprawling organizations, leaders cannot be everywhere at all times, making it imperative to seamlessly embed sustainability across all operations and all jobs, no matter their title or task. It's our firm conviction that this integral approach ensures sustainability remains an ever-present and unwavering focus. We firmly advocate a transformative shift in how we do business and perceive sustainability. Sustainability is no longer a peripheral concern or an optional Corporate Social Responsibility (CSR) project. The present demands that we elevate sustainability, embedding it as a central pillar of our business strategies. This transformation is about not only minimizing consumption, but actively redefining business frameworks that benefit society, champion circularity and positively influence the world. It's imperative for businesses to boldly venture down this path as hesitance could lead to irrelevance.

We also believe that a human-centred approach is the very essence of effective leadership and change management. Central to this philosophy is the practice of active listening – a genuine, in-depth engagement with the perspectives and sentiments of others. This human-centric philosophy naturally extends to a suite of skills we consider invaluable. Communication is the cornerstone, requiring clarity, active engagement and tailored messaging. Emotional intelligence and empathy allow for richer, more meaningful interactions, while adaptability and resilience demonstrate a steadfast commitment even in the face of challenges. Conflict resolution and negotiation skills ensure smooth sailing in turbulent waters, and visionary thinking helps us keep the long-term impact in sight. Embracing teamwork, collaboration and cultural awareness ensures we resonate across diverse groups, while problem-solving skills help navigate any challenges that arise.

Discovering the transformative power of collective action was a game-changer for Lisen, as she explains in the case study that follows.

CASE STUDY Sustainability is everyone's job

I fondly look back at my job as sustainability manager at a time when sustainability was more of a sideliner than the focal point it has become today. At that time, despite recognizing its importance, most (other) companies did not actively manage sustainability.[2] I realize my experience probably resonates with many in similar roles today. Working together with a small team, my responsibilities were diverse, ranging from waste management to sustainability-related media and partnership relations. My days were filled with a wide range of activities: drafting strategic plans for sustainable store formats, creating recycled textile collections, training colleagues in sustainability practices and staying updated on environmental legislation. While my schedule was flooded with opportunities for impactful change, this experience also highlighted a crucial insight shared by many sustainability leaders: tackling sustainability with a handful of people is far from ideal. It neither harnesses the full potential of the organization nor aligns seamlessly with its broader goals and capabilities.

There was a moment of clarity when I understood that working together would multiply our efforts and effect. The interest in sustainability was there; what was missing was a broader awareness and skill set across the retail country organization. So, I pivoted. Thereafter, nearly 80 per cent of my time was invested in cultivating this awareness and competence. Together with key stakeholders, I held workshops, refined our HR processes to include sustainability criteria and collaborated closely across functions. With a coherent strategy, shared responsibilities and a roadmap, the vision became increasingly achievable. The transformation was monumental.

Together, we made considerable strides in both the climate and circularity agendas of the organization, even as we continued to invest in creating a more equitable society. A more detailed overview of how sustainability was embedded throughout this organization and into every function is found in Chapter 7. This movement happened thanks to the hard work of the entire organization, not a few individuals. And what I have brought with me is the realization that this is a marathon, not a sprint.

What we hope this book will give you

Throughout these pages, we invite you to delve deeper into the concept of embedded sustainability, unravel its vast potential and glean insights into how it can be effectively implemented within your sphere of influence. Now more than ever, we must embed sustainability into the DNA of our operations, challenging the status quo and catalysing a transformation towards a more resilient, inclusive and sustainable future. The book touches upon why a sustainability transformation is important, but the focus is on how to make it happen: we have aimed to provide a step-by-step guide, or 'CSO handbook', that you can revert to for guidance and support when needed. We don't think the book needs to be read from beginning to end; instead, you can dip into the chapters relevant for your transformation journey.

We hope to broaden your understanding of sustainability, revealing its extensive connections with various aspects of our world. Our goal is to illustrate the interconnections – not only the challenges but also the ways sustainability influences every facet of an organization. We aim to empower you with the insight and strategies needed to effectively integrate and embed sustainability within your organization, guiding you in leading transformative change – no matter where in your organization you are placed. We know first-hand that there are many conflicting messages and goals in an organization. Hopefully, this book will provide you with guidance on how teams across the entire organization can align around a common purpose.

Working towards a better world is arguably the most critical mission one can undertake. To endure, despite sometimes losing hope, is essential. We have therefore – and this is perhaps unique to this book – dedicated a section of the book (see Chapter 10) to resilience and health, recognizing the substantial demands of this role.

Interviews and case studies

The central theme of this book is that sustainability is not a niche domain but, rather, vital across all sectors and professions. It's crucial for everyone, whether they are working in waste management, education, banking or any other sector, to embrace sustainability for its full potential and benefits to be realized in both organizational and societal contexts. We illustrate this through concrete examples and interviews with diverse individuals leading social and environmental impacts in various sectors and functions. These interviews were conducted during 2021 and 2022, with people mainly from our own networks.

These stories aim to provide practical examples of sustainability in action and inspire readers. The goal is to show that everyone has a role in this collective mission and to encourage readers to share these inspiring tales within their organizations, reinforcing the idea that every person is key to driving meaningful change. Moreover, throughout the book, we also delve into insights from various companies and organizations and draw upon and share experiences from our own work. We hope this approach will provide a rich tapestry of real-world examples, illustrating the application of sustainability principles across different contexts and industries.

Limitations of the book

While there are abundant resources available – books, platforms and courses – that go deep into the specific legislation and frameworks for sustainability, it's crucial to recognize that this is a rapidly evolving field. What's current and state-of-the art today could very well be outdated tomorrow. The pace of change in sustainability regulations and best practices is so fast that a comprehensive guide could become obsolete almost as soon as it's printed.

That's why the purpose of this book isn't to provide an exhaustive overview of every legal and structural detail. Instead, we're focusing on what we believe has enduring value: the leadership skills and practical tools you'll need to embed sustainability into the very DNA of your organization. This book aims to provide you with the agility and insight to adapt to new sustainability landscapes as they emerge. We want to help you not just navigate but thrive amid change, inspiring those around you to become part of the solution. It's about equipping you with the vision and strategies to lead your organization through the complexities of sustainability, no matter how those complexities may evolve.

Structure of the book

This book is divided into three distinct parts, each meticulously designed to guide and support you as a sustainability leader on your journey to integrate sustainability into your organization.

Part 1: Understanding our world and the evolution of sustainability: The first part lays the foundational groundwork, focusing on broadening your understanding of the world we live in and the evolving landscape of sustainability. It delves into the historical development of the sustainability field, offering insights into how it has transformed and expanded over time as well as giving numerous hands-on examples of companies that have already come far in their sustainability transformation journey. This part also covers the role of the individual: how you and me – no matter if we are leading sustainability in an organization or have another job completely – are instrumental in making companies succeed in their sustainability transformation.

Part 2: Practical integration of sustainability: The second part of the book is where theory meets practice. It walks you through the tangible process of embedding sustainability into your organization. This section is rich with practical advice, providing a plethora of tools and real-life examples that illustrate how to effectively integrate sustainable practices into various aspects of your organization. Thus, in these six chapters, you will learn more about the different tools and concepts that can help you on the sustainability transformation journey.

Part 3: Leadership and self-care in sustainability: The final part serves as an enabler, focusing on the principles of leadership necessary to drive sustainable change. It addresses the personal challenges that often accompany this journey, offering guidance on self-care and resilience. This section acknowledges that while the path to sustainability can be demanding, maintaining your well-being is crucial for sustained success and impact. This part is therefore about guiding you, as an individual change agent, on how to build capacity and resilience to create the change necessary, and how to learn from other individuals who are already on this journey.

Collectively, these three parts comprise the essence of *Embedding Sustainability*. Our hope is that this book not only bolsters your capabilities as a leader but also strengthens the sustainability stance and performance of your organization. We aim to empower you with the knowledge, skills and inspiration needed to make a meaningful impact in the ever-important field of sustainability.

Endnotes

1 Throughout this book, we will use CSO, sustainability manager and head of sustainability interchangeably, as companies use many different titles that mean more or less the same thing.

2 How companies manage sustainability, McKinsey, 1 March 2010. www.mckinsey.com/capabilities/sustainability/our-insights/how-companies-manage-sustainability-mckinsey-global-survey-results (archived at https://perma.cc/B3MW-SSU4)

PART 1
Understanding our world and the evolution of sustainability

The field of sustainability is massive and complex, and it includes a wide range of interdependent topics. These topics evolve over time, and therefore it is fundamental for sustainability professionals to adapt and stay updated with the latest trends and challenges. As society and organizations continue to address social and environmental challenges, the role of sustainability leaders will consequently continue to evolve and expand over time.

Part 1 of this book is structured into three comprehensive chapters, each designed to provide a foundational understanding of the key aspects of sustainability in the context of modern leadership and business practices:

1. **Global sustainability challenges:** We start by presenting the major sustainability challenges the world is currently facing. This chapter examines environmental, social and economic issues on a global scale, providing an overview of the critical challenges that need to be addressed, and underlines the interdependence between social, economic and environmental topics.

2 **The evolving role of sustainability leadership:** This chapter delves into how the role of sustainability leaders has transformed over time. It covers the expanding scope of responsibilities, the shifting dynamics within organizations, and the increasing importance of integrating sustainability into core business strategies. It stresses how important it is that we as employees get engaged in sustainability, no matter which job function we hold.

3 **The business case for sustainability:** This chapter makes a compelling case for why sustainability is not just a moral imperative, but also a business one. It outlines the important role of the corporate sector in enabling society's transition to a just, fair and more sustainable or regenerative state. This chapter aims to equip leaders with the arguments and evidence needed to advocate for sustainability initiatives within their organizations.

Each of these chapters is designed to support you in gaining a comprehensive understanding of sustainability. They offer insights, practical tools and real-life examples to help you navigate the complexities of sustainability in your role as a leader or a business professional. By the end of Part 1, you will have a solid foundation to understand the broader context in which sustainability operates and how it can be effectively integrated into business strategies and practices.

Global sustainability challenges

01

In a rapidly evolving field such as sustainability, comprehensive guides are at risk of becoming out of date within a few days of their circulation. Keeping this pace in mind, this chapter is designed to offer you a high-level perspective, focusing on the broader strokes that have more enduring relevance. While the nitty-gritty of legislation is undeniably important, our aim here is to point you towards valuable sources for that information and highlight the long-term trends that are shaping the sustainability landscape. This will ensure that you are not just well informed but also well prepared to adapt and evolve in a field characterized by rapid changes. By understanding the overarching themes and trajectories, you'll be better positioned to lead with vision and wisdom, making meaningful contributions to sustainability that stand the test of time. This chapter is enriched with multiple case studies to reinforce the core message.

The global context

We are making progress...

Even if it might not feel like it when you read or watch the news, Professor Hans Rosling states that the world is getting better and safer and that humans are healthier and live longer than ever.[1] Decades of development work have been fruitful, and compared to a hundred years ago, many people have been lifted out of poverty and enjoy an improved quality of life. For example, a century ago, the global child mortality rate was much higher than it is today. Thanks to medical advancements and public health initiatives, more children now live past their fifth birthday than ever before.

Rosling's data highlights that in the 1800s, only a few countries had child mortality rates lower than 10 per cent, but now, most nations have achieved this milestone. Additionally, global literacy rates have improved significantly over the past hundred years. While most of the world's population was illiterate in the early twentieth century, today over 86 per cent of adults worldwide can read and write.

Moreover, climate scientists Johan Rockström and Owen Gaffney point out that although we have crossed six out of nine planetary boundaries,[2] there are significant positive systems changes in motion.[3] They highlight that these movements are following an exponential pathway, rather than a linear one. That means that although change might start small and slow, it can grow in importance in a relatively short amount of time. With regards to *political powers*, Rockström and Gaffney mention more substantial commitments on climate among the more prominent economic regions: Europe, China and the US.[4] Looking at the *financial aspect*, today solar power is the cheapest energy source, which creates strong financial incentives to transition. The entire energy transition has solid economic advantages. Energy costs are high, and we are detaching ourselves from the running costs by investing in renewable sources. Finally, *technical innovations* present massive opportunities through, for example, 5G, biotechnology and artificial intelligence (AI).

Although we should not rely on technology to solve everything, we must utilize the potential of innovations to maximize their benefits for solving our social and environmental challenges. 'Fridays for Future' is perhaps the most prominent and substantial example of a fast-growing *people's movement*. It started with the Swedish activist, Greta Thunberg's school striking outside the Swedish parliament. Within just a couple of years, it had grown to millions of people worldwide, striking for stricter legislation on greenhouse gas emissions. Looking at such examples, we can be confident that it has the potential to grow massively during the coming years. According to Rutger Bregman, a historian and author of the book *Humankind*, we are underestimating the power and goodwill of people in climate science.[5] We can overcome the humanitarian and climate crisis with sufficient awareness and guidance. People are good, and we will do good things in the right environment.

To summarize, compared to a few years back there has been a massive development in legislation, classification systems and methods to support the transition and movement towards sustainable development goals. Over the past few decades, we've witnessed notable progress in poverty reduction and diminished child mortality rates. While the concept of exponential change can be hard to grasp, it's crucial to trust that transformative shifts are under way. Even if we can't see it every day amid the noise of challenges, countless positive developments are unfolding. We strongly encourage the sharing and communication of these positive perspectives. It's crucial to recognize the positive momentum on a grand scale. There's immense power in collective optimism; our firm belief is that one positive action has the potential to ignite a cascade of further positive actions. This idea that positive news stories bring people together is backed up by research: 'News stories that focused on solutions were shown to boost a person's belief in their ability to make a difference.'[6]

... while still dealing with a multi-crisis situation...

At the same time, we are facing a severe humanitarian and environmental crisis. Halfway to the 2030 deadline for the Sustainable Development Goals (SDGs), the 2023 SDG Progress Report reveals that only 15 per cent are on track, emphasizing the urgent need for increased investments and action. The report, published in July 2023, highlights how challenges like the climate crisis, economic strains and the aftermath of the Covid-19 pandemic are hindering progress, especially for the most vulnerable.[7] Secretary-General António Guterres cautions, 'Unless we act now, the 2030 Agenda will become an epitaph for a world that might have been,' emphasizing the urgency of immediate action.[8]

Since the 1990s, and particularly since 2010, fewer people have been living in extreme poverty, which means earning less than $2 a day.[9] But this positive trend was arrested because of the Covid pandemic, ongoing conflicts in some countries and climate change. Ongoing geopolitical conflicts across the world – the war that broke out in Ukraine in 2022 and the humanitarian crisis as a result of civil war in Syria since 2011 to name a few – present severe setbacks, mainly in terms of humanitarian work and environmental destruction. The war in Ukraine also impacted the global food and energy market, causing heavy price jumps and increased costs of living. The world is inherently unequal, with disparities in wealth, opportunity and access to resources varying greatly across different regions and communities.[10] Women, young people and those with low-paying or non-regular jobs, especially in cities, are struggling the most. According to the UN, the Covid pandemic took the world back a decade in terms of development work.[11]

In many regions, there is an increasing polarization, coupled with threats to freedom of speech and democracy.[12] This threatens to destabilize nations and groups and erode the foundation of open societies, driving divisions among populations. Technological advancements, especially in AI, while offering incredible opportunities for progress,[13] also pose significant risks by potentially concentrating power, manipulating information and invading privacy.[14]

... *often driven by climate change and biodiversity loss...*

Climate change and inequalities are the biggest challenges of our time.[15] The Intergovernmental Panel on Climate Change (IPCC) warns that the climate breakdown will present more severe effects than predicted and that there is only a slim chance of avoiding its worst consequences.[16] At the time of writing, in 2023, the climate was already changing, and we had reached an average global temperature increase of about 1.1 degrees Celsius. Research by Berkeley Earth even shows that in 2023, for the first time, the global annual average was above 1.5 degrees, the limit set out by the Paris Agreement.[17] Even in the most optimistic scenario where we would rapidly decarbonize our economies by 2030, the warming effect of the greenhouse gases emitted has locked in some degree of changing climate, at least in the short term. The effects of climate change are both severe and varied, touching every facet of society. The evidence is clear: glaciers are melting, sea levels are rising and weather patterns are shifting, causing heatwaves, droughts, floods, rising sea levels, storms and wildfires. And many animal and plant species are becoming extinct.[18]

Activities such as burning fossil fuels, deforesting large areas and farming livestock are key contributors to the shifting climate and rising global temperatures. Major contributors to these emissions include energy consumption, transportation, electricity, heating, construction, agriculture and deforestation. Despite increased awareness, greenhouse gas emissions, driven by our current economic model, continue to rise.[19] These emissions trap heat, subsequently changing climates both on land and in our oceans.

The IPCC estimates that these unavoidable climate impacts will drive 32–132 million people into extreme poverty in the next decade alone, as many areas around the world are at risk of becoming uninhabitable.[20] For instance, Kiribati, an island nation in the Pacific, is already grappling with the effects of rising sea levels. In anticipation, the nation's leader has procured land in Fiji as a potential relocation spot for its 100,000 inhabitants.[21] And across the globe, the summer of 2023 brought extreme weather events, causing severe damage and losses, both material and in human lives. If global temperatures surge by an average of 3 degrees, which is a plausible scenario given current trends, sea levels could inundate areas home to 10 per cent of the world's population. Research by Climate Central suggests that cities such as Amsterdam, New Orleans, Venice and Bangkok might face severe threats as early as 2030.[22]

Humans have always relied on ecosystems for essentials like clean air, water, food and shelter. However, climate change, primarily caused by human-induced greenhouse gas emissions, is globally impacting ecosystems. Oceans are absorbing more carbon dioxide, leading to coral reef damage, reduced fish habitats and vulnerable coastlines. Farming communities are seeing decreased crop yields, risking global food supplies. Climate change is anticipated to exacerbate natural disasters and weather extremes, with warmer temperatures increasing droughts and storm intensities. While these issues will impact all, the poorest will be most affected. Nature operates as a vast, interconnected system. Hence, disruptions in one area can ripple out, affecting ecosystems globally. For instance, it was shown in 2021 that the Amazon rainforest, a vital sink for our carbon emissions, had started releasing more carbon than it was absorbing, due to rampant deforestation. Without the protective influence of the Amazon, our trajectory towards irreversible climate change accelerates.[23] Similarly, forests in Russia, home to the planet's largest expanse of natural forests (23 per cent of global forest cover), face threats from illegal logging and wildfires. As temperatures rise, Russia's permafrost layers are beginning to thaw.[24]

While much attention has been given to climate change, the issue of bio diversity loss is often overlooked. Biodiversity, encompassing all life forms from genes to ecosystems, is the bedrock of our existence, providing vital resources like food, water, and medicine. Our planet's diverse ecosystems, including forests, wetlands and oceans, play a crucial role in absorbing over half of all carbon emissions, thereby mitigating climate change impacts. Ecosystems provide countless benefits to society, such as clean drinking water, carbon storage, storm protection and food from agriculture.[25]

From 1970 to 2012, wildlife population reduced by 58 per cent.[26] In 2015, 50 million acres of forests were lost, marking a significant increase from 2001.[27] This decline in biodiversity stems from human actions such as poaching, overfishing, deforestation and plastic pollution in oceans. Human activities, primarily land conversion for agriculture, coupled with climate change, endanger numerous species and entire ecosystems. For example, deforestation has turned parts of the Amazon rainforest from carbon sinks to carbon sources, and rising ocean temperatures threaten to obliterate most remaining coral reefs. This decline in the diversity of plant and animal life undermines ecosystem resilience and adaptability. The consequences reach beyond environmental collapse; they pose immediate risks to human societies, economies and even individual well-being. Biodiversity loss could eliminate species with medicinal potential, disrupt essential natural services like water purification and make us more susceptible to diseases. In essence, diminishing biodiversity jeopardizes both our environment and our way of life.[28]

In summary, the loss of biodiversity compromises the health of ecosystems, posing direct and indirect threats to human survival and well-being. Efforts to conserve trees, bees or lions aren't just about safeguarding individual species. Despite our urban-centric lives, our well-being is inextricably linked to healthy ecosystems. As highlighted in our interview (later in this chapter) with Julika Riegler, the communications director of the International Fund for Animal Welfare (IFAW), the interconnected nature of ecosystems means that a disturbance in one region can ripple across the globe. We must treat nature as our sanctuary, not as merely a resource to exploit at will. After all, nature isn't just a segment of our society; it underpins society's very existence.

Efforts to combat climate change and biodiversity loss are interwoven. While forests still cover 30 per cent of our land, peatlands, though accounting for just 3 per cent of global land, store double the carbon of all forests. Similarly, mangroves can sequester carbon at rates up to four times higher than terrestrial forests. By enhancing nature's capacity to absorb emissions, we can achieve about one-third of the necessary greenhouse gas emission reductions in a decade. Internationally, two key agreements, the UN Framework Convention on Climate Change (UNFCCC) and the Convention on Biological Diversity (CBD), address these intertwined crises. Recent milestones include the Kunming-Montreal Global Biodiversity Framework of 2022, which aligns with the Paris Agreement's goals to combat both biodiversity loss and climate change. The agreement includes ambitious targets like conserving at least 30 per cent of the world's land, fresh water and oceans, while also respecting the rights of Indigenous peoples and local communities.[29]

> We need to get business, government, and individuals to understand that nature is not only wonderful, but also economically valuable. Indeed, nature is the fundamental underpinning to human well-being. One way is to connect nature to what concerns people most – how to make lives better, protect health, create

jobs, and strengthen the economy. Whether they grew up in the city or the country, and no matter what they've studied or read, every person shares those concerns.[30]

... and an outdated linear economic model

Our current economic system is at the heart of several environmental crises, including raw material scarcity, climate change and biodiversity loss. This system largely follows a linear model: we extract resources, use them to create products and then dispose of these products, often without considering reuse or regeneration. Such an approach leads to the depletion of natural resources and significant environmental damage.[31]

The environmentalist and author Paul Hawken, in *The Ecology of Commerce*, highlights the critical need to rethink our entire economic approach. He suggests adopting sustainable practices like biomimicry, efficient resource use, minimizing waste and ensuring social justice.[32] The problem of plastic pollution is starkly illustrated by the fate of discarded plastic bottles, which can linger in landfills for up to 450 years. Over 8 million tons of plastic waste enter our oceans annually, causing long-term environmental harm. Of the world's plastic waste, which amounts to 8.3 billion metric tons since its creation, only about 9 per cent has been recycled.[33] While recycling efforts are valuable, a more comprehensive solution lies in shifting to a circular economy. This model focuses on the perpetual cycle of use and reuse, essentially eliminating the concept of waste. We will dig deeper into circularity in chapters 3 and 5.

Ellen MacArthur

In 2005, Ellen MacArthur became the fastest solo sailor to circle the globe. This intense journey, where she was entirely reliant on limited resources, provided her with a profound understanding of the concept of 'finite'. Drawing parallels between her experience at sea and the world's economy, she recognized that our linear system of consumption was unsustainable. Ellen realized that, just as she had a finite number of supplies on her boat, the world operates with limited resources, from metals in our gadgets to the sand in our buildings. Inspired, she founded the Ellen MacArthur Foundation, aiming to shift our economy from its current wasteful trajectory to a circular model, where resources are reused, waste is eliminated and natural systems are regenerated.[34]

The interconnectivity of sustainability topics

While climate change and biodiversity loss are two environmental challenges, it is important to realize that sustainability is broader than the environment alone. When we mention 'sustainability', what exactly are we referring to? While definitions range from broad to narrow, we favour a more comprehensive perspective. This holistic approach encompasses both social and environmental facets, rather than zeroing in on one specific aspect of sustainability. The widely accepted definition states: 'Meeting the needs of the present without compromising the ability of future generations to meet their own needs.' This understanding stems from the UN Brundtland Commission in 1987.[35] Thus, sustainability has grown to encompass a wide range of social, environmental and economic considerations, and it is poised to continue expanding with the advancement of legislation and escalating societal and environmental demands. Throughout this book, we'll use 'sustainability' and 'social and environmental impact' interchangeably, referencing this all-encompassing view of the challenges we face.

'Nature is our global life support system. Without it our economies cannot function, our societies cannot survive. Yet clean air, healthy soils, or any of the countless value that nature provides rarely make it onto a government balance sheet or a company financial statement.'[36] This perspective isn't new. Native Americans, for instance, have long embraced this mindset following the Seventh Generation Principle,[37] which emphasizes the importance of considering the implications of our actions for future generations. This principle advocates making decisions that sustain the world for seven generations into the future, influencing not just environmental policies but also relationships. Adopting this wide lens on sustainability is vital. Our social and environmental challenges are intrinsically linked. While nature's preservation is a worthy goal on its own, our very existence hinges on a flourishing environment and the services it offers. Essential necessities like clean air and wholesome food are non-negotiable. Trees and plants purify our air, while a consistent climate nurtures the food we consume. Sustainability also encompasses the idea of decoupling – severing the ties between environmental degradation and economic growth. The objective? Achieving economic expansion and job generation without sacrificing environmental health or social welfare. Put another way: one cannot care about children, but not nature. Or about health, but not climate. Or poverty, but not biodiversity. It is all interconnected.

CASE STUDY How we are all interconnected

Julika Riegler, global communications and marketing at IFAW,[38] shows how important it is for businesses to include biodiversity conservation in their practices, involving collaboration between companies, NGOs and conservation experts. She believes that protecting biodiversity is key not only for the environment but also for social and economic stability, and that it should form part of business strategies for a real, lasting effect.

For example, Julika points out that harming bees affects humans and communities. Bees are vital for pollinating crops, and their decline, due to pesticides and habitat loss, can lead to lower crop yields. This affects the agricultural economy, leading to higher food prices and shortages, impacting both farmers and communities. She also discusses the importance of whales in marine ecosystems. Whales contribute to ocean health by providing essential nutrients for phytoplankton, crucial for marine life and oxygen production. A decrease in whale numbers can disrupt this cycle, reducing phytoplankton, affecting fish populations and the fishing industry, and impacting global climate regulation.[39]

On the one hand, people are negatively impacted by climate change...

Environmental degradation and poverty are deeply interlinked. The world's top one per cent are responsible for more than half of total emissions, while the bottom half contributes under 10 per cent.[40] This disparity is stark, as economically disadvantaged communities lack the resources to shield themselves from climate change's repercussions. The world's poorest populations face the most significant threats from climate change.

As urban populations grow, pollution can magnify, as seen in many cities around the world.[41] Rapid population growth in such cities has led to increased exposure to pollutants from various sources. The world's poorest are more likely to live near pollution sources and have inadequate waste management services, leading to numerous environmental, health and economic consequences. Around 2 billion people globally lack waste collection services. In many low-income countries, this deficiency results in the burning or dumping of waste, intensifying environmental and health hazards. The World Health Organization (WHO) identifies climate change as a paramount challenge to human health.[42] For example, asthma is made worse by air pollution, causing many deaths, especially in polluted urban environments.[43]

CASE STUDY A changing climate is changing our health conditions

Dr Maria Wolodarski, an oncologist from Stockholm's Karolinska University Hospital, highlights this interconnectedness of health and climate. Environmental sustainability is crucial for human survival and overall public health. As the planet grapples with climate change, humans face dire health risks, from heat-related illnesses to respiratory problems, malnutrition and the spread of diseases. If the planet's health deteriorates, our own well-being and survival are directly threatened.

Maria was introduced to the idea of sustainability early in her life, through her grandmother's tales of the luxury of fresh and clean water and food when she was growing up, in the 1920s. When Maria became a mother herself, she realized that addressing climate change was not just about individual consumption, or just about the bigger picture, but about the here and now, and her child's future. This reflection led her to initiate personal lifestyle changes, such as minimizing flying and meat consumption.

Yet, she yearned to make a broader impact, particularly leveraging her professional platform. As a doctor, she realized that she has a unique voice in society, with the ability to inform the public, politicians and other decision makers about the impacts of climate change on health. She was also well positioned to raise awareness of the double role healthcare plays: as part of the problem, with its emission-intensive activities, and as part of the solution, with the responsibility to highlight the co-benefits of a transition. While climate change might seem distant to some, its repercussions on health are immediate and tangible. Our concerns for personal health and the well-being of loved ones, and the high costs and consequences of poor public health, underscore the value of prevention. This awareness fosters a collective interest in proactive health measures. For Maria, tackling climate change was akin to engaging in highlighting the health benefits of a transition and highlighting the responsibility of healthcare to reduce its own emissions and take a more active role in the transition and adaptation. Maria's story emphasizes that one need not be in an obvious position to make a difference in sustainability. From her story, it's clear that there is potential for impact regardless of one's professional background.[44]

Poorer communities often find themselves working in climate-sensitive industries such as farming and fishing, and often reside in fragile coastal housing or areas prone to extreme weather events. Small island nations, for instance, face existential threats from rising sea levels and extreme weather. In addition, as the demand for natural resources increases, impoverished individuals are often pushed to participate in environmentally harmful practices, like logging, to earn an income.[45] As an example, the demand for palm oil, which is present in many products, has caused significant deforestation in tropical rainforests, especially in Indonesia. Here, Indigenous communities frequently lose their homes, and local farmers who are under economic pressure clear vast stretches of forests for low-yield crops.

The relationship between health, sustainability and obesity is intricate, highlighting disparities in food access. While some communities face food scarcity, with limited access to nutritious options, others are inundated with processed, unhealthy foods that are cheaper but lead to health issues like obesity, particularly among socio-economically disadvantaged groups. This situation underscores a significant flaw in our food system, where cost does not equate to nutritional value, impacting societal health and hindering sustainability efforts. Addressing this challenge requires a comprehensive strategy that encompasses reformed food systems for fair access to healthy food, community education on nutrition, and policies that promote sustainable, health-focused food production and distribution. Achieving balance in these areas is crucial for social justice and environmental sustainability.[46]

Vulnerable groups, like women, children, the elderly and minority communities, bear the brunt of these negative impacts. Women, particularly in low-income and lower-middle-income countries, are heavily reliant on natural resources for their livelihoods, yet face unequal access. This dynamic is exacerbated during environmental crises, such as droughts or floods, when women's responsibilities for securing food, water and fuel intensify, often at the cost of their own and their daughters' education and well-being. Climate change acts as a threat multiplier, amplifying social, political and economic tensions, especially in fragile settings, thereby increasing women's and girls' vulnerability to gender-based violence, including sexual violence, trafficking and forced marriages. Disasters related to climate change often result in higher mortality and injury rates among women due to existing gender inequalities in information access, mobility, decision making and resources. Lastly, climate change poses significant health risks to women and girls, limiting access to healthcare and exacerbating issues related to maternal and child health, further entrenching gender disparities.[47]

Moreover, climate-related issues, such as in areas where rising temperatures and extreme weather events have diminished the viability of farming, compel many to migrate.[48] The UN Refugee Agency (UNHCR) forecasts increased socio-economic tensions and mass migrations as a consequence of climate change, anticipating a refugee population of 200 million by 2050 – double the current number.[49] Ironically, these climate migrants might encounter resistance when trying to move to wealthier countries, which are major contributors to climate change. In essence, as the environment degrades, the impoverished bear the brunt of the consequences, and are often driven to further harm their surroundings by economic pressures. Thus, the UNHCR recognizes climate change as a foremost threat to global peace. In reality, many people are migrating not in pursuit of better opportunities but out of sheer necessity. Environmental disruptions exacerbate living conditions, strain food resources and heighten political tensions, leaving many with no choice but to leave. A stable climate is essential, not just for addressing humanitarian concerns, but for ensuring quality of life for all.

CASE STUDY Human rights and the reality of war and migration

Lama Abdulrahman is a human rights lawyer living in Berlin. But how she got there is a remarkable story of adaptability, resilience and the pursuit of justice. As a child, Lama dreamt about becoming a successful businesswoman in Damascus, Syria. However, one day war broke out and everything changed. Lama's world was turned upside down and she realized that business life was not what she wanted to pursue. Her people were dying. So, instead, she decided to study human rights law, to create justice and support those who do not have a voice.

After graduating, she managed to go to Berlin, Germany, as a Syrian migrant. In her role as a pro-bono lawyer, Lama leads the 'Know your rights' programme, a beacon of hope for countless refugees navigating the maze of European legal systems. Empowering them with knowledge and skills, from understanding the healthcare system to setting up businesses, the programme epitomizes the essence of sustainable development. Testimonials from participants affirm the transformative impact of such initiatives.

Lama's insights on the misconceptions surrounding refugees bring to the fore a pivotal point: the overarching narratives, often shaped by media and popular sentiment, don't always align with reality. A 2018 study by the Organization for

Economic Co-operation and Development (OECD) shattered many prevailing myths, highlighting the invaluable contributions of migrants to the economies of the countries in which they live.[50] In addressing these misconceptions, Lama's work aligns with the broader sustainability goals of fostering inclusive societies, built on knowledge, awareness and empathy. This is something we desperately need as migration will increase as a consequence of a changing climate. Lama Abdulrahman's trajectory – from a child in Damascus to a human rights lawyer in Berlin – highlights the intertwined nature of personal journeys with broader socio-political dynamics.[51]

Water is a critical resource for agriculture and human survival. As our planet continues to warm and undergo climatic changes, many regions are experiencing prolonged droughts and reduced access to fresh water. These challenges are expected to intensify in the coming years, leading to greater competition over this essential resource. Thus, we are only at the beginning stages of conflicts related to water scarcity. In areas where water sources cross national boundaries or are shared among communities, the potential for disputes is particularly high. Examples include tensions in the Nile River Basin and disputes between countries like India and Pakistan over river water. Moreover, a vicious cycle has emerged: as fish stocks near shores are depleted due to fish populations migrating to cooler waters as well as overfishing, fishermen are compelled to venture further out to sea. This not only endangers marine ecosystems by stripping them of essential species, but also puts fishermen at risk due to the increased dangers of deep sea fishing. Longer trips yield lower profits, making it harder for these fishermen to sustain their livelihoods. This reinforces the cycle, as desperate fishermen take even greater risks and further deplete fish stocks.[52] Moreover, overfishing and illegal fishing have led to conflicts between nations competing for dwindling fish stocks. For instance, tensions have arisen in the South China Sea over fishing rights.

... while others are negatively impacted in the short term by the transition away from fossil fuels

As we pivot towards an environmentally sustainable economy, it's imperative that this transformation aligns with broader societal goals such as creating quality employment opportunities, promoting social inclusion and eliminating poverty. The path to sustainability won't necessarily benefit everyone equally from the outset. Consider workers deeply entrenched in the fossil fuel industry. Their livelihoods, identities and fortunes are tied to a sector undergoing significant change. Similarly, traditional car mechanics might view the rise of electric vehicles, which demand less frequent servicing, with apprehension. Such transitions underscore the importance of providing alternative avenues for these individuals to earn decent livelihoods. Without concerted efforts in re-training, skill enhancement and job creation, we risk sidelining significant segments of the population. This not only compounds humanitarian concerns but might lead to political and societal disruptions. In 2018, as a testament to proactive transitioning, Spain allocated €200 million to aid mine workers in transitioning to new jobs as coal mines shuttered.[53]

The 'yellow vests' protests in France, which began in 2018 and lasted until autumn 2019, and the agricultural demonstrations in the Netherlands in 2019 serve as stark reminders of the repercussions of overlooking inclusivity. While these protests were rooted in specific issues like nitrogen emission policies and fuel taxes, they also reflect deeper complexities involving individualism, consumerism, rural–urban divides and tensions between citizens and the state or the elite. These movements underscore the importance of considering the diverse needs and perspectives of people in the broader sustainability transformation, highlighting the need for inclusive and empathetic approaches to address these multifaceted challenges. As aptly noted by Simone Tagliapietra in *The Guardian*, 'The world won't be greener until it's fairer. Climate action must be paired with safeguards for the vulnerable.'[54] When the burden of funding a sustainable future falls disproportionately on specific groups, it's paramount to ensure they're also recipients of the benefits.

The International Labour Organization (ILO) argues that a green economic transformation holds potential as a catalyst for growth, both in developed and emerging economies.[55] Such a transformation can yield 'green jobs' that not only support environmental sustainability but also make significant strides towards poverty alleviation and societal inclusion. When we talk about green jobs, it's not limited to new, emergent sectors, but also extends to transforming traditional roles to align with sustainable practices. When executed with foresight and inclusivity, this shift towards both environmental and societal sustainability can be a robust instrument for job creation and enhancement, fostering social justice and poverty reduction.

Sustainability challenges across different continents

Sustainability challenges manifest differently across regions and sectors, influenced by various factors like economic development, social structures and geographic conditions. The global North–South divide is a key aspect of this variability, with industrialized nations in the Global North having a significant impact on climate change and environmental degradation, which disproportionately affect the less developed Global South. Regions in the Global South face greater climate impacts despite their lower contribution to global emissions, underscoring the necessity for equitable and region-sensitive approaches in global sustainability.

Working in a global context offers first-hand insight into the diverse and complex societal and environmental challenges that vary across regions. For instance, wars or conflicts in an operation's region can impact supply, production, transportation and customer relations, underscoring how priorities can shift dramatically in crisis situations.[56] While these are trivial matters in the context of the larger conflict, they serve as tangible examples of the direct and immediate impacts of such events. It's not feasible to discuss waste management infrastructure when bombings are an immediate threat. Similarly, it's a luxury to talk about implementing cutting-edge renewable energy solutions when basic utilities, like access to electricity or clean water, aren't even assured. These situations highlight the importance of understanding local contexts and the unique challenges they present, in order to ensure that solutions are not only sustainable but also relevant and timely.

It is of course very difficult to generalize, since the regions discussed in the following sections are so large, but a few high-level issues are highlighted. Each of these challenges requires tailored solutions that consider local contexts, resources and needs while also fitting into a broader global strategy for sustainability. Unfortunately, political corruption acts as a barrier to true progress and is a topic that cuts across many regions.

Africa

In many parts of Africa, access to clean water and sanitation is a pressing issue, exacerbated by climate change, which is also causing desertification and threatening arable land. Additionally, the continent faces challenges in developing sustainable energy infrastructure that can accommodate rapid population growth without further contributing to global emissions. Under-investment in infrastructure and the energy transition are part of the problem. Poverty remains a crucial challenge in most parts of Africa, exacerbating other issues like access to clean water and education.[57] Social unrest and political instability, often stemming from resource scarcity or ethnic tensions, further complicate sustainability efforts. LGBTQ+ rights are also a significant concern, with many countries still criminalizing homosexuality.[58]

Asia

Asia is grappling with multiple sustainability challenges. Air pollution is a severe problem in many large cities due to industrial emissions and increased vehicle use. Deforestation, particularly in South East Asia, is another significant issue, contributing to loss of biodiversity and increased carbon emissions.[59] Rapid industrialization also raises questions about equitable labour practices and social responsibility.[60] Social unrest related to governance and freedom of speech is an issue in some parts of Asia. Gender inequality and limited LGBTQ+ rights are other social sustainability concerns.[61] Migrant labour practices, especially in the Gulf States, face criticism for inequitable conditions.[62] In Asia, women face systemic discrimination, affecting their educational and employment opportunities,[63] while smallholder farmers confront the pressures of climate change and market volatility. Coastal and Indigenous communities grapple with threats to their homes and cultural heritage due to environmental changes and displacement.[64] Rapid urbanization, while presenting opportunities, places strain on the urban poor, and children face exploitation risks while the elderly navigate healthcare and financial challenges.[65]

On the positive side, there is substantial progress and investments being made in renewable energy, especially across China. India, on the other hand, has immense solar potential, but many poorer areas are locked into coal, with substantial investments needed to unlock this opportunity.

Australia and Oceania

Water scarcity is a severe issue in Australia, impacting agriculture and leading to bushfires.[66] These are frequent and devastating events, especially during the hot, dry summer months. They have significant environmental, economic and social impacts, with the 2019–2020 fire season being particularly catastrophic, resulting in loss of life, destruction of property and extensive damage to the country's unique ecosystems.[67] Coral bleaching, caused by warmer ocean temperatures, affects the Great Barrier Reef and other essential marine ecosystems in the region.[68]

Social issues in Australia and Oceania often revolve around the rights and treatment of Indigenous peoples. Issues related to refugees and asylum seekers are also pressing, as is the recognition and acceptance of LGBTQ+ rights.[69]

Europe

In Europe, one major issue is resource efficiency, as many countries aim to transition towards a circular economy to reduce waste and carbon footprint. Climate change also looms large, with the melting of Alpine glaciers and increased flooding being significant concerns. Migration, refugees and escalating inequalities also remain pressing challenges.[70] As recognized by the UN, the significant influx of refugees, especially evident during 2015, alongside persistent economic disparities within European nations, has heightened social tensions, prompting essential discussions on integration, the preservation of national identities and equitable resource distribution.[71] Additionally, the spectre of polarization looms large in European societies, leading to increased social unrest in various contexts. Gang violence has escalated in certain urban areas, with gangs actively recruiting young individuals and, alarmingly, even children.[72] Terrorism, spurred by radical ideologies, has unfortunately been a recurring challenge in several European cities.[73]

Meanwhile, the European Union (EU) is vigorously pursuing the gold standard in data protection and ethical AI applications, ensuring that tech growth resonates with human values.[74] While much of Europe leads in LGBTQ+ rights, discrimination continues in certain regions, mirroring the broader issue of social inequality and the expanding wealth chasm.

North America

North America's vulnerability to climate-related disasters has become increasingly apparent, with forest fires, flooding, hurricanes and oil leaks in the Mexican Gulf becoming more frequent and severe. Issues of waste management, especially plastic pollution in oceans, complement concerns around food waste and the pressing need to transition to sustainable agriculture.[75] Amid these environmental challenges, societal dynamics are equally complex. Racial inequality, systemic poverty and immigration remain contentious, driving considerable debate and sometimes causing polarization and social unrest. While significant progress has been made as regards LGBTQ+ rights, especially in the US and Canada, hurdles persist, notably in more conservative regions, reflecting the broader landscape of social disparities in North America.[76]

South America

Deforestation in the Amazon rainforest is a critical sustainability issue that impacts global carbon sinks and local biodiversity.[77] Water scarcity is also increasingly a concern, particularly in regions heavily reliant on agriculture. Social inequality and poverty are pervasive issues. Indigenous rights, particularly related to land use and cultural preservation, are another significant concern. The situation in terms of LGBTQ+ rights vary widely, with some countries being quite progressive and others lagging behind.

In Central America, historic and ongoing conflicts with guerrilla movements have deeply influenced social and political landscapes, particularly in nations like Nicaragua and El Salvador. Additionally, many Central Americans, driven by factors ranging from socio-economic challenges to violence, are migrating north, a trend that poses humanitarian and geopolitical challenges. Across both South and Central America, women continue to advocate for equal rights and representation, confronting issues such as gender-based violence, limited reproductive choices and barriers in the political and economic spheres.[78]

Creating a just transition

The gap between rich and poor people is growing, both between countries and within many countries. This affects chances and opportunities for many people. For example, a Credit Suisse report tells us that the richest one per cent of people in the world have almost half of all the money globally.[79] At the same time, over half of all people have only a tiny bit more than one per cent of the money. But being unequal isn't just about money. It's also about things like being a man or a woman, how old you are, where you come from, your skin colour, any disabilities, whom you love, your social class and your religion.

What happens when society is not equal? Besides it being unfair, research shows that when there's a big gap between rich and poor, there are more health problems, more crime, less happiness and slower business growth. In short, more fighting and less working together. On the other hand, in places where everyone is more equal, people trust each other more, work together better and come up with new ideas.[80] The OECD states that if we make things more equal, everyone will benefit, and our businesses will do better.[81] Thus, if we can limit the increase in world temperature to 1.5 °C, life will be better for everyone, especially those with the least money. In the book *Breaking Boundaries* by Johan Rockström and Owen Gaffney, it is stated that if we can make the world more equal, we will be able to solve climate change.[82]

International efforts are under way to move beyond using gross domestic product (GDP) as the sole measure of a country's progress and to develop more comprehensive metrics that better reflect economic performance, social progress and well-being. The reliance on GDP, a system established in the past, has been criticized for its inability to fully capture the health of countries and societies. This shortcoming is especially evident in its failure to predict or adequately address crises like the global financial crisis of 2008. New approaches aim to create dashboards of indicators that not only track economic growth but also assess its sustainability, distributional equity and impact on individuals' quality of life. These efforts are part of a broader movement to inform policy decisions with data that encompasses well-being and social progress, going beyond traditional economic measures.[83]

Senator Ed Muskie said in 1970: 'The only kind of society that has a chance [is] a society that will not tolerate slums for some and decent houses for others, rats for some and playgrounds for others, clean air for some and filth for others.'[84] These sustainability challenges – and the need to move towards a just, fair and sustainable society – require a collective effort by business, government civil society and citizens. As the challenges – and their solutions – are complex and complicated, the only way we can solve them is by working together across different kinds of organizations, as each organization plays a unique role. Addressing the intertwined challenges of biodiversity loss, climate change and poverty might seem daunting, but everyone has a role to play in finding solutions. For example, public–private partnerships can present possible solutions for driving development forward. In essence, while the challenges are vast, by working together and combining expertise from various fields, we can work towards holistic and sustainable solutions.[85] This involves cross-sector collaboration to address pressing issues:

- **Health and sanitation:** Around 2.3 billion people around the world rely on burning materials, like coal and biomass, for cooking and heating according to a study in 2023, leading to toxic fumes that caused approximately 3.2 million deaths per year in 2020.[86] By transitioning to cleaner energy, we can both improve health and conserve forests. Moreover, in many developing countries, inadequate sanitation leads to water pollution, causing diseases and contributing to the high mortality rate of children under five. This not only affects human health but also the biodiversity of rivers. Collaborative efforts between health experts, ecologists and behavioural scientists can lead to the discovery of ways to enhance sanitation and prevent river pollution.
- **Agriculture:** The world's poorest often work in agriculture, a sector vulnerable to climate change and extreme weather events. There are initiatives by agriculture specialists to introduce practices that rejuvenate soil and combat climate change effects. The challenge is to amplify the adoption of these sustainable practices.
- **Livelihoods:** Activities such as clearing rainforests for agriculture, as seen in the palm oil industry in Indonesia, may provide immediate income but jeopardize long-term ecological balance and livelihood sustainability. Similar patterns are evident in places like the Amazon and global fisheries. Restoring a marine ecosystem requires a delicate balance, especially when local communities rely on fishing for their livelihoods. Introducing a recycling facility might modernize waste management, but what becomes of the informal waste collectors who depend on sorting waste and selling the recyclable materials? If an affordable energy product becomes obsolete, is its final resting place a landfill? The intricacies of poverty and environmental preservation are tightly interwoven. Issues such as overfishing, deforestation and pollution stem from human activities and have significant repercussions for both individuals and the environment.[87] Multidisciplinary teams aim to restore ecosystems while also reducing the allure of unsustainable resource extraction.

CASE STUDY Addressing the root causes of migration

Eva Iveroth's journey from supporting refugees in Jordan to her role at the Swedish Environmental Protection Agency underscores the crucial link between humanitarian and environmental crises. Growing up in Tanzania, Eva developed a deep passion for helping the less fortunate. Working with the UNHCR in

Jordan, she encountered refugees whose stories often highlighted a key issue: environmental degradation, particularly droughts driven by climate change, as a significant factor in forced migration.

Her experiences confirm that environmental degradation, like climate-induced droughts, often drives migration. While recognizing that migration is driven by various factors, Eva acknowledged the central role of environmental issues. This realization led her to shift her focus towards environmental protection. Eva now aims to tackle these root causes through her work in international environmental policy-making. Her role involves not only guiding policy but also collaborating with the private sector to foster sustainable solutions that benefit vulnerable communities worldwide.[88]

The critical role of the business sector

Businesses are already experiencing significant negative environmental and social impacts, and this will only increase. Climate change and biodiversity loss are disrupting supply chains, causing shortages and increasing costs for accessing raw materials. As extreme weather events become more frequent, businesses face physical damage to assets and infrastructure, leading to significant financial losses.[89]

The business sector is increasingly being recognized as having a crucial role in global development and poverty reduction. For businesses, these environmental and social challenges offer a dual opportunity: to contribute positively to global sustainability and, at the same time, to innovate and adapt for future resilience.[90] We strongly believe in the corporate sector's ability to create positive change due to its size and problem-solving skills. Moreover, the corporate sector is a big contributor to the world's greenhouse gas emissions.[91] For example, between 1988 and 2017, 71 per cent of the world's total greenhouse gases resulted from only 100 large companies.[92]

Paul Hawken stated, 'Business is the only mechanism on the planet today powerful enough to produce the changes necessary to reverse global environments and social degradation.'[93] First and foremost, organizations and businesses can choose to be responsible entities by ensuring they contribute positively to a sustainable world. It's essential that their operations add value to the global community while minimizing or eliminating negative externalities. Their business models should be sustainable, as their influence extends beyond their immediate operations, shaping society and setting precedents that individuals and smaller entities often look to for guidance. When an organization embraces sustainability, it does more than just minimize its ecological footprint; it casts a vision for what responsible enterprise looks like and provides a blueprint for others to follow.

The avenues through which organizations can make a difference are broad and expansive. A positive work culture fosters employee happiness and well-being, serving as a cornerstone for broader organizational change. Culture and values become the lens through which every decision is made, creating a virtuous cycle of positive impact. Products and services can be designed with a purpose that extends beyond mere functionality, becoming solutions that genuinely improve lives. Add to this a sustainable value chain, and you have an ecosystem that amplifies impact at every touchpoint.

CASE STUDY Pioneering public health and corporate sustainability

Therese Noorlander's career path stands as a compelling example of dedication to public health and sustainability. Initially immersing herself in the public sector, Therese dedicated years to driving change in health and environmental practices. Her profound desire to make a significant impact led her to explore collaborations between prevention and sustainable healthy living measures and the business world.

A notable connection during this phase was engagement with the entity of Coca-Cola in the Netherlands, a relationship that revealed to Therese the potential of influencing sustainability from within a corporate structure. This realization prompted a bold career move: joining the Coca-Cola Company. The first to oversee responsibilities for communication and sustainability in the Netherlands, later on Therese developed into the role of Sustainability Director for Europe. While her decision to transfer from the public to the private sector was met with scepticism and surprise, with many viewing her as an outlier in her field, Therese was guided by a clear vision. She understood that her impact on sustainable practices could be exponentially greater from within the corporate sphere than from an external partnership position. At Coca-Cola, Therese's unique blend of public health expertise and a deep commitment to sustainability allowed her to implement significant changes. The change and impact were welcomed by the company and the teams she worked with.

Therese Noorlander's journey highlights the profound impact that can be achieved from various sectors, emphasizing the power of working within an organization. Her transition from the public sector to a corporate role underlines the potential to drive substantial change from the inside when the time is right. This case study illustrates that while external advocacy and partnerships are valuable, the influence wielded from within a company can often be more direct and consequential. Therese's story is an inspiration to those looking to make a difference, demonstrating that impactful sustainability efforts can be pursued successfully from multiple angles and within various frameworks.[94]

To address inequalities within their sphere of influence, businesses can adopt a multifaceted approach. This can start with equitable hiring practices that focus on diversity and inclusion, while also offering transparent wages and growth opportunities. Companies can also use their purchasing power responsibly by vetting suppliers for ethical labour practices. Making products and services more accessible through affordable pricing models or localized investments can have a significant impact on underserved communities. Employee well-being can be promoted through comprehensive benefit packages and work–life balance initiatives. Finally, it's essential for businesses to measure their social impact and share this openly for accountability. By incorporating these strategies into their core operations, companies can transition from being passive bystanders to active participants in reducing social and economic inequalities.

A company in the construction industry can negatively impact local biodiversity by destroying natural habitats during the development of new properties. To counteract this, the company could adopt sustainable construction methods such as green roofing or set aside areas as protected habitats. Additionally, they could work with environmental experts to perform biodiversity assessments before construction, ensuring minimal impact on local fauna and flora. This approach not only conserves the existing ecosystem but also enhances the company's reputation as a responsible and sustainable business.

To provide another example, Lisen and her team collaborated with the World Wide Fund for Nature (WWF) on an innovative project in Oaxaca, Mexico, emphasizing shade-grown coffee cultivation.[95] Conventional coffee farming often involves clearing large tracts of land, leading to significant deforestation and habitat loss. This not only disrupts local ecosystems but also negatively impacts biodiversity, particularly bird species. However, the shade-coffee-method, where coffee grows under the canopy of native trees, not only bolsters local biodiversity but also conserves water in the region.

More than an environmental solution, this approach has economically uplifted smallholder farmers in Oaxaca. With coffee beans maturing slower, resulting in richer flavours and increased yields, farmers have secured both immediate and long-term sustainable incomes. This initiative, blending ecological care with community upliftment, showcases the tangible benefits businesses can bring to both biodiversity and local economies.

Emerging technology enabling the sustainability transition

As we look towards 2030 and beyond, the collective actions in these areas – exponential solutions, AI, transparency and blockchain technology – offer promising pathways to addressing the climate crisis (and other sustainability-related crises as well). Although they are technologies that have the potential to do severe harm, these innovations and initiatives, grounded in sustainability and social responsibility, are not only necessary but also achievable, providing hope and direction for a more sustainable and equitable world. While we can't rely only on technology to solve climate change, it's an important part of the solution. We need to use technology in a way that includes everyone and benefits the whole society. When presenting these solutions, we, as authors, do not claim to be experts in the field of future trends and technology. However, we find it important, interesting and relevant to include this information to provide a comprehensive view.[96]

Exponential solutions

Throughout this book, numerous solutions and sustainable business models will be explored, many of which are currently in pilot stages or operating on a small scale. It's important to recognize the inherent potential in these initiatives to scale up rapidly – a phenomenon known as exponential growth. Typically, we associate exponential growth within the realm of sustainability with negative trends, such as the rise in carbon emissions or the alarming decrease in biodiversity. However, it's crucial to understand that exponential growth can also manifest itself positively. The same rapid expansion that characterizes these negative trends can apply to sustainable solutions, allowing them to quickly escalate in scale and impact. This perspective shifts our focus from the often daunting, negative aspects of sustainability to a more optimistic view, emphasizing the swift and transformative potential of sustainable practices. Therefore, exponential change, a concept explored in Rebecka Carlsson's book on climate solutions, offers a beacon of hope and drives momentum in our urgent quest to meet the SDGs.[97]

The Exponential Roadmap Initiative presents solutions that are exponentially scalable.[98] This initiative is grounded in the principle that addressing climate change effectively requires solutions that can grow rapidly in scope and impact, mirroring the urgent and escalating nature of the climate crisis itself. Project Drawdown is yet another resource that provides scalable and actionable solutions to combat climate change.[99] It highlights how, with the right tools and approaches, we can effectively address this global crisis. Green technologies like solar and wind power have seen costs decrease over time. When technology is ready, and investments in manufacturing are made, costs decrease, leading to market changes. Technologies transition from being exciting to being economically viable, and consumer preferences change. These tipping points are happening in society, with increasing investments in green energy globally.

By 2030, green energy technologies will have further developed and become more efficient. The costs of energy from solar, wind, water and geothermal sources will have decreased even more, making it logical for developing countries to leapfrog to renewable sources instead of relying on dirtier ones. Battery technology and other energy storage methods will likely have advanced significantly in technical and cost terms, further leveraging the transition. However, the transition will not be pain-free, as while economic barriers for batteries, solar and wind power are removed, other challenges remain, such as political will, improvements in power grids, public attitudes towards solar and wind (NIMBY, or 'not in my backyard', challenges) and the availability of necessary metals.

Transparency

Radical transparency, aided by advancements in satellite technology, is emerging as a powerful tool in holding various actors accountable for their environmental impacts. Satellites orbiting the Earth are continuously gathering global data, which is crucial for monitoring environmental changes and human activities. This satellite data, along with other terrestrial measurement systems, enables us to track melting glaciers and weakening ocean currents, and provide us with detailed information on natural disasters like fires and floods. This technology also aids in identifying illegal activities, such as environmental violations or unauthorized deforestation, and in monitoring sensitive natural areas.

Organizations like Climate TRACE are working to meticulously disclose global emissions data, employing the concept of radical transparency.[100] Similarly, NASA's OCO-2 Project measures atmospheric carbon dioxide and maps methane, a significant contributor to climate change.[101] NASA's identification of super emitters is a critical step in addressing these hidden sources of greenhouse gases. The UN is also utilizing satellite technology for environmental monitoring that aims to identify major methane leaks and inform governments and companies for timely action. This level of surveillance and accountability is becoming the norm, making it increasingly difficult for companies and countries to engage in destructive practices or greenwashing.[102]

Due to these developments, operations that harm the planet will likely face greater scrutiny, and organizations will find it prudent to earnestly transition towards greener and more ethical operations. The trend towards open emission data will make it difficult for entities to avoid living up to their environmental goals and promises. It also promises to encourage and reward entities that elevate their climate ambitions, as genuine action becomes increasingly recognizable and commendable, while the opposite becomes punishable.

EXAMPLE Traceability in wool fashion

Sheep on Repeat is a groundbreaking project aimed at enhancing traceability in the wool fashion industry. By implementing a QR-code system, it allows for the tracking of wool products from sheep farms to final garments, addressing the fashion industry's transparency and sustainability challenges. This initiative emerged in response to new EU regulations promoting responsible textile production and consumption. The project's goal is to trace wool items from origin through resale and reuse, using the GS1 standards for universal product identification. This comprehensive approach involves collaboration with various industry players, like Axfoundation[103] and Filippa K, and utilizes the VirtualRouteZ digital platform for data sharing. Key objectives include establishing sustainability standards, empowering stakeholders and aligning with EU Digital Product Passport requirements to foster a circular economy.

Artificial intelligence

AI is another frontier for exponential change. AI and emerging technologies like 5G, quantum computing and the Internet of Things (IoT) are poised to revolutionize various sectors by 2030. It could develop advanced, personalized medical treatments; automate and optimize transport systems; enhance financial decision making; and boost manufacturing productivity. A critical aspect of this technological evolution is the green transition, with AI playing a significant role in optimizing renewable energy use, enhancing electric vehicle technology and improving agricultural practices for sustainability. Its applications range from fundamental climate research and monitoring to reducing emissions and fostering innovation and transformation in climate adaptation. The potential use of AI also goes beyond environmental benefits:[104]

- In the **energy sector**, AI can optimize the production, distribution and consumption of renewable energy sources like solar and wind power. AI's data analysis of weather patterns can predict energy production more accurately, allowing for better integration of renewable sources into the power grid. Machine learning algorithms can manage energy needs and optimize energy use in buildings, reducing costs and emissions.
- In **transportation**, AI is key in developing electric and autonomous vehicles. It can optimize routes, reduce fuel consumption and emissions, and improve traffic management. AI-driven advances in battery technology and smart charging infrastructure can extend the range and lifespan of electric vehicles, making them more accessible and viable for mass adoption.
- In terms of **social equality**, AI can be used to analyse large data sets to identify and address various forms of social inequality. For example, it can help in monitoring and analysing social trends related to gender, race and economic status, providing insights that can inform policies to promote equality. AI-driven tools can also help in removing biases in hiring processes, promoting a more diverse and inclusive workforce.[105]
- AI can support **smallholder farmers** by enabling access to information that would otherwise be difficult to acquire, such as tailored advice on optimal farming techniques. It can bridge knowledge gaps by answering questions about crop care, pest management and market access, fostering an environment for better-educated and healthier populations in poorer countries. These advances in AI-driven agricultural insights contribute to social impact by potentially increasing crop yields, reducing the need for chemical inputs and improving overall farm sustainability. Moreover, AI can enhance decision making and resource management, leading to more resilient farming practices and communities.[106]

Blockchain technology

Decentralized blockchains (for example, Bitcoin), built on the foundation of Distributed Ledger Technology (DLT),[107] could be a versatile tool for various applications that promote sustainability and social responsibility. When sufficiently decentralized among various actors, the key strength of blockchain technology is its ability to trace and verify products through every step of a supply chain. This immutable record-keeping capability ensures that every phase, from production to retail, can be securely tracked and authenticated. Such transparency is crucial for verifying claims related to environmental and social responsibility, such as confirming that a product is made without child labour, that it adheres to fair trade principles or that it maintains a low-carbon footprint.

In the context of the food industry, for example, blockchain can track the journey of products from farm to table. This enables consumers to verify claims about organic farming practices, ethical sourcing and the overall environmental impact of their purchases. Leading companies like Carrefour and Walmart, in collaboration with IBM, are already using blockchain for this purpose, demonstrating its practical application in enhancing food safety and sustainability.[108] By 2030, the adoption of distributed trust through blockchain is expected to become a standard in designing systems for increased traceability, transparency and trust. This shift will further challenge and reduce greenwashing, promoting a marketplace where truly sustainable and socially responsible practices are the norm.

EXAMPLE BanQu

BanQu, a social enterprise with the mission to lift 100 million people out of extreme poverty by 2028, exemplifies the social impact potential of blockchain. BanQu's approach focuses on creating an equitable economy where every brand can prove the provenance of its products, every consumer can make ethical purchasing decisions and every participant in the supply chain, including labourers, is given visibility and recognition. This model of transparent, ethical supply chains supported by blockchain technology, not only empowers consumers with information but also ensures fair treatment and compensation for workers, contributing significantly to poverty alleviation and social equity.[109]

Summary and key take-aways

This chapter provided a detailed overview of both the progress and challenges in global sustainability. It highlighted positive advancements as well as critical multicrises, including climate change, biodiversity loss, the outdated linear economic model and deep-rooted inequalities. The chapter emphasized the interconnected nature of these issues and the human role in exacerbating them. A central concept was a just transition, advocating for a fair and inclusive path towards global sustainability, considering disparities across regions. We also highlighted the increasing role of AI and technology in achieving social and environmental benefits, while stressing the importance of the ethical development and inclusivity of these tools.

Picturing the path forward, we're faced with two divergent futures: one overshadowed by pollution, plastic-suffocated oceans and a dwindling wildlife population; or, in contrast, a world teeming with biodiversity, where businesses are in harmony with nature and societies underpinned by equity and justice. The turning point? Wholeheartedly embracing sustainability, transitioning from linear practices to circular methodologies and placing planetary well-being above mere profits. So, let's embrace the positive changes occurring, draw inspiration from them and push forward, fully aware that the steps we take today lay the foundation for a sustainable and inclusive future. As a leader in this transformation, your influence can make this vision a reality. Keep the positive momentum going; it's contagious and could be the catalyst that turns aspirations into concrete actions.

Endnotes

1 Hans Rosling (2019) *Factfulness, Ten reasons we are wrong about the world and why things are better than you think*, Hodder Stoughton, London

2 Stockholm Resilience Centre. All planetary boundaries mapped out for the first time, six of nine crossed, 13 September 2023. www.stockholmresilience.org/research/research-news/2023-09-13-all-planetary-boundaries-mapped-out-for-the-first-time-six-of-nine-crossed.html (archived at https://perma.cc/QT62-67RE)

3 Johan Rockström and Owen Gaffney (2021) *Breaking Boundaries: The science of our planet*, DK, London

4 Globally, more voters than ever in history will head to the polls as at least 64 countries (plus the European Union) – representing a combined population of about 49 per cent of the people in the world – are meant to hold national

elections, the results of which, for many, will prove consequential for years to come. See Koh Ewe. The Ultimate Election Year: All the Elections Around the World in 2024, *Time*, 28 December 2023. https://time.com/6550920/world-elections-2024/ (archived at https://perma.cc/P3YY-8M8Z)

5 Ruger Bregman (2021) *Humankind: A hopeful history*, Bloomsbury, London

6 Positive news stories bring people together, study finds, Positive News, 18 November 2016. www.positive.news/society/media/positive-news-stories-bring-people-together-study-finds/ (archived at https://perma.cc/Q2DM-K49Q); Jodie Jackson. Publishing the positive: Exploring the motivations for and the consequences of reading solutions-focused journalism, University of East London, 2016. docplayer.net/61036226-Publishing-the-positive.html (archived at https://perma.cc/7M9Q-8VXZ)

7 Stocktaking: What it will take to achieve the Sustainable Development Goals, UN Web TV, 17 September 2023. webtv.un.org/en/asset/k1g/k1gp8ozc3g (archived at https://perma.cc/XX6N-W25E)

8 UN News. The SDGs Report 2023: Special Edition, 2023, p. 2. unstats.un.org/sdgs/report/2023/ (archived at https://perma.cc/ZT3X-PZQN)

9 Nishant Yonzan, Daniel Gerszon Mahler and Christopher Lakner. Poverty is back to pre-COVID levels globally, but not for low-income countries, World Bank, 3 October 2023. https://blogs.worldbank.org/en/opendata/poverty-back-pre-covid-levels-globally-not-low-income-countries (archived at https://perma.cc/AF28-QF5U); Poverty and Inequality Platform, World Bank. https://pip.worldbank.org/home (archived at https://perma.cc/XTE8-FL9P)

10 Andrew Stanley. Global inequalities, IMF, March 2022. www.imf.org/en/Publications/fandd/issues/2022/03/Global-inequalities-Stanley (archived at https://perma.cc/Z3NN-DDXJ)

11 UN Department of Economic and Social Affairs (DESA). UN report finds COVID-19 is reversing decades of progress on poverty, healthcare and education, 2022. www.un.org/nl/desa/un-report-finds-covid-19-reversing-decades-progress-poverty-healthcare-and (archived at https://perma.cc/UAQ2-DVHS)

12 Political divisions deepen globally, University of St Andrews News, 8 December 2021. news.st-andrews.ac.uk/archive/political-divisions-deepen-globally/ (archived at https://perma.cc/35PH-H65F)

13 Explainer: How AI helps combat climate change, UN News, 3 November 2023. news.un.org/en/story/2023/11/1143187 (archived at https://perma.cc/J98C-FKKC)

14 Bernard Marr. The 15 biggest risks of artificial intelligence, *Forbes*, 2 June 2023. www.forbes.com/sites/bernardmarr/2023/06/02/the-15-biggest-risks-of-artificial-intelligence/ (archived at https://perma.cc/U7F9-REKT)

15 Climate change is one of the biggest challenges of our times, European Environmental Agency. www.eea.europa.eu/themes/climate/climate-change-is-one-of (archived at https://perma.cc/3ABF-9SR5)

16 Climate change widespread, rapid, and intensifying – IPCC, IPCC Newsroom, 9 August 2021. www.ipcc.ch/2021/08/09/ar6-wg1-20210809-pr/ (archived at https://perma.cc/G4PG-ZGZP)

17 Berkeley Earth. Global Temperature Report for 2023, 11 January 2024. berkeleyearth.org/wp-content/uploads/2024/01/EMBARGOED-Global-Temperature-Report-for-2023-Berkeley-Earth.pdf (archived at https://perma.cc/Q65N-MVDR)

18 What is climate change? UN Climate Action. www.un.org/en/climatechange/what-is-climate-change (archived at https://perma.cc/CXZ4-QS2H)

19 Indicators of global climate change 2022: Annual update of large-scale indicators of the state of the climate system and human influence, Earth Systems Science Data, 8 June 2023. essd.copernicus.org/articles/15/2295/2023/ (archived at https://perma.cc/2WZ3-BATW)

20 Kelly Levin, Sophie Boehm and Rebecca Carter. 6 Big Findings from the IPCC 2022 Report on Climate Impacts, Adaptation and Vulnerability, World Resources Institute, 27 February 2022. www.wri.org/insights/ipcc-report-2022-climate-impacts-adaptation-vulnerability (archived at https://perma.cc/4KDC-YK8K)

21 Oliver Milman. 'No safe place': Kiribati seeks donors to raise islands from encroaching seas, *The Guardian*, 18 November 2022. www.theguardian.com/environment/2022/nov/18/cop27-kiribati-donors-raise-islands-sea-level-rise (archived at https://perma.cc/G9RB-BCM6)

22 John Keefe and Rachel Ramirez. Our underwater future: What sea level rise will look like around the globe, CNN, 12 October 2021. edition.cnn.com/2021/10/12/world/3-degrees-sea-level-rise-climate-central/index.html (archived at https://perma.cc/T8C8-7L72); This is what 3°C of global warming looks like, *The Economist*, 30 October 2021. www.economist.com/films/2021/10/30/this-is-what-3degc-of-global-warming-looks-like (archived at https://perma.cc/4AYF-XU5Z)

23 Damian Carrington. Amazon rainforest now emitting more CO2 than it absorbs, *The Guardian*, 14 July 2021. www.theguardian.com/environment/2021/jul/14/amazon-rainforest-now-emitting-more-co2-than-it-absorbs (archived at https://perma.cc/N4WK-8YXY)

24 Katarina Kertysova and Akash Ramnath. How permafrost thaw puts the Russian Arctic at risk, IPI Global Observatory, 22 November 2021. theglobalobservatory.org/2021/11/how-permafrost-thaw-puts-the-russian-arctic-at-risk/ (archived at https://perma.cc/7UGW-PHF6)

25 Lorin Hancock, What is biodiversity? World Wide Fund for Nature (WWF). www.worldwildlife.org/pages/what-is-biodiversity (archived at https://perma.cc/25H9-7CCX)

26 WWF. Living Planet Report 2016, 2016. www.worldwildlife.org/pages/living-planet-report-2016 (archived at https://perma.cc/8MC7-9EAJ)

27 Bobby Magill. A Nebraska-Sized Area of Forest Disappeared in 2015, Climate Central, 24 July 2017. www.climatecentral.org/news/mississippi-sized-area-of-forest-disappeared-21641 (archived at https://perma.cc/7TJV-ATYY)

28 Biodiversity: Our strongest natural defense against climate change, UN Climate Action. www.un.org/en/climatechange/science/climate-issues/biodiversity (archived at https://perma.cc/2JL5-ULML)

29 Biodiversity: Our strongest natural defense against climate change, UN Climate Action. www.un.org/en/climatechange/science/climate-issues/biodiversity (archived at https://perma.cc/2JL5-ULML)

30 Mark Tercek. Money Talks – So Let's Give Nature a Voice, *Earth Island Journal*, 2013, Summer. www.earthisland.org/journal/index.php/magazine/entry/money_talks_so_lets_give_nature_a_voice/## (archived at https://perma.cc/LPE8-63Y3)

31 What is a circular economy? Ellen Macarthur Foundation. www.ellenmacarthurfoundation.org/topics/circular-economy-introduction/overview (archived at https://perma.cc/6KND-L2EZ)

32 C Sundarapandian. From linear to circular: How Paul Hawken's principles can help build a sustainable future, About Paul Hawken, Ecology of commerce, LinkedIn, 1 May 2023. www.linkedin.com/pulse/from-linear-circular-how-paul-hawkens-principles-can-help-c/ (archived at https://perma.cc/RF5N-SANA)

33 Laura Parker. A whopping 91% of plastic isn't recycled, *National Geographic*, 20 December 2018. www.nationalgeographic.com/science/article/plastic-produced-recycling-waste-ocean-trash-debris-environment (archived at https://perma.cc/XFL3-RMER)

34 About us, Ellen's story, Ellen Macarthur Foundation. www.ellenmacarthurfoundation.org/about-us/ellens-story (archived at https://perma.cc/VJ8E-Q2N5)

35 Sustainability, UN, www.un.org/en/academic-impact/sustainability (archived at https://perma.cc/J2HS-4J8U)

36 Inger Andersen. Valuing nature, Green Economy Coalition. www.greeneconomycoalition.org/themes/valuing-nature (archived at https://perma.cc/V8MS-BRSM)

37 This principle is rooted in the ancient Haudenosaunee (Iroquois) philosophy embodied in the Great Law of the Haudenosaunee Confederacy

38 See www.ifaw.org (archived at https://perma.cc/D7CP-548H)

39 Interview conducted November 2021

40 Richest 1% emit as much planet-heating pollution as two-thirds of humanity, Oxfam, 20 November 2023. www.oxfam.org/en/press-releases/richest-1-emit-much-planet-heating-pollution-two-thirds-humanity (archived at https://perma.cc/SCS8-S62S)

41 Lu Liang and Peng Gong. Urban and air pollution: A multi-city study of long-term effects of urban landscape patterns on air quality trends, *Scientific*

Reports, 2020, 10. www.nature.com/articles/s41598-020-74524-9 (archived at https://perma.cc/E95E-VYFJ)

42 Climate change, WHO, 12 October 2023. www.who.int/news-room/fact-sheets/detail/climate-change-and-health (archived at https://perma.cc/H33M-5DXF)

43 Damian Carrington. 'Remember me': Ella's law would be fitting legacy after London air pollution death, says mother, *The Guardian*, 10 February 2023. www.theguardian.com/environment/2023/feb/10/ellas-law-rosamund-kissi-debrah-air-pollution-death-london#:~:text=Ella%E2%80%99s%20fame%20is%20tragic%3A%20she,as%20a%20cause%20of%20death (archived at https://perma.cc/C6LZ-RKBC)

44 Interview conducted February 2021

45 Acumen course: Designing for Environmental Sustainability and Social Impact. acumenacademy.org/course/designing-environmental-sustainability-social-impact/ (archived at https://perma.cc/N5LS-9XJW)

46 Transforming food systems to reduce global inequality and improve food safety and health, WHO, January 2023. https://cdn.who.int/media/docs/default-source/universal-health-coverage/who-uhl-technical-brief-template---food-safety.pdf?sfvrsn=6681d1e3_3&download=true (archived at https://perma.cc/T4FQ-6YYU)

47 Explainer: How gender inequality and climate change are interconnected, UN Women, 28 February 2022. www.unwomen.org/en/news-stories/explainer/2022/02/explainer-how-gender-inequality-and-climate-change-are-interconnected (archived at https://perma.cc/F8PP-XYUT)

48 Witnessing climate change: The voices of El Salvador, UN Development Programme (UNDP), 8 June 2023. climatepromise.undp.org/news-and-stories/witnessing-climate-change-voices-el-salvador (archived at https://perma.cc/JC9A-9KR2)

49 Tim Gaynor, Climate change is the defining crisis of our time and it particularly impacts the displaced, UNHCR stories, 30 November 2020. www.unhcr.org/news/stories/climate-change-defining-crisis-our-time-and-it-particularly-impacts-displaced (archived at https://perma.cc/SH6D-PXDN)

50 OECD/European Union. Settling In 2018: Indicators of Immigrant Integration, 9 December 2018. www.oecd-ilibrary.org/social-issues-migration-health/indicators-of-immigrant-integration-2018_9789264307216-en;jsessionid=V2WZAcnNTxrfGMAXfv8WYhsbhZeI784JNF35NpTb.ip-10-240-5-96 (archived at https://perma.cc/5TQQ-FMUH)

51 Interview conducted February 2022 (online)

52 Overfishing, WWF. www.worldwildlife.org/threats/overfishing (archived at https://perma.cc/KE7D-YHBS)

53 European Commission. 2022 Country report: Spain, 23 May 2022. commission.europa.eu/system/files/2022-05/2022-european-semester-country-report-spain_en.pdf (archived at https://perma.cc/6U3D-3KSS)

54 Simone Tagliapietra. The world won't be a greener place until it's a fairer one, *The Guardian*, 9 April 2021. www.theguardian.com/world/commentisfree/2021/apr/09/world-greener-fairer-climate-crisis-social-contract-poor-vulnerable (archived at https://perma.cc/7MW4-3YH3)

55 Green jobs, International Labour Organization (ILO). www.ilo.org/asia/projects/WCMS_099647/lang--en/index.htm (archived at https://perma.cc/4M9Y-XYQW)

56 Rafaela Lindeberg and Clara Hernanz Lizarraga. H&M, Inditex stores close in Israel following Hamas attacks, Bloomberg, 10 October 2023. www.bloomberg.com/news/articles/2023-10-10/israel-h-m-inditex-stores-close-following-hamas-attacks (archived at https://perma.cc/7583-WRSY)

57 A Abrams, K Carden, C Teta and K Wågsæther. Water, sanitation, and hygiene vulnerability among rural areas and small towns in South Africa: Exploring the role of climate change, marginalization, and inequality, *Water*, 9 October 2021. consensus.app/papers/water-sanitation-hygiene-vulnerability-among-rural-areas-abrams/67ca88b457735d4c8772468b4bd379b6/?utm_source=chatgpt (archived at https://perma.cc/3H9G-C4QS)

58 Graeme Reid. Progress and setbacks on LGBT rights in Africa: An overview of the last year, Human Rights Watch, 22 June 2022. www.hrw.org/news/2022/06/22/progress-and-setbacks-lgbt-rights-africa-overview-last-year (archived at https://perma.cc/36K3-78WJ); UN Economic Commission for Africa (UNECA). New and Emerging Challenges in Africa Summary Report, 2011. sustainabledevelopment.un.org/index.php?page=view&type=400&nr=502&menu=1515

59 Olivia Lai. Deforestation in Southeast Asia: Causes and solutions, Earth.org, 7 March 2022. earth.org/deforestation-in-southeast-asia/ (archived at https://perma.cc/EXY9-MNXX)

60 Asia's wicked environmental problems, Asian Development Bank, February 2012. www.adb.org/publications/asias-wicked-environmental-problems (archived at https://perma.cc/NZ83-EJKR)

61 LGBT rights, Human Rights Watch. www.hrw.org/topic/lgbt-rights (archived at https://perma.cc/R79M-7F52)

62 Labor migration in the Arab states, ILO. www.ilo.org/beirut/areasofwork/labour-migration/WCMS_514910/lang--en/index.htm (archived at https://perma.cc/46CX-PH2M)

63 Gender equality and discrimination in Asia and the Pacific: 12 things to know, Asian Development Bank, 18 September 2012. www.adb.org/features/12-things-know-2012-gender-equality (archived at https://perma.cc/6CSP-79YS)

64 Audrey Tan and Francesco Ricciardi. Climate threat: Rising sea levels and stronger storms highlight the need for coastal resilience, Asian Development Bank, 12 July 2023. blogs.adb.org/blog/climate-threat-rising-sea-levels-and-stronger-storms-highlight-need-coastal-resilience (archived at https://perma.cc/CHJ7-A5EF)

65 East Asia and Pacific Cities: Expanding opportunities for the urban poor, World Bank. www.worldbank.org/en/region/eap/publication/east-asia-and-pacific-cities-expanding-opportunities-for-the-urban-poor (archived at https://perma.cc/M3NZ-SJC8)
66 Jon Heggie. Failing rains and thirsty cities: Australia's growing water problem, *National Geographic*, 2019. www.nationalgeographic.com/environment/article/partner-content-australia-water-problem (archived at https://perma.cc/5R9C-CX3L)
67 Thailynn Munroe and Rod Taylor. 4 things to know about Australia's wildfires and their impacts on forests, World Resource Institute, 10 January 2020. https://www.wri.org/insights/4-things-know-about-australias-wildfires-and-their-impacts-forests (archived at https://perma.cc/TS72-XR6R)
68 Coral bleaching: What it is, how it happens and what we're doing to help, Great Barrier Reef Foundation. www.barrierreef.org/the-reef/threats/coral-bleaching (archived at https://perma.cc/73FS-6DJM)
69 Human rights and aboriginal Torres Strait islanders peoples, Australian Human Rights Commission. humanrights.gov.au/sites/default/files/content/letstalkaboutrights/downloads/HRA_ATSI.pdf (archived at https://perma.cc/M9DB-VX6P)
70 Migration, European Parliament. www.europarl.europa.eu/news/en/headlines/priorities/migration (archived at https://perma.cc/F793-YWPD)
71 Europe and the refugee crisis: A challenge to our civilization, UN Academic Impact, September 2023. www.un.org/en/academic-impact/europe-and-refugee-crisis-challenge-our-civilization (archived at https://perma.cc/FHH3-ULTG)
72 Sweden is suffering a grim wave of gang violence, *The Economist*, 13 November 2023. www.economist.com/europe/2023/11/13/sweden-is-suffering-a-grim-wave-of-gang-violence (archived at https://perma.cc/7C57-8PNY)
73 Infographic: Terrorism in the EU: Facts and figures (2021), European Council. www.consilium.europa.eu/en/infographics/terrorism-eu-facts-figures/ (archived at https://perma.cc/5DRP-M7HV)
74 A European approach to artificial intelligence, European Commission. digital-strategy.ec.europa.eu/en/policies/european-approach-artificial-intelligence (archived at https://perma.cc/4TNA-CYZ7)
75 Events: Billion-dollar weather and climate disasters, National Centers for Environmental Information, 2023. www.ncei.noaa.gov/access/billions/events/US/1980-2023?disasters[]=all-disasters (archived at https://perma.cc/P5TZ-KFSL)
76 North America Human Rights Issues country by country, Amnesty International. https://www.amnesty.org/en/countries/ (archived at https://perma.cc/8FWE-LYAD)
77 What are the biggest drivers of tropical deforestation? WWF, Summer 2013. www.worldwildlife.org/magazine/issues/summer-2018/articles/what-are-the-

biggest-drivers-of-tropical-deforestation (archived at https://perma.cc/7XWV-RDJV); National Geographic Education, Amazon deforestation and climate change. education.nationalgeographic.org/resource/amazon-deforestation-and-climate-change/ (archived at https://perma.cc/ELZ3-8HXB)

78 Amnesty International. Americas regional overview, 2022. www.amnesty.org/en/location/americas/report-americas/ (archived at https://perma.cc/T6LE-C6AC)

79 Credit Institute. Global wealth report, leading perspectives to navigate the future, 2022. www.credit-suisse.com/media/assets/corporate/docs/about-us/research/publications/global-wealth-report-2022-en.pdf (archived at https://perma.cc/YQ55-NNRN)

80 Johan Rockström and Owen Gaffney (2021) *Breaking Boundaries: The science of our planet*, DK, London

81 Inequality puts our world at risk, Organization for Economic Co-operation and Development (OECD). www.oecd.org/inclusive-growth/#inequality-puts-our-world-at-risk (archived at https://perma.cc/2USU-QWYP)

82 Johan Rockström and Owen Gaffney (2021) *Breaking Boundaries: The science of our planet*, DK, London

83 Beyond GDP, OECD. www.oecd.org/inclusive-growth/#beyond-gdp (archived at https://perma.cc/9T7Z-PSED)

84 Jedediah Britton-Purdy. The green new deal is what realistic environmental policy looks like, *The New York Times*, 14 February 2019. www.nytimes.com/2019/02/14/opinion/green-new-deal-ocasio-cortez-.html (archived at https://perma.cc/6SZK-MJTV)

85 Charlotte Mack-Heller. 5 examples of cross-sector collaboration for conservation, climate change, and sustainability, Resonance, 22 April 2021. www.resonanceglobal.com/blog/5-cross-sector-collaboration-examples-for-conservation-and-climate-change-impact (archived at https://perma.cc/KKS5-L3M2)

86 WHO. Household air pollution, 15 December 2023. www.who.int/news-room/fact-sheets/detail/household-air-pollution-and-health (archived at https://perma.cc/QW7C-KBW4)

87 Systems change, Ashoka. www.ashoka.org/en-nrd/systems-change (archived at https://perma.cc/K37M-Q9RX)

88 Alexis Gazzo. Why biodiversity may be more important to your business than you realize, EY, 25 April 2022. www.ey.com/en_gl/assurance/why-biodiversity-may-be-more-important-to-your-business-than-you-realize (archived at https://perma.cc/XVW4-9T57)

89 Interview conducted December 2021

90 How do you leverage the strengths and resources of each sector in a cross-sector partnership? LinkedIn, 29 February 2024. www.linkedin.com/advice/0/how-do-you-leverage-strengths-resources (archived at https://perma.cc/E7XQ-N938)

91 Global emissions, Centre for Climate and Energy Solutions. www.c2es.org/content/international-emissions/ (archived at https://perma.cc/H8KP-X7V3)

92 New report shows just 100 companies are source of over 70% of emissions, CDP, 10 July 2017. www.cdp.net/en/articles/media/new-report-shows-just-100-companies-are-source-of-over-70-of-emissions (archived at https://perma.cc/8FBE-AMGF)

93 James Epstein-Reeves and Ellen Weinreb. Paul Hawken: Programming a new operating system for civilization, *The Guardian*, 23 September 2013. www.theguardian.com/sustainable-business/paul-hawken-profile (archived at https://perma.cc/8SVS-8JZ7)

94 Interview conducted October 2021

95 WWF Mexico and WWF Nature Pays, IKEA, www.ikeasocialentrepreneurship.org/en/partnerships/accelerating-for-impact/wwf (archived at https://perma.cc/4D3N-F2YB)

96 Judith Wolst et al. 20 trender mot 2030: En rapport om Teknik, hållbarhet och framtid [20 trends towards 2030, a report about technology, sustainability and the future], March 2023. www.mot2030.se/?ref=judithwolst.se (archived at https://perma.cc/2FVT-LTVM)

97 Rebecka Carlsson, exponential climate solutions, 2020. www.rebeckacarlsson.se (archived at https://perma.cc/7MJW-Y8KT)

98 See exponentialroadmap.org (archived at https://perma.cc/78LU-QTBL)

99 Paul Hawkens, Project Drawdown. https://drawdown.org/ (archived at https://perma.cc/LAC4-4H2B)

100 See climatetrace.org (archived at https://perma.cc/2RWQ-QXJ3)

101 Quick facts, NASA. ocov2.jpl.nasa.gov/mission/quick-facts/ (archived at https://perma.cc/928W-KTTT)

102 UN announces high-tech, satellite-based global methane detection system, UN Environment Programme (UNEP), 11 November 2022. www.unep.org/news-and-stories/press-release/un-announces-high-tech-satellite-based-global-methane-detection (archived at https://perma.cc/V3SS-UX3T)

103 The fiber traceability initiative: Towards full traceability in fashion, Axfoundation. www.axfoundation.se/en/projects/sheep-on-repeat-en (archived at https://perma.cc/X6ZK-H2RT)

104 AI for good global summit, aiforgood.itu.int (archived at https://perma.cc/64CV-34C7)

105 V Eubanks (2018) *Automating Inequality: How high-tech tools profile, police, and punish the poor*, St Martin's Press, New York

106 AI for all, *The Economist*, January–February 2024, p. 10

107 Judith Wolst. Rapport: Vad sjutton är blockkedjor? & vad kan de användas till? [Report: What the Hell Are Blockchains? & what can they be used for?], 22 November 2022. www.judithwolst.se/rapport-vad-sjutton-ar-blockkedjor-och-vad-kan-de-anvandas-till/ (archived at https://perma.cc/9PMS-BNSD)

108 Nicky Morris. Carrefour extends food traceability blockchain, Ledger Insights, 6 August 2018. www.ledgerinsights.com/carrefour-food-traceability-blockchain/ (archived at https://perma.cc/8M8F-D5EZ); Robert Hackett. Walmart and 9 food giants team up on IBM blockchain plans, Fortune, 22 August 2017. fortune.com/2017/08/22/walmart-blockchain-ibm-food-nestle-unilever-tyson-dole/ (archived at https://perma.cc/9WTV-JZM8)

109 See www.banqu.co/about (archived at https://perma.cc/3NVM-C7B8)

The evolving role of sustainability leadership

02

If you're reading this book, chances are you're deeply invested in sustainability and eager to make a meaningful impact. We believe that engaging and contributing as employees, through our organizations and companies, is one of the most effective ways to achieve sustainability transformation. Hence, this book focuses on the role individuals can play within organizations, through their everyday work.

A lot of focus is placed on the role of the CSO or sustainability manager, with their sustainability teams, but this book also covers other roles in the corporate sector, as we firmly believe that a successful sustainability transformation can only happen when people across the entire organization are involved and contributing. Again, the emphasis here is on the notion that meaningful change occurs and is propelled through the collective efforts of organizations and businesses, as opposed to isolated, individual actions. Every individual has a role to play and can contribute to positive change in different ways.

Ways for you and me to contribute to sustainability

In the book *Tomorrow's Economy*, author Per Espen Stoknes introduces four distinct roles individuals can adopt to effectively contribute to sustainability, offering a practical framework for personal engagement in environmental and societal change. We can act as consumers, owners/

Figure 2.1 The four roles of sustainable development that individuals can play

1. Consumer The classic example is to be a consumer: to vote with one's wallet and to live as sustainably as possible through one's day-to-day shopping behaviour.	**2. Owner** Another role is to be an engaged owner: to review the placement of one's pensions and savings and to ensure that the money is invested in more sustainable sectors and companies.
3. Engaged citizen Engaged citizens use their voting power to select the most sustainably dedicated politicians and decision makers, and to use their voice collectively.	**4. Employee** Finally, the fourth role is to be an engaged employee and to influence organizations and systems through one's everyday profession.

investors, citizens and employees.[1] Most likely you will act in the capacity of all four roles over your lifetime. All four distinct roles are essential in transitioning to a more sustainable and equal society where key actors in finance, regulations, civic society and businesses are aligned, enabling the necessary transition to take place.

As illustrated in Figure 2.1, we can influence the political space through democratic voting. We can initiate change through financial investments by consciously setting aside our savings for more environmentally or socially responsible investments. And as consumers, we can make a significant difference by reducing our consumption and supporting sustainable products and brands. While individuals strive to make conscientious choices, the impact can often feel negligible when weighed against systemic challenges. Surely, it's important to remember that collective action begins with individual efforts. Your role, no matter how modest, forms a critical part of a larger, influential movement towards a sustainable future. However, acting alone can be heavy and lonely, while working together with others can be motivating and spur systems change. Working together with others can be done on community level, through advocacy, on social media and through organizations and workplaces.

Thus, while the first three roles have already received some recognition, we believe that the fourth role – *to act as an employee through our organizations*

– requires more attention. It could, of course, also be a role outside the organization, for example a consultancy agency supporting an organization to become more sustainable. The point is that the impact is happening through work and organizations, rather than individuals striving on their own. The role we all can play through our professions is crucial: we can create more impact together, through organizations and businesses, to achieve structural changes than by acting alone as private individuals.

CASE STUDY Use your professional skill set to create a positive change

Kali Andersson is a licensed psychologist, environmental activist and permaculture designer. Inspired by a TV programme she watched when she was a child, she took the reins in her personal life to advocate for sustainability. Every day, she cycled a commendable 36 km to work; she embraced a vegan diet and exclusively consumed local, homemade produce. 'I dedicated myself wholly, cycling and crafting my own essentials. However, it often felt like a solitary battle,' Kali recounts.

Her professional journey took her first to the field of psychology, aiming to aid individuals traumatized by destructive workplaces. She found, however, that after recovery many would return to the very environments that had once broken them. The cyclical nature reminded her of the endless battles against environmental deterioration. Although her personal commitment to sustainability was unwavering, she felt the weight of the challenge when broader societal change seemed stagnant. Diving deep into research on climate change, sociology and behavioural dynamics, Kali experienced an epiphany. She recognized the untapped potential of psychology in fostering the behaviour change vital for environmental conservation. 'What if my expertise in psychology could be a powerful tool for the climate?' she wondered. With renewed vigour and purpose, Kali co-founded the Climate Psychologists.[2] This innovative initiative aimed to reshape societal views on sustainability by harnessing psychological strategies. Their reach grew, encompassing workshops and lectures with politicians, business leaders and educators. Their work has even resulted in a guidebook on sustainability and behaviour science, called climate psychology.

Kali firmly believes that while individual efforts like hers at the consumer level are commendable, the real change springs from collective action and systemic shifts. As she succinctly states, 'We cannot merely buy our way out of problems rooted in consumption. Systematic change is paramount.' Reflecting on the sustainability journey ahead, Kali emphasizes resilience and perseverance. Drawing on her rich background in psychology, she contends that navigating uncertain terrains while advocating change is of the essence. 'It revolves around grasping what we can modify, mustering the courage to initiate the change, and discerning the contrast between the two,' she elaborates. In Kali's narrative, the multifaceted nature of sustainability emerges, revealing how even a seemingly unrelated field, like psychology, can substantially inform and impact the discourse on environmental conservation. For leaders in sustainability, Kali's insights underline the need to harness diverse organizational skills to promote sustainable practices.

At its core, Kali's story is a clarion call, emphasizing that everyone, irrespective of their professional lineage or designation, can bring a unique perspective to the sustainability discourse. It beckons CSOs to envision sustainability not just as a strategy but as a transformative movement pivoted on behaviour change, where each stakeholder's role is vital.[3]

By influencing and driving change through our workplaces, we can transform the core of value chains and sectors to contribute to the global SDGs and a better future for all. The SDGs are a set of 17 universal targets aimed at ending poverty, protecting the planet and ensuring prosperity for all by 2030.[4] As an in-house designer, engineer or logistical specialist, one can, for example, improve the sustainability characteristics of the company's products, the packaging and/or the transport of the products. Working in marketing and sales, one can develop tools and methods to steer sales towards the more sustainable alternatives, and so forth. We will elaborate more on how one can influence through various functions in Part 2.

The growing sustainability job market

Employees increasingly look for sustainability and purpose when joining organizations

The interest in jobs with a positive impact and a focus on sustainability has grown tremendously. Recent research shows that organizations that intend to contribute positively to society and the environment attract the most talent.[5] Students and others are interested in contributing to solving social and environmental challenges, but they often do not see the opportunities ahead of them. Most people still think that if they want to contribute to a better world, they must work for UNICEF or Greenpeace, or possibly in a dedicated sustainability manager role in the private sector.

In the past, employees were looking for jobs that offered stability, career opportunities, solid incomes and good pension frameworks. In 2008, when Lisen joined a corporate trainee programme in Norway, the hiring manager was promoting the financial and pension package as the most critical workplace benefit. Lisen was pretty surprised, as she had never been driven by salary, fancy titles or pension packages; the company spirit and people had always attracted her. Pay and stability are, of course, still the essential aspect for many when it comes to work. But for a growing, fortunate group who can choose their work path, the employee wish list is very different. Research shows an apparent movement towards more meaningful and sustainable professions.[6]

Although the extent to which sustainability is vital to employees and candidates vary among different age groups and genders, there is an increasing interest and awareness across those groups. According to the latest studies conducted by Edelman on the *belief-driven employee* in 2021, the expressed ambition and actions companies take regarding environmental and societal matters are deal-breaking factors in an employee staying at a job or a candidate accepting a job offer.[7] The research, conducted in seven markets – Brazil, China, Germany, India, Japan, the UK and the US – covered a total of 7,000 employees. According to the study, employees are looking for more fulfilling jobs. They want to work for socially engaged organizations and to be part of an inclusive culture. According to the study, 62 per cent of the subjects are compelled to take a job offer from *organizations that demonstrate a solid commitment to social and environmental impact*. Seventy-one per cent of employees consider social impact opportunities a deal breaker or an encouraging factor. Social impact opportunities include working for a bigger purpose, having a meaningful job that shapes society and having opportunities to address social problems.

Another study, carried out in 2021 by the IBM Institute for Business Value (IBV), showed that 71 per cent of employees viewed environmentally sustainable organizations as more attractive employers.[8] More than two-thirds of them were more likely to apply for and accept jobs with environmentally and socially responsible organizations and nearly half surveyed would accept a lower salary to work for such organizations. As these ratios are very high, a disclaimer might be required: these studies do not unfold to what *degree* companies and organizations should focus on sustainability.

CASE STUDY Impact through business

Sarah Garcia, leading the market development and growth agenda at B Lab Europe, has a background marked by a striking transition. Raised in Guadalajara, Mexico, she was acutely aware of the stark inequalities around her. Her father used their daily drives through the city's diverse landscapes to teach her valuable lessons about empathy and gratitude. These early experiences ignited Sarah's drive to create a more inclusive and sustainable world.

Initially, Sarah gravitated towards NGOs and international human rights law, believing this was the best avenue for positive change. Her experiences in Ethiopia and Peru provided her with a deep understanding of the struggles in marginalized communities. However, her career took a pivotal turn during an eye-opening internship at the Dutch Entrepreneurial Development Bank (FMO). It was there that she realized the private sector's immense potential to drive meaningful change.

As a result, Sarah shifted her focus to sustainability within the private sector. Now, at B Lab Europe, Sarah plays a crucial role in helping multinational companies embrace sustainability and inclusivity through a rigorous certification process. Working across various industries, she is encouraged by the growing commitment to sustainability she observes. Sarah is convinced that transforming large corporations can create widespread positive changes across different sectors.

Sarah Garcia's transition from NGOs to the business world highlights the broad scope of impact in sustainability. It's not confined to NGOs and the public sector; businesses, with their extensive reach in raw materials, transportation and production, are integral to this movement. Sarah's journey underlines the importance of embedding sustainable practices in every aspect of business operations for a truly impactful change.[9]

Demand for sustainability talent is growing among employers

This apparent trend driven from an employee perspective is, fortunately, matched by an increasing demand for competence from the job market. To mention a few examples, the number of CSOs at US publicly traded companies grew sixfold between 2011 and 2023, with more CSOs appointed in 2021 than in the previous five years combined.[10] With less than 15 per cent of companies having a CSO in place (in 2021), there is a significant and growing demand for sustainability leaders.[11] PwC announced in June 2021 that it would invest $12 billion over five years to create 100,000 new jobs. Those jobs are aimed at helping clients to manage the climate and diversity reporting.[12] LinkedIn reports indicate a greening of jobs, meaning that jobs are becoming more green or sustainable; this suggests that sustainability is fast becoming an essential aspect of every job. In 2021, LinkedIn's chief economist, Karin Kimbrough, stated that millions of new jobs would be created, and existing jobs would change, due to government and company pledges to become carbon neutral.[13]

Estimates in 2018 from the ILO showed that 24 million new jobs would be created globally by 2030 because of sustainable practices adopted and implemented.[14] The Future of Jobs Report 2023, by the World Economic Forum (WEF), reveals that hiring for green roles has surpassed overall hiring rates globally for four consecutive years. In a slowing labour market, green jobs – such as sustainability analysts, specialists and managers – are increasingly appealing and secure options for job seekers. These roles have consistently been among the fastest growing globally, as per LinkedIn's annual 'Jobs on the Rise' lists.[15] These jobs will be established in various sectors, including innovation and technology, clean energy, and climate change mitigation, such as erosion control.

A 2021 report by Swedish Enterprises highlights the urgent need for competencies and people within several critical sectors, such as the industry and transport sector, to manage the energy transition and the sustainability goals set by the Swedish government. The report highlights that there will be new competence needs and that companies and other organizations must prepare to ensure they gain the necessary expertise.[16] Several organizations have published different sustainability job lists to provide an idea of the future job market. Our Kids' Climate (read the case study of Frida Berry Eklund in Chapter 7) and the Climate Club have, together with experts, developed a list of 101 professions that are needed to reach the SDGs. These jobs include existing professions that will increasingly contribute to sustainability and new functions that will meet the growing demand.

Different types of sustainability jobs[17]

Existing jobs and professions

Existing jobs are those functions and professions that exist today but will have an increasing focus on sustainability. As social and environmental commitments will become an integrated part of organizations, every position will have a role to play. Eventually, as mentioned in the LinkedIn report, this could be any job, since all organizations that aim to grow need to address sustainability in their area. In Part 2 and Part 3 of this book, examples of doctors, marketeers, psychologists and economists will be mentioned.

New types of jobs

Next to the currently existing jobs, there will be a growth of new types of professions. There is quite an exciting list of new opportunities: ocean-bound plastic engineer, algae farmer, climate mitigation planner and tiny-house architect, to mention a few. Other lists cite urban farming, wave producers to harness the energy generated by the seas, and hydrologists to improve access to clean drinking water. And many more people with competence in sustainability and social impact will be needed.

Thus, as we enter the era of the Fourth Industrial Revolution – the next phase in the digitization of the manufacturing sector – the job market is undergoing a transformative shift. This new phase is characterized by a move towards digitization and the integration of advanced technologies like AI, robotics and cloud computing in manufacturing. This revolution is not only enhancing productivity and sustainability, but also significantly altering job roles and skills requirements. As a result, there's a growing emphasis on upskilling and reskilling the workforce to meet these evolving demands. Industry 4.0's impact is widespread, affecting every industry, with a projected value creation of $3.7 trillion by 2025, reshaping businesses and employment landscapes globally.[18]

The Future of Jobs Report 2023 highlights the digital revolution and green transition as key drivers reshaping the global job market.[19] Autonomous and electric vehicle specialists, AI and machine learning experts, and environmental protection professionals are among the fastest-growing jobs. Conversely, roles like bank tellers and data entry clerks face decline due to digitalization and automation. The report anticipates a net decrease of 14 million jobs globally, with significant job creation in non-technological roles like heavy truck drivers and vocational education teachers. The green transition is expected to create millions of jobs, but reskilling and upskilling efforts are lagging behind this growth.

A large percentage of these jobs will be created due to the greening of the economy, but it is important to underline that it is not only the energy sector that will require this competence. Product designers will be expected to understand sustainable product design, circular product principles and the product's life cycle impact, from both a social and an environmental perspective. Investment and insurance analysts need to understand how to assess a business's exposure to social and environmental risks and make recommendations accounting for these risks. Data engineers will increasingly focus on reducing their computing infrastructure's energy load. Teachers need to secure competence development among their students. Psychologists can support the behaviour change journey, and entrepreneurs need to develop business models that contribute to a more inclusive and sustainable society.

Sustainability roles within an organization

A first step in achieving integration is to examine the various roles within the organization. While the end goal is that sustainability should be fully embedded in every function of the organization, a starting point is to have someone (such as a sustainability leader or CSO) dedicated to orchestrating this transformation. This approach ensures that there is a clear focus and leadership in driving the sustainability agenda, facilitating a more structured and effective integration of sustainable practices across various departments and operations. Such a dedicated role can serve as a catalyst for change, helping to align organizational strategies with sustainability objectives and laying the groundwork for their eventual full integration into all organizational activities. Sustainability teams should evolve from leading to facilitating, helping each department adopt sustainable practices. Organizational structures differ: some have a comprehensive team under a CSO, while others have just a few roles focused on sustainability.

- **CSO:** At the forefront of sustainability leadership, the CSO assumes the highest-ranking position, directly reporting to the CEO. The CSO is responsible for shaping the organization's sustainability strategy, setting ambitious goals and driving its implementation across all levels and functions. This role requires strong leadership skills, a comprehensive understanding of sustainability principles and the ability to align sustainability initiatives with the organization's overall business objectives.[20] This is still a relatively new role, as the first CSO was appointed only in 2004.[21]

- **Sustainability manager:** This role can be found at various levels within an organization, depending on its size and structure. These professionals play a central role in integrating sustainability practices into day-to-day operations and decision-making processes. They collaborate with cross-functional teams to develop and execute sustainability initiatives, monitor progress and ensure compliance with relevant standards and regulations. Sustainability managers are instrumental in fostering a culture of sustainability throughout the organization and are often responsible for engaging stakeholders both internally and externally.
- The terms 'sustainability manager' and 'CSO' are occasionally used interchangeably, but their roles can vary significantly depending on the organization's structure. In some instances, the CSO acts as the global lead, overseeing the company's overarching sustainability strategy, while sustainability managers may operate at the national level, implementing and adapting the global objectives to local contexts and requirements.
- **Sustainability developer:** As organizations strive for continuous improvement and innovation in sustainability, the role of a sustainability developer is useful. These professionals explore emerging trends, technologies and business opportunities that align with sustainability objectives. They assess the potential impact of new initiatives, identify areas for improvement and develop strategies to enhance the organization's environmental and social performance. Sustainability developers work closely with R&D teams, industry partners and external experts to drive innovation that contributes to both sustainability and business growth. Sustainability developers can also be placed in the procurement or supply function, responsible for supporting suppliers and partners, to achieve Scope 3 commitments.
- **Compliance specialist:** This person plays a crucial role in sustainability management by ensuring the organization meets sustainability standards, legal requirements and best practices. They audit, advise on compliance strategies and help implement corrective actions and monitoring systems. By training business units and aiding in the adoption of compliance measures, they promote ethical and responsible operations. However, the

daily maintenance of these standards falls on the business developers and operational teams, emphasizing the importance of continuous adherence beyond periodic audits.

- **Sustainability analyst:** This role harnesses data to enhance sustainability outcomes, creating key performance indicators (KPIs), tracking goals and generating reports. Sustainability analysts' work, such as assessing the climate impacts of materials, guides strategic material and product choices, which are crucial for future sustainability efforts. Through data analysis, they facilitate informed decision making, spotlight improvement opportunities and communicate successes, supporting the company's sustainability strategy.

The roles mentioned above are not exhaustive, and organizations may create customized positions tailored to their specific sustainability goals. When designing and managing the sustainability organization, it is essential to have clear governance and accountability across the roles so that each role is clear and an effective part of the total. This also enables constructive collaboration between the different team members. Additionally, the integration of sustainability into an organization's DNA requires collaboration and coordination among various roles, fostering a holistic approach to embedding sustainability within business practices.

Tool: Matrix management

In many organizations, which operate in a matrix structure, country sustainability managers report to their national teams and also form part of a matrix team. Striving for a balance between a universally applicable global strategy and regional adaptability is central in forging a unified and effective global sustainability narrative. To optimize the matrix management model, strive to foster a community spirit. This community should serve as a hub for exchanging challenges, successes and innovative practices, providing a dynamic support system for both moral encouragement and pragmatic solutions. In this structure, individuals with sustainability responsibilities, social ambassadors and members of green groups all converge to form a vibrant community. They exchange ideas and learn from one another, forming a matrix that's not just about reporting lines or organizational charts, but also about fostering strong connections and a shared mission.

The role of the sustainability leader

The success of sustainability transformation is a collective effort, requiring collaboration across all organizational functions, including finance, supply chain, operations and marketing. This book advocates for integrating sustainability into every role and task, with Chapter 6 presenting a case study on embedding sustainability in job descriptions.

While focusing on the role of sustainability managers and leaders who aim to drive sustainability, we emphasize the need for clear roles, responsibilities and authority for these positions. Without clarity and strategic placement within the organization, sustainability initiatives may falter. We further explore the critical elements of the CSO role in Chapter 10.

As environmental and social sustainability gain importance, many organizations are introducing roles like sustainability officers or managers. Unlike established roles such as sales managers or chief financial officers (CFOs), the sustainability role often lacks a standardized description, making it imperative for organizations to clearly define these positions, grant appropriate authority and strategically integrate them into their structure for effective sustainability management.

Areas of responsibility

In some organizations, the sustainability leader may be responsible for implementing sustainability policies and practices, like waste reduction or renewable energy initiatives. In others, they may be responsible for ensuring the company meets relevant legal requirements, handling corporate social responsibility programmes or even integrating sustainability considerations into every aspect of the organization's operations, from procurement to marketing. The responsibilities can vary drastically from one organization to another. As the title of this book suggests, we argue that while these responsibilities lie under the CSO, it is crucial to secure the implementation of every area into relevant functions.

The role of a sustainability leader is diverse and dynamic, often encompassing a wide range of tasks that may vary greatly from day to day – this contributes to its appeal.[22] Here are some of the responsibilities and tasks that were on the table for us during our tenure as global and national sustainability managers:

- **Developing strategic frameworks:** This involves establishing the strategic sustainability direction of the company, while aligning it with the business strategy and the purpose of the company. It could include, for example, enabling workshops and dialogues at all levels of the organization about whether the company, and its purpose, is fit for the future. An important part of the strategy work is securing adequate funding and investment processes across the organization to enable the development and implementation work.

- **Innovation management:** From reviewing proposals for green technologies to exploring new business models like a circular economy, the CSO's role is to stay at the forefront of innovation that can drive sustainability. An important part of this is to be a forward-thinker, keeping an eye on international policy changes, scientific reports on climate change and emerging green technologies that can impact or enhance the company's sustainability efforts.
- **Cross-departmental communication:** Ensuring sustainability goals are integrated into all aspects of the business requires regular communication with various departments. This might include collaboration with the supply chain for sustainable sourcing, with product development for eco-design or with HR for employee engagement in sustainability. It might also involve sustainability training programmes outlining the importance of individual and collective action.
- **Stakeholder engagement:** This ranges from presenting to the board of directors about sustainability agendas to engaging with customers and local communities, which may involve organizing community service events, participating in local environmental initiatives or leading corporate social responsibility programmes. Whether it's collaborating with NGOs on conservation projects or working with other businesses on joint sustainability ventures, building strategic partnerships is key.
- **External communication:** Crafting a compelling sustainability narrative for the public is a key part of the job. This involves working with marketing to promote the company's sustainability efforts and shape its public image as a responsible business. When sustainability-related issues arise, such as supply chain disruptions due to environmental concerns or public outcry over corporate practices, the CSO is at the helm of problem solving and crisis management.
- **Reviewing and analysing sustainability metrics:** This involves not just looking at numbers but interpreting complex data sets to gauge the effectiveness of sustainability initiatives, carbon footprints and the life cycle impacts of products or services. The CSO needs to understand the story behind the metrics to make informed decisions.

Sustainability leaders do not want to be accountants

An article by Marshall Chase emphasizes the growing concern among sustainability professionals, who find themselves increasingly mired in data management.[23] This trend is driven by evolving standards and regulations, alongside the increasing legal demand to be able to substantiate sustainability claims. Chase paints a vivid picture of the current landscape, where the balance between data accuracy and actionable sustainability initiatives is tipping precariously. He warns of the dangers of sustainability roles becoming too focused on data, metaphorically likening it to fixating on the speedometer while speeding towards a cliff, instead of focusing on avoiding the imminent danger. The trend presents a significant challenge for the sector, as it struggles to strike a balance between the need for data integrity and the imperative for tangible sustainability efforts. This scenario highlights a crucial labour trade-off: every moment spent on data collection could be a missed opportunity for real, impactful action.

Chase also scrutinizes the actual impact of data. In some cases, existing data might be sufficient for taking decisive action, making the pursuit of additional data an exercise in redundancy. This observation raises critical questions about the real value of enhanced data in driving more effective sustainability outcomes.

Looking towards potential solutions, Chase suggests that attracting more people to the accounting profession with links to sustainability could be a way forward. This mirrors our belief that instead of trying to find sustainability people with all the necessary skills across, for example, accounting, marketing, product design and so forth, people already holding these jobs should get sustainability tasks and responsibilities integrated into their job descriptions. For example, many companies are already separating out reporting tasks from the team driving organizational change.

Placement

Where the sustainability role fits within the organization's structure is often unclear. Should it be a standalone department, or should it be a function within an existing department like operations, HR or marketing? The placement of this role can significantly affect its visibility, influence and effectiveness. Often, sustainability managers report to marketing or communications managers. Being part of one specific function gives them quite limited exposure to the overall issues they shall deal with. And they might be steered to focus on such topics rather than the holistic sustainability agenda. Waste management, compliance and energy consumption might, for example, be less valued than awareness creation.

Today, in large global organizations, CSOs increasingly and typically report directly to the CEO.[24] As the role of the CSO cuts across the entire organization, and is about strategy, innovation and transformation, we believe that the role should report to the CEO or chief operating officer (COO). This will give the CSO an umbrella view of the organization and bring the role close to top management and their decisions; it will therefore not be seen as forming part of any specific department. The CSO needs to move between all departments depending on the focus topic or where things are falling behind. For example, if the role sits in the communications department, there is a risk that the focus will shift towards PR and public affairs activities – sustainability activities that improve the reputation of the organization. If the role is in the legal department, on the other hand, there is a risk of the CSO mainly having a risk minimization mindset and focusing on legal compliance. If in operations, the CSO might focus on operational efficiency. The CSO needs to be active across all these areas and, therefore, should report to the CEO.

Mandate

Whether you are leading a small team, managing a national entity or in charge of inspiring change in a global organization, your mandate's scope will determine the strategies and actions required to achieve your sustainability goals. Each mandate, depending on its scale and influence, carries unique implications, and it's crucial to discern them at the earliest. Level of mandate often depends on the maturity, size and geographical spread of an organization. Within large international organizations, the sustainability matrix often contains team members with all the different levels of mandate, as you often find people working with sustainability at the global office, on country level and at unit level.

Mandates at different levels

Local-level mandate

If you are working in a larger organization, your mandate differs depending on where in the structure you are. If you are leading a small team, your mandate might involve creating a culture of sustainability within a small group of individuals.

When dealing with sustainability on a local scale, the focus often zooms in on the smaller, everyday practices. It is about getting the basics right, with small steps, leading to big impact. Consider, for example, the discussions we often found ourselves navigating, as co-workers pondered whether using a dishwasher or opting for single-use cups is the more sustainable choice. These might seem like small considerations, but they play a critical role in our sustainability journey, as these are the hands-on concerns that employees sit with. So as symbolic as they might be in the total footprint of a large production company, addressing them enables employees to feel that they can take action within their sphere of influence. However, it is always important to put these activities into the bigger context.

National-level mandate

On a larger scale, if you're responsible for a national entity or a multinational corporation, your role might entail creating systemic changes. Here, you might have to drive policy reforms, initiate large-scale green initiatives and foster an organizational culture that values sustainability. In such a case, the task is often complex and multidimensional, involving a range of stakeholders, from employees and customers to investors and policy-makers. Handling sustainability on a national level means dealing with a lot more – more units, more people and more complicated processes like handling products, services, production lines, transport and supply chains. This kind of big-picture management demands a thorough approach. Here's the key: doing your homework is crucial. You'll need a deep understanding of all the moving parts in your organization to create a strategy that works.

Your approach will also depend on the type of organization you're in. If you're part of a global entity, your job might involve making sure the national units align with wider global sustainability goals. It's like fitting your piece into a larger puzzle – ensuring your strategies not only follow the big-picture goals but also address local challenges and opportunities. If your organization is purely national, your strategy might be a bit more independent, but it's still important to be aware of global sustainability trends. That way, your local efforts will reflect both the challenges at home and contribute to worldwide sustainability conversations. Should you navigate the integration of numerous sub-brands, it is imperative to engage each respective brand management team, ensuring the coherent infusion of the sustainability strategy at every brand tier. The emphasis is on crafting a strategy that is both strong and flexible. Leaders managing at a national level need to create strategies that mesh with larger, potentially global, goals while also being finely tuned to address specific local needs and opportunities.

Global mandate

Stepping into a global role amplifies both your challenges and opportunities, demanding not just steering the sustainability strategy but also ensuring its complete, impactful deployment throughout the organization's entirety, bridging multiple nations and the full spectrum of the value chain. Your duty surpasses being a sustainability leader; you become a global catalyst for sustainable development, unifying multiple strategies while respecting varied cultural attitudes and navigating diverse legal frameworks.

In your journey to deeply embed sustainability, marrying strategic foresight with solid, actionable operations is paramount, especially in your pivotal role as a global CSO. It's more than crafting and guiding strategy; it's about ensuring it seamlessly integrates across every element of the organization, considering the multifaceted nature of diverse units and structures. The nuanced complexities of your role oblige you to fortify a clear and unwavering vision and strategy, safeguarded within a sturdy organizational foundation. Essential too is the necessity for your leadership to shape a robust organization, one that can deftly transpose the broad strategic road map into every unit, securing unity and consistency across myriad organizational levels and geographical horizons.

While it's important to focus on high-level strategies like developing impactful metrics and reshaping business models, it's equally crucial to engage in and demonstrate practical actions in your daily environment. Such engagement at various levels ensures that no action is too small or insignificant in contributing to sustainability. Thus, leadership in sustainability is reflected not only in strategic achievements but also in daily, simple actions. Embrace every aspect of sustainable practices – from waste sorting to considering your travel and eating habits, and even trying plant-based options in the canteen. These actions, though they may seem minor, play a significant role in setting an example for your team. It's the combined effort of everyone that truly embeds sustainability into the organization's fabric.

CASE STUDY Level of mandate

Kirsten van Zandwijk is the Sustainability and Partnership Director for the Association of Southeast Asian Nations (ASEAN) and South Pacific at Coca-Cola. That means she has a regional responsibility for sustainability. In her role, Kirsten not only ensures that the global strategy of Coca-Cola is adhered to at a minimum compliance level, especially in regions where challenges are prevalent, but also endeavours to surpass expectations wherever feasible. Her operational terrain spans across various countries in South East Asia and the Pacific, like Singapore, Malaysia and the Philippines – where plastic waste, in particular in coastal communities, is paramount – and Australia, where distinct challenges prevail.

Kirsten's role is twofold: ensuring that each country under her jurisdiction is facilitated and supported to deliver on Coca-Cola's sustainability commitments, and forging synergies and partnerships that drive change beyond the organizational level. She embodies a philosophy that surpasses basic compliance, advocating for transformative changes on the ground and crafting strategies that consider regional cultural and infrastructural disparities. Her work embodies the 4 principle that sustainability isn't solely a global objective but is most impactful when tailored and enacted at regional and local levels, making a concrete difference where it's needed most.[25]

Authority

The level of authority given to the sustainability role is another source of confusion. Are they a part of the executive management team, having the same authority as the marketing manager? Or do they operate in an advisory capacity, providing guidance but not making decisions? The lack of clarity can lead to conflicts or misunderstandings about who has the final say on sustainability-related issues. As the topic has tended to be the last thing on the agenda, it requires someone sitting at the decision table, being responsible for sustainability.

If your role is not embedded within the management team, forging robust connections to upper-level leadership becomes crucial. While stakeholder management and relationship building perennially sit at the heart of change management, it's imperative in this context to guarantee that those representing your sustainability initiatives at the decision-making table are not only well versed in the subject matter but also genuinely engaged. Ensuring that these key individuals are both knowledgeable and committed will underpin the effective representation and advancement of your sustainability agenda.

Thus, an essential initial step is a thorough understanding of your organization's primary objectives and those of its various units. Discerning whether the aim is to cut costs, boost sales, expand, innovate, rebrand, develop new products or merely sustain current operations is pivotal during the assessment phase. This knowledge enables you to customize and weave your sustainability message and strategy seamlessly into the units' plans. Identifying these objectives allows you to align sustainability initiatives in a manner that not only supports but potentially enhances these goals. For instance, if a unit is focused on reducing costs, introducing energy-saving initiatives could be a sustainable action that also lowers expenses. On the other hand, if the objective is rebranding or innovation, sustainability can be positioned as a cornerstone, demonstrating forward-thinking and responsibility. By dovetailing your sustainability strategy with the diverse goals of organizational units, you not only reinforce their objectives but also establish sustainability as an indispensable thread in the organization's overall tapestry.

Skills and capabilities

The role of sustainability manager is multifaceted and thus requires skills and capabilities across many levels: systems change (we will elaborate on this in Part 2), leadership and implementation skills. The University of Cambridge Institute for Sustainability Leadership (CISL) has created a framework focusing on developing and expanding leadership capacity[26] and Forum for the Future has designed systems change capabilities, arguing that in order to address current and future complex challenges the number of people who can think and act systemically and implement radical change need to increase.[27] Moreover, in a 2021 study by Deloitte, strategic thinking, communication, influence, education and the ability to drive change were stated as more valuable skills than technical and legal knowledge.[28] This underscores the evolving nature of the role, from being technical and operational to strategic and transformative.

Systems change capabilities[29]

- **Systemic diagnosis:** This includes being able to look at the challenges facing us in a holistic way, having a broad understanding of sustainability while also using tools such as systems thinking and mapping, futures inquiries and human-centred research. We also believe that communicating with and understanding the needs and perspectives of various stakeholders – including employees, customers, investors, regulators and the community – is vital. A CSO must build consensus and integrate stakeholder feedback into sustainability strategies. They must build relationships with other CSOs, industry leaders and policy-makers to stay ahead of trends and collaborate on industry-wide sustainability efforts.
- **Strategy design:** We need to use our understanding of the system dynamics to create design principles and models that help us plan and make choices about where and how to intervene. A CSO must envision and shape the organization's sustainability agenda. This involves setting long-term goals, understanding market trends and aligning sustainability initiatives with business objectives.
- **Innovation for impact:** The innovations we need in order to further the transition to sustainability go beyond technologies, products and services, and commercial enterprises; they include our mindsets, values, beliefs, new forms of organization and collaboration – and in all sorts of combinations that we don't yet know.
- **Collaboration and engagement:** At the heart of systemic change is the assumption that it cannot be achieved alone. A systems change agent will be able to facilitate, build partnerships and create coalitions and will seek to influence and engage wider audiences in the change.

Leadership skills

System change is both complex and uncertain, as we are trying to navigate into an unknown future. Underpinning the other capabilities is the need for individual change agents to be able to reflect, learn and continually develop their skills and resolve to implement systems change. You will read more about this in Chapter 10, where we highlight the importance of people skills, emotional intelligence and empathy and compassion.

Moreover, successful sustainability leadership requires the ability to inspire and mobilize collective action within an organization. Effective sustainability leaders view their organization as a holistic system, integrating sustainability into every department. They need to be intrapreneurs, adept at change management and rallying teams around sustainable practices, without necessarily delving into every detail of sustainability processes. Adaptive skills are also critical, as leaders navigate unique sustainability challenges in sectors ranging from agriculture to finance. A study by the Weinreb Group interviewed leading CSOs about what competencies make them effective, and these areas were highlighted:[30]

- **Adaptability:** As a CSO, you should be able to engage with different departments, like marketing, sales or logistics, and gain their support for sustainability initiatives.
- **Persistence:** Organizations, especially large ones, might resist change. CSOs must be determined to drive culture change and shift ingrained mindsets.
- **Focus:** Don't try to tackle every issue at once. Have the knowledge and business understanding to identify what's most important to your company and where the biggest sustainability opportunities lie.

A growth mindset, as defined by psychologist Carol Dweck, embraces challenges and believes abilities can improve with effort and practice.[31] Dweck emphasizes the importance of mindset interventions and cautions against a false growth mindset, which misinterprets the concept by focusing solely on effort. The nine differences between fixed and growth mindsets cover aspects like responses to challenges, feedback, views on intelligence and success, and attitudes towards learning and effort. From our experience, having – or practicing and developing – a growth mindset is a key leadership skill for any CSO.

Positive storytelling skills

Often, our discussions revolve around what we shouldn't do, emphasizing risks and painting grim pictures of the future. This approach fosters a culture of fear. However, where are we directing our energies? What are our aspirations and dreams? Instead of merely forecasting doom, we should craft visions that inspire and magnetize. If we uphold an enticing vision, talent and financial capital will naturally gravitate towards it, turning that vision into a self-fulfilling prophecy. As a CSO in an organization, your pivotal role is to articulate this compelling vision – vividly illustrating it, making it accessible to all and ensuring it's so alluring that everyone yearns to contribute. By doing this, you're not just setting a goal; you're igniting a movement. Once that's in place, your job is to pave the way, ensuring individuals have the resources and freedom to align their efforts with this collective aspiration.

Thus, despite all the environmental and social concerns facing us, it is important to maintain a positive outlook. Let's continue to amplify the good, celebrate the progress and inspire each other to build a better future. Christiana Figueres, the architect of the Paris Agreement, states that society is 'paralyzed and obsessed about the consequences of climate change.'[32] According to her we need a vision of what the future could look like, in terms of more inclusive economies, cleaner cities, improved health and so forth.

Operational/technical skills

As much as sustainability is about leadership and systemic change, it is at the end of the day also about being able to implement the change, thus making it happen in the day-to-day of an organization. Some skills that we perceive as important are:

- **Project management:** Implementing sustainability initiatives often requires managing multiple projects simultaneously, each with its own set of objectives, timelines and resources.
- **Data analysis and interpretation:** A CSO needs to measure and quantify sustainability efforts, analyse data for actionable insights and communicate the benefits and outcomes effectively to both internal and external audiences.
- **Financial acumen:** A CSO needs to understand the financial implications of sustainability initiatives, including budgeting and cost-benefit analysis, and identify opportunities for cost savings or revenue generation through sustainable practices.
- **Risk management:** Understanding how environmental and social issues translate into financial and operational risks for the company is important.
- **Knowledge of environmental regulations and standards:** Staying abreast of local and international environmental laws, as well as voluntary sustainability standards (like ISO 14001, the Global Reporting Initiative and the SDGs), is crucial to ensure compliance and industry leadership.

Summary and key take-aways

To summarize, there are many roles individuals can play to contribute to sustainability. We, however, believe that one of the most effective ways for individuals to contribute to the sustainability transition is through their everyday work as employees across various organizations. A strong sustainability track record is an important tool for employers to attract talent, and employees want to contribute. Employers are increasingly looking for this talent. However, employers are also realizing that it is not only about hiring into specific sustainability jobs; rather, sustainability skills and capabilities must be embedded into many job positions. While we firmly believe that integrating sustainability across all different job functions in an organization, and positioning sustainability as a collaborative effort, is critical for a successful sustainability transformation, we also see the need for a sustainability manager who holds the transformation together.

We have shown that for a sustainability leader to be successful, a certain level of responsibility, authority, placement and integration is required, as well as specific skill sets and capabilities. It is important that we move away from the current unclarity about what the role entails, and instead align and standardize what leading sustainability in a corporate setting means. In summary, driving sustainability change demands leaders who balance in-depth sustainability knowledge with strategic foresight and have the ability to galvanize their organization towards a shared vision for a sustainable future.

Endnotes

1 Per Espen Stoknes (2022) Tomorrow's Economy: A guide to creating a healthy green growth, MIT Press, Cambridge, MA. Stoknes uses 'worker' in his model, but we have modified this to 'employee' for the purposes of this book
2 Kali Andersson, Klimatpsykologerna, www.klimatpsykologerna.se (archived at https://perma.cc/8W44-2UFW)
3 Interview conducted February 2022
4 See sdgs.un.org (archived at https://perma.cc/3AEA-ZG5Y)
5 Justin McCarthy. Environmental record a factor for most US job seekers, Gallup, 13 April 2021. news.gallup.com/poll/346619/environmental-record-factor-job-seekers.aspx (archived at https://perma.cc/V86S-PRCA); Rich Lesser, Derek Kennedy Marjolein Cuellar, Elizabeth Lyle, Suketu Shah, Simon Bamberger and SK Missert. Put talent at the top of the sustainability agenda, BCG, 11 January 2023. www.bcg.com/publications/2023/prioritize-talent-within-sustainability-agenda (archived at https://perma.cc/A66L-L3FY)

6 Anthesis Group Insights, 2021. www.anthesisgroup.com/sustainability-vital-for-employee-attraction/ (archived at https://perma.cc/Q5VH-4UZ7)

7 Richard Edelman. The belief-driven employee, Edelman Trust Barometer, 31 August 2021. www.edelman.com/trust/2021-trust-barometer/belief-driven-employee/new-employee-employer-compact (archived at https://perma.cc/Q3MY-4EPP)

8 McBride Sustainability. The Power of Corporate Sustainability: Attracting Top Talent, LinkedIn, 23 May 2023. https://www.linkedin.com/pulse/power-corporate-sustainability-attracting-top-talent/ (archived at https://perma.cc/WR5H-26VG)

9 Interview conducted October 2021

10 Weinreb Group. 2023 Weinreb Group Chief Sustainability Officer Report, 2023. https://weinrebgroup.com/wp-content/uploads/2023/03/2023-CSO-Report.pdf (archived at https://perma.cc/L8PN-ZWWT)

11 The chief sustainability officer will rise to prominence in coming years as business priorities align with role responsibilities, according to first-of-its-kind survey, Deloitte, news release, 2021. www.deloitte.com/ke/en/about/press-room/the-chief-sustainability-officer-will-rise-to-prominence.html (archived at https://perma.cc/9PY9-NPH2)

12 PwC announces new strategy: The New Equation, PwC Media Centre, 13 August 2021. www.pwc.com/id/en/media-centre/press-release/2021/english/pwc-announces-new-strategy-the-new-equation.html (archived at https://perma.cc/66DZ-LPND)

13 Karin Kimbrough. The world is going green: That means a transformation for workers everywhere, LinkedIn, 11 February 2021. www.linkedin.com/pulse/world-going-green-means-skill-transformation-workers-karin-kimbrough (archived at https://perma.cc/RK9H-DMPV)

14 24 million jobs to open up in the green economy, International Labour Organization (ILO), press release, 14 May 2018. www.ilo.org/global/about-the-ilo/newsroom/news/WCMS_628644/lang--en/index.htm (archived at https://perma.cc/K5MC-AXUT)

15 The future of jobs is green: How climate change is changing labour markets, World Economic Forum (WEF), 1 May 2023. www.weforum.org/agenda/2023/04/future-of-jobs-is-green-2023-climate-change-labour-markets/ (archived at https://perma.cc/NQH5-3N4A)

16 Svenskt näringsliv rapport, 26 October 2021. www.svensktnaringsliv.se/sakomraden/utbildning/rapport-stort-kompetensbehov-for-att-klara-klimatutmaningen_1175886.html (archived at https://perma.cc/H7D3-NQ26)

17 Rich Lesser, Derek Kennedy, Marjolein Cuellar, Elizabeth Lyle, Suketu Shah, Simon Bamberger and SK Missert. Put talent at the top of the sustainability agenda, BCG, 11 January 2023. www.bcg.com/publications/2023/prioritize-talent-within-sustainability-agenda (archived at https://perma.cc/A66L-L3FY)

18 What are Industry 4.0, the Fourth Industrial Revolution and 4IR?, McKinsey Explainers, 17 August 2022. www.mckinsey.com/featured-insights/mckinsey-explainers/what-are-industry-4-0-the-fourth-industrial-revolution-and-4ir (archived at https://perma.cc/QFE3-NPB6)

19 WEF. Future of Jobs Report 2023, 30 April 2023. www.weforum.org/publications/the-future-of-jobs-report-2023/ (archived at https://perma.cc/AFV3-9778)

20 Chief value creator?: The changing role of the chief sustainability officer (CSO), IPSOS, 11 July 2023. https://www.ipsos.com/en/chief-value-creator-changing-role-chief-sustainability-officer-cso (archived at https://perma.cc/RE73-YD92)

21 In 2004, DuPont appointed Linda Fisher with the title of VP Safety, Health and Environment and Chief Sustainability Officer

22 ACCP. Fourth Annual CSR Insights Survey, Summer 2023. accp.org/resources/csr-resources/4th-annual-csr-insights-survey/ (archived at https://perma.cc/LS46-MGQA)

23 Marshall Chase. Sustainability professionals shouldn't (and don't want to) be accountants: Don't make them, Greenbiz, 31 October 2023. www.greenbiz.com/article/sustainability-professionals-shouldnt-and-dont-want-be-accountants-dont-make-them (archived at https://perma.cc/YHX7-WS77)

24 The rise of the CSO, Korn Ferry, www.kornferry.com/insights/featured-topics/people-planet-profit/the-rise-of-the-chief-sustainability-officer (archived at https://perma.cc/K2MV-WMLL)

25 Interview conducted February 2021

26 Cambridge Institute for Sustainability Leadership (CISL). Leadership for a Sustainable Future, 2023. www.cisl.cam.ac.uk/news-and-resources/publications/leadership-sustainable-future (archived at https://perma.cc/8TUJ-TB8A)

27 System change capabilities, School for System Change. www.forumforthefuture.org/system-change-capabilities (archived at https://perma.cc/JX6K-3E2G)

28 Deloitte, The future of the CSO, February 2021. www2.deloitte.com/content/dam/Deloitte/bg/Documents/financial-services/gx-fsi-future-of-the-cso-report.pdf (archived at https://perma.cc/9H4U-SGCM)

29 System change capabilities, School for System Change. www.forumforthefuture.org/system-change-capabilities (archived at https://perma.cc/JX6K-3E2G)

30 Weinreb Group. 2023 Weinreb Group CSO Report, 2023. weinrebgroup.com/wp-content/uploads/2023/03/2023-CSO-Report.pdf (archived at https://perma.cc/KQ8L-4KLB)

31 Dr Carol Dwech (2017) *Mindset: Changing the way you think to fulfil your potential*, updated edition, Hachette, London

32 Emily Holden. 'Individual actions do add up': Christiana Figueres on the climate crisis, *The Guardian*, 5 March 2020. www.theguardian.com/environment/2020/mar/05/christiana-figueres-climate-crisis (archived at https://perma.cc/87U7-CEG2)

The business case for sustainability

03

In this chapter, we go deeper into the role of businesses, sharing examples across different business sectors. Sustainability is no longer a 'nice-to-have' but has become a 'must-have' across all sectors of the economy.[1] The call to action is clear: whether you are in food or fashion, supply-driven or demand-driven, your organization must find a path to sustainable operations. Yet, the path towards sustainability is not one-size-fits-all; it varies greatly depending on your sector and your business model. As a leader within this space, your role is to navigate sector-specific challenges and opportunities, crafting a sustainability strategy that's both adaptive and deeply integrated into your organization's culture and decision-making processes.

Moreover, as we proceed on this shared journey towards a more sustainable future, we must remember that it requires not just an unwavering commitment but also innovative thinking and adaptive leadership. These will be the hallmarks of tomorrow's sustainability leaders – those who will lead the way in catalysing impactful and enduring change.

The evolving role of corporate sustainability

The image of sustainability, in society at large and in the corporate sector, has changed significantly since the term first came about. Initially, it was seen as an inconvenient necessity. On an individual level, sustainability was introduced with high costs. Sustainability wasn't presented as the next cool gadget or trendy, eco-friendly product. It was more like swapping your soft, luxurious toilet paper for sandpaper, or switching your quick-to-brighten light bulbs for energy-saving ones that took seemingly forever to light up. It was about giving up certain comforts for the greater good of the planet. It involved tough decisions and trade-offs, rather than improvements.

Similarly, when sustainability entered the business conversation, it was met with anxiety and discomfort, and perceived as a burden. For many top managers and decision makers, sustainability was seen as a threat to their conventional ways of operating, which usually focused on short-term profits, efficiency and growth rather than the long-term social and environmental impact coupled with long-term prosperity for the company. Companies adopted sustainability mainly as a way to satisfy regulations or boost their public image.[2] Back then, sustainability investments were considered added expenses rather than strategic investments. They demanded significant financial, time and energy resources to execute, and it was not clear how they would directly positively impact the company's profits. This created the idea that sustainability was costly and not an essential part of business planning and operations.[3] The complexity of implementing sustainable practices thus scared many companies. Understanding and managing the complicated environmental, social and economic aspects of sustainability were challenging. Plus, incorporating new technologies and practices into existing operations could be disruptive and inconvenient. Moreover, there was a lack of understanding and knowledge about sustainability. Many companies found themselves investing a lot of time and personnel to grasp what sustainability meant, how it could be incorporated into their business, and how to measure and report their progress.

However, both the reality and narrative around sustainability has dramatically changed over time. The content, depth and breadth of working with sustainability today, versus 20 years ago, are very different. Corporate sustainability has evolved from being a peripheral CSR initiative to becoming a core component of the highest-level strategic agenda in many organizations. This shift is well documented in books such as *Net Positive* by Paul Polman and Andrew Winston.[4] Today, in progressive organizations, sustainability is viewed not as an expensive burden, but as a strategic necessity. It's a crucial part of twenty-first-century business, and top managers need to recognize its worth and potential to shape their companies' future. Today, it is not merely an optional act of corporate benevolence, but a crucial strategy in the game of business. This transformation has been driven by a profound shift in societal values and expectations, along with the stark realities of our environmental predicaments. Stakeholder demands, regulatory requirements, risk management and the discovery of new market opportunities have all made sustainability an important business consideration.[5]

In his book *Tomorrow's Economy*, Per Espen Stoknes presents a five-step staircase of integrating sustainability within a business.[6] Many organizations go through the phases outlined in the rest of this section, also when entering

Figure 3.1 Overview of different steps when embedding sustainability in an organization[7]

Corporate social responsibility The outreach step presents traditional CSR work, philanthropic donations or, for example, engaging in carbon offsetting.
A house in order/efficient operations Having your house in order is about operations in the owned workplaces and buildings, including energy consumption and waste management, as well as improving social conditions. It also includes co-worker travel and commuting.
Supply chain and compliance Setting social and environmental requirements for suppliers, and ensuring that there are both support and control systems in place to verify compliance, is a key responsibility of the supply chain/procurement teams.
Communications and marketing Having come some way on the journey, companies realize that they have stories to tell and a role to play in advocacy and influencing stakeholders around them.
Business model/strategic role Shifting the entire business model to an impact-first model means that the company's very existence serves to create positive social and environmental impact. Carefully assess the offer to ensure that non-sustainable products are replaced with better alternatives. Social enterprises are examples of such models.

the sustainability space today versus getting started 20 years ago. The sector or geography you operate within will most likely determine where you start on the below step-by-step sustainability evolution ladder. Not all geographical markets have the same capacity to prioritize sustainability. In some emerging or resource-strapped economies, immediate concerns like poverty alleviation or infrastructure development often take precedence over long-term sustainability goals. In these cases, it becomes the responsibility of more mature markets to offer support, whether it's through technology transfer, financial assistance or collaborative initiatives. The aim should be to make sustainability not just an option, but the most feasible and attractive choice for all markets, levelling the playing field and ensuring that sustainable practices become the new normal globally.

A business can be at different stages in its journey towards integrating a purpose-driven approach into its business model (see Figure 3.1). This progression is often iterative rather than linear, adapting as the company and its operating environment evolve.

Phase I: Corporate social responsibility or charity focus

This traditional approach typically involved companies contributing to charitable causes or participating in community projects, separate from their main business activities. It was seen as a way to enhance corporate image, rather than being integrated into the strategic framework of the organization.

Phase II: Efficient operations

About 20 some years ago, many organizations realized the importance of incorporating sustainability measures in their business practices to address growing environmental concerns. Energy efficiency and waste management were obvious starting points – tangible, measurable aspects of business operations that could have significant environmental impact and cost implications. Sustainability leaders at that time were often working in siloed, operational roles and they mainly focused on compliance with environmental regulations, waste reduction and resource conservation. Those holding these roles often came from maintenance or engineering backgrounds. The roles were about how to better run operations, stores, factories and warehouses, rather than truly reflecting on how products were made or what the purpose of the organization was.

Another key motivator was risk avoidance. Seeking to evade scandals and negative publicity, companies proactively managed risks, guiding their past decisions towards more responsible and sustainable operations. Many companies have moved out of this phase, but many still start here even though the world around us and the requirements on organizations have evolved a lot.

Phase III: Supply chain and compliance

Thereafter, companies increasingly realized that a lot of an organization's environmental and social footprint is connected to how products are made. Which materials are being used, where are these materials sourced from and how are the factories operated where these products are made?[8]

In the 1990s, several companies faced criticism when investigations revealed the use of child labour and bad working conditions. This revelation highlighted the urgent need for companies to monitor and ensure ethical practices not only within their direct operations but across their entire supply chain. To respond to these challenges, companies began establishing codes of conduct. Such codes laid out the minimum requirements expected from suppliers, covering aspects from child labour and working conditions to environmental considerations.[9] Auditors and sustainability developers were hired to secure compliance. Over time, however, there was a shift towards forging stronger supply chain partnerships and steering towards a development-centric, supportive direction. It's about collaborating, improving and growing together.[10]

Phase IV: Communications and marketing

As sustainability gained popularity, its role evolved into a marketing and communication-oriented phase, focusing on showcasing an organization's environmental efforts to stakeholders and ensuring the brand is seen as responsible. This shift was driven by changing consumer attitudes, as consumers started to demand not only sustainable products but also responsible corporate behaviour. Sustainability leaders are now tasked with effectively communicating these efforts, highlighting the significant impact of communication. Organizations influence societal values and practices by promoting sustainability, moving it from a sideline to a central societal issue. They play a vital role in shaping a sustainable future, balancing economic growth with environmental and social health. However, the risk of greenwashing looms; this will be further explored in Chapter 9.

Phase V: Strategic and purpose-led

Increasingly, sustainability has grown into a business-critical topic and is becoming an integrated part of businesses and organizations. The scope of what organizations can achieve depends on several aspects. But, overall, it extends to delivering products and solutions that don't merely serve the lives of people but enhance them. It's about aligning the core business strategies with purpose, culture and values that resonate far beyond the walls of the organization.

The emerging fourth sector of the economy marks a transformative shift in addressing global challenges.[11] This sector, known as 'for-benefit' enterprises, merges the market-driven approach of the private sector with the social and environmental objectives of the public and non-profit sectors. An example of this is B Corporations (B Corps), which are businesses certified for meeting high standards of social and environmental performance, accountability and transparency.[12] B Corps exemplify how companies can be a force for good, focusing on profit for a purpose. They are at the forefront of this transformative sector, demonstrating how businesses can effectively address social and environmental issues while maintaining profitability. This approach is vital in steering the global economy towards more sustainable and equitable practices. These organizations are increasingly pivotal in solving pressing social and environmental issues. They represent a diverse array of business models, from social enterprises and sustainable businesses to cooperatives and benefit corporations, all aiming to leverage profit for a greater purpose.

The role of sustainability leaders has evolved into a crucial, strategic position, often at the level of the CSO, who is actively involved in investment and decision-making processes. CSOs are central in incorporating sustainability into their organization's core – from strategy and operations to culture and stakeholder engagement – moving beyond compliance to drive significant change management. Similar to the digital manager's role in spearheading digital transformation, CSOs aim to weave sustainability so deeply into the organizational fabric that their role may ultimately become redundant or integrated into other senior leadership roles.

The future of sustainability leadership will likely further move towards the strategic framework of organizations. The people leading the sustainability transformation within the organization become the 'sense-makers in chief,' guiding the entire organization's sustainability vision, setting a clear road map and ensuring that every business decision aligns with this vision.[13] In this future scenario, the sustainability leader functions as the spider in the web of relationships – with legislation, investors, customers and employees – to shape the organization's sustainability narrative and drive meaningful action.

Moreover, what we know for sure is that the sustainability leadership of today is not the leadership blueprint for tomorrow. Yesterday's sustainability heroes may not necessarily be the ones of tomorrow, depending on how the landscape changes. For organizations, sustainability is not a static goal but a moving target. Hence, it is vital to set ambitious and visionary targets, while constantly stretching the boundaries of their sustainability work and ambitions. Adapting to change and pushing the envelope should be ingrained in the organizational DNA, driving the organization to achieve a more sustainable business model and, ultimately, a more sustainable world.

Today's business case for sustainability

The business case for sustainability is nowadays often compelling. Recent research and practical experiences have shown that sustainability can actually improve financial performance.[14] Companies find they can cut costs, become more operationally efficient, improve branding and reputation, spur innovation, be prepared for current and future legislation and attract and keep investors as well as the best employees – all of which can give them a competitive edge and increase long-term value.[15]

Firstly, sustainable operations can offer *direct financial returns*.[16] Consider the case of renewable energy. Yes, the initial costs can be high, but the return on investment (ROI) over time can be even more considerable, as fossil fuel costs rise and renewable technology continues to improve. The same applies for energy efficiency. The first efforts often show quick ROI as the organization becomes better at managing its energy use and stops wasting energy across its processes and operations. Remember, the best money spent is that which is not spent at all. In other words, becoming effective and using less energy, while producing the same outcome, is the most effective way to spend your money.

Secondly, sustainability has become a significant *brand value creator*.[17] Modern consumers are more discerning and values-driven (read: more critical and demanding), often seeking products and services from companies that align with their personal beliefs about the environment and social responsibility. They are expecting companies to not just provide more sustainable products and services, but also demonstrate a strong commitment to environmental and social stewardship. Moreover, employees are increasingly looking to work for companies that prioritize sustainability. Consequently, sustainable practices can drive customer loyalty, employee engagement and overall brand value – and often open up new markets and customer segments.

Moreover, sustainability often drives *innovation* by pushing companies to develop new products, services and processes that are environmentally friendly and socially responsible. This can lead to the discovery of more efficient, cost-effective and sustainable ways of operating, creating a competitive advantage.[18] And it is increasingly a *licence to operate* as companies that demonstrate a commitment to sustainability are more likely to earn and maintain their social licence to operate from local communities, governments and regulatory bodies. This acceptance and approval by stakeholders is critical for long-term operational stability and success.

There is also the *cost of inaction*. Companies that make their profit exploiting externalities and thus neglect to build sustainability into their business model may find themselves facing increasing raw material costs, supply chain disruptions, regulatory penalties and consumer backlash. If businesses don't start to implement circular material flows, they could be looking at a future where their key resources are scarce or even unavailable.[19] Thus, the cost of doing nothing can be immense, both in terms of human well-being and economic consequences, on societal but also company level:[20]

- **Refugees and migrants:** Failing to welcome and integrate refugees and migrants can lead to increased social tensions, higher crime rates and the loss of potential economic contributors. It might also tarnish a country's international reputation, making diplomatic relations strained and potentially impacting trade and other collaborations. Not addressing issues in conflict zones can lead to wider regional instabilities, large-scale refugee crises and the potential for spillover of violence.[21] Therefore, integration of refugees and migrants isn't just a humanitarian concern but has direct and indirect implications for the business community.[22]
- **Rising inequalities:** Increased economic inequalities can lead to social unrest, decreased overall economic growth and reduced social mobility. Economies can become more vulnerable to shocks, and societies can become more polarized, leading to political instability. Furthermore, inaction may hinder opportunities for innovation and growth by overlooking the diverse talent and perspectives that vulnerable groups may offer.
- **Destroying ecosystems:** Ecosystem degradation can lead to reduced agricultural yields, loss of valuable biodiversity and diminished natural buffers against extreme events like hurricanes or floods. The loss of biodiversity can also impact medicine, as many drugs are derived from natural compounds. Moreover, over-extraction and non-sustainable use of raw materials can lead to scarcities, resulting in increased prices and potential conflicts over resources. Thus, overburdening the earth's resilience capacity – its ability to absorb shocks like natural disasters or climate change – can have catastrophic consequences.

In a globalized world, businesses can't afford to operate in isolation from societal issues. This perspective was a real eye-opener for us, especially when considering current investments in areas like social welfare and youth, and helping those who are marginalized in the labour market. The same holds true for climate change. If we don't make these investments today, the future costs – both material and human – will be incalculable. The challenge lies in the fact that these negative impacts are often diffused across society, making the need for private entities and companies to act less apparent and immediate. This diffusion of responsibility can lead to collective inaction where the urgency to address these issues is not felt until the consequences become more direct and severe. It is, therefore, crucial for businesses to recognize that the cost of inaction can far outweigh the investment required to operate sustainably, not just for their own longevity but for the broader societal good.

Moreover, when discussing the business case for sustainability transformations, the concepts of *sunk cost* and *stranded asset* are important. A sunk cost refers to money that has already been spent and cannot be recovered. It's a concept in economics and business decision making, emphasizing that such past expenses should not affect future decisions, as these costs remain constant regardless of the outcome of current actions. The concept of sunk costs thus revolves around the past investments we've made, and the fallacy ensues when we let those irrecoverable costs dictate our future decisions, instead of considering what's best moving forward. Stranded assets, on the other hand, are about the risk of sitting with assets that are unusable or less valuable due to changes in, for example, regulatory frameworks or consumer demands. This mindset poses a significant barrier to innovation and transition, especially when we're striving to pivot towards sustainable solutions.

EXAMPLE Embracing change for a better future

Embracing change, even when it means moving past significant investments (such as in a product, system or lifestyle), is crucial in the journey towards sustainability.[23] Take, for instance, someone trained in geology and oil drilling and another person specializing in virgin material textile production. Their inclination might be to preserve the status quo because they've invested time, effort and resources in mastering their fields. Similarly, we might resist acknowledging the obsolescence of a gasoline-powered car or a high-priced property we own. On a grander scale, we've even constructed economic welfare measurement systems, like GDP, that prioritize the value of freshly produced goods and services rather than actual well-being.

We believe that there is a common set of behaviours that create blind spots for companies, often hindering them from acting, even when the business case for sustainability is increasingly clear. There is the common continuity bias, where we assume that the future will be like the past, even though we know that the only thing that is constant is change. Businesses often calcify around a successful business model, which leads to cognitive entrenchment and a tendency to downplay threats to the model and overestimate current competitive advantage, instead of truly reflecting on consumer and societal needs and daring to go against the norm. Moreover, companies often lack skills and experience in understanding and evaluating existential or systemic risks, such as climate change, and are often not trained in recognizing their dependencies on natural and social value or truly appreciating the impact of exponential change on the business. All these often lead to companies not taking the necessary action or waiting too long. Moreover, the tendency of businesses to talk in terms of win-win – thus trying to convert complex, uncertain systemic risks into linear, reductionist (often financial) metrics – makes them less able to spot and act upon the systemic shifts that are at play. This highlights the limits of 'making the business case' – in traditional business language – as, fundamentally, business as usual will not work considering the multiple issues we are facing. These issues will most likely converge, creating tipping points and seismic shifts. Companies thus need to build capabilities to better cope with uncertainty and complexity.[24]

Real-life examples across different sectors

For us leaders in sustainability, the power of a good example can't be overstated – it offers not just a road map but also a source of inspiration and validation. Leading organizations in the field of sustainability serve as real-world case studies that showcase what's possible when you combine innovation, commitment and strategic thinking. They challenge us to look beyond conventional approaches, offering practical, tested solutions that can be adapted to our own unique organizational contexts.

Don't just admire these trailblazers; dissect their success stories to extract actionable insights. Dive into how they overcome challenges, adapt to changes and consistently align their mission with measurable impact. This analysis serves as a rich resource for you to refine your own sustainability strategies, initiatives and stakeholder engagements. Utilize their experiences to bolster your own toolkit, tailoring their best practices to fit the specific needs and nuances of your organization. In doing so, you're not just amplifying your potential for success; you're also fostering a culture of continuous learning and positive impact that permeates every layer of your organization.

Energy from the sun (and wind)

Solar panels are perhaps the obvious example of a good business case for sustainability. Solar panels have become an increasingly compelling sustainability and financial business case due to a combination of factors: decreasing costs, increasing energy prices, technological advancements, policy incentives and growing environmental awareness. These factors have made it both economically viable and environmentally beneficial for businesses and individuals to invest in solar power. By investing in solar power, businesses can not only save money on their energy costs but also contribute to a more sustainable and resilient energy system.[25]

- **Decreasing costs:** According to Our World in Data, the price of solar energy dropped nearly 90 per cent between 2009 and 2019, and since 1976, the price of solar has decreased by 99.6 per cent.[26] Land-based wind power saw a 70 per cent price reduction over 10 years, making green energy sources the cheapest options in most places on Earth. Battery technologies have experienced similar cost reductions, with a learning rate of close to 20 per cent. This is primarily due to the economies of scale achieved through increased manufacturing volume, technological advancements and global competition in the solar panel industry. Improvements in the production process and the increasing efficiency of solar cells have also contributed to lowering costs. Additionally, the shift towards automation and more efficient supply chains has reduced production and delivery costs.[27]
- **Increasing energy prices:** In many parts of the world, the cost of traditional energy sources (such as fossil fuels) is rising. This is due to a combination of factors, such as depleting resources, higher extraction costs and increased regulatory pressures to internalize the environmental costs of carbon emissions. As traditional energy becomes more expensive, solar energy becomes a more financially attractive option.
- **Technological advancements:** Solar technology continues to improve, increasing the efficiency and lifespan of solar panels. This means that for the same investment, solar panels can now generate more energy and last longer than before, improving the ROI.

- **Policy incentives:** Many governments around the world have implemented policies and incentives to encourage the adoption of solar power. These include subsidies, tax credits, feed-in tariffs and renewable portfolio standards. These policies can significantly reduce the upfront cost of solar panel systems and improve their financial viability.
- **Growing environmental awareness:** As awareness of environmental issues such as climate change grows, more businesses and individuals are seeking to reduce their carbon footprint. Investing in solar panels is one way to achieve this and can also help enhance a company's reputation as a sustainable and socially responsible business.

As an illustration of transformative leadership in sustainability, consider the example of Ørsted.[28] Once one of Europe's most coal-intensive energy companies, Ørsted has evolved into a global leader in sustainable energy. This dramatic shift wasn't just a change in operations; it was a redefinition of their core competence and purpose around energy. However, instead of continuing to rely on fossil fuels, they pivoted to sustainable energy sources. This pivot wasn't just about mitigating harm; it was a profound move towards making a positive impact on global sustainability. The company transitioned from being part of the problem to being a significant contributor to the solution, exemplifying the kind of transformative change that is possible.

Walmart's installation of solar panels at its Apple Valley distribution centre in California serves as a business case for renewable energy investment. This project, the company's largest solar power initiative, consists of over 5,300 ground-mounted solar panels covering nearly seven acres, capable of generating one megawatt of power – enough to power 175 homes. Scott Kubicek, the general manager of the distribution centre, highlights that the project aligns with Walmart's goal of being powered entirely by renewable energy, emphasizing that increasing solar energy use is both environmentally beneficial and makes good business sense.[29]

A business case in solar installation from Africa is the Kenyan company Sun King (formerly Greenlight Planet). They offer solar home systems (SHSs) that replace harmful kerosene lanterns, providing lighting, phone charging and power for electrical appliances in off-grid areas. Customers can afford these solutions through small daily payments, with a typical payback period of up to 12 months.[30] Another example is the Senegalese-based company Oolu, which installs and maintains solar systems for commercial and industrial clients across West Africa, offering a cost-saving alternative to diesel generators. Additionally, off-grid solar energy in Africa is used in agriculture, powering appliances for irrigation, refrigeration and processing. Companies like Kenya-based SunCulture are scaling solutions to help smallholder farmers improve efficiency and adapt to climate change. Solar Sister, also in Africa, is yet another example of solar as a business case, innovating in the solar energy space. This organization empowers women in rural African communities by training them to become clean energy entrepreneurs. Solar Sister provides these women with the skills and tools to distribute solar lighting and energy products in their communities, addressing energy poverty while promoting gender equality and economic empowerment. By focusing on a network of women, Solar Sister facilitates the spread of sustainable energy solutions, enhancing both environmental and social outcomes in underserved areas.[31]

Driving on electricity

Companies like Tesla have shown that sustainability makes business sense in the car industry. Electric vehicles (EVs) are not only more energy-efficient but also require less maintenance, contributing to overall cost savings. Furthermore, as governments worldwide push for reduced carbon emissions, incentives and subsidies are often provided for EV manufacturing and purchasing.

In Norway, there has been a boost of EV for many years now.[32] The success story of Norway's EV market is rooted in a powerful synergy between governmental incentives and commercial innovation. The government has supported the EV market by providing a suite of attractive benefits such as tax exemptions and infrastructure development, significantly reducing both the initial and ongoing costs of EV ownership.[33] These initiatives are further bolstered by the nation's robust charging infrastructure, which assuages consumer concerns over range limitations. Alongside these governmental measures, the private sector has been integral in driving the adoption of EVs, taking advantage of the country's green energy production, which is predominantly from hydropower. In a society known for its environmental consciousness and prosperity, these strategic collaborations have led to a broad societal acceptance of EVs. Furthermore, a clear policy direction towards phasing out internal combustion engine vehicles by 2025 has also provided market certainty and set a global example of what can be achieved when government and businesses work together towards sustainability.

China's EV sales have significantly outpaced other countries, and this surge is expected to continue. The widespread adoption of EVs in China is primarily driven by economics and consumer preferences, and not environmental concerns. This shift is leading to a decline in oil demand, signalling a potential end to the era of oil dominance. China has managed to rapidly develop a network of charging stations and create an appealing offer to consumers, and is actively searching for more sustainable ways of EV manufacturing and battery recycling. The transition to electric vehicles is seen as a key factor in China's future energy consumption and its role in the global oil market.[34]

Paris is an example of a city that is supporting a green transition. Numerous cycling lanes have been added and upgraded in recent years to ensure safety and convenience for cyclists. The city has been implementing significant measures to promote the use of EVs, including setting up charging stations throughout the city and providing financial incentives for the purchase of EVs.[35] Like Norway, Paris has also set clear policies for phasing out internal combustion engine vehicles in the near future, making it another example of a city committed to a sustainable future.

Rethinking the food ecosystem

Each step in the complex food ecosystem (from farms to fork, comprising farming, processing, distribution, retail and consumption) carries its own unique sustainability challenges and opportunities. Thus, sustainability in the food sector requires a systemic end-to-end approach that considers every link in the food chain. For instance, farming practices have to be adapted to reduce water use and chemical inputs while improving soil health. Distribution and retail operations need to tackle food waste, energy efficiency and packaging. At the consumption level, a shift towards plant-based diets or reduced meat consumption can have significant sustainability benefits.[36]

Meat and dairy production in particular present a unique set of sustainability challenges. The livestock sector is one of the largest contributors to global greenhouse gas emissions, with cattle production accounting for the majority of these emissions.[37] Additionally, manure management and feed production further contribute to the sector's carbon footprint. Tackling these emissions is a significant challenge, but also an opportunity for innovative solutions and practices. Animal welfare is a key concern in the meat and dairy industry. Intensive farming often prioritizes productivity at the expense of animal health and well-being. To address this, there must be a shift towards more humane farming practices that respect animal welfare, with measures such as enhanced living conditions, responsible handling and care for animals. Deforestation is another major issue linked with meat and dairy production. Large areas of forests, especially in regions like the Amazon, are frequently cleared to make way for pastures and to grow feed crops such as soy, which directly contributes to biodiversity loss and increases carbon dioxide levels in the atmosphere.

Organic and regenerative farming methods can offer farmers increased profits in the long run. While they might require more labour, these techniques can lead to healthier soil and crops, more resilient ecosystems and, potentially, premium product pricing due to growing consumer demand for organic and sustainably produced food. A concrete example is the Better Cotton Initiative (BCI), where multiple corporates have collaborated with the WWF to improve cotton production and the lives of farmers.[38] BCI aims to holistically support farming communities by improving social, environmental and economic factors. This comprehensive strategy includes better soil and water management, reduced pesticide use and increased resilience to climate change. These improvements have led to greater yields, better working conditions and increased financial security. The initiative also focuses on gender empowerment and reducing inequality among farming communities.

Moreover, the issue of food waste is a significant global challenge, leading to unnecessary resource depletion and contributing to environmental degradation. Much of this waste occurs due to inefficient supply chains, overproduction and consumer habits, emphasizing the need for systemic changes in how food is produced, distributed and consumed. Implementing solutions such as improved food storage techniques, consumer awareness campaigns and more effective distribution networks can significantly reduce food waste and its associated impacts.[39]

CASE STUDY Sopköket

In the capital city of Sweden, Stockholm, Sopköket (the Waste Kitchen) stands as a testament to what is possible when entrepreneurial drive aligns with sustainability. Founded by the passionate entrepreneur Filip Lundin at the young age of 23, this unique establishment turns potential food waste into healthy and delicious dishes, served through their catering and frozen meals business.

Established in 2015, Sopköket was Filip's dream realized. Not only does the catering rescue surplus food, it also ensures that any unsold meals find their way to those in need. The figures are impressive; by March 2022, they had managed to utilize 89,000 kg of food that would have otherwise been wasted and donated more than 56,000 meals. In addition, the business provides employment opportunities to migrants in Sweden, acknowledging the invaluable culinary skills and service orientation they bring with them.

Filip and his team face a unique challenge daily: they never truly know what ingredients they'll receive. This unpredictable nature demands creativity and flexibility in the kitchen, giving rise to inventive dishes that are often born from spur-of-the-moment decisions. Yet, no dish makes it to the menu before receiving the seal of approval from Filip's discerning grandmother. Sopköket's journey has involved other challenges too. Operating in a system that often leans towards waste rather than circularity presents obstacles. The existing legislative framework sometimes incentivizes waste, and changing this will require systemic shifts and examples like France, where food waste from supermarkets is prohibited.[40] Yet, there are upsides too, with Sopköket's innovative approach garnering attention and setting the pace for others to follow.

Filip is not just an entrepreneur; he is an educator, sharing the endless possibilities of creating businesses from food waste. He mentions that, often, these 'wasted' products are even better than their fresher alternatives. He gives the example of how orange juice made from older oranges rescued from supermarkets can often be sweeter and more flavourful than juice made from fresher ones. It challenges the traditional consumer mindset that often seeks the most aesthetically pleasing products, leaving behind those that are slightly imperfect yet still perfectly good.[41]

Greening the money

We're part of a system that values quick profits over long-term good. This doesn't help us when we're trying to do things that are better for the planet and people. So, we need to change the system, step by step. We need to make decisions that are good for the future, not just for right now. Finance holds a transformative power in guiding the world towards sustainable development. While individuals strive for sustainable lifestyles, their investments, often unbeknownst to them, might support industries counteracting these efforts. This paradox underlines a stark need for financial transparency and ethical investment.

The linchpin to realigning our financial contributions with our values lies in understanding the influence of banks, pension funds and insurance companies. These institutions, by diverting funds from harmful industries to responsible and sustainable ventures, can effectuate significant environmental and social change. Notable campaigns such as Make My Money Matter emphasize the substantial impact of sustainable pension investments.[42] They advocate for transparency and the redirection of funds towards creating a sustainable future. Similarly, the insurance industry, directly confronting the realities of climate change, is progressively investing in sectors that mitigate environmental risks. The banking sector is witnessing an evolution, with increased customer demand for sustainability and accountability, prompting even the largest asset managers, like Blackrock, to consider environmental, social and governance (ESG) criteria in their investment strategies.

By supporting local communities, championing gender equality in finance and tackling financial exclusion, banks and financial institutions can foster a more equitable society. Beyond traditional economic metrics, the EU's exploration of 'beyond GDP' measures suggests a growing recognition that financial decisions must align with broader social and environmental well-being.[43] In sum, finance is not just about the accumulation of wealth; it's about directing financial flows to cultivate a sustainable and just world. Moreover, the Greening Cash Action Guide is a practical guide to reduce emissions from one's cash holdings in banks, align financial activities with sustainability efforts and transform the financial sector.[44] It emphasizes the importance of considering the carbon footprint of financial supply chains, including cash, investments and pension funds, to meet global temperature rise targets. The guide also includes a checklist for adherence to the standards of the Partnership for Carbon Accounting Financials (PCAF), which offer a structured methodology for assessing and disclosing greenhouse gas emissions associated with financial activities.[45]

CASE STUDY Fair Finance, Jakob König

Jakob König, leading Fair Finance Guide (FFG) in Sweden, shows how finance can be combined with ethical values to support the SDGs Jakob started his career in an investment bank, where he realized that the focus on profit didn't align with his values. This led him to focus on ESG in investments. He noticed that traditional methods weren't effective in ensuring ethical practices in companies, which inspired him to start FFG.

FFG looks closely at how financial institutions finance and invest in companies, focusing on their impact on human rights and climate. It has revealed important information about investments in the controversial arms trade and harmful environmental projects, helping consumers and policyholders to make better financial choices. Jakob points out that there's enough money globally to achieve the SDGs, like ending hunger and improving living standards. The key challenge is to direct the money towards sustainable projects and to transform companies to sustainable business models. Since FFG started, more banks are meeting international sustainability criteria, thanks to clearer goals and reports from banks and more customers asking about sustainability.

Jakob remains cautiously optimistic. He compares the current state of the financial sector to the textile industry two decades ago, when the sector struggled with managing the most severe issues, like child labour and heavy pollution suppliers and controls. He advocates for a thorough review and reform of financial systems to ensure investments contribute to sustainability. FFG encourages financial institutions to think carefully about their investment strategies. It's a model for organizations worldwide to keep improving their sustainability efforts, aligning finances with ethical and sustainable practices.[46]

Green buildings

Incorporating sustainability in the construction industry through green building practices can result in significant energy and water savings, reduced waste and improved indoor air quality. Such practices can reduce operational costs, increase property values and meet regulatory requirements. These gains are often relatively direct and have short ROIs.

For example, Ibuku, a pioneering architectural and design firm based in Bali, has taken the concept of green building to new heights with their innovative use of bamboo as a primary construction material.[47] The bamboo houses designed by Ibuku go beyond just using a sustainable material; they reflect a holistic approach to green buildings, incorporating principles of biomimicry and smart design to optimize energy use and take advantage of natural resources. The homes are crafted to fit harmoniously into their surroundings, mirroring the forms and patterns found in nature, which not only contributes to their aesthetic appeal but also enhances their environmental performance. Their designs allow for natural ventilation and cooling, reducing the need for energy-intensive air conditioning. The strategic positioning of windows and spaces helps to maximize natural light during the day, reducing the need for artificial lighting.

Furthermore, bamboo as a construction material has a very low carbon footprint. It grows rapidly, absorbs carbon dioxide at higher rates than trees and, if harvested correctly, can be a truly renewable resource. In addition, the firm also ensures that the bamboo is treated with natural salts to make it resistant to insects, and it is used in ways that make the structures robust and enduring.[48] Ibuku's bamboo homes showcase a potent combination of traditional materials, great design and sustainable practices. They offer an interesting example of how innovative green building practices can contribute significantly to sustainability, while also providing functional, comfortable and visually stunning spaces for human habitation. Incorporating green design principles such as those employed by Ibuku has not only environmental benefits but also significant financial advantages. The strategic use of natural light reduces reliance on artificial lighting, lowering electricity costs. Similarly, capitalizing on natural airflows for ventilation decreases the need for air conditioning, contributing to additional energy and cost savings. The use of locally sourced, rapidly renewable materials like bamboo can also lower construction costs. While the upfront cost may sometimes be higher due to the specialized knowledge required for such unique construction techniques, the long-term savings derived from reduced operational costs often more than compensate for this initial investment. In addition, the longevity of properly treated bamboo structures can match or even exceed that of conventional materials, which translates to lower maintenance and replacement costs.

Sales of heat pumps, which are vital for reducing building emissions, have seen a remarkable increase, with double-digit growth for two consecutive years as of 2023. In some European markets, this surge has reached as high as 50 per cent. Notably, sales of heat pumps are now outpacing those of gas furnaces in the US. However, while this progress is commendable, governments have been less successful in promoting other types of building retrofits. Consequently, we are still far from achieving a comprehensive set of policies that would completely eradicate emissions from buildings.[49]

New ways of using products (circularity)

Circularity is a thrilling aspect of sustainability, infusing creativity and innovation into business practices. It is about moving from a linear business model to closing the loops of materials. It challenges companies to reimagine the life cycles of their products and services, turning waste into resources and ensuring that everything has a purpose and place in the cycle. Circularity demands a profound transformation, delving deep into the heart of operations and upending traditional linear models of production and consumption. By striving for a circular approach, businesses are not just making incremental changes; they are radically redefining their operational DNA. Thus, with a strategic shift towards circularity, businesses can not only deepen their relationships with existing customers but also discover new markets. Whether it's offering after-sales services, exploring the resale market or initiating a product-as-a-service model, the possibilities are vast. The challenge, of course, is maintaining the circular flow of materials, especially when there is a geographical separation in terms of where products are made and where they're consumed.

Reflecting on the example from the introduction, where circular economy practices were possible in Dharavi's slums without technology or investments, it's inspiring to imagine the transformative impact when innovation, technology and investments are introduced simultaneously to enhance circularity.

EXAMPLE Product innovations for sustainability

The examples given here range from scalable solutions already making significant impacts to ground-breaking innovative pilots questioning why wasteful practices were ever accepted, thus showcasing a broad spectrum of circular initiatives across different sectors. Some prompt a reflective question: why haven't these common-sense solutions been our standard practice all along? This challenges us to reconsider past wastefulness and underscores the importance of adopting sustainable practices from the outset.

Coca-Cola

Coca-Cola's Universal Bottle, introduced in Latin America and now expanding globally, is a reusable plastic bottle used across multiple soda brands. Customers return these bottles after use, and Coca-Cola collects them for refilling and reuse, significantly reducing plastic use and environmental impact. This bottle can be reused up to 25 times, cutting down plastic usage by 90 per cent. The concept represents an innovative approach to tackle the issue of single-use plastic, aligning with Coca-Cola's commitment to sustainable practices, including their goal to make all packaging recyclable by 2025 and to use 50 per cent recycled material by 2030. The success of this project in Latin America has led to its introduction in South Africa, with plans to expand further, offering a practical and sustainable packaging solution.[50]

Interface

Interface, a leading carpet tile manufacturer, pioneered a remarkable shift towards circularity in their industry. Recognizing the environmental toll of traditional carpet production, the company embarked on a mission to redesign its entire product life cycle. Interface introduced a closed-loop system, where old carpet tiles are reclaimed to create new ones, reducing the need for virgin materials. By innovating in both design and manufacturing processes, they not only minimized waste but also positioned themselves as trailblazers for sustainable practices in the flooring industry. Their efforts exemplify how businesses can turn challenges into opportunities, transforming industries with visionary sustainable models.[51]

Parently

Parently is an innovative company that offers rental services for children's products. Recognizing that children outgrow items quickly, the company provides a sustainable and cost-effective alternative to constantly buying new products. Customers can subscribe or rent specific items as needed, allowing them to save money, enjoy flexibility and reduce their environmental impact.[52]

The rise of such service-based models is evident across various sectors. From tools to vehicles, sports equipment, household appliances, gardening tools, clothing, furniture and more, there's a growing trend towards renting rather than owning, signifying a shift towards more sustainable consumption patterns.

Sellpy

Large brands have a significant role to play in advancing circularity by leveraging their extensive customer reach and platforms to shift consumer behaviour towards sustainable practices. These brands can enable circularity and reuse on a large scale, making it a mainstream practice rather than a niche concept. One example is Sellpy, now part of the H&M Group. They focus on extending the lifespan of garments through circular business models like repair, reuse and remake. These models not only contribute to climate goals but also offer affordable sustainable fashion options and job creation opportunities. By adopting such measures, companies like H&M can significantly influence consumer habits and drive the transition to a more sustainable and circular fashion industry.[53]

Other examples

The following are some examples from a range of industries:[54]

- Stockholm Data Parks partners with Stockholm Exergi to recycle excess heat from data centres, transforming it into district heating and contributing to the circular economy. This initiative traded over 116 GWh of heat in 2021, enough to warm 1,500 modern apartments.
- Cashewmeetly and Axfood developed a sustainable plant-based meat from cashew apples, a previously discarded by-product of cashew nut processing in Africa. In this way they are addressing the issue of food waste while meeting the rising demand for cashew nuts.
- Timber on Top focuses on adding to existing buildings using bio-based materials for sustainability, as seen in the renovation of Trikåfabriken in Stockholm. This conserves resources and extends buildings' lifespans.
- Fiskeby Board's unique process in Scandinavia recycles 100 per cent return fibre for new cardboard packaging, including drink cartons and coated materials, reducing energy use by 40 per cent and cutting carbon dioxide emissions significantly. This showcases a move towards more sustainable production in the paper industry.
- LKAB Berg & Betong conducted a large-scale test of entirely cement-free concrete using GGBS and waste lime from their own operations. This resulted in concrete that adheres to circular principles and has low carbon dioxide emissions, highlighting innovative steps towards reducing environmental impact in mining operations.

The concept of the sharing economy is increasingly seen as a crucial tool in transitioning from a throwaway model to a circular society. This model emphasizes using resources rather than owning them, as exemplified by platforms that connect supply and demand. High-profile examples include Uber and Airbnb, as well as others like Foodora, Voi, KRY, Rover, Upwork, Coursera, ShareDesk and TipTapp. The foundation of this business model is creating value by facilitating trust between parties in new ways, primarily through digital platforms. These platforms, often based on the online-to-offline (O2O) model, have exploded in popularity, enabling users to order services digitally but experience them in the physical world. The sharing economy extends beyond personal services to sectors like agriculture, where technology can aid in resource sharing.

By 2030, platforms for shared resources are anticipated to be one of several solutions for moving away from throwaway models, with success going to those who effectively link supply and demand in new industries and areas.[55] The platform model is expected to expand into more industries, creating trust between new actors, integrating payment and contracts into solutions, and matching supply and demand using AI. The evolution will continue in both business-to-consumer (B2C) and consumer-to-consumer (C2C) models and extend into business-to-business (B2B) scenarios, as seen in agriculture. Examples in the B2B domain include Equipment Share for construction equipment rentals, Flexe for on-demand warehousing, V-Industry for making 3D printing accessible, Open Energy for green energy trading between companies, Tradeshift for logistics and supply chain collaborations, and Kwipped for renting various equipment.

EXAMPLE A holistic approach to solving a multifaceted problem

Pranshu Singhal is leading a significant e-waste recycling initiative in India through his organization, Karo Sambhav. His approach involves transforming the hazardous and unregulated e-waste recycling system into a safe, efficient and responsible process. This change is crucial, given India's status as the world's fourth-largest e-waste producer and the prevalent use of unsafe recycling methods by the informal sector. His strategy leverages legislative changes and builds a network involving stakeholders like NGOs, the informal sector, industry bodies and government agencies. Pranshu's efforts focus on raising awareness, incentivizing responsible recycling and integrating informal recyclers into a formal, transparent system. Karo Sambhav's impactful work includes collaborating with schools, bulk consumers and electronic producers to foster responsible e-waste management and meet extended producer responsibility (EPR) guidelines. Through a mobile app, the initiative also facilitates e-waste collection and recycling for the wider community. Pranshu's model has reached several cities and states in India, significantly reducing e-waste in landfills. His successful approach is now being considered for replication in other industries and countries, to address the global e-waste challenge.[56]

Industrial symbiosis

Industrial symbiosis is a concept within industrial ecology where different industries collaborate to optimize resource use and reduce environmental impact. It's based on the principle of mimicking natural ecosystems, where the waste or by-product of one process becomes the raw material for another. This approach fosters a more circular economy, minimizing waste and maximizing resource efficiency. Examples of industrial symbiosis have been recorded all over the world, including in Brazil, Mexico, Argentina, Colombia and Costa Rica. Overall, industrial symbiosis is about creating a collaborative network where businesses mutually benefit from each other's activities, leading to more sustainable and efficient industrial practices.[57] Key features of industrial symbiosis include:

- **Resource sharing:** Companies share resources like water, energy, materials and infrastructure. This collaboration can lead to significant reductions in costs and environmental footprint.
- **Waste as resource:** Waste produced by one company is used as an input for another. For example, heat generated as a by-product in one industrial process might be used to power another facility.
- **Innovation and cooperation:** It encourages innovation as companies work together to find new ways to use by-products or share resources. This cooperation can lead to novel technologies or processes.
- **Economic and environmental benefits:** Industrial symbiosis can lead to economic benefits for the participating companies through cost savings and new revenue streams. Environmentally, it reduces waste and emissions, contributing to more sustainable industrial practices.
- **Networking and knowledge exchange:** It fosters a network of businesses and organizations that exchange materials, energy, water and by-products. The sharing of knowledge and best practices is also a crucial element.

EXAMPLE Working together for mutual benefit in Kalundborg

A classic example of industrial symbiosis is found in Kalundborg, Denmark. This industrial ecosystem involves a web of public and private enterprises that exchange materials, energy, water and by-products in a closed-loop system. The synergy started spontaneously in the 1960s and has evolved into a well-structured system. In Kalundborg, a coal-fired power plant generates electricity and steam. The excess heat from this plant is used to heat 3,500 local homes and a nearby fish farm, while the steam is used in a pharmaceutical plant. The power plant also supplies fly ash (a by-product of burning coal) to a cement company and gypsum (a by-product of their flue gas desulfurization unit) to a wallboard manufacturer. Additionally, a refinery and a biotech company are part of this network, exchanging various streams of water, steam and energy.

This symbiosis allows these companies to use resources more efficiently, leading to significant reductions in energy consumption, water usage and waste generation. This not only benefits the environment by minimizing pollution and conserving resources, but also provides economic advantages to the involved parties through cost savings and additional revenues. The Kalundborg model is often cited as a pioneering example of how industrial symbiosis can contribute to sustainable development.[58]

Greening the fashion runway

The fashion industry faces several different types of sustainability challenges, as it needs to address issues like overproduction, short product life cycles, waste and poor labour conditions. Sustainable solutions include the use of eco-friendly materials, circular design principles and ethical labour practices, and encouraging consumers to buy less and choose well. It's a much more consumer-facing challenge, requiring not just changes in production practices but also shifts in consumer behaviour.[59] Compare these sectors with a supply-driven business, such as raw material extraction or a manufacturing company. Here, the sustainability challenges may be more direct, such as reducing emissions, improving energy efficiency or managing waste. The solutions often involve technological innovations and operational efficiencies. At the same time, such businesses also face indirect challenges, such as managing the sustainability performance of their suppliers and ensuring responsible sourcing.[60]

Looking ahead to 2030, a crucial shift is anticipated in the industry, pivoting from unsustainable practices to a model that champions sustainability. A key part of this transformation is the concept of circularity, which involves reselling, upgrading or recycling existing garments. The market for second-hand or 'pre-loved' fashion is already growing three times faster than traditional retail.[61] Companies like Patagonia have made sustainability a key part of their business strategy. By using recycled materials and encouraging customers to repair and recycle their products, these companies reduce their environmental impact and appeal to consumers who are increasingly conscious of sustainability. Major fashion companies like H&M, Zara and Uniqlo are embracing this trend, not only as their responsibility towards sustainability but also as a growth strategy. However, the challenge remains to integrate circular fashion more deeply into core business operations, moving beyond symbolic gestures to create significant impact.

Digital product IDs and blockchain technology are set to revolutionize how fashion companies track and manage their garments. Start-ups like Lablaco and EON are creating scalable solutions enabling companies to monitor the condition of their products and offer attractive terms for resale.[62] This tech-driven approach not only simplifies the resale process but also opens up new revenue models for manufacturers. By 2030, it's expected that selling clothes will be as commonplace as buying them, facilitated by technology that makes the process as easy as a click of a button. This shift towards a more sustainable and circular fashion industry is poised to significantly reduce the environmental impact of our clothing consumption while creating new opportunities for consumers and companies alike.[63]

CASE STUDY i-did, a slow-fashion social enterprise

Mireille Geijsen, founder of i-did, transitioned from graphic designer to sustainability innovator, embodying the essence of social enterprise. i-did's business model centres around social inclusion and circular textiles, creating products from recycled materials while employing those distanced from the labour market. i-did's mission is twofold: to provide sustainable employment opportunities for people who have been long-term unemployed and to address the textile waste issue in the country. And by taking unused human capital and waste material, they have created a growing business case. For people struggling with long-term unemployment due to multiple life issues, i-did offers comprehensive guidance, coaching and work-based learning experiences. They aim to empower these individuals by developing their job skills and assisting them back into the labour market. On the other hand, i-did also targets the significant textile waste problem in the Netherlands, which sees about 330 million kg of old textiles discarded each year. They work towards reducing this textile mountain by transforming old textiles, like corporate or consumer clothing, into recycled felt. Within their workshops, participants contribute to the creation of beautifully crafted items like bags, interior design pieces and accessories, all made from this recycled felt. This hands-on experience not only provides them with practical skills but also instills a sense of accomplishment and self-esteem, which are crucial for their reintegration into the workforce.

As a social enterprise, i-did operates with a keen focus on delivering maxmum sustainable and social impact. All profits generated by the organization are reinvested into their mission, reflecting their commitment to not just economic gain, but social betterment and environmental responsibility as well. Through their unique approach, i-did is creating a more inclusive and sustainable world, one job and one piece of recycled textile at a time.[64]

Social enterprises: Founded to do good

Social enterprises like i-did are businesses that have a specific social and environmental mission at their core. They aim to generate profit through the sales of products or services, but, unlike traditional businesses, their primary focus is on creating positive societal impact and reinvesting the profit into the business.[65]

For example, a social enterprise might sell ethically sourced, sustainable coffee, with a portion of their profits going towards supporting fair trade farming communities. This includes providing jobs to people who are vulnerable or marginalized. For example, social enterprises may hire people who are distant from the labour market, providing them with income and training, while making sustainable products. The key to profitability for a social enterprise, just like any business, lies in the successful execution of its business model. Social enterprises must be efficient, innovative and market-driven to succeed, even as they maintain their focus on their social mission.

EXAMPLE Tony's Chocolonely and Fairphone

Tony's Chocolonely was founded in 2005 by Teun van de Keuken, a Dutch journalist who was shocked to discover the prevalence of child labour and slavery in cocoa farming. Teun initially tried to draw attention to this issue through a television programme, but felt that the impact was limited. He then decided to create a chocolate company committed to making slave-free chocolate the industry norm. Tony's Chocolonely works directly with cocoa farmers in West Africa, ensuring they are paid a living wage and promoting sustainable farming practices. The company's chocolate bars are also designed to be unevenly divided, a visual reminder that the profits within the chocolate industry are unfairly distributed.[66]

Fairphone stands as a beacon for businesses looking to integrate circularity. Hailing from the Netherlands, this social enterprise is more than just a phone company. They've designed modular phones that encourage users to replace parts, not the whole device. Beyond product design, Fairphone educates its users on the importance of sustainable consumption. They've also made a point of sourcing materials from conflict-free zones, underlining their commitment to both environmental and social sustainability. Their mission is two-fold: create sustainable, modular products and raise awareness about responsible consumption in the wider community.[67]

These companies demonstrate that having a purpose beyond profit can mobilize both consumers and employees, creating a loyal community around the brand. Additionally, the focus on sustainability and ethical sourcing proves that it is not only possible but also advantageous to align commercial success with social and environmental responsibility. Furthermore, Fairphone's modular design concept can inspire traditional businesses to think about product life cycles and circular economy principles. Chocolonely's direct relationship with cocoa farmers is a valuable model for establishing equitable and sustainable vendor relationships in any industry. By partnering with or doing business with such social enterprises, traditional companies can amplify their own impact, moving the needle further towards a sustainable and equitable global economy.

Summary and key take-aways

This chapter outlined the evolution of sustainability from a perceived burden to a profitable business strategy. We urge sustainability leaders to draw inspiration from leading examples to blend profitability with social responsibility, showcasing sustainability as a wise business choice. We also presented an optimistic stance on sustainability as both a strategic necessity and a morale booster, encouraging collaboration across sectors and emphasizing that even small efforts contribute to broader sustainability goals. The chapter suggested that aligning business strategies with sustainability not only fulfils an ethical duty but also offers a competitive advantage, opening avenues for business growth and partnerships.

Endnotes

1 Mattei Nikki. Sustainability is no longer a 'nice to have' – it is a necessity, LinkedIn, 2 August 2023. www.linkedin.com/pulse/sustainability-longer-nice-have-necessity-nikki-mattei-/ (archived at https://perma.cc/54Z9-FVFT)

2 Md. Tareq Bin Hossain, Chamhuri Siwar, Mazlin Bin Mokhtar and Abul Bashar Bhuiyan. Historical development of corporate social responsibility: A review on early studies, Historical Research Letter, 2014, 14, 14–18. core.ac.uk/download/pdf/234668602.pdf (archived at https://perma.cc/2TC6-JL6T)

3 Bruce M. From charity to responsibility: A brief history of corporate social responsibility (CSR), LinkedIn, 2 April 2023. www.linkedin.com/pulse/from-charity-responsibility-brief-history-corporate-social-msimanga/ (archived at https://perma.cc/4VW7-NLSP)

4 Paul Polman and Andrew Winston (2021) *Net Positive: How courageous companies thrive by giving more than they take*, Harvard Business Review Press, Boston. Also see Chrissa Pagistas (2022) *Chief Sustainability Officers at Work: How CSOs build successful sustainability and ESG strategies*, Apress, New York

5 Mario Paysse. 5 reasons sustainability is beneficial for business – not just the environment, *Forbes*, 1 September 2022. www.forbes.com/sites/forbesbusinessdevelopmentcouncil/2022/09/01/5-reasons-sustainability-is-beneficial-for-business-not-just-the-environment/ (archived at https://perma.cc/6EV2-FNXY)

6 Per Espen Stoknes (2022) *Tomorrows Economy: A guide to creating healthy green growth*, MIT Press, Cambridge, MA

7 An alternative way to structure organizations is presented in Cambridge Institute for Sustainability Leadership (CISL). CISL's Business Transformation Framework Preliminary Diagnostic, 19 October 2023. www.cisl.cam.ac.uk/

news-and-resources/publications/cisls-business-transformation-framework-preliminary-diagnostic (archived at https://perma.cc/Q9BW-MEBS)

8 Yann Bouchery (2018) *Sustainable Supply Chains: A research-based textbook on operations and strategy*, Springer, Cham

9 Lynn S Paine, Rohit Deshpandé, Joshua D Margolis and Kim Eric Bettcher. Up to code: Does your company's conduct meet world-class standards? Harvard Business Review, December 2005. hbr.org/2005/12/up-to-code-does-your-companys-conduct-meet-world-class-standards (archived at https://perma.cc/P2Q4-UB2F)

10 How to create a supplier code of conduct and examples of what to include, WorldFavor blog. blog.worldfavor.com/how-to-create-a-supplier-code-of-conduct-examples-of-what-to-include (archived at https://perma.cc/MUQ4-DU87)

11 What is the fourth sector? Fourth Sector Group. www.fourthsector.org/what-is-the-fourth-sector (archived at https://perma.cc/9ACQ-HEN3)

12 Make business a force for good, B Corporation. www.bcorporation.net (archived at https://perma.cc/GJ5C-2RGM)

13 Deloitte. The Future of the Chief Sustainability Officer: Sense-Maker in Chief, February 2021. www2.deloitte.com/content/dam/Deloitte/bg/Documents/financial-services/gx-fsi-future-of-the-cso-report.pdf (archived at https://perma.cc/9H4U-SGCM)

14 Sheila Bonini and Steven Swartz. Profits with purpose: How organizing for sustainability can benefit the bottom line, McKinsey, July 2014. www.mckinsey.com/~/media/McKinsey/Business%20Functions/Sustainability/Our%20Insights/Profits%20with%20purpose/Profits%20with%20Purpose.ashx (archived at https://perma.cc/L86X-CX4R)

15 Michael E Porter and Mark R Kramer. Creating shared value: How to reinvent capitalism – and unleash a wave of innovation and growth, Harvard Business Review, January–February 2011. hbr.org/2011/01/the-big-idea-creating-shared-value (archived at https://perma.cc/3DJH-E5S5)

16 Duc Cuong Pham, Thi Ngoc Anh Do, Thanh Nga Doan, Thi Xuan Hong Nguyen and Thi Kim Yen Pham. The impact of sustainability practices on financial performance: Empirical evidence from Sweden, Cogent Business and Management, 2021, 8 (1), #1912526. doi.org/10.1080/23311975.2021.1912526 (archived at https://perma.cc/7T49-KJN7)

17 Andreas Staubli and Christophe Bourgion. Sustainability isn't about value preservation: It's about value creation, interview, PwC. www.pwc.ch/en/insights/sustainability/sustainability-is-about-value-creation.html (archived at https://perma.cc/95BY-R775)

18 Ram Nidumolu, CK Prahalad and MR Rangaswami. Why sustainability is now the key driver of innovation, Harvard Business Review, September 2009. hbr.org/2009/09/why-sustainability-is-now-the-key-driver-of-innovation (archived at https://perma.cc/95CW-HBJV)

19 Stefan Premer. The hidden cost of corporate climate inaction, GreenBiz, 30 August 2023. www.greenbiz.com/article/hidden-cost-corporate-climate-inaction (archived at https://perma.cc/M7JR-FST8)

20 Simon Stiell. The cost of inaction is far greater than the cost of action, UN. www.un.org/en/climatechange/thought-leaders-simon-stiell (archived at https://perma.cc/J362-KDCD)

21 The role business can play in tackling the refugee crisis, Unilever, 20 June 2017. www.unilever.com/news/news-search/2017/role-business-can-play-in-tackling-the-refugee-crisis/ (archived at https://perma.cc/JK86-PEVQ)

22 Mark R Kramer and Marc W Pfitzer. The ecosystem of shared value, Harvard Business Review, October 2016. hbr.org/2016/10/the-ecosystem-of-shared-value (archived at https://perma.cc/37H2-LKL8)

23 Christine Johnson. How understanding sunk costs can help your everyday decision making processes, Harvard Business School Online, 3 November 2016. online.hbs.edu/blog/post/how-understanding-sunk-costs-can-help-your-everyday-decision-making-processes (archived at https://perma.cc/WUJ2-YTG5)

24 Building on input from Ben Kellard, director of business strategy at the CISL

25 The business case for commercial solar, The Energy Experts, 13 June 2023. theenergyexperts.com.au/the-business-case-for-commercial-solar/ (archived at https://perma.cc/9BB6-Q9KA)

26 Solar (photovoltaic) panel prices, Our World in Data. https://ourworldindata.org/grapher/solar-pv-prices (archived at https://perma.cc/H2GC-ZYVQ)

27 BatteryBits Editors. Scale and the economic mechanisms of learning rate: Applying lessons from solar to the battery industry, Medium, 25 July 2023. medium.com/batterybits/scale-and-the-economic-mechanisms-of-learning-rate-applying-lessons-from-solar-to-the-battery-f96c823e2105 (archived at https://perma.cc/A3RH-A9FF)

28 See https://orsted.se/om-oss/darfor-heter-vi-orsted (archived at https://perma.cc/TXF9-73L3)

29 Walmart announces the completion of Apple Valley distribution center solar project, press release, Webwire, 19 January 2010. www.webwire.com/ViewPressRel.asp?aId=111174 (archived at https://perma.cc/UCA2-8G5N)

30 The solar energy start-up Africa, Briter Bridges, 17 January 2023. briterbridges.com/stories/2022/10/20/the-solar-energy-startup-landscape-in-africa (archived at https://perma.cc/F7KM-EEUL)

31 See solarsister.org (archived at https://perma.cc/4UWJ-YPET)

32 Sandra Wappelhorst. The end of the road? An overview of combustion engine car phase-out announcements across Europe, ICCT (International Council on Clean Transportation), May 2020. theicct.org/sites/default/files/publications/Combustion-engine-phase-out-briefing-may11.2020.pdf (archived at https://perma.cc/24LU-PGAW)

33 Electrical vehicles, EEA (European Environmental Agency), October 2023, modified 10 January 2024. www.eea.europa.eu/en/topics/in-depth/electric-vehicles (archived at https://perma.cc/UW67-54JB)
34 Bloomberg News. Electric Cars Are Driving China Toward the End of the Age of Oil, 21 December, 2023. www.bloomberg.com/graphics/2023-china-ev-roadtrip-oil-turning-point/?embedded-checkout=true (archived at https://perma.cc/FC49-J4LT)
35 Feargus O'Sullivan. Inside the new plan to make Paris 100% cyclable, Bloomberg, 22 October 2021. www.bloomberg.com/news/articles/2021-10-22/how-paris-will-become-100-cyclable (archived at https://perma.cc/FYS3-CVKN)
36 Stockholm Resilience Centre. The planetary health diet, 17 January 2019. www.stockholmresilience.org/research/research-news/2019-01-17-the-planetary-health-diet.html (archived at https://perma.cc/V3PP-V6GH)
37 UN Food and Agriculture Organization (FAO). Tackling climate change through livestock: A global assessment of emissions and mitigation opportunities, 2013. www.fao.org/3/i3437e/i3437e.pdf (archived at https://perma.cc/C3H4-C9LR)
38 See bettercotton.org (archived at https://perma.cc/7PGJ-SEWM)
39 International Day of Awareness on Food Loss and Waste Reduction, 29 September, UN. www.un.org/en/observances/end-food-waste-day (archived at https://perma.cc/Y5HF-GT83)
40 France's law for fighting food waste, Zero Waste Europe fact sheet. zerowasteeurope.eu/wp-content/uploads/2020/11/zwe_11_2020_factsheet_france_en.pdf (archived at https://perma.cc/D4DZ-JUP9)
41 Interview conducted March 2022
42 See makemymoneymatter.co.uk (archived at https://perma.cc/W7BJ-MP94)
43 Beyond GDP, UN Systems Chief Executives Board for Coordination (CEB). unsceb.org/topics/beyond-gdp (archived at https://perma.cc/LB96-BBYY)
44 Greening Cash Action Guide, Exponential Roadmap. exponentialroadmap.org/wp-content/uploads/2023/08/Greening-Cash-Action-Guide.pdf (archived at https://perma.cc/BWK6-Y62R)
45 See https://carbonaccountingfinancials.com (archived at https://perma.cc/2Y4G-G3LX)
46 Interview conducted January 2022
47 See ibuku.com (archived at https://perma.cc/7AFT-GQ8M)
48 Shreeya Khadka. Why is bamboo the sustainable architectural design and construction material of the future? GreenESA, 12 December 2020. www.greenesa.com/news/bamboo-sustainable-material-of-the-future (archived at https://perma.cc/S9B5-7G9U)
49 Generation Investment Management. The Sustainability Trends Report 2023, 14 September 2023. str2023.generationim.com/chapters/introduction?utm_medium=google_ads&utm_source=primary&utm_campaign=google_ad&utm_content=copy1 (archived at https://perma.cc/SMF9-QM9U)

50 A reusable drinks bottle design for multiple brands: Universal bottle, Ellen MacArthur Foundation, 7 October 2021. www.ellenmacarthurfoundation.org/circular-examples/a-reusable-drinks-bottle-design-for-multiple-brands-universal-bottle?utm_term=exclude&utm_source=exclude (archived at https://perma.cc/XZ5Z-2TVH)

51 Sustainability is in our DNA, Interface. www.interface.com/AU/en-AU/sustainability/sustainability-overview.html (archived at https://perma.cc/U2CC-V4EL)

52 See https://www.parently.se/pages/safunkardet-1 (archived at https://perma.cc/G792-3SGL)

53 Designing products for circularity: H&M Group, Ellen MacArthur Foundation, 14 December 2021. www.ellenmacarthurfoundation.org/circular-examples/hm-group (archived at https://perma.cc/9H32-67PM)

54 100 examples of circular economy solutions, Hagainitiativet. www.hagainitiativet.se/100-exempel-pa-cirkular-ekonomi/ (archived at https://perma.cc/95GN-VLBA)

55 Blake Morgan. No Ownership, No Problem: An updated look at why millennials value experiences over owning things, *Forbes*, 2 July 2019. www.forbes.com/sites/blakemorgan/2019/01/02/nownership-no-problem-an-updated-look-at-why-millennials-value-experiences-over-owning-things/?sh=1ee0538c522f (archived at https://perma.cc/9KY4-Z3KV)

56 Pranshu Singhal, Ashoka. www.ashoka.org/en-nrd/fellow/pranshu-singhal (archived at https://perma.cc/GR8F-HHNV)

57 Sabrina De Gobbi. Industrial symbiosis networks as part of a circular economy: Employment effects in some industrializing countries, ILO research brief, April 2022. www.ilo.org/wcmsp5/groups/public/---dgreports/---inst/documents/briefingnote/wcms_844753.pdf (archived at https://perma.cc/5UTT-GHDG)

58 Kalundborg symbiosis, Hållbarhetsguiden. hallbarhetsguiden.se/?guide=kalundborg-symbiosis-effective-industrial-symbiosis-sv-translation (archived at https://perma.cc/9VU4-ER7R)

59 What do we mean by a sustainable closet? Sustainable Closet. www.asustainablecloset.com/sustainabilityfacts (archived at https://perma.cc/84B8-TTL3)

60 Infinite X, Circular Fashion. Fast fashion: The environmental and social impacts you need to know, LinkedIn, 31 March 2023. www.linkedin.com/pulse/fast-fashion-environmental-social-impacts-you-need-know-infinite-x/ (archived at https://perma.cc/66Z7-LXYA)

61 Sarah Butler. Online marketplaces report surge in sales of secondhand goods, *The Guardian*, 29 November 2023. www.theguardian.com/business/2023/nov/29/online-marketplaces-report-surge-in-sales-of-secondhand-goods (archived at https://perma.cc/M2NR-7LXD)

62 See lablaco.com (archived at https://perma.cc/BC8A-ZKUF) and www.eon.xyz (archived at https://perma.cc/5DZJ-E4N7)

63 Henrik Evrell. 20 trender mot 2030 [20 trends towards 2030], Judith Wolst blog, March 2023. www.judithwolst.se/rapporter/ (archived at https://perma.cc/WW6B-UXRK)

64 Interview conducted October 2021

65 All about social enterprise, Social Enterprise UK. www.socialenterprise.org.uk/all-about-social-enterprise/ (archived at https://perma.cc/VF34-XEDE)

66 See tonyschocolonely.com/us/en/our-mission (archived at https://perma.cc/45R3-FAP9)

67 See www.fairphone.com/en/story/ (archived at https://perma.cc/2VFG-FVB3)

PART 2
Practical integration of sustainability

Welcome to Part 2, where our journey takes a practical turn. Here, we shift gears from understanding sustainability, as well as individuals' and organizations' roles in the sustainability transformation, to actively embedding it into organizations, ensuring that good intentions transform into meaningful actions.

Our methodology for embedding sustainability within an organization is structured yet adaptable, echoing well-established management models like 'plan, do, check, act' (DPCA).[1] We'll explore pathways, from pinpointing where we stand to crafting effective strategies, engaging pivotal stakeholders and ensuring our progress is measurably impactful. At its core, it's about understanding your operational environment and the challenges therein, envisioning where you want to be, mobilizing people and resources to achieve this vision and then engaging in a cycle of reporting, learning and improvement. We'll provide clear steps and practical tips, as well as tools, examples and real-life case studies – reflective learning from our experiences and those interviewed for this book – thus providing clear, real-world insights to guide and inspire. All of this is designed to offer practical tips and food for thought as you embark on the journey to embed sustainability across your organization.

Each of the following six chapters are dedicated to an element of the implementation and embedding process: assessment, strategy, integration, stakeholder management, reporting and communications. Our strategic framework is a collective, iterative process with multiple feedback loops, each step vital for fully integrating sustainability within the organization. The process begins with an assessment, identifying the organization's sector, business orientation and current performance levels. A baseline is established by answering the question, 'Who are we as an organization?'; and the organization's current standing is determined by asking, 'What is our performance benchmark?' Thereafter, we focus on setting future objectives, defining clear goals and creating a strategic pathway towards these objectives. Integrating the strategy into the organizational structure ensures that sustainability becomes a thread running through the entire organization. This phase involves responsible individuals being identified for each aspect of the strategic framework and ensuring active stakeholder engagement and effective change management. We emphasize the synergy of top-down leadership and bottom-up engagement, fostering grassroots initiatives and ensuring that sustainability remains a focus for everyone. A robust reporting framework, emphasizing a theory of change, complemented by monitoring, evaluation and continuous learning, is also key. Communication, using effective, tailored communication strategies, is integral. Advocacy also plays a crucial role in driving change beyond the organization's immediate boundaries.

We view this as a continuous cycle, with learning being a constant, especially given the ever-changing nature of the world and sustainability challenges. Chapter 6 will specifically explore the integration of sustainability into the organization's fabric. In contrast, other chapters, such as those on strategy, will focus on embedding sustainability more deeply into the business model itself. Consequently, we suggest in chapters 4 and 5 that the responsibility for sustainability initiatives should extend beyond just a sustainability leader, involving relevant functional departments closely related to the issue at hand. This multidisciplinary approach to sustainability will become clearer as you progress through the chapters. For a sustainability leader, staying informed and adaptable isn't just a one-time task, but a continuous commitment.

Endnote

1 Plan, do, check, act, Lean Enterprise Institute. www.lean.org/lexicon-terms/pdca/ (archived at https://perma.cc/NL7V-E9SA)

Assessment and orientation of sustainability performance 04

Begin with a critical assessment of your current sustainability status and performance, to connect aspirations with reality and to guide the tactical deployment of your sustainability initiatives. Two essential assessments require your attention as you set out to embed sustainability in your organization:

1. **Orientation:** This is about pinpointing your current position and defining your type of organization, industry and geographical context. There are four sub-steps in this process:
   - **(a)** Comprehending the specifics of the organization's internal landscape
   - **(b)** Understanding the context within which the organization exists
   - **(c)** Gaining a thorough understanding of the specific environments and geographical markets where the organization conducts its operations
   - **(d)** Reviewing the existing sustainability frameworks that are available that can guide and support your organization.
2. **Performance:** Evaluate your organization's performance by measuring the progress you've achieved. To do this, you need to follow these three steps:
   - **(a)** Conducting a robust materiality assessment
   - **(b)** Reviewing your current environmental and social performance
   - **(c)** Drawing conclusions from the information provided by the orientation and performance stages.

Figure 4.1 shows these steps.

Figure 4.1 Outline of steps and useful tools to assess your organization's sustainability readiness

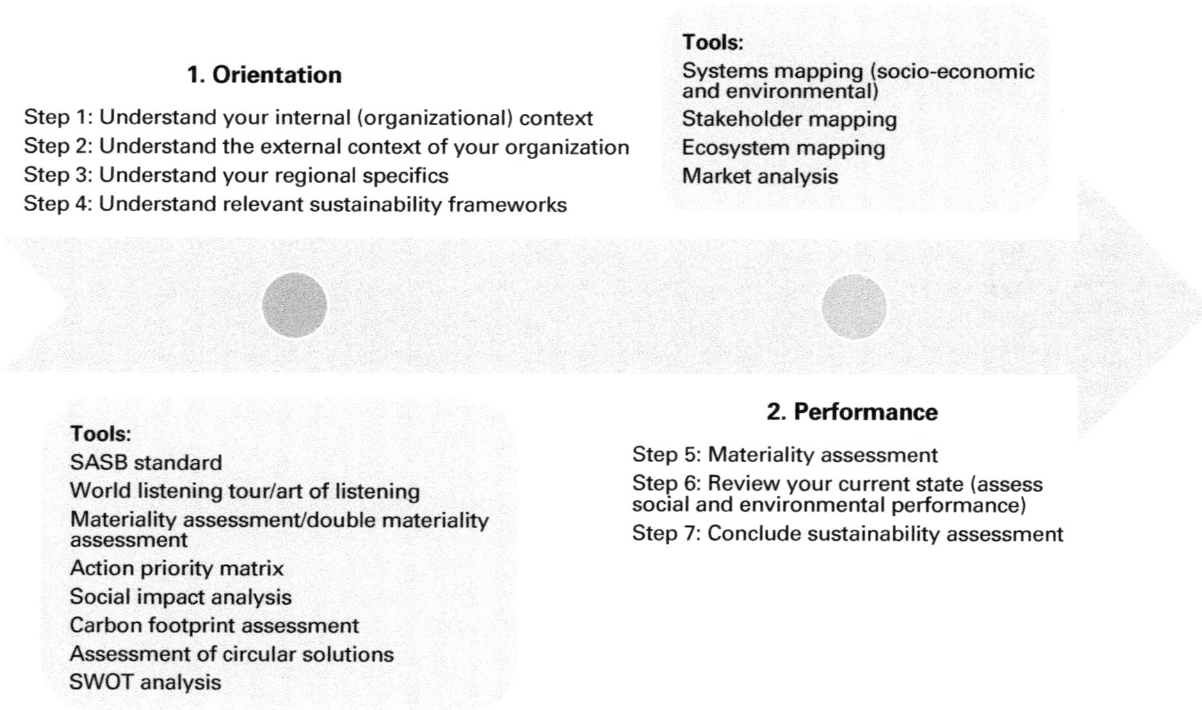

There is a surplus of tools available to support you when assessing where your organization is on its sustainability journey. We will highlight some in this chapter. These tools are tailored to help you effectively align your sustainability efforts with your organization's unique context and objectives. However, when delving into assessment, it's easy to become completely absorbed as there are so many different tools and approaches available. We therefore recommend using the 80/20 principle as a general guideline. It refers to the Pareto Principle, which is a common concept in business and economics, stating that you will have the greatest impact if you understand where your organization is having its biggest footprint.[1] The principle suggests that roughly 80 per cent of effects come from 20 per cent of the causes. In the context of sustainability for production and material-heavy companies, it implies that a significant portion (likely around 80 per cent) of the company's environmental impact – in terms of greenhouse gas emissions and material footprint – is caused by a relatively small proportion (about 20 per cent) of the materials and processes used.

Orientation

Let's start with orientation, a step that involves understanding the organization and the larger system you're part of. There are several steps to take while you orient yourself, starting with understanding the internal context of your organization and continuing with understanding the external context and system your organization operates within. Thereafter, you need to understand geographical and sectorial implications and, finally, which legislation and international frameworks are available.

Step 1: Understand your internal (organizational) context

Evaluating the present sustainability performance of an organization calls for a thorough and multidimensional enquiry into its past and present practices; it is thus important to orient yourself as regards the internal organizational context:

1 **Historical context:** When contemplating whether the organization has a history of working with sustainability, it's pivotal to assess which aspects have been prioritized. An entity might be seasoned in implementing sustainable manufacturing processes but new to social responsibility

initiatives, or the other way around. It's also crucial to identify whether past initiatives have been people-oriented or compliance-driven. Have business-oriented individuals driven sustainability as a side task to meet compliance or market needs? Or has there been dedicated sustainability staff with relevant expertise? Consider whether the initiatives have predominantly been shaped by in-house talent or if external experts have been roped in to impart specialized knowledge and insights. How mature is the organization in its sustainability work and what is the level of quality of the sustainability deliverables so far?

2 **Strategy and aspiration:** Understand your organization's purpose: why does it exist, and what value does it provide? How is this value delivered to your stakeholders? Assess whether your impact is predominantly positive or if your strategies primarily focus on mitigating negatives, like reducing greenhouse gas emissions. Establishing this baseline helps to form a foundation upon which you can build your sustainability initiatives, ensuring they are coherent with your core business functions and value propositions. Scrutinizing the existence and effectiveness of a sustainability strategy is vital. This involves evaluating whether there is a clear, actionable plan in place that spells out the organization's sustainability goals and whether these aspirations are anchored in a realistic understanding of the organization's capabilities and the external environment.

3 **Data as a prerequisite:** Ensuring your organization has the essential data for sustainability assessments is crucial. Evaluate whether you have systems for data collection, know who is monitoring it and understand how it is analysed to inform decisions. This approach not only aligns with regulatory compliance but also enhances the transparency and credibility of your sustainability efforts among stakeholders. It is crucial that we use science-based targets to ensure accuracy and precision in our evaluations. By using quantitative, evidence-based measures, we can accurately monitor progress, identify areas for improvement and devise effective strategies that align with our sustainability objectives.

4 **Internal awareness and engagement:** Understanding the internal pulse regarding sustainability, meaning gauging the level of awareness and engagement among employees and leadership, is foundational for planning future initiatives. An enquiry into whether the team is versed in sustainability matters and to what extent they are actively involved in existing projects provides insights into the internal sustainability culture and can also hint at the potential success of future initiatives. The key is

securing unequivocal support from top-tier management and the board. With their endorsement, initiating and advancing sustainability efforts becomes a feasible endeavour.

5 **Sustainability structure:** At the outset, it's crucial to determine whether sustainability structures already exist within an organization. This means looking at whether there are dedicated teams or individuals steering sustainability efforts and whether the existing operational model supports the efficient roll-out of sustainability projects. If the organization is lacking in this area, strategizing on how to embed a viable sustainability structure becomes a primary objective. While having these structures is undoubtedly beneficial, their absence doesn't impede progress.
6 **Driving and hindering forces:** Identifying the accelerators and roadblocks within the sustainability journey of an organization is key. Driving forces could include a keen market for sustainable products, internal enthusiasm or beneficial regulations. Conversely, obstacles might comprise budget constraints, resistance to change among staff or a lack of expertise in sustainability management. We often notice that companies find it easier to make sustainability commitments when they are doing well (increasing revenues and strong growth trajectory), but when things get tougher, pockets tighten. Recognizing these elements can aid in fortifying the strategy by leveraging strengths and safeguarding against weaknesses.

By carefully dissecting each of these questions, leaders can construct a well-informed overview of the organization's current standing in its sustainability journey. This, in turn, shapes a fertile ground from which a robust, contextually apt sustainability strategy can spring, embedding sustainability holistically and effectively into the organization's DNA. In addition to the above, we believe that the organizational structure, ownership structure and size of the organization are three areas that impact the sustainability transformation process.

Organizational structure

The organizational structure has a significant influence on your mandate. If you're in a franchise model, where franchisees must align with a certain concept, it becomes vital to ensure that sustainability is becoming part of the franchise's core DNA. It implies that all branches will align their practices with your sustainability vision. Contrarily, in an organization with several brands, each brand might have its own sustainability approach, although under the broader sustainability vision of the parent organization. Or, for instance, if you're part of the main office in a multi-brand setup, your mandate could involve integrating sustainability into the organization's core values. You'd be responsible for developing a universal sustainability framework that all brands can adapt and adopt in their unique context.

Ownership structure

Ownership structures, encompassing family-owned, foundation-based or shareholder-owned entities, significantly sculpt the trajectory of sustainability strategies and the mandate of the sustainability team. The nature of ownership and corresponding reporting mechanisms undeniably influence your mandate, shaping both the strategy's depth and its execution.[2] Companies that are publicly traded on a stock exchange have increased regulatory scrutiny, higher transparency requirements and a more diverse shareholder base which may demand greater accountability in sustainability practices. Listed companies often need to adhere to strict ESG criteria that investors and regulators expect, and they must regularly disclose their sustainability performance. In contrast, non-listed, or private, companies are not subject to the same level of public scrutiny and may have more flexibility in their approach to sustainability. They might not face the same pressure from shareholders for immediate results and can potentially take a longer-term view on sustainability investment. They might thus choose to adopt rigorous sustainability practices to align with their values, meet customer expectations, attract talent or prepare for future regulations.[3]

Organizational size

Sustainability as a concept is universal, but its application varies depending on the scale and structure of an organization. Smaller organizations often possess certain inherent advantages. For one, they tend to be more agile, allowing for swift decision making and facilitating the rapid roll-out of sustainable strategies. Given the size of these entities, individuals within them usually wield a significant influence over the organizational direction and its execution. Additionally, the streamlined nature of smaller organizations means there's less bureaucracy to wade through, which results in leaner processes, faster action and minimal red tape. Their relatively flat structures also grant them more flexibility, offering greater freedom to test out and implement novel sustainable measures. Moreover, since there's typically no centralized sustainability team, it can be easier to embed sustainability thinking across all departments and roles, ensuring a cohesive approach. However, there are challenges unique to smaller organizations. Their limited size often means fewer resources at their disposal, particularly in comparison to their larger counterparts. The journey to sustainability might also feel isolated initially, especially in the absence of a dedicated team to steer these efforts. Lastly, while smaller organizations can swiftly enact changes, the overall impact of these changes might be on a smaller scale due to their restricted operational reach.

Larger organizations bring with them a set of strengths and challenges distinct from those of their smaller counterparts. On the upside, they often command vast resources, both financial and human, which can be directed towards sustainability efforts. They usually benefit from structured support in the form of a centralized or matrixed sustainability team, providing expertise and impetus for sustainable transitions. The scale of these organizations means that even minor sustainable shifts can culminate in a substantial aggregate impact. Furthermore, these corporations typically have robust infrastructures in place, which can underpin larger sustainability projects and provide a sturdy base upon which innovative initiatives can take root. However, navigating sustainability in such vast set-ups isn't without its hurdles. The magnitude and diverse nature of larger organizations can amplify the complexity of sustainability undertakings. Additionally, the inevitable bureaucratic challenges that come with size may stall or slow down initiatives, especially those that necessitate substantial overhauls. There's also the looming threat of structural inertia. If a clear sustainability framework isn't ingrained deeply within the organization's DNA – covering its processes, structures, KPIs and overarching business model – there's a risk of backsliding. This risk is particularly pronounced if pivotal sustainability proponents depart or transition into different roles.[4]

Regardless of an organization's size, there's immense value in understanding and learning from the approaches of other-sized entities. Larger corporations often develop robust sustainability frameworks, offering a wealth of insights for smaller businesses. By adapting these blueprints to their context, smaller enterprises can accelerate their sustainability efforts. Meanwhile, the agility, direct stakeholder engagement and holistic integration seen in smaller organizations can provide lessons for larger companies, inspiring them to foster a more nimble and unified sustainability approach. By leveraging shared platforms and networks, organizations of all sizes can collaborate, share challenges and solutions, and drive towards a unified goal of universal sustainability. Businesses, especially large corporations, wield significant influence in shaping societal norms and public policy. By taking a stand on key issues, companies can catalyse broader societal change, often leveraging their brand, resources and networks to advocate progressive policies and sustainable practices. This power to drive change extends beyond the immediate business environment, affecting communities, influencing industry standards and sometimes even shaping national or global conversations on important issues.[5]

Step 2: Understand the external context of your organization

It is now time to review the world the organization is operating within – that is, the overall organization's ecosystem, which includes the stakeholders and the systems in which the business operates. The process typically involves identifying key stakeholders and the system's components, understanding how they interact and then developing strategies that address their needs and goals in a manner that promotes sustainability.[6]

Before doing so, let's dive a bit deeper into what a system means. Systems refer to interconnected sets of elements that work together, like how different parts of a car work together to get it moving. Systems thinking is a way of understanding how things influence one another within a whole. Systems change means making adjustments, or transformations, in this set of connected elements to improve how they work together or to solve problems that are created by the way the system currently operates.[7]

In organizations, it means looking at the company not just as separate departments or teams, but seeing how they are connected and how changes in one area can affect others. Essentially, it's like looking at a spider web – if you touch one part of the web, the whole web moves, demonstrating that everything is linked in some way. Thus, in an organization, systems change might involve altering the underlying structures that contribute to ongoing issues, rather than simply addressing the issues themselves. For instance, consider a company struggling with employee burnout. Rather than only offering wellness programmes, a systems change approach might involve reassessing workloads, modifying expectations, restructuring teams or amending policies to encourage a healthier work–life balance. Here, the goal is to modify the foundational structures (like workload distribution, expectations and policies) to prevent burnout from occurring in the first place, illustrating that systems change seeks to address the root causes of problems by transforming the underlying systems and structures that cause them.

Tool: System mapping tools

System mapping tools show how the organization is part of a broader ecosystem, which can include its industry, its market and the social, economic and environmental systems in which it operates. Understanding this ecosystem can help a business identify the direct and indirect impacts and dependencies it has on the environment and society, and where it can make changes to promote sustainability. As much as it is about the business ecosystem, it is also about dependencies on nature and climate, enabled through frameworks such as the Task Force on Climate-related Financial Disclosures (TCFD) and the Taskforce on Nature-related Financial Disclosures (TNFD).

Systems mapping can be done using a causal loop diagram (CLD)[8] or a systems influence diagram,[9] which visualizes the feedback loops and dependencies within your system. It helps to visualize the different components of a system and the relationships and feedback loops between them. For example, in a clothing manufacturing business, a systems map might include the sources of raw materials (like cotton farms), the manufacturing process, transportation, customer usage and end-of-life disposal or recycling. This map can help the business identify key leverage points where it can make changes to reduce its environmental impact, such as by sourcing more sustainable raw materials, improving energy efficiency in manufacturing or implementing a recycling programme.

Tool: Stakeholder mapping

In Chapter 7, we go deeper into stakeholder management, but we mention it here, as mapping your stakeholders is part of the assessment stage. An effective stakeholder map should ideally be crafted in collaboration with pertinent team members, ensuring comprehensive coverage of every stakeholder and aspect.[10] Stakeholders include anyone who has an interest in or is affected by the business. They can range from employees, customers, suppliers, investors and local communities, to government agencies, NGOs and even future generations who might be impacted by the business's environmental footprint. Stakeholder mapping helps you to understand and categorize stakeholders based on their influence and interest in your business.

A common tool for this process is a stakeholder map, which helps to visualize stakeholders based on their power (or influence) over the business and their interest in the business's activities. For instance, investors and owners might have high power and high interest, while local communities may have high interest but relatively low power. This map allows you to tailor your communication and engagement strategies to meet different stakeholder needs and expectations, such as providing regular financial reports for investors or organizing community engagement initiatives for local communities.

Step 3: Understand the regional specifics you are operating within

An important part of the organizational context is related to geographical and cultural contexts, as sustainability is not a one-size-fits-all phenomenon; it is multidimensional, multifaceted and context-dependent. There is an element of complexity in executing sustainability initiatives across diverse national and cultural landscapes where varying degrees of progress and perceptions around sustainability are prevalent. Working in an international context, we have had first-hand experience of these challenges. It is also one of the more frequently asked questions we get from others: how to implement sustainability across various countries and cultures. We will give a couple of examples in this chapter.

The sustainability landscape is notably fragmented. In some nations, sustainability efforts are just beginning to gain traction, with infrastructure for recycling or environmental protection non-existent. From China's sprawling industrial landscapes to the tech-inclined quarters of American metropolises, the conceptualization and practice of sustainability and social impact reveal distinct nuances. In certain nations, all waste is directed to landfills, fostering a perception that waste sorting is futile due to the absence of adequate infrastructure. In other countries, sustainability has become an integral part of societal norms and business practices. These nuances are inextricably linked to regional disparities, cultural variations and socio-economic dynamics. At the same time, this diversity in advancement and understanding of sustainability poses a significant challenge for multinational corporations seeking to embed sustainability into their global strategies.

Although regions may navigate their own unique challenges and leverage different customer preferences, the underlying trials – particularly regarding how sustainability is integrated and operationalized in businesses, notably integrating initiatives into business plans, securing budgets, acquiring approvals for pilots and tests and ensuring the hiring of adept teams – often reverberate with commonality. This underscores the essence that, while the journeys may be individual, the challenges and the destination – a more sustainable future – are shared. Thus, the tapestry of global sustainability is interwoven with threads of distinct regional narratives, each enriching the collective journey towards a sustainable, equitable and inclusive future.

In conclusion, it is important for a global sustainability leader to be aware of these challenges when assessing the organization. You must also, when crafting the strategy, ensure that it is both globally applicable and permits regional adaptability to cater to the specific challenges and opportunities inherent to each locale. Your strategy should set a basic standard that every area can meet at a minimum. It should also allow them the freedom to do more or even excel, depending on their own situations and abilities.

Tool: Market analysis

To effectively navigate this evolving terrain, businesses must pay close attention to market trends in sustainability and conduct thorough competitor analysis. These might differ substantially between regions. Understanding overall market trends and customer interests is crucial for any organization, particularly in the context of sustainability. Understanding where other players stand and how they are positioning themselves in terms of sustainability will guide you to identify gaps and opportunities in the market. Are they ahead in some areas or trailing behind in others? What does 'good' look like in your industry? Additionally, knowing the expectations of your customers in your segment helps you align your sustainability efforts with market demands. This doesn't mean copying what others are doing, but rather learning from their successes and failures, adapting best practices to your unique context and continually striving to do better.

Finding your organization's unique space in sustainability might involve identifying areas where you can lead or areas that are notably neglected by others. This demands a genuine and transparent approach to avoid being perceived as engaging in greenwashing. Your strategy should genuinely reflect your sustainability efforts, ensuring that your external communications are firmly rooted in actual practices and achievements and that your aspirations are backed with a solid plan and commitment. This transparency not only fosters trust among your stakeholders but also solidifies your position in the market, enabling you to navigate through the sustainability journey authentically and effectively. By integrating this knowledge into your strategic planning, you can ensure that your sustainability efforts are both responsive to market needs and ahead of the curve.

Step 4: Understand relevant sustainability frameworks

Addressing social and environmental challenges effectively requires an understanding of the global frameworks that foster international and cross-sector collaboration. As sustainability cannot be achieved solely by states, NGOs, corporates or isolated individuals, it demands concerted efforts from every individual and organization. These collaborations are guided by robust frameworks and agreements that underscore the importance of collective action. Below you will find an introductory glance at these guiding principles and structures.

International, regional and national legislation

The legislative environment that encompasses your operations includes local, national, regional and international legislation, as well as other standards and guidelines to ensure smooth operation, safeguard reputation and fulfil responsibilities to all stakeholders. Examples of other types of standards include industry standards and certifications such as ISO standards,[11] the Rainforest Alliance[12] and the Forest Steward Council (FSC).[13] It could be ethical standards such as the Guiding Principles on Business and Human Rights,[14] Fair Trade[15] or others set out by the UN Global Compact.[16] You might also want to have a look at cultural and social sensitivity and anti-corruption and bribery acts.

International treaties and guidelines

UN Sustainable Development Goals (SDGs)

Perhaps the most critical and well-known global agreement is the 2030 agenda for sustainable development, which all UN member states adopted in 2015. Agenda 2030 comprises 17 SDGs and 169 specific targets. The goals are built on the Millennium Development Goals from 2000, which mainly focused on reducing poverty and improving access to education.[17] The SDG framework is more extensive than its predecessor, covering the broader Brundtland definition of sustainability. Next to poverty reduction, the SDGs include the removal of inequalities and emphasize peace, partnerships and solving the climate crisis. The SDGs also acknowledge that ending poverty must be in line with strategies that improve social impact within the limits of the planet.[18]

The UN Global Compact

This is a voluntary initiative that encourages businesses worldwide to adopt sustainable and socially responsible policies. It operates on 10 principles encompassing human rights, labour, the environment and anti-corruption. By participating, companies can benefit from a framework for developing sustainable business practices while being part of a global movement towards a more stable, equitable and sustainable world. The UN Global Compact offers a rich community of stakeholders and many courses and tools relevant to organizations working with sustainability.[19] It has introduced an interim digital platform for the 2023 Communication on Progress (CoP) submission. The enhanced CoP allows participating companies to measure and demonstrate progress on the 10 principles and the SDGs. Members can submit a sustainability report in lieu of the CoP questionnaire for 2023, with the CoP becoming mandatory from 2024.[20]

United Nations Guiding Principles on Business and Human Rights (UNGPs)

This framework outlines how states and businesses should implement their human rights obligations and responsibilities. It is centred on three pillars: the state duty to protect human rights, the corporate responsibility to respect human rights, and access to remedy for victims of human rights abuses.[21]

Other frameworks and models

The SDGs and the wedding cake model

All 17 goals are fundamental for our global social welfare. Environmental scientist Johan Rockström and environmental economist Pavan Sukhdev from the Stockholm Resilience Centre have designed a wedding cake model to depict the interconnectedness of the economy, society and our planet's boundaries. This model positions environmental sustainability as its foundational layer, with social goals in the middle and economic aspects at the top. It conveys the idea that our planet's environmental parameters limit and define the possibilities for economic growth, essentially emphasizing that sustainable human existence is only viable within these confines.[22]

The planetary boundaries model

The planetary boundaries model, spearheaded by Johan Rockström and a team of scientists, outlines nine crucial thresholds that humanity must respect in order for future generations to flourish. These are climate change, biosphere integrity, ocean acidification, freshwater consumption, land system change, chemical pollution, stratospheric ozone depletion, biogeochemical flows and atmospheric aerosol pollution. While some boundaries remain safely within their limits, others are alarmingly close to being breached. Critically, these boundaries are interlinked, and violating one can have cascading effects on the others. As detailed in the book *Breaking Boundaries*, the challenges of addressing poverty, hunger, inequality and diseases magnify when these boundaries are compromised.[23] Exceeding these limits exacerbates phenomena like heatwaves, droughts, floods and rising sea levels, with the gravest repercussions befalling the most vulnerable populations.[24]

The doughnut model

Kate Raworth, an economist, introduced the 'doughnut model', bearing resemblance to Rockström's concept. This visual representation, shaped like a doughnut or lifebuoy, merges both planetary and humanitarian constraints. The doughnut's core signifies fundamental social needs, such as healthcare, education and housing, while its outer crust depicts the planet's limits. Raworth argues that true economic prosperity is achieved when all 12 social foundations are met without exceeding any of the nine ecological limits, ensuring equilibrium for both humans and nature.[25]

Project Drawdown

Project Drawdown is a non-profit organization that seeks to help the world 'draw down' greenhouse gases in the atmosphere. It provides a comprehensive plan to reverse global warming by focusing on 100 solutions, ranging from clean energy to food waste reduction. The project compiles and disseminates research to help individuals, communities and organizations understand and implement these solutions. Next to providing hope, it can function as inspiration for and guidance as to what types of solutions your organization can contribute to.[26]

Exponential Roadmap

Exponential Roadmap aims to accelerate action against climate change by focusing on the most effective, scalable solutions. Its road map provides a strategic outline to halve greenhouse gas emissions by 2030 through rapid innovation and adoption of sustainable technologies. It primarily targets policy-makers and businesses, offering them actionable strategies to achieve these goals. The framework offers guidelines for transparent reporting and accountability, boosts employee engagement and helps in optimizing resource allocation for sustainability.[27]

We Mean Business

We Mean Business is a global coalition of businesses committed to mitigating climate change. The initiative collaborates with influential platforms and policy-makers to push for a low-carbon economy. By focusing on corporate commitments and policy advocacy, it aims to make businesses a leading force in the global transition to sustainable practices.[28]

B Corporations

B Corporations, or B Corps, are businesses globally recognized for meeting rigorous standards of social and environmental performance, accountability and transparency. These companies undergo a comprehensive certification process, ensuring they not only aim for profitability but also make a positive impact on society and the environment. By embracing this model, B Corps demonstrate a commitment to balancing profit with purpose, often leading the way in sustainable business practices and corporate responsibility.[29]

TCFD

This framework, also mentioned in Part 1, focuses on improving and increasing reporting of climate-related financial information. Companies use the TCFD to disclose the financial impacts of climate risks and opportunities, guiding investors, lenders and insurers in making informed decisions.[30]

TNFD

Similar to the TCFD, but focused on nature, the TNFD aims to provide a framework for organizations to report and act on evolving nature-related risks. It helps businesses understand the financial impacts of their interaction with nature, like biodiversity loss and ecosystem degradation.[31]

PAS 808

PAS 808 provides principles-based guidance for purpose-driven organizations (PDOs), outlining worldviews, principles and behaviour necessary to contribute to a sustainable future, manage resources and stakeholders effectively and ensure profitability. It offers a high-level approach to embed sustainability throughout the business, aligning it with other standards and practices.[32]

ISO 37000 (Governance of Organizations)

ISO 37000 provides guidelines for effective organizational governance. It can be used to ensure that sustainability is a core aspect of governance structures, helping organizations make decisions that are ethically sound and environmentally responsible.[33]

Dollar Street by Gapminder

If you are aiming to educate and train your team on global inequalities, Gapminder's Dollar Street is an invaluable resource. This tool offers a vivid, real-world illustration of how people live at different income levels across various countries. It uses photographs and data to paint a compelling picture of everyday life in diverse economic conditions, effectively bridging the gap between abstract statistics and tangible human experiences. By exploring Dollar Street, you and your team can gain a deeper, empathetic understanding of global disparities and the lived realities behind income statistics.[34]

Performance

When starting the important journey of evaluating your organization's sustainability performance, it's crucial to carefully review your current state. Whether your organization is a well-established business or a blooming start-up greatly shapes this review. The evaluation covers both physical aspects, like performance, and more intangible ones, like team engagement and skills. Each of the described tools and assessments are instrumental in providing a thorough understanding of an organization's sustainability performance, offering insights into areas of strength and opportunities for improvement. By applying these tools, organizations can create a robust and dynamic sustainability strategy that is responsive to both internal and external factors.

Step 5: Review key issues material to your organization (materiality assessment)

A materiality assessment is a structured exercise which assists organizations in pinpointing the sustainability issues that are most pertinent to both the business and its stakeholders. It aids in identifying and prioritizing the ESG issues that can have substantial impacts on the company and that are of paramount importance to its stakeholders.[35] Thus, a materiality assessment can serve as a pivotal tool in shaping a strategy that is both aligned with the company's context and responsive to the concerns and expectations of its stakeholders, ensuring that the sustainability initiatives are impactful, relevant and value-driven. It acts as a guide, enabling organizations to effectively do the following:

- **Allocation of resources:** Adequately channelling resources towards issues that have high significance.
- **Strategic alignment:** Ensuring that sustainability efforts are strategically aligned with corporate objectives.

- **Stakeholder communication:** Efficiently communicating with stakeholders, ensuring transparency and reporting on matters that are of paramount importance to them.

CASE STUDY Defining double materiality

Double materiality pertains to a dual-faceted impact consideration, exploring both financial materiality and non-financial materiality:

- **Financial materiality** involves how sustainability issues impact the financial performance and position of an organization. In the context of sustainability, financial materiality assesses how ESG factors can impact a company's financial performance, risks and valuation. This concept helps organizations and investors understand which sustainability issues are most likely to affect financial outcomes and should, therefore, be prioritized and reported. For example, in the case of a manufacturing company, financial materiality might highlight the risk of increased production costs due to carbon pricing, making it essential to invest in energy-efficient technologies and sustainable practices to maintain profitability and attract environmentally conscious investors.
- **Non-financial materiality** relates to how the organization's activities impact the environment and society at large. The concept amplifies the traditional materiality assessment by not only concentrating on aspects material to the company but also considering the broader socio-environmental impacts and dependencies, thereby reinforcing the integral role of sustainability.

Double materiality provides enhanced risk management: understanding and addressing both financial and non-financial materialities allows organizations to foresee, mitigate and communicate risks effectively. It enables strategic decision making, as the comprehension of impacts and dependencies associated with double materiality fortifies strategic decision making, anchoring it in a framework that assures sustainable and responsible business conduct. And it lays the groundwork for improved reporting: with double materiality in play, reporting transcends fiscal performance to envelop broader impacts, thereby offering a more comprehensive view to stakeholders and bolstering transparency and accountability.[36]

When performing a materiality assessment, we recommend following the following steps.

1. Identify potential issues

This step is about compiling a list of potential ESG issues that could impact the organization. Typically, this task is led by the organization's sustainability team, owing to their specialized knowledge in sustainability issues. However, try to involve a range of departments – like operations, finance, HR and marketing – to ensure all potential ESG aspects are considered. ESG topics could encompass areas like environmental conservation, labour practices, governance policies and more.

The process starts with reviewing industry standards and benchmarks, such as the Global Reporting Initiative (GRI) or the Sustainability Accounting Standards Board (SASB), to identify common ESG issues in the industry. Analysing sustainability reports and public disclosures of competitors and industry leaders also provides insights into relevant ESG topics. A regulatory scan helps in understanding the impact of current and future laws on the organization's operations.

Tool: SASB Standards

The SASB Standards are a vital tool connecting businesses with investors on the financial impacts of sustainability. They provide industry-specific guidance on sustainability risks and opportunities affecting a company's financials across various time horizons. In August 2022, the International Sustainability Standards Board (ISSB) of the International Financial Reporting Standards (IFRS) Foundation assumed responsibility for these standards, ensuring their continued evolution and relevance in today's economy. This move signifies a growing global emphasis on integrating sustainability into financial reporting, recognizing that managing sustainability issues effectively is crucial for long-term business success. The materiality topics are divided into five dimensions: environment, social capital, human capital, business model and innovation, and leadership and governance. Each of these consists of different issues:[37]

1 **Environment:** This covers greenhouse gas emissions from various sources, air quality management (excluding greenhouse gases), energy consumption impacts with an emphasis on efficiency, water use and wastewater strategies, waste and hazardous materials management (excluding certain emissions) and impacts on ecosystems and biodiversity (excluding climate change effects).

2 **Social capital:** Topics include managing business–community relationships with a focus on human rights, customer privacy (excluding cybersecurity),

data security risks, accessibility and affordability of services, product quality and safety, consumer welfare (including health concerns), and ethical marketing and product labelling.

3 **Human capital:** This addresses labour practices, including workers' rights and labour relations, workplace health and safety through safety management and audits, and fostering diversity and inclusion while combating discrimination.
4 **Business model and innovation:** This encourages ESG integration into product design and life cycle, resilience in changing environmental and social conditions, ESG risk management in supply chains, materials sourcing efficiency, and addressing the physical impacts of climate change on business operations.
5 **Leadership and governance:** This focuses on ethical business conduct and avoiding conflicts, managing monopolistic and anti-competitive practices, compliance with legal and regulatory frameworks, and critical incident and systemic risk management strategies to mitigate potential long-term effects and large-scale systemic risks.

Material topics depend on what sector you are in and what type of organization you lead. Utilizing tools like the SASB Standards gives insights into the materiality specific to various sectors. Depending on what you produce and what your business model is, different issues will be material to your operations. For instance, a textile producer might prioritize facets like sustainable material use, ethical supply chain management, energy and water usage efficiency, waste management, fair labour practices and addressing the entire product life cycle. On the other hand, a service organization would focus on elements like employee well-being, rigorous data protection, equal employment opportunities, sustainable procurement practices, local community engagement, ensuring customer satisfaction and managing energy efficiently within their facilities.

For example, the hotel industry, which has its own set of challenges and concerns, is largely driven by customer preferences based on service quality, price, loyalty programmes and more. Significant components of their operations revolve around energy consumption and water use. Hotels not only have a direct environmental footprint through energy use, leading to greenhouse gas emissions, but also face risks associated with water scarcity. The threat of climate change brings about challenges like inclement weather and flooding, especially for coastal properties, impacting operations and even insurance premiums. Furthermore, the industry's impact on local ecosystems can't be ignored. Unsustainable practices can endanger natural attractions, impacting both the environment and business. Concurrently, proper environmental care can enhance tourist attractions, driving more room bookings. Another crucial aspect for hotels is labour. A contented workforce is essential for delivering top-notch service. Yet, the industry often grapples with job satisfaction issues, leading to high turnover and possible legal repercussions. Fair wages and anti-discrimination efforts can be both ethically right and cost-effective.[38] A final example is that of professional services companies, like consultancies, and advertising and creative agencies, whose material topics often are about the advice (and financial loans) they provide to their clients. The impact of what they do for their clients is often much bigger than just focusing on their own operational footprint, which tends to be quite small (offices and business travel).[39]

2. Engage stakeholders

Maintaining robust relationships with relevant stakeholders is a recurrent theme in sustainability, and it's woven into the core of many discussions in this book because of its paramount importance. Engaging with stakeholders not only enhances your strategies by incorporating diverse perspectives, but also fortifies relationships that could be vital in navigating through potential future challenges. Involving them in different phases of your sustainability journey can sharpen your initiatives and ensure they're relevant. And, when challenges do arise, those well-nurtured relationships can pivot from being merely transactional to becoming a collaborative force, helping you navigate through difficulties towards continuous improvement and sustainable development. Thus, solicit inputs from internal and external stakeholders through surveys, interviews and workshops to understand their concerns and priorities regarding sustainability matters. Remember, your stakeholders can be allies in both triumph and trial, aiding you to be better and smarter in your sustainability endeavours.

Tool: 'World listening tour'

A productive way of not only mapping, but also understanding, what your stakeholders expect of you is to listen and learn from the people around you. In the face of evolving global challenges, particularly in sustainability, leadership demands more than authoritative decision making; it requires a paradigm shift to inclusivity, understanding and genuine engagement. One of the initial and most impactful steps a leader can take is embarking on a 'listening tour'. This isn't merely a series of meetings, but rather an earnest journey of learning and empathetic engagement.

For this listening tour, one can categorize the focus into three key areas: internal engagement, external outreach and industry interaction.

- **Internal engagement:** Meetings with internal teams provide invaluable ground-level insights. Leaders should approach these interactions with openness, posing questions that invite honest reflection on current practices, successes and areas needing improvement. By understanding the daily experiences of those within the company, leaders can gain a nuanced perspective of internal operations and morale.
- **External outreach:** Dialogue with external partners, suppliers and even customers can reveal the company's impact in broader strokes. These discussions can uncover how the company's sustainability efforts (or lack thereof) are perceived and the ripple effects of its operational choices. It also helps in understanding market demands and the areas where the company can expand or improve its sustainability efforts.
- **Industry interaction:** Perhaps most intriguingly, leaders shouldn't shy away from engaging with competitors. Understanding their approaches to similar challenges can spark new strategies and foster a healthy competitive environment where the ultimate goal is collective sustainability.

In coaching, there are three levels of listening. The third level, termed active listening, goes beyond merely hearing the words spoken. It involves tuning into body language, tone and underlying emotions. This deep form of listening can be a transformative tool when aiming to genuinely grasp the current state of your stakeholders and organization.[40] This means not merely hearing words but comprehending the experiences and insights behind them and their implications. It involves recognizing non-verbal cues, reading between the lines and synthesizing this information to form a comprehensive picture.

After listening, the leader's role morphs into one of strategic synthesis and action. It's about taking the diverse insights, concerns and suggestions collected during the tour and weaving them into an actionable, forward-thinking plan for sustainable growth. In this journey, leaders transition from authoritative figures to facilitators of collaborative growth, learning from the past and present to build a more sustainable, inclusive future.

During this evaluation and planning stage, getting advice from external experts can be a game changer. An outside perspective can offer an unbiased evaluation of your organization, revealing insights that may be missed from an inside view. Even the most casual conversations can offer valuable insight into your organization's priorities and focus. Consider the chats around the coffee machine. Are they about the sustainability of paper cups versus glass and dishwasher usage? Or maybe they dive into bigger issues like energy use and end-of-life concerns? Both types of conversations have their value. They show the range of sustainability awareness and concerns within your organization. It's key to respect these discussions when they come up, and equally important to focus your energy where it can make the most impact.[41]

3. Prioritize issues

Evaluate and rank the identified issues based on their importance to stakeholders and the potential impact on the business. Utilize a materiality matrix to visualize and prioritize these aspects. Many discussions may arise during this exercise, and they form an integral part of the process. Engaging in these dialogues uncovers diverse perspectives, challenges assumptions and paves the way for a more thorough and collective understanding among all participants. Navigating through these discussions is vital in forging a well-rounded and inclusive sustainability strategy and ensuring it is resilient, adaptable and broadly supported across different stakeholders and the management team. It's not merely about reaching agreements but rather about weaving a tapestry of varied insights to drive impactful, sustainable change within the organization.

Tool: Issues Ranking/Matrix

To categorize materiality issues within an action priority matrix, as shown in Figure 4.2, you should first divide the matrix into four distinct quadrants. The top right quadrant is for issues with both high business impact and high stakeholder concern, which represent the priority issues that require your immediate attention. The top left quadrant is for issues with low business impact but high stakeholder concern. These are issues that stakeholders deem essential, but they might have a less direct impact on the business's bottom line or operations. Conversely, the bottom right quadrant is for issues with high business impact but low stakeholder concern, which are critical for your business operations but might not be on the forefront of stakeholders' minds. Lastly, the bottom left quadrant is reserved for issues with both low business impact and low stakeholder concern, which can be considered as low priority.

Figure 4.2 Action priority matrix[42]

Low business impact, high stakeholder concern	High business impact, high stakeholder concern
Low business impact, low stakeholder concern	High business impact, low stakeholder concern

Once you've categorized the issues, it's crucial to prioritize and address them accordingly. Begin by concentrating on the top right quadrant, as the issues there are vital for both the business and the stakeholders. For these priority issues, it's advisable to plan specific strategies and initiatives. This could involve allocating appropriate resources, setting clear and measurable objectives and determining KPIs to track progress and ensure effective management of the identified concerns. We acknowledge that this can be quite challenging, given constraints such as limited resources, time and expertise, complexity and potential opposition.

4. Validate and review

Validate the findings with the executive leadership team and key stakeholders to ensure alignment with organizational objectives and strategies. Periodically review and refresh the materiality assessment to accommodate evolving priorities and contexts. It is thus not a one-and-done task, but rather a living document and ongoing work. The assessment should evolve over time, reflecting changes in both the internal and external environments and adapting to new insights, challenges and opportunities that arise.

5. Integrate into strategy

Incorporate the prioritized sustainability issues into the corporate strategy, aligning them with business goals, risk management and reporting initiatives. You will learn more about this step in Chapter 5.

Step 6: Assess your environmental and social performance

Once you have reviewed the internal and external context of your organization and performed a comprehensive materiality assessment, it is important to assess the more technical aspects of sustainability, on both the social and environmental sides. What are the social and environmental issues that are key to your organization? And what is your status – that is, how are you doing today across, for example, social, climate and circular solutions?

Tool: Social impact analysis

Exploring the social side of sustainability takes us into a complex network of impacts that a business might have during its life and throughout its whole value chain. The social impact – both positive and negative – weaves through various stakeholders: from co-workers, customers, communities and workers to suppliers, partners and sub-suppliers – as well as more indirect stakeholders, be it the families with children living close to factories or even future generations. Understanding and defining the current social impact necessitates a thoughtful and robust analysis, using varied tools and frameworks that can effectively gauge and elucidate these influences.[43]

Assessing these impacts involves creating a thorough stakeholder-inclusive assessment that not only determines the current situation but also influences strategy development to enhance positive impacts and mitigate negative ones. Hence, exploring the present impact becomes a crucial stepping stone towards crafting a future where the business operates in harmony with its social and environmental contexts, heralding a future of sustainability and social responsibility. In this context, integrating a comprehensive social impact analysis (SIA) can be useful, serving as a lens through which the consequences and influences of a company's activities, projects or policies on society are brought to the foreground.[44] It provides a robust foundation for better decision making by identifying unforeseen social impacts, anticipated consequences and potential conflicts that may arise due to business operations. Thus, a systematic approach, ensuring your business amplifies its positive influence on society and the environment, becomes imperative.[45] Other tools, like the social return on investment (SROI) and the B impact assessment, can provide valuable insights into the social value being created,[46] while guidelines from the GRI offer a pathway for transparently reporting your economic, environmental and social impacts. The outcome of a business's actions might already be positive, such as providing stable employment or investing in local communities. Conversely, negative impacts – perhaps obscured within the supply chain, like labour rights issues – must be identified and addressed.[47]

Tool: Carbon footprint assessment

The Greenhouse Gas (GHG) Protocol is widely recognized as the most comprehensive and broadly accepted standard for measuring and managing greenhouse gas emissions in the business sector.[48] Developed by the World Resources Institute (WRI) and the World Business Council for Sustainable Development (WBCSD),[49] the GHG Protocol classifies corporate greenhouse gas emissions into three 'scopes':

- **Scope 1:** Direct emissions from owned or controlled sources
- **Scope 2:** Indirect emissions from the generation of purchased electricity, steam, heating and cooling consumed by the reporting company
- **Scope 3:** All other indirect emissions in a company's value chain, such as those from business travel, transportation and distribution, and purchased goods and services. Scope 3 often represents over 90 per cent of a company's emissions.[50]

The Carbon Disclosure Project (CDP),[51] the Science Based Targets initiative (SBTi)[52] and the GHG Protocol collectively guide corporate environmental sustainability and greenhouse gas emissions management and enable businesses to align their emissions reduction goals with the Paris Agreement's objective to limit global warming. The CDP's platform for environmental impact disclosure helps companies understand and manage risks, crucial for setting and tracking science-based targets. SBTi offers guidance and validation for emissions reduction targets aligned with climate science, utilizing the GHG Protocol's standards for measuring and reporting emissions. This synergy ensures that corporate climate actions are transparent, consistent and based on the latest science, with the GHG Protocol's classification of emissions into Scope 1, 2 and 3 providing a comprehensive framework for assessment and strategy development. Together, these frameworks enable businesses to effectively manage emissions, comply with regulations and communicate progress to stakeholders, fostering robust and transparent sustainability practices. These three guidance documents enable organizations to enhance their reputations and meet stakeholder expectations, and can lead to cost savings through energy efficiency and resource management, fostering long-term business resilience and demonstrating corporate responsibility leadership.

Tool: Life cycle assessment

Life cycle assessment (LCA) is a method used to evaluate the environmental impacts associated with all the stages of a product's life, from raw material extraction through materials processing, manufacture, distribution, use, repair and maintenance, and disposal or recycling.[53] It's a useful tool to identify the stages where the product or process is having the most significant environmental impact and where improvements can be made. By understanding the full life cycle of their products, companies can make informed decisions about materials, processes and designs that are more sustainable. Additionally, an LCA can guide effective waste reduction strategies and help businesses communicate their environmental efforts transparently to customers, building trust and enhancing their brand's reputation for sustainability.[54]

Tool: Material flow analysis

Production and material-heavy companies in particular should assess which key materials are being used in the organization and the volumes of these. Therefore, by applying the 80/20 principle mentioned early in this chapter, a company can focus its sustainability efforts on identifying and improving the key materials and processes that contribute most significantly to its footprint. This approach allows for more efficient and effective resource allocation, as it targets the areas where changes can have the greatest impact on reducing emissions and material waste. In essence, it's about prioritizing efforts on the most impactful areas to achieve the most substantial environmental benefits.

Tool: Assessment of circular solutions

Determining your organization's status concerning materials management and circularity involves a detailed examination of your current practices, especially regarding recycling and take-back schemes. Transitioning from a linear model to a circular economy isn't just a shift; it's a transformative journey that will recalibrate how resources flow through your business operations. Remember, there are myriad approaches to making this transition – akin to the metaphorical ways of slicing an elephant. Perhaps you're already employing elements of circularity, such as repair services, which extend the life cycle of products. Exploring tools and resources from renowned institutions like the Ellen MacArthur Foundation could provide further insights and guidelines to refine your strategies and practices in embracing a circular economy. The circular model emphasizes regenerative practices, and even small steps towards recycling, reusing and reducing will position your business more sustainably within its ecosystem.[55]

Step 7: Draw conclusions and prepare for strategy development

Having completed the orientation and performance assessment, which includes in-depth analyses of materiality and double materiality, it's time to contextualize these findings. This step involves interpreting what these results signify for your organization. Are you leading the way, or do you have ground to make up? Consider what these outcomes mean in the grander scheme of things and pinpoint exactly where your organization stands on its sustainability journey right now.

Tool: SWOT Gap analysis

A SWOT (strengths, weaknesses, opportunities, threats) analysis is a useful tool to create a picture of where you stand as an organization. It is important to perform the SWOT with several people across the organization – and even with external stakeholders – to avoid getting a narrow view on the company. For example, different departments might have different views; some might see a circular economy as a threat to the business, whereas another department might see it as a business opportunity. We have witnessed this transformation first-hand in leadership journeys: individuals who were initially obstructing progress transitioned to becoming champions at the forefront of change. Bringing these groups together to discuss different views is also an important part of the learning journey.

Utilizing these tools is not a one-time effort but a continual process that requires updates and application at various stages. For instance, stakeholders' perspectives on sustainability, as well as their perception of threats and opportunities, may shift over time. It's inherent in the journey of change that certain stakeholders may initially exhibit reluctance, perceiving numerous aspects as challenges. However, with time, they may assimilate and not only adopt a positive stance but potentially evolve into ambassadors. Thus, patience emerges as a pivotal virtue in this context. This evolution of people's mindsets offers a promising outlook for the future.

Summary and key take-aways

In this chapter, we've navigated through the realms of systems thinking and mapping, visualizing the network within which your organization operates. Acknowledging and understanding the symbiotic relationship your business has with various elements within this system – such as stakeholders, socio-economic dynamics and environmental aspects – is pivotal. This systemic view not only illuminates your place within this web of interactions, but also highlights potential influence points, areas of collaboration and emerging opportunities.

Moreover, we delved into a comprehensive assessment of your performance as an organization. Utilizing an array of tools and frameworks, we've demonstrated how you can not only unearth your tangible impacts but also unveil areas that may need recalibration, refinement or even a transformation. This type of assessment provides a comprehensive, nuanced understanding of where your business stands, shining a light on both triumphs and challenges. A key part of this assessment phase is performing a (double) materiality assessment, as it helps to identify sustainability issues pivotal to an organization and its stakeholders, and helps to depict how sustainability issues affect the organization and how the organization's activities influence society and the environment.

As highlighted in this chapter, sustainability topics are broad and complex. This book underscores the notion that the responsibility for sustainability extends beyond a single leader; it should be woven into and led by relevant functional areas within the organization. But how can this be effectively implemented? A collaborative materiality assessment is an excellent starting point. Gathering all key stakeholders together ensures a comprehensive review of significant topics identified during the assessment. This collective approach paves the way for effectively allocating resources and assigning dedicated teams to each identified area of focus. For more details and examples of which functions could drive certain topics, see Chapter 6. Ultimately, this book advocates for sustainability as a shared responsibility, enriching the entire organization through the concerted efforts of diverse functions.

Now, you've laid down the initial stones on your path towards sustainability. These elements, steeped in self-awareness and systematic understanding, will underpin the strategy and actions in the subsequent stages of your sustainability journey.

Endnotes

1 Kevin Kruse. The 80/20 rule and how it can change your life, *Forbes*, 7 March 2016. www.forbes.com/sites/kevinkruse/2016/03/07/80-20-rule/ (archived at https://perma.cc/59QV-YGVU); Lydie SA Yiougo and Dorothee Spuhler. Material flow analysis, SSWM university course. sswm.info/sswm-university-course/module-4-sustainable-water-supply/further-resources-water-sources-software/material-flow-analysis-%28mfa%29 (archived at https://perma.cc/94LB-Z7XR)

2 Umeå school of business and statistics. Sustainability Performance and Ownership Structure on the Nordic Market, Spring 2021. www.diva-portal.org/smash/get/diva2:1574088/FULLTEXT01.pdf (archived at https://perma.cc/T97B-BAC5)

3 Peter Englisch. Family businesses have an opportunity to lead on ESG, PwC, 28 July 2021. www.pwc.com/gx/en/issues/reinventing-the-future/take-on-tomorrow/family-business-and-esg.html (archived at https://perma.cc/M4KS-8AS4)

4 Sustainability in small vs large businesses: Differences, challenges, and strategies, Future Tracker, 27 June 2023. www.futuretracker.com/post/sustainability-in-small-vs-large-businesses-differences-challenges-and-strategies#:~:text=In%20the%20world%20of%20small,in%20ways%20larger%20businesses%20cannot (archived at https://perma.cc/94NQ-V4X8)

5 Nazila Vali. Harnessing power business advocate change, UN Development Programme (UNDP) blog, 23 December 2019. www.undp.org/blog/harnessing-power-business-advocate-change (archived at https://perma.cc/8VBJ-J97K)

6 What are ecosystem maps? Interaction Design Foundation. www.interaction-design.org/literature/topics/ecosystem-maps (archived at https://perma.cc/SE82-C47X)

7 About systems change, Catalyst 2030. https://catalyst2030.net/what-is-systems-change/ (archived at https://perma.cc/C938-SPMW)

8 Colleen Lannon. Causal loop construction: The basics, The Systems Thinker. thesystemsthinker.com/causal-loop-construction-the-basics/ (archived at https://perma.cc/GMM4-KM25)

9 Influence diagrams, Open University. www.open.edu/openlearn/mod/oucontent/view.php?id=65668&section=3 (archived at https://perma.cc/323B-9GXZ)

10 What is stakeholder mapping? How to map stakeholders. www.stakeholdermap.com (archived at https://perma.cc/62V9-LX2Q)

11 See www.iso.org/standards.html (archived at https://perma.cc/95KR-JH4X)

12 See www.rainforest-alliance.org (archived at https://perma.cc/GZ66-RT93)

13 See se.fsc.org/se-sv (archived at https://perma.cc/4F6G-XSSR)

14 Office of the UN High Commissioner for Human Rights (OHCHR). Guiding Principles on Business and Human Rights, 2011. www.ohchr.org/sites/default/files/documents/publications/guidingprinciplesbusinesshr_en.pdf (archived at https://perma.cc/3ZHJ-2ZB8)

15 See www.fairtrade.net (archived at https://perma.cc/Q5SZ-DCB7)

16 See unglobalcompact.org (archived at https://perma.cc/QZ4C-CWVS)

17 See www.un.org/millenniumgoals/ (archived at https://perma.cc/5HZR-UGKP)

18 See sdgs.un.org/goals (archived at https://perma.cc/7SXC-2QMJ)

19 See unglobalcompact.org (archived at https://perma.cc/QZ4C-CWVS)

20 Communication on progress, UN Global Compact. unglobalcompact.org/participation/report/cop (archived at https://perma.cc/4ERD-JMGB)

21 UN Guiding Principles, Business and Human Rights Resource Centre. www.business-humanrights.org/en/big-issues/un-guiding-principles-on-business-human-rights/ (archived at https://perma.cc/6GWJ-2N97)

22 Stockholm Resilience Centre. The SDGs wedding cake, 14 June 2016. www.stockholmresilience.org/research/research-news/2016-06-14-the-sdgs-wedding-cake.html (archived at https://perma.cc/ZU9D-MNUE)

23 Johan Rockström and Owen Gaffney (2021) *Breaking Boundaries: The science of our planet*, DK, London

24 Stockholm Resilience Centre. Planetary boundaries, 24 March 2024. www.stockholmresilience.org/research/planetary-boundaries.html (archived at https://perma.cc/2VHQ-M9NN)

25 Kate Raworth. What on earth is the doughnut? https://www.kateraworth.com/doughnut/ (archived at https://perma.cc/CL6P-6XPU)

26 See drawdown.org (archived at https://perma.cc/DJU2-DPBX)

27 See exponentialroadmap.org (archived at https://perma.cc/78LU-QTBL)

28 See www.wemeanbusinesscoalition.org (archived at https://perma.cc/K5JP-6WES)

29 See www.bcorporation.net (archived at https://perma.cc/GJ5C-2RGM)

30 See www.fsb-tcfd.org (archived at https://perma.cc/QW7J-T5WH)

31 See tnfd.global (archived at https://perma.cc/4JLV-XPM7

32 PAS808: Purpose-driven organisations, British Standards Institution (BSI), 2024. www.bsigroup.com/en-IN/Standards-and-Publications/pas-808/ (archived at https://perma.cc/QYE4-V4AY)

33 ISO/TC309: Governance of organizations. committee.iso.org/ISO_37000_Governance (archived at https://perma.cc/QXR7-8UGL)

34 Dollar Street, Gapminder. www.gapminder.org/dollar-street (archived at https://perma.cc/GQ29-2997)

35 KPMG Sustainable Insight. The Essentials of Materiality Assessment, 2014. assets.kpmg.com/content/dam/kpmg/pdf/2014/10/materiality-assessment.pdf (archived at https://perma.cc/6GCT-7438)

36 Lorenzo Fantini, Jannik Leiendecker and Benedetta Testino. The new double materiality assessment: A toolbox for companies, BCG White Paper, February

2023. media-publications.bcg.com/New-Double-Materiality-Assessment-final-21.02.23.pdf (archived at https://perma.cc/83N5-57KJ)
37 Exploring materiality, SASB. sasb.org/standards/materiality-map/ (archived at https://perma.cc/BU6U-TYPN)
38 Willy Legrand. ESG and hospitality: An evolving sustainability context, Hotel Yearbook, 2023. www.hotelyearbook.com/article/122000226/esg-and-hospitality-an-evolving-sustainability-context.html (archived at https://perma.cc/H659-3EK9)
39 Ellen Ormesher. 'Take responsibility for your clients': UN backs crackdown on adland's climate impact, The Drum, 20 June 2022. www.thedrum.com/news/2022/06/20/take-responsibility-your-clients-un-backs-crackdown-adland-s-climate-impact (archived at https://perma.cc/2XQY-489B)
40 Glenn Llopis. 6 ways effective listening can make you a better leader, *Forbes*, 20 May 2013. www.forbes.com/sites/glennllopis/2013/05/20/6-effective-ways-listening-can-make-you-a-better-leader/ (archived at https://perma.cc/7FHT-WC49)
41 Désirée Crawford. The art of active listening, Beyond Leadership Coaching. beyondlsc.com/en_AU/beyond-leadership-coaching-blog/the-art-of-active-listening/ (archived at https://perma.cc/78KJ-JVY2)
42 The action priority matrix, Mindtools. www.mindtools.com/agst6d0/the-action-priority-matrix (archived at https://perma.cc/6EYB-2T5Q)
43 Social impact assessment guide, SOPACT. university.sopact.com/article/social-impact-assessment (archived at https://perma.cc/V4SG-G3QL)
44 Social impact assessment, International Association for Impact Assessment (IAIA). www.iaia.org/wiki-details.php?ID=23 (archived at https://perma.cc/E98Q-M2F6)
45 Social impact assessment, International Institute for Sustainable Development (IISD). www.iisd.org/learning/eia/wp-content/uploads/2016/05/SIA.pdf (archived at https://perma.cc/K9RK-4FQT)
46 Social return on investment (SROI) methodology and sensitivity analysis of the case studies, UNDP. www.undp.org/sites/g/files/zskgke326/files/migration/eurasia/Appendix-SROI-methodology_ENG.pdf (archived at https://perma.cc/DLA6-J9JC)
47 Resources Library: A guide to social return on investment 2012, Social value UK. socialvalueuk.org/resources/a-guide-to-social-return-on-investment-2012/ (archived at https://perma.cc/QEW7-JREJ)
48 See ghgprotocol.org (archived at https://perma.cc/N88K-34TA)
49 See www.wbcsd.org (archived at https://perma.cc/WUH4-QYM2)
50 Scope 3 Frequently Asked Questions, GHG Protocol, June 2022. ghgprotocol.org/sites/default/files/2022-12/Scope%203%20Detailed%20FAQ.pdf (archived at https://perma.cc/E9G8-T6AB)
51 See www.cdp.net/en (archived at https://perma.cc/N8P8-6KFZ)
52 See sciencebasedtargets.org/ (archived at https://perma.cc/U9S5-ZRS9)

53 Life cycle assessment, EEA glossary, www.eea.europa.eu/help/glossary/eea-glossary/life-cycle-assessment (archived at https://perma.cc/C4LG-6SZC)

54 What is life cycle assessment (LCA)? Rochester Institute of Technology, blog, 2 July 2020. www.rit.edu/sustainabilityinstitute/blog/what-life-cycle-assessment-lca (archived at https://perma.cc/L3FP-4FXW)

55 Atalay Atasu, Céline Dumas and Luk N Van Wassenhove. The circular business model: Pick a strategy that fits your resources and capabilities, Harvard Business Review, July–August 2021. hbr.org/2021/07/the-circular-business-model (archived at https://perma.cc/K2VW-VAP7)

Purpose and strategy

05

When developing a strategic roadmap for sustainability, we suggest the four steps below. Every step comes with associated tools, and together they form a comprehensive approach to integrating sustainability into an organization's core strategy. Each step shown in Figure 5.1 builds upon the previous one, creating a strategic foundation that ensures sustainability is woven into the fabric of the organization's purpose, ambition, strategy and material actions:

1. **Purpose:** This step is about establishing the fundamental 'why' behind the organization's existence – beyond just profits. This involves formulating a clear vision and a compelling narrative that can mobilize and create a movement, aligning the organization's operations with its deeper values and principles.
2. **Ambition level:** This involves understanding where the organization fits within the market and deciding whether to be a leader, setting sustainability standards, or – as a follower – adopting established best practices.
3. **Sustainability strategy:** Develop a sustainability strategy by using the theory of change to outline the desired outcomes and the steps needed to achieve them.
4. **Materiality:** Bring key material topics from the previous materiality assessment into your strategy.

Figure 5.1 Purpose and strategy

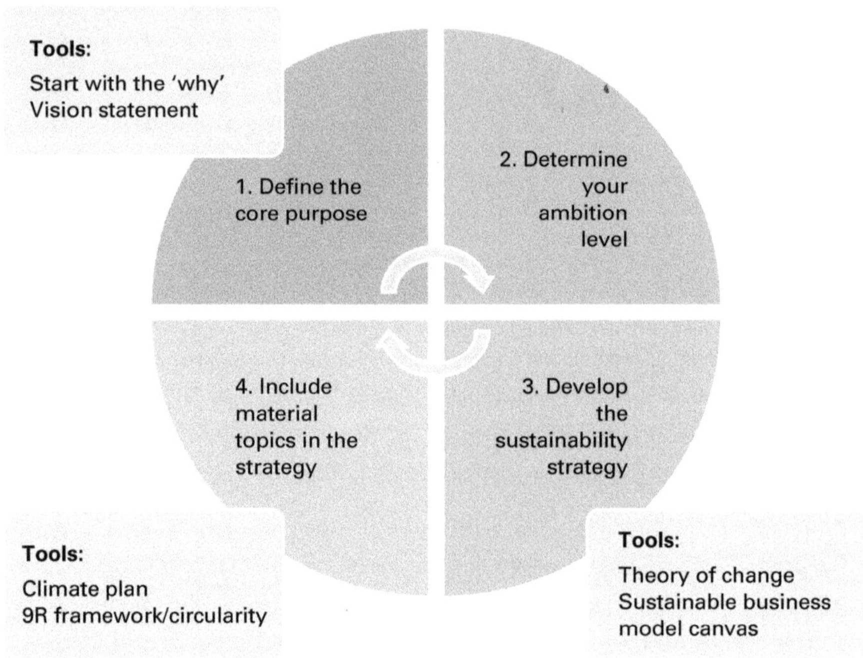

The societal role of organizations: Impact, identity and existence

As mentioned in the beginning of this book, every organization, irrespective of its size or sector, plays a role in the tapestry of society. This role is not just about economic contributions or employment generation; it's about the imprint the organization leaves on the world. Is the organization actively working towards creating a better world? Is its focus merely on minimizing negative impacts? Or is it even just focusing on maximizing returns and ignoring its negative impact completely? These distinctions are not just a matter of public relations or branding – it strikes at the very heart of an organization's identity and its reason for existence.

An organization that aims to contribute to a better world actively seeks to create positive change. It doesn't just limit its harms or comply with the bare minimum standards; it innovates and pushes boundaries to leave a lasting, positive legacy. Such organizations typically prioritize stakeholder value over just shareholder value, considering the well-being of communities, the environment and future generations. These organizations could, for example, be social enterprises, founded by people seeking to solve societal challenges as their starting point. For such enterprises, alignment with their vision isn't a step that's added later – it's the foundation on which they are built. In these organizations, the ethos of sustainability is naturally integrated into every strategic decision, operational process and organizational practice. This organic, innate alignment gives them a unique advantage in the journey towards sustainability, fostering a model where profit and purpose harmoniously coexist. On the other hand, organizations that focus on 'doing less bad' typically centre their strategies around risk mitigation. While they might make efforts to reduce their negative impacts, their primary aim isn't necessarily to drive positive societal change. Their efforts are often reactive, driven by regulations, consumer demands or market pressures, rather than a proactive vision of societal betterment.

Ultimately, an organization's chosen role in society mirrors its fundamental principles, leadership philosophy and strategic objectives. On a deeper level, this choice becomes pivotal to its legacy, determining whether the organization is a fleeting participant or one that imprints a lasting, beneficial impact on history's timeline. When deciding to take the more ambitious route, you embark on a journey that requires dedication, commitment and, most importantly, integration of sustainability with your organization's purpose and strategy, especially since the journey involves navigating against the current of established systems and structures, like short-term profit motives and linear models. This challenging path demands perseverance and a strategic approach to transform traditional paradigms.[1]

Step 1: Define the core purpose of your organization

As we delve into the process of embedding sustainability within your organization, reflect on your organization's core purpose. What is the fundamental 'why' behind your organization's existence? This question is not just philosophical – it's the key to inspiring and motivating your team. Simon Sinek, an author and speaker renowned for his TED Talk 'Start with the Why', suggests that organizations should 'start with why', an idea that essentially underlines the importance of aligning strategy and vision with the organization's fundamental purpose.[2] Sinek's model means first understanding the deeper purpose, or 'why'. The 'how' pertains to the methods, strategies and values a business will employ to achieve its sustainable goals. Lastly, the 'what' delves into the tangible actions, products or services that reflect the company's sustainable ethos. Sinek's model is pivotal, as it underscores the importance of starting with a strong purpose-driven foundation for genuine and effective sustainable practices. And it is crucial for the entire change management process involved in undertaking a sustainability transformation.

Based on the understanding of your organization's purpose, you can start designing your sustainability strategy, which should either be incorporated into your business strategy or be a supporting part of the business strategy. Sustainability is about who you choose to be as a company, and is thus an extension of your business strategy, not a stand-alone strategy. Moreover, sustainability fundamentally means a large-scale transformation process for most organizations. However, this does not mean that incremental change does not have a role. Depending on previous performance and external demands, organizations might need to make only incremental changes in some areas, while in others, comprchensive and deep cross-organizational change is needed. Developing a strategy involves not just planning the steps towards your sustainability goals, but also establishing a narrative that resonates authentically with your stakeholders and enhances your brand positioning. This approach not only invites everyone to join in on your journey but also embeds your sustainability ambitions at the heart of your organizational identity and business strategy.[3]

When we apply this principle to sustainability, an important question arises: how can we align the vision of our sustainability strategy with the purpose of our organization? The answer to this lies in ensuring that your organization's contribution to sustainability is intrinsically linked to your core business and mission.

Your sustainability strategy should not merely be an adjunct to your operations. Instead, it should be an integral part of the organizational fabric, seamlessly woven into every aspect of your business. This integration empowers your sustainability initiatives to contribute directly to the overall vision and the core existence and growth of your organization. How to do that in different contexts is something we will further unfold in this chapter. As an illustration, consider a company that manufactures eco-friendly cleaning products. Their core purpose may be to enrich lives by providing products that create clean, healthy home environments while minimizing environmental impact. Their sustainability strategy, in this case, could revolve around using renewable materials, reducing waste and promoting recycling. These actions align with the company's core purpose and contribute directly to its growth and profitability.

In the report 'Leading with a Sustainable Purpose' by the Cambridge Institute for Sustainability Leadership (CISL), it is highlighted that unlike other business units – which might directly dive into setting goals – the domains of sustainability and purpose delve much deeper into understanding the 'why' behind actions and embedding this understanding throughout the journey.[4] The report emphasizes that adapting a company's strategy to its external environment is pivotal for identifying potential new markets and needs. Particularly in a rapidly and fundamentally changing landscape, aligning a company's purpose and strategy with the underlying trends and societal expectations is not just advantageous but essential for sustained success and survival. This alignment aids in navigating through complexities, managing risks and capitalizing on opportunities. It enables companies to understand their social and environmental dependencies, such as the viability of supplier communities or the accessibility of resources like water for consumers, and to leverage this understanding to bolster resilience, protect assets and uncover new sources of value. Given the current climate, in which businesses are urged to reconsider their role within society, the report raises a pertinent question: 'how can organizations develop alignment and integration between their purpose and strategy to facilitate the transition to a sustainable economy?'

Tool: Start with the 'why'

To develop a purpose or 'why' for a business using Simon Sinek's approach, it's essential to consider the broader societal role and the positive impact the business can make in the world. In that process, you could consider taking the following steps:

1. **Reflect on the origin:** Delve into the reasons behind the inception of the business. What passion, problem or societal gap led to its creation? For BlackRock, it is 'To help more and more people experience financial well-being'. Coca-Cola has 'Refresh the world. Make a difference'[5] and for Patagonia, it is 'We're in business to save our home planet'.[6]
2. **Understand the value:** Ascertain the genuine value the business offers its clientele and the world. This isn't merely about tangible products or services but extends to emotional and transformative benefits that enrich

lives. For a bank, it could be empowering individuals with the knowledge to make informed financial decisions, giving them the confidence and security to navigate their financial future. It could also be to use financial means to reallocate funding to make the world more sustainable and increase social impact.

3 **Societal contribution:** Reflect upon the role your business plays in society. As an actor in the community, what can your business do to foster a better world? What unique contributions can you make that go beyond profit?

4 **Envision the impact:** Visualize the expansive influence your business might exert on the local community, the broader industry and, potentially, the world. This encompasses environmental, social and economic dimensions.

5 **Articulate the belief:** Define your 'why' in terms of a profound belief or core principle. For instance, rather than stating, 'We sell high-quality skincare products', you could formulate this in a more meaningful way to address the importance of feeling confident and empowered in one's own skin and body.

In alignment with PAS 808's guidance on purpose-driven organizations (PDOs), these steps help articulate a business's purpose in a way that resonates with its commitment to sustainability and its stakeholders, ensuring the 'why' reflects both internal motivations and external societal contributions. This approach, consistent with PAS 808, emphasizes the importance of aligning the organization's mission with sustainable practices and stakeholder well-being, creating a business that not only thrives economically but also contributes positively to society and the environment.[7]

Pinpointing the 'why' may involve comprehensive dialogues, workshops or external consultations. To uncover an organization's purpose, workshops and co-creation sessions should focus on existential questions like 'Why are we here?', 'What value do we add to society?' and 'How can our heritage shape our future?' These discussions encourage deep reflection, helping team members understand and articulate the organization's core mission and how its history can inform its future trajectory.[8] Some enterprises collaborate with expert consultants or mentors specializing in guiding organizations to unearth and define their purpose. While Simon Sinek's philosophy offers a fundamental methodology, discovering one's purpose doesn't depend on a universal 'tool'. It will be a distinct expedition for every organization, interwoven with its unique history, vision and aspirations.[9]

Tool: Formulate a vision and create a movement that people want to be part of

Creating a vision statement involves collecting diverse input from stakeholders, reflecting on the organization's core values and long-term goals, and engaging in brainstorming sessions. This process leads to drafting a concise, inspiring vision statement, which is then refined through feedback. Finally, the statement is finalized and communicated to guide and inspire all members of the organization. It's an evolving element that is adapted as the company grows. A vision statement is not static; it should be revisited and potentially revised as the organization evolves and grows.[10]

Understanding what drives people within the organization isn't only a nice-to-have; it's a cornerstone of effective leadership, especially when steering your organization towards sustainability. Do employees find motivation in financial incentives, such as a yearly bonus or a performance-based reward system? Or does the notion of meeting company targets and contributing to the organization's growth energize them? Perhaps it's the prospect of creating a positive environmental and social impact that truly moves them. In most cases, it's a blend of these elements.

Once you've comprehended what motivates your people, you can collaboratively shape a sustainability vision and movement that aligns with these motivations. It's about positioning sustainability not as an add-on to the existing organizational culture, but as a fundamental part of it. Relating back to setting a clear vision and ambition, you should tailor this vision in a way that resonates with your workforce. Create a narrative that allows employees to see how their roles and actions contribute to the larger sustainability objectives. Show them how their everyday decisions and tasks can drive significant positive change, not just for the organization but for society at large. When employees see their roles through the lens of this transformative vision, they feel more invested in the cause. It's no longer about doing a job; it's about contributing to a mission they believe in. This shift in perception can fuel a sense of purpose and motivation that transcends traditional rewards and recognition, fostering a unified, organization-wide commitment to sustainability.

In short, integrating sustainability into the core identity of your organization is about understanding your people, aligning your sustainability vision with their motivations and creating an inclusive movement that they're proud to be part of.

Step 2: Determine your ambition level (all-in or incremental change)

In shaping a future-oriented sustainability approach, understanding 'where the organization is' paves the way for determining 'where you want to be'. This involves not just comprehending your current sustainability position, but also knowing how you're perceived in the market and what your reputation is among stakeholders. If sustainability is already synonymous with your brand, wonderful! Your journey can evolve from this foundation. If not, it's a signal to switch gears and set a new course.

Considering where you'd like to be involves strategic choices: do you make a gradual transition, evolving step by step, or do you make a bold leap towards sustainability, openly acknowledging the magnitude and timeframe of this shift? The decision to lead or follow reflects an organization's values, ambition and desired impact. Leaders in sustainability don't just craft ambitious strategies; they execute them swiftly, outpacing their peers. This leadership garners numerous advantages. A proactive approach enhances brand perception and cements customer loyalty. It also positions the company at the forefront of advocacy, shaping industry norms and practices. Moreover, such leadership often sidelines competitors, especially those sluggish in their sustainability pursuits, and becomes a beacon for top talent, refining the organizational structure and capabilities. However, the mantle of leadership isn't without its challenges.

It demands dedication, significant resources and the bravery to innovate. On the other hand, opting to follow in the sustainability journey offers its own set of merits. Followers can capitalize on the foundational work of leaders, navigating with the benefit of their insights and lessons, thus potentially sidestepping pitfalls. An ecosystem further along its sustainability path presents followers with a richer array of partners and suppliers already versed in sustainable practices. This position allows them a more concentrated internal business strategy, relying on established benchmarks. But there's a stark warning for followers: they must maintain momentum. Falling too far behind not only risks market relevance but also obsolescence.

Ultimately, the broader goal of sustainability is societal transformation, emphasizing the scaling of effective solutions. This shift isn't just a business imperative; it's a societal one, centred on enriching lives, uplifting the vulnerable, championing environmental well-being and fostering collective prosperity. Organizations that don't contribute constructively to this narrative risk fading into obscurity. As we navigate this journey, every entity must introspectively assess its desired role: to trailblaze towards a sustainable future or to build upon the pathways established by pioneers. Regardless of the chosen path, unwavering commitment to a better, more sustainable world is paramount.

Understanding the trajectory of your organization's sustainability journey is a central question to begin with. Is your goal merely to comply with the existing regulations, or is it to position your company as a leader in sustainable business practices? We highly recommend the latter – fully commit and create an ambitious, transparent strategy for sustainability. The reason is that this journey is not about lessening the harm your organization inflicts on the environment by a meagre percentage. Instead, your objective should be to make a positive, significant impact.

EXAMPLE IKEA switching to LED lights

Back in 2013, while most retailers stocked their shelves with a mix of incandescent, low-energy and newly introduced LED light bulbs, IKEA spotted an opportunity. LED lights, though around six times pricier than traditional bulbs, are far more energy-efficient, using 80 per cent less energy. Additionally, their lifespan is impressive, lasting up to 80 years. In contrast, traditional bulbs, while cheaper, primarily generate heat, with only a fraction of energy being used for lighting.

Faced with a crossroads, IKEA chose a daring path. Rather than incrementally shifting their focus, they decided to discontinue older light options and concentrate solely on LEDs. This bold step allowed IKEA to streamline its business operations, drive volume towards LEDs and dramatically reduce prices – eventually offering LEDs for as low as €1. By focusing exclusively on LEDs, IKEA simplified its inventory and supply chain processes, leading to more efficient operations and enabling the company to pass cost savings on to customers.

This strategic move exemplifies the power of commitment in sustainability. By going all-in, IKEA not only secured profitability but also made a significant environmental impact. Had they taken a gradual approach, they might have faced fiercer competition, missed the dramatic price drop and, possibly, confused customers with too many choices. This IKEA story underscores that decisive action in sustainability can yield both business success and meaningful change.[11]

Step 3: Develop your sustainability strategy

Setting targets

Striking a balance between ambitious moonshot goals and realistic strategic objectives is a pivotal aspect of crafting a sustainability strategy. Moonshot goals are visionary objectives that aim to solve significant challenges with radical solutions and breakthrough technology. They serve to inspire and mobilize action on a grand scale. However, while these aspirational objectives are important for driving innovation and progress, they must be complemented with realistic, attainable (SMART) targets.[12]

A well-rounded sustainability strategy recognizes the importance of setting incremental and achievable targets that create a roadmap for progress. These targets should be grounded in current capabilities and resources, with a clear understanding of the operational steps needed to achieve them. This dual approach ensures that while a company reaches for transformative change with moonshot thinking, it also maintains a steady trajectory of improvement through attainable, measurable and time-bound objectives.

Oftentimes, companies set various targets to be 'less bad'. It may be to use 20 per cent less fossil fuels or to reduce the amount of chemicals in their products. However, first of all, targets to be 'less bad' are not very motivating for co-workers. Secondly, goals referring to 80 or 90 per cent goals tend to create unclarity in the organization. Most people think of themselves as being in the last 10 to 20 per cent, believing that they do not need to lead the change. By setting out 100 per cent positive sustainability objectives, you provide a sense of clarity and direction. Take, for instance, a commitment to transition entirely to renewable energy sources; this leaves no room for ambiguity about investing in fossil fuel projects, regardless of their scale. Similarly, setting a zero-tolerance policy on human rights violations eliminates any uncertainty about the organization's stance and actions in such matters.

Clear targets energize your team, mobilize resources and rally everyone behind a clear, defined cause. That being said, remember that total transformation will not happen overnight. It is crucial to develop a road map for your sustainability journey. You might need to start with the basics in certain areas, gradually moving towards more sophisticated, innovative strategies as your capacity and understanding evolve.

Balancing immediate targets with long-term visions: The retailer's dual strategy

In the fast-paced world of retail, time is often of the essence. With the dynamic nature of consumer demands and trends, retailers are acutely tuned to the rhythm of short-term cycles, from quarterly down to the hourly shifts in market dynamics. These frequent goals are essential for tracking immediate performance, optimizing inventory, refining marketing strategies and responding agilely to consumer preferences. They act as the pulse, giving retailers a snapshot of their health and efficiency at any given moment.

Yet, while this continuous feedback loop is invaluable, successful retailers recognize that vision can't be confined to the immediate horizon. Long-term goals – ones that stretch over, say, a decade – play a pivotal role in shaping a retailer's overarching direction and identity. These goals might encompass strategic market positioning, expansion plans, technology adoption or sustainability initiatives, among others. They are the north star, guiding decisions and providing a larger context for those day-to-day operations.

In essence, the duality of these short- and long-term goals creates a harmonious balance. While the immediate targets ensure efficiency, responsiveness and profitability, the long-term vision ensures relevance, growth and sustainability in an ever-evolving marketplace. It's akin to a ship navigating through a vast ocean: while the crew manages daily operations, it's the captain's charted course that determines the ultimate destination.

Stand-alone strategy or full integration

A question we often get is whether an organization should have a stand-alone sustainability strategy or one that is integrated into its overall strategy. The answer depends largely on the organization's maturity level. For organizations that already have sustainability principles deeply embedded in their business model, values and mission, there may not be a need for a separate sustainability strategy. In such cases, specific plans addressing areas like diversity or road maps focusing on circularity might suffice. However, for organizations still in the nascent stages of embracing sustainability, a dedicated strategy that clearly outlines all sustainability-related topics can serve as a comprehensive guide, highlighting the complete road map.

Regardless of the approach, it's essential that sustainability initiatives align with the core of the business and are appropriately managed within their respective domains. It's crucial to ensure that the sustainability strategy doesn't become an isolated document, unread by anyone outside of the sustainability sector. Instead, it should be a dynamic document utilized by everyone in the business. While the sustainability strategy may bring together all sustainability-related topics in one place, these themes should also be integrated into other strategies. Just as we advocate in this book for the sustainability organization and its operations to be ingrained throughout the company and incorporated into its core business purpose and model, the same principle applies to the strategy. It should be as integrated as possible into the business's core and, if necessary, accentuated through a centralized strategy.

Tool: Theory of Change

Transformative journeys, especially those that steer a business towards sustainability, are fraught with complexities and necessitate a structured, well-thought-out pathway. In the realm of change management, particularly in crafting and managing a shift towards more sustainable practices, the Theory of Change (ToC) emerges as a paramount tool, sculpting a lucid framework that lays down a strategic route from the present state to the desired future. It is a comprehensive model that helps businesses to chart a course from their current state to a more aspirational, sustainable future by providing a structured framework. This methodology does not merely define the desired impact and the steps needed to achieve it, but rather deciphers the underlying mechanisms that must be activated to trigger the desired change.[13] Let's delve a bit deeper:

- **Impact:** Identifying the ultimate impact or the 'why' behind your initiatives is the starting point. This could range from reducing environmental footprints to enhancing societal well-being. This is long term.
- **Outcomes:** These are the specific, short- to medium-term effects that collectively steer the path towards the ultimate impact. The outcomes reflect the changes in conditions, behaviour or perceptions that need to occur in order for the long-term goals to be realized.
- **Outputs:** Signifying the tangible, direct results of activities, outputs could encompass various aspects like workshops, policy changes or developed products/services. The outputs are direct results of the actions.
- **Activities:** These are the actions, initiatives or programmes that need to be executed to generate the desired outputs and, subsequently, drive the anticipated outcomes and impact.

The ToC encourages a practical, achievable approach to strategy, facilitating real change by integrating your sustainability efforts into a coherent, strategic framework. It highlights the importance of continuous adaptation and learning; businesses are therefore urged to periodically update their ToC to reflect new insights and achieve ongoing improvement. Breaking down the journey into these segments ensures that every initiative, activity and desired outcome is meticulously articulated, providing a blueprint that guides all sustainability endeavours. This elucidates not only the end points (impact) but also the waypoints (outputs and outcomes) that pave the road towards that impact.

The ToC also serves as a strategic framework that defines your sphere of influence, distinguishing between what your business can directly control, such as internal practices, and broader goals like societal change. It acts as a strategic guide, ensuring that every action taken is deliberate and impactful and aligns with your sustainability vision. For a sustainability strategy, reflect on:

- **Control:** Direct management of internal sustainability practices
- **Enable:** Collaboration within the value chain for wider sustainable practices
- **Influence:** Advocacy for broader societal and environmental change.

By strategically navigating these spheres, businesses can maximize their sustainable impact, underscoring the power of collective, purposeful action to achieve more than can be done by individual efforts alone.

Exploring the ToC approach

The ToC approach begins by identifying the desired impact, followed by outlining the outcomes and outputs and, finally, detailing the activities required to achieve these goals. To illustrate this concept at a high level, consider the following example in the context of sustainability and purpose-driven impact:

- **Impact:** To create a positive impact on society and the environment by promoting healthy diets, reducing environmental harm and encouraging physical activity through healthy products and solutions.
- **Outcomes:** The primary outcomes include widespread adoption of healthier diets, a significant reduction in environmental harm related to

food production and consumption, and increased physical activity among the target population.

- **Outputs:** Key outputs to achieve these outcomes involve increasing public awareness of the benefits of healthy products and solutions, enhancing accessibility and consumption of nutritious foods and motivating more individuals to engage in physical activities.

Actions could include the following:

1. **Awareness campaign:** Launch a comprehensive awareness campaign utilizing various media platforms to educate the public on the importance of healthy eating and regular physical activity. This campaign will highlight the environmental benefits of choosing sustainable and healthy food options.
2. **Healthy product offering:** Develop and offer a range of healthy, environmentally friendly food products that are easily accessible to a wide demographic. This could include organic, locally sourced items and plant-based alternatives, ensuring that these products meet high nutritional standards and have a lower environmental footprint.
3. **'Move-more' activities:** Organize community-based events and initiatives, such as 'move-more' challenges, fitness classes and active lifestyle workshops, to encourage people to incorporate more physical activity into their daily routines. Partner with local organizations and influencers to increase reach and engagement.
4. **Access and education programmes:** Implement programmes aimed at ensuring everyone, especially those in underserved communities, has access to healthy foods and understands how to incorporate them into their diets. This might involve partnerships with schools, community centres and local markets to provide educational resources and affordable healthy food options.

By executing these actions, the initiative aims to transform public attitudes and behaviour towards health and sustainability, leading to healthier diets, reduced environmental harm and a society that values and prioritizes movement and physical well-being.

This example demonstrates how working backwards from a desired impact through outcomes, outputs and activities can create a clear and structured path for achieving sustainable and purposeful change.

Tool: Sustainable Business Canvas

We recommend using the Sustainable Business Canvas as a strategic tool to help integrate sustainability into the business model. It's an adaptation of the traditional Business Model Canvas, but it's specifically focused on ensuring that sustainability is at the core of business planning and operations. The Sustainable Business Canvas is structured around nine steps, each with key questions to guide businesses in developing a sustainable business model. Although the main target user is a start-up, more established businesses can benefit from working with the tool when developing their sustainability approach. The Sustainable Business Canvas includes nine components: team, sustainability, customers, trends and scalability, unique value proposition, branding and storytelling, partnerships, processes and optimization, and financial goals and models.[14]

Step 4: Bringing in your materiality study

As emphasized in Chapter 4, the foundation of your strategy is rooted in your materiality study, ensuring that your actions and messages resonate deeply with issues crucial to your organization and its stakeholders. At a foundational level, it's essential to embed several broad themes in your sustainability strategy, due to their widespread relevance across various sectors. Key areas include climate, addressing both mitigation and adaptation; biodiversity, championing the protection of ecosystems and species; circularity, emphasizing resource efficiency; and social impact, prioritizing a positive imprint on communities and individual lives.

Adapting the depth and specifics of these topics based on insights from your materiality study guarantees a strategy that is all-encompassing and honed to drive substantial, meaningful change. It's noteworthy that, despite varied outcomes from the materiality assessment based on organizational types, the aforementioned topics remain universally relevant for all businesses. For a deeper dive into these sustainability challenges, refer to Chapter 1.

Climate

Addressing climate change is perhaps easier than other topics within the sustainability strategy, as it is a structured endeavour with numerous tools and methodologies available, for example the SBTi and the Exponential

Roadmap.[15] However, the subject is still inherently technical and offers scope for in-depth exploration. Our aim here is to provide a comprehensive overview. For those interested in delving deeper, numerous specialized courses are available.

The process begins by prioritizing the reduction of direct emissions. This encompasses Scope 1 emissions, which are the direct emissions from sources owned or controlled by the organization, like company vehicles or facilities. You have already conducted an assessment of this through the tools discussed in Chapter 4. Alongside this, attention is also given to Scope 2 emissions, which are the indirect emissions resulting from the generation of energy that the organization purchases, such as electricity or heating. Scope 1 emissions, or direct emissions from owned or controlled sources, often stem from company-owned vehicles like cars or trucks utilized for deliveries, business operations or even employee commutes. They can also originate from on-site power equipment like generators or boilers, and even something as common as refrigerant leaks from the office's air conditioning systems. On the other hand, Scope 2 emissions, which account for indirect emissions from the generation of purchased energy, arise from the electricity that the office consumes. This includes the energy driving the lights, computers and air conditioning. It's crucial to understand that while the office doesn't emit these gases directly, the power plants producing the electricity do. Additionally, if a business taps into district heating or cooling, the emissions related to that energy production would fall under Scope 2. To proactively address and reduce these emissions, businesses can consider measures like transitioning to more fuel-efficient vehicles, enhancing building insulation, switching to energy-efficient appliances and lighting, and opting for electricity sourced from renewable energy providers. Addressing both these scopes ensures a comprehensive approach to minimizing an organization's immediate carbon footprint.

Mitigating value chain emissions is a fundamental phase in a comprehensive sustainability strategy. Often referred to as Scope 3 emissions, these encompass all external emissions that are not owned or directly controlled by the company but are integral to its operation. Scope 3 emissions can be both upstream (related to inputs for the company, such as sourcing of raw materials or manufacturing of products they buy) and downstream (related to how customers use and dispose of their products). To paint a clearer picture, consider a clothing retail business. For such a company, upstream Scope 3 emissions might arise from the cultivation of cotton, including the emissions from tractors, fertilizers and transportation of the raw cotton to the mills. The processing of that cotton into fabric, the manufacturing of clothing and the transportation of the finished product to the store – all these processes contribute to the company's indirect carbon footprint. Meanwhile, downstream emissions could be tied to how consumers use the clothing (like washing and drying) and, eventually, how they dispose of it, whether through regular waste, recycling or composting.

The 1.5 °C Supply Chain Leaders initiative underscores the importance of businesses not only addressing their direct emissions but also influencing and working with their suppliers and partners to reduce the broader carbon footprint.[16] By being part of such initiatives, businesses can ensure they are at the forefront of sustainability, influencing change not just within their operations but throughout their entire value chain. Participating companies might, for example, set requirements for their suppliers to adopt more sustainable farming practices, use renewable energy or reduce waste in the manufacturing process. In doing so, they're championing a ripple effect of positive change throughout the industry.

An integrated climate approach also necessitates embedding climate considerations into a company's core strategy. This involves not just minimizing one's carbon footprint, but also proactively offering climate-positive solutions, aligning the company's overall vision and offerings with the ambitious 1.5 °C target. To ensure your targets are in line with current scientific requirements to combat climate change, we suggest you collaborate with the SBTi. This will involve setting targets that align with the Paris Agreement, getting them validated by SBTi experts and regularly reporting progress to ensure accountability and transparency. Integrating the SBTi's expertise provides credibility to your climate action efforts. The SBTi offers multiple benefits to companies; for example, by getting targets scientifically verified, you enhance their credibility. Furthermore, this commitment boosts the confidence of various stakeholders, from investors to customers. Importantly, as climate science progresses, the SBTi continuously refines its criteria, ensuring businesses remain aligned to the latest scientific requirements.[17]

Tool: Quick guide to building a climate plan[18]

This approach can be encapsulated as 'optimize, electrify, decarbonize'. The carbon footprint across the value chain of a company can vary based on its business model, operational practices and the nature of the products or services it offers. For different types of companies, the largest carbon footprints can be found in different stages of their value chains. Each company's footprint can evolve over time, influenced by operational changes, sourcing decisions, technological innovations and more. Tools like life cycle assessments (LCAs) prove invaluable in this context, helping companies pinpoint and address their most significant emission sources.

For instance, a typical retailer often has the majority of its carbon footprint stemming from the extraction, production and transportation of goods. The raw materials in clothing, such as cotton farming or synthetic fibre production, or in electronics, like the mining of metals, are significant contributors. Add to this the logistics: transporting goods from manufacturers to distribution centres and then retail outlets can have a vast footprint, especially if international or air transport is involved. Then there's the energy consumption of the physical stores, encompassing everything from lighting and refrigeration to heating and cooling. On the other hand, tech companies present a different scenario. Those offering cloud services are heavily reliant on data centres which consume a massive amount of energy, making this a substantial portion of their carbon footprint. Tech hardware companies face challenges with the production of devices, such as computers and smartphones, where the extraction of essential metals and minerals and the manufacturing process contribute significantly to emissions. The energy that devices consume during their usage phase also can't be overlooked. Switching our lens to the agriculture or food production sector, the picture shifts again. Here, the cultivation phase dominates, especially when considering the use of fertilizers, pesticides and machinery. This is especially pronounced for meat and dairy producers, given the enteric fermentation in ruminants. The production of animal feed, along with the emissions it brings, also plays a significant role. And, of course, the carbon footprint contribution of transportation and refrigeration of perishable products cannot be understated.

Biodiversity

To proactively address biodiversity within a strategic framework, companies first need to evaluate their ecological footprint, understanding the ecosystems and species impacted by their operations. This has already been described in previous chapters.

Decision makers often overlook the significance of their impacts and dependencies on natural capital, leading to potentially risky and ineffective choices. The value of natural capital has traditionally been neglected or inconsistently addressed in decision making. The Natural Capital Protocol offers a standardized framework for understanding and evaluating the effects on and dependencies with natural capital. The Protocol comprises four stages, with nine steps that guide the integration of natural capital value into organizational decisions.[19] Although presented linearly, it's an adaptable and iterative process. The stages address the following:

1 **Frame (why?):** Recognize business and stakeholder risks and opportunities linked to natural capital and determine the relevance of assessment.
2 **Scope (what?):** Define the assessment's goal and, through materiality, select key impacts and dependencies from a business and stakeholder perspective.
3 **Measure and value (how?):** Quantify and assign value to the significant impacts and dependencies on natural capital.
4 **Apply (what next?):** Analyse, validate and incorporate the assessment results into business processes to guide decisions.

Thus, it is about integrating biodiversity considerations into existing business processes, such as procurement, product development and site management. An organization could collaborate with environmental NGOs, academics, local communities and other stakeholders to gain insights, knowledge and validation. Engage with customers and suppliers to understand their perspectives and expectations. Consider certifications that address biodiversity, such as the Rainforest Alliance or Biodiversity in Good Company. Sustainable sourcing is paramount; businesses should prioritize raw materials that don't contribute to habitat destruction. Pollution reduction, especially in waste management and harmful discharges, aids in safeguarding aquatic biodiversity. Embracing a circular economy by maximizing resource efficiency can further alleviate pressure on ecosystems. Simultaneously, companies should actively combat climate change by reducing carbon emissions and supporting initiatives like reforestation, which in turn can also help biodiversity. Collaborative endeavours, partnering with conservation-focused NGOs and engaging with local communities can enhance conservation outcomes. Continuous monitoring, target-setting and transparent reporting of biodiversity initiatives will ensure accountability and alignment with broader conservation goals.[20]

EXAMPLE Biomimicry in business

Biomimicry, the practice of emulating nature's time-tested patterns and strategies, offers companies a powerful tool to integrate biodiversity principles into their strategies. Biomimicry involves learning from and replicating nature's forms, processes and ecosystems to create sustainable and regenerative designs. It advocates for valuing nature not for what can be extracted but for the insights it offers.

Fredrik Moberg isn't just a researcher; he's on a mission to bring nature into our modern solutions through biomimicry. From the coral reefs to consulting firms, his journey is nothing short of an adventure, exploring the rich, sustainable solutions hidden within nature's intricate designs. His book The Inventive Planet[21] and his co-founded consultancy, Albaeco,[22] are not just platforms but voices championing the concept that learning from nature, rather than exploiting it, can weave sustainability into our future development and well-being.

Dipping his toes into multiple roles – researcher, educator and consultant– Fredrik translates the complex language of science into tangible, actionable insights for businesses and broader society. His optimism, despite the stark realities of our environmental crises, propels him to embed sustainable, nature-inspired methodologies into various industries, urging a system-wide transformation towards green practices. In essence, Fredrik Moberg paints a future where nature is not just observed but emulated, crafting a path where every stride towards development is in sync with the natural world.[23]

Circularity in business strategy

Circularity is indeed a thrilling aspect of sustainability, infusing creativity and innovation into business practices. It is about moving from a linear business model to closing the loops of materials. It challenges companies to reimagine the life cycle of their products and services, turning waste into resources and ensuring that everything has a purpose and place in the cycle. Organizations searching for such opportunities can start by conducting an internal resource audit to understand their excess resources or needs. Mapping the value chain, including suppliers, customers and even competitors, can reveal potential synergies. Engaging in industry networking events and leveraging online platforms dedicated to industrial symbiosis can facilitate connections with complementary partners. Collaborating with local governments, agencies and research institutions can provide additional insights and expertise. Initiating small-scale pilot projects can test the viability of these partnerships. It's important to develop a solid business case for each opportunity, clearly outlining the economic, environmental and social benefits. Establishing clear agreements and processes for resource exchange is crucial, as is continuously monitoring the performance and being adaptable to change.[24]

Your approach to circularity will hinge on your specific industry, your sector and the foundational elements of your business model. However, certain universal principles apply.

Product longevity

Aim for products that endure, that are designed for longevity and, if possible, for multiple users over time. Take, for instance, home appliances – those indispensable kitchen comrades like refrigerators and ovens, which have an uncanny knack for throwing in the towel the moment their warranty breathes its last. Crafting these household heroes to last beyond the celebrated 'warranty period' does more than save consumers from the dreaded appliance-shopping escapades; it weaves trust into the brand's fabric. Imagine a world where your trusty washing machine, rather than conspiring with the calendar, hums along faithfully, challenging time itself.

Conversely, certain products which are subject to wear and hygiene concerns, like toilet brushes, may not benefit from an extended lifespan. It's more practical to design these for appropriate durability, accepting that they will be replaced periodically to maintain sanitary conditions. The key is to balance longevity with practicality, ensuring that the product life cycle aligns with its function and user requirements.

Circular infrastructure

This is about more than just your products. Think of your buildings, materials, transport systems – every asset in your business should lean towards sustainability. Envision a workplace where the buildings themselves are paragons of sustainability, constructed with materials birthed from the cradle of circularity, destined for rebirth at the end of their cycle. It's a place where the walls tell stories of reclaimed wood, the windows are a testament to recycled glass, and even the bricks might have a past life. Transport systems within this circular haven are not mere vessels of transit but ambassadors of efficiency, perhaps powered by renewable energy sources or designed to share, reduce and recycle energy within a smart grid. These are not the gas-guzzling chariots of yore but the sleek, green conveyances of the future. In this circular realm, even the cafeteria's food waste is not wasted; it's a resource, a valuable input for compost that nurtures the community garden which, in turn, provides fresh produce for the cafeteria. It's an elegant loop, a harmonious dance of resources that keeps giving.

Value retention

Aim to keep products or materials at their highest utility and value throughout their life. Start with reuse, then refurbish, remanufacture and, only then, recycle. The mantra here is 'reduce, reuse, refurbish, remanufacture, recycle' – in that order:

1. The journey starts with the simple act of **reusing**, finding new ways to employ an item when its initial purpose is served. An office desk, for instance, once a stage for computers and paperwork, could find its second act as a crafting table in a school.
2. Next up is **refurbishment** – giving products a makeover, perhaps updating that same desk with fresh paint or new hardware to extend its life.
3. **Remanufacturing** takes it a step further, where the item is not only cosmetically revived but also technologically updated, keeping it relevant in a modern setting and delaying its date with the recycling bin.
4. Only when a product has danced through the cycles of reuse, refurbishment and remanufacturing should it bow gracefully into the **recycling** process. This stage meticulously deconstructs and salvages materials, ensuring they remain in the economic loop, ready to be reborn as the building blocks for new products.

This hierarchy isn't just about being thrifty; it's a profound shift in the consumption narrative. It's the art of maintaining the essence, the utility and the value of materials without allowing them to degrade into waste. It's about seeing the potential in every product to live multiple lives and to serve multiple purposes, and in doing so, challenge the very concept of obsolescence. This value retention ethos is a keystone in the archway leading to a future where nothing is wasted and everything is valued far beyond its first use.

Considerate product design

Think about the following in terms of the design of your products:

- **Material source:** Think about where your materials come from. Are they responsibly sourced? Ensure that their extraction or creation doesn't harm ecosystems or communities. Are they made of recycled components?
- **Life cycle thought:** A product's design should encapsulate foresight for its entire lifespan. From the drawing board to the end of its life, consider how each component can be maximized for durability. Design with disassembly in mind, allowing products to be easily taken apart. This not only facilitates repair and refurbishment but also aids in recycling parts that can no longer be used. By planning for the future of the materials used in your products, you embed the principles of circularity right at the conception stage, setting the stage for a closed-loop system where materials continually flow through cycles of use and reuse.

Consumer engagement models

Consider the following:

1. **Flexible ownership:** Could customers rent the product or buy it second-hand? Challenge the traditional 'buy-and-own' model by offering alternatives. Could your products be part of a rental or leasing service, thus staying under your care while providing utility to the customer? This way, you not only extend the life cycle of the products but also retain the ability to ensure their optimal performance. Additionally, consider certified pre-owned options, which give products a second life and offer customers a cost-effective alternative.
2. **Maintenance and care:** Offer services that allow customers to refurbish or repair their products, ensuring they last longer and serve better. Emphasize longevity by providing maintenance services. A product that's well cared for is a product that lasts. Offering repair services or even DIY repair kits encourages consumers to mend rather than discard. This not only extends the product's life but also deepens the customer's relationship with the product and the brand. Regular maintenance checks could also be an avenue, ensuring that products are always performing at their best.
3. **Post-usage strategy:** After its primary life, can the product be returned, resold, recycled or even donated? Plan for the product's life after the consumer is done with it. Can it be returned to you for refurbishing or remanufacturing? Is there a take-back scheme that allows customers to return products at the end of their life cycle for responsible recycling or

safe disposal? Perhaps there's an opportunity for the product to be resold or donated, creating social value. By establishing a post-usage plan, you ensure that products do not end up in landfills and instead find new purposes, new homes or new forms, thereby continuing the cycle of utility.

Tool: The circular economy framework of the Ellen MacArthur Foundation

In this framework, three design principles are presented: eradicating waste and curbing pollution, keeping products and materials in circulation (maximizing their utility) and, finally, restoring and rejuvenating the natural environment. Further strengthened by a shift towards renewable energy and materials, the circular economy establishes a robust system beneficial for businesses, society and our planet.[25]

Within circularity, the distinction between technical and biological material flows is crucial. Technical materials are non-biodegradable and are designed to be reused, repaired and recycled without losing their quality and functionality. They circulate within the economy, ideally in a closed-loop system, minimizing waste and the need for new resources. On the other hand, biological materials are biodegradable and can safely re-enter the environment after use. They can decompose and are intended to be returned to the Earth, often as compostable substances that can help regenerate natural systems.

Although it may seem necessary in some cases, one should strive to avoid mixing these two types of materials, because the contamination of biological materials with technical ones can hinder the composting process and the ability of biological substances to return to the ecosystem. Similarly, the presence of biological materials in technical streams can reduce the quality of recycled products and complicate the recycling process. Proper segregation ensures that each type of material can be processed efficiently in its respective cycle, thereby maintaining the integrity of circularity within the sustainability framework.

Tool: The 9R framework

A potentially helpful tool when designing your circular approach is the 9R framework.[26] The 9R framework is a comprehensive approach, encompassing strategies that businesses can adopt to shape their circular strategies effectively. It includes refuse, reduce, reuse, repair, refurbish, remanufacture, repurpose, recycle and recover.

This framework helps businesses move beyond traditional linear models (take-make-dispose) by encouraging them to consider alternative ways to use and reuse materials and products. By incorporating these principles, companies can reduce waste, extend product life cycles and create more sustainable and efficient processes. Applying the 9R framework can lead to innovations in product design, production methods and business models, fostering a transition towards a more sustainable, circular economy. This approach not only benefits the environment but can also offer economic advantages through cost savings, new revenue streams and enhanced brand reputation.

Social impact

Navigating the 'people' aspect of sustainability is multifaceted and should be tailored to an organization's context, defined by its operations and location. Yet, the universal ambition remains unchanged: bettering the lives of all people connected to the business. A thorough materiality assessment and comprehensive stakeholder mapping provide a foundational understanding, revealing how businesses touch lives – from individual persons to entire communities. Key strategic areas to address are discussed in the rest of this section.

In terms of responsible business and societal resilience, consider the following aspects:

- **Championing human and children's rights:** This can be done by embedding the UN Guiding Principles on Business and Human Rights and UNICEF's Children's Rights and Business Principles.[27] This means actively integrating these frameworks into company policy and throughout the value chain. It also involves being a vocal advocate for these rights in the broader business community and society. For more insights into this topic, read the interview with Lama Abdulrahman in Chapter 1.
- **Upholding ethical standards:** This ranges from fighting corruption to ensuring ethical data management and transparent tax practices. Such integrity is non-negotiable and must be ingrained in the business's operations.
- **Navigating societal challenges:** Climate and health crises need to be addressed with strategies that protect employees and partners throughout

the supply chain. For climate crises, this could mean creating adaptive measures that ensure business continuity during extreme weather events, such as floods or hurricanes. Companies might invest in robust infrastructure, diversify supply sources or develop emergency response plans that prioritize the safety of their workers and the integrity of their supply chains. In the case of health crises, like a pandemic, businesses must pivot to protect their workforce and partners. This could involve instituting remote work policies, enhancing workplace safety measures or providing health support, and clear communication to all members of the supply chain. The goal is to maintain operations while ensuring that every person connected with the business is informed, supported and safeguarded against health risks.

- **Proactively engaging with local communities:** This means leveraging the company's role, influence and expertise to make a positive impact, whether it's through educational initiatives, local economic development or environmental conservation. This approach helps build a resilient society where businesses and communities thrive together.

It is important to promote decent work across the value chain:

- **Committing to decent work:**[28] This process begins with the basics – ensuring that all employees earn a living wage. This is a wage that not only meets the legal minimums but allows workers to afford a standard of living that includes basic needs like food, housing, healthcare, education and savings for unexpected events. Companies must also use their influence to encourage and sometimes require that their business partners, suppliers and distributors commit to similar standards, thus advocating for economic justice throughout their value chain. The possibility to do so varies, of course, depending on the company's size and importance.
- **Safe and rights-respecting workplaces:** The push for decent work environments entails guaranteeing safety and human rights in the workplace. This commitment must be unwavering regardless of local standards and extend to all global operations. It also means looking forward and adapting workplaces to be sustainable and to contribute to a net-zero economy. As part of this future-proofing effort, companies should invest in upskilling and reskilling programmes to ensure that their workforce is prepared for the transitions that a circular, net-zero economy demands.
- **Ethical recruitment and worker rights:** Decent work also encompasses ethical recruitment practices that protect workers from exploitation and

human trafficking. It involves ensuring that workers have the right to collective bargaining, which can help them negotiate fair pay, benefits and working conditions. Moreover, supporting the freedom of association means respecting the rights of workers to join or form trade unions, as well as the right not to do so if they choose. These principles are foundational to a respectful and democratic workplace where the voices of employees at all levels are heard and valued.

Championing equality, diversity and inclusion (EDI) can be done in the following ways:

- **Reflecting diversity:** A key element of EDI is the recognition and celebration of human differences across all levels of the company. This means ensuring that the workforce mirrors the varied demographics of the locations where the company operates. By doing so, a business taps into a wealth of perspectives and experiences, fostering creativity and innovation. Moreover, this diversity in the workplace helps to establish a strong connection with the community and the customer base, enhancing both the business's relevance and its impact.
- **Equal opportunities and non-discrimination:** Equality in the workplace is about more than just fair treatment – it's about actively preventing discrimination, whether based on race, gender, age, disability, orientation, religion or any other characteristic. This involves implementing and enforcing policies that promote equal opportunities in hiring, promotions and professional development. Ensuring that every individual has the same chance to succeed and thrive within the company is not just ethically imperative but also beneficial for the organization's growth and success.
- **Inclusive culture and environment:** An inclusive work environment is one where everyone feels valued and supported, irrespective of their background or identity. It includes designing accessible workplaces that accommodate all individuals, including those with disabilities. It's also about cultivating a company culture that recognizes and respects individual needs and boundaries, promoting work–life balance through family-friendly policies and ensuring that children's rights are protected. This approach to inclusivity should also engage younger employees, who often bring fresh insights and energy, helping to drive the company forward in a competitive business landscape.

EXAMPLE Becoming a leader in social impact

Companies can champion and lead on the social impact agenda by transforming challenges into opportunities to become leaders. Here are some examples of how they can do this:

- **Embrace transparency:** Companies like Patagonia and Everlane have turned transparency into a selling point. By disclosing their supply chain and production costs, they've built trust with consumers and set new industry standards.
- **Employee empowerment:** Starbucks, for example, provides comprehensive health benefits and tuition assistance to its employees, even part-timers. This initiative not only aids in employee retention but also positions the company as a leader in employee welfare.
- **Inclusive hiring practices:** Microsoft has programmes specifically designed to hire people with autism. By doing so, they tap into a unique talent pool, push diversity and become an example for other corporations.
- **Engage in social entrepreneurship:** TOMS Shoes, with its 'One for One' model, donates a pair of shoes for every pair sold. This approach transforms the challenge of global poverty into a business opportunity and strengthens their brand. Timberland has partnered with Other Half Processing, a social enterprise that produces sustainable hides and leather. Other Half Processing utilizes by-products from sustainably raised animals, promoting zero waste and supporting farmers, ranchers and Native American communities. This partnership aligns with Timberland's commitment to sustainable fashion, advancing environmental preservation and healthier lifestyles while expanding support for regenerative farming practices in the community.[29]
- **Stakeholder collaboration:** Companies can engage stakeholders, including NGOs, local communities and governments, to co-create solutions. Coca-Cola, for example, has partnered with the WWF to promote water conservation.
- **Skills-based volunteering:** Many tech companies, including Accenture, encourage their employees to use their specific skills to support non-profits or social enterprises. This not only serves the community but also boosts employee morale.

- **R&D for societal issues:** Companies like Johnson & Johnson invest in research for diseases that predominantly affect the poor, turning global health challenges into areas of leadership.

Steps to conclude your strategy

When developing a sustainability strategy, one may strive for a one-pager that encapsulates high-level ambitions and principles, assuming the integration of sustainability into all organizational aspects. Yet, in their early sustainability stages, organizations often require a more detailed strategy. This typically includes a road map based on a theory of change, outlining clear objectives and principles that are adaptable across different organizational levels, from global to local or corporate to unit-specific plans.

The essence of this strategy is its ability to be broken down into actionable steps, ensuring coherence and understanding of each department's role in achieving the overall sustainability goals. It's not merely a document but a living guide influencing decision making and operations at all levels. A comprehensive strategy, covering both social and environmental sustainability aspects, provides a holistic view of the organization's ambitions. It serves as a central reference, aiding in consistent communication, progress tracking and stakeholder understanding, thereby enhancing the organization's sustainability performance and bolstering its reputation as a responsible entity.

Having crafted your strategy, it's vital to remember the importance of the inclusive approach you've employed, engaging stakeholders at every juncture. Now, it's time to refine and validate. Firstly, conduct a rigorous stress test on the strategy. Does it possess the ambition to inspire and galvanize? Does it aptly address the pertinent challenges? It's essential to ensure your strategy holistically encompasses materiality topics, integrates science-based targets and presents actionable steps. Additionally, align the strategy with your organization's broader strategic vision. Benchmarking against peer companies can be invaluable at this stage. This will not only help you ascertain that you're focusing on the right issues but will also position you at the forefront, where you aim to lead.

Following this, facilitate the transformation of the strategy into tangible action plans. Securing the endorsement and advocacy of senior leadership will be pivotal in propelling the strategy forward. Their role in communicating and championing the vision cannot be understated. Lastly, establish a robust implementation framework. This will enable you to continuously gauge your performance, ensuring you remain on course and achieve the intended impact.

Summary and key take-aways

In this chapter, we delved into the multifaceted journey of crafting a sustainability strategy. We began by exploring the underlying motivations and purpose, and discussed varying ambition levels – from transformational shifts in business models to gradual, stepwise enhancements. Utilizing the ToC emerged as a fundamental tool in this process. We underscored the significance of materiality, pinpointing critical subjects that the strategy should encompass. Further, we provided insights into the effective launch and holistic implementation of the strategy across the organization.

The chapter emphasized the imperative of integrating sustainability, not as a mere peripheral addition but as an intrinsic component of the overall business strategy. Such an approach ensures that the strategy is rooted deeply within the organizational purpose. It recognizes the constraints and possibilities within the planetary boundaries and the social contract that binds an organization to the broader society.

Drawing from this perspective, the sustainability dimension of the business strategy emerges from the organization's materiality assessment. This helps identify specific areas along the value chain where the organization not only has a substantial impact but also holds the potential for transformative positive contributions. This exercise also helps to clarify which departments and teams are responsible for specific sustainability-related tasks.

Endnotes

1 How to make sustainability a part of your company DNA, UN Global Compact. unglobalcompact.org/take-action/20th-anniversary-campaign/how-to-make-sustainability-a-part-of-your-company-dna (archived at https://perma.cc/KW26-9VL3)

2 Simon Sinek (2011) *Start with Why: How Great Leaders Inspire Everyone to Take Action*, Penguin, London, simonsinek.com/books/start-with-why/ (archived at https://perma.cc/D8WL-EANU); Simon Sinek. Start with why:

How great leaders inspire action, TEDx Talk, YouTube, 2009. www.youtube.com/watch?v=u4ZoJKF_VuA (archived at https://perma.cc/286E-7PGN)

3 PAS 808: Purpose-driven organisations: Worldviews, principles and behaviours, Embedding Project. embeddingproject.org/resources/pas-808-purpose-driven-organisations-worldviews-principles-and-behaviours/ (archived at https://perma.cc/YVD8-VCAB)

4 Cambridge Institute for Sustainability Leadership (CISL). Leading with a Sustainable Purpose: Leaders' Insights for the Development, Alignment and Integration of a Sustainable Corporate Purpose, November 2020. www.cisl.cam.ac.uk/resources/sustainability-leadership/leading-with-a-sustainable-purpose (archived at https://perma.cc/W4CT-2WRQ)

5 Best purpose statement examples from the Fortune 500, Purposebrand, 16 August 2021. purposebrand.com/blog/best-purpose-statements-fortune-500/ (archived at https://perma.cc/P6EB-T4MJ)

6 Patagonia's mission statement, www.patagonia.com.hk/pages/our-mission (archived at https://perma.cc/J24R-DVBS)

7 PAS 808: Purpose-driven organisations: Worldviews, principles and behaviours, Embedding Project. embeddingproject.org/resources/pas-808-purpose-driven-organisations-worldviews-principles-and-behaviours/ (archived at https://perma.cc/YVD8-VCAB)

8 Tom van de Cruys. Give meaning to your organization and unlock the power of purpose, Purpose Alliance. purposealliance.org/services/purpose-discovery/ (archived at https://perma.cc/W38E-TRGP)

9 Hubert Joly. Creating a meaningful corporate purpose, Harvard Business Review, 28 October 2021. hbr.org/2021/10/creating-a-meaningful-corporate-purpose (archived at https://perma.cc/9UYP-FZAP)

10 Sean Peek. What is a vision statement? Business News Daily, 16 January 2024, www.businessnewsdaily.com/3882-vision-statement.html (archived at https://perma.cc/8LDA-X932)

11 Jonathan Bardelline. Lights out for IKEA incandescent lights, GreenBiz, 4 January 2011. www.greenbiz.com/article/lights-out-ikea-incandescent-bulbs (archived at https://perma.cc/ZG27-LVS8)

12 Kat Boogaard. How to write SMART goals, Atlassian blog, 26 December 2023. www.atlassian.com/blog/productivity/how-to-write-smart-goals (archived at https://perma.cc/6KLB-ZHHK); Definition of goals, targets and objectives, Australian Transport Assessment and Planning, www.atap.gov.au/framework/goals-objectives-targets/2-defining-goals-objectives-targets (archived at https://perma.cc/XR3X-YAAT)

13 United Nations Development Group (UNDP). Theory of Change, unsdg.un.org/sites/default/files/UNDG-UNDAF-Companion-Pieces-7-Theory-of-Change.pdf (archived at https://perma.cc/C4K8-SRDD)

14 See www.sustainablebusinesscanvas.com (archived at https://perma.cc/8GYY-N33B)

15 See sciencebasedtargets.org (archived at https://perma.cc/C54G-GLST); exponentialroadmap.org (archived at https://perma.cc/78LU-QTBL)
16 See https://exponentialroadmap.org/supply-chain-leaders/ (archived at https://perma.cc/68FJ-PKRM)
17 Set a target, SBTi, sciencebasedtargets.org/step-by-step-process (archived at https://perma.cc/8TVQ-R7GJ)
18 Sphera solutions, sphera.com; Stefan Premer. 6 steps to develop a robust climate strategy, Greenbiz, 7 June 2022. www.greenbiz.com/article/6-steps-develop-robust-climate-strategy (archived at https://perma.cc/JGW9-RNGY)
19 Natural Capital Coalition, Natural Capital Protocol Principles and Framework. capitalscoalition.org/wp-content/uploads/2021/07/NCC_Framework.pdf (archived at https://perma.cc/G3YB-ECXC)
20 Biodiversity: Why set science-based targets for species and ecosystems? SBTi. sciencebasedtargetsnetwork.org/our-mission/issue-hubs/biodiversity/ (archived at https://perma.cc/8D6S-3S5D)
21 Fredrik Moberg (2021) *Den uppfinnelserika planeten*, Natur & Kultur, Stockholm. www.nok.se/titlar/a7/den-uppfinningsrika-planeten/21a97033-9488-4f9e-a8b6-6e894b279b9d (archived at https://perma.cc/8XWL-ZPUF)
22 See www.albaeco.se (archived at https://perma.cc/73DG-QLH3)
23 Interview conducted September 2022
24 Jukka Teräs and Nelli Mikkola. What is industrial symbiosis? Nordregio, nordregio.org/nordregio-magazine/issues/industrial-symbiosis/what-is-industrial-symbiosis/ (archived at https://perma.cc/HDY8-PQLU)
25 What is a circular economy? Ellen MacArthur Foundation. www.ellenmacarthurfoundation.org/topics/circular-economy-introduction/overview (archived at https://perma.cc/6KND-L2EZ)
26 Jason Graham-Nye. The circular economy: How it can lead us on a path to real change, World Economic Forum (WEF), 17 May 2022. www.weforum.org/agenda/2022/05/the-circular-economy-how-it-can-be-a-path-to-real-change/ (archived at https://perma.cc/WMK4-ZXW9)
27 The Convention on the Rights of the Child: The children's version, UNICEF. www.unicef.org/child-rights-convention/convention-text-childrens-version (archived at https://perma.cc/M7FV-J74C); Children's Rights and Business Principles, UNICEF. www.unicef.org/documents/childrens-rights-and-business-principles (archived at https://perma.cc/R68N-CFUP)
28 Decent work, ILO. www.ilo.org/global/topics/decent-work/lang--en/index.htm (archived at https://perma.cc/3BYW-Y4VW)
29 See www.otherhalfprocessing.com (archived at https://perma.cc/3374-N9PJ)

Organization: Integration and governance

06

The purpose of this book is to show how an organization can move from centralized sustainability to a position where everyone in the organization wants to, and understands how to, contribute to sustainability. Sustainability is an extensive field, covering areas as diverse as legal compliance, human rights, environmental conservation, material analysis, sourcing, engineering, packaging and design, among others. The breadth and depth of this discipline have thus invited an important question: can the sustainability function be the responsibility of a single person?

Simply put, the answer is no. The scope of sustainability is too vast, both in terms of workload and the expertise required, to be managed by a single person. Yet, many organizations still place the burden of sustainability on the shoulders of a sole individual or a very small, centralized team. Our book argues against such an approach as it is neither realistic nor efficient. By understanding the diverse roles in sustainability and their interconnections, we can pave the way for effective and impactful sustainable practices across industries.

Important ways to embed sustainability into your organization outlined in this chapter follow these four steps, which are also shown in Figure 6.1:

1. **Culture** as an enabler: Creating a culture that supports sustainability
2. **Human-centred design** (HCD) as an enabler: How to use this thinking as a tool
3. **Engagement** as an enabler: How to engage through various sustainability forums
4. **Structure** as an enabler: How to build a governance model and integrate sustainability into job functions.

Figure 6.1 Four steps to embed sustainability

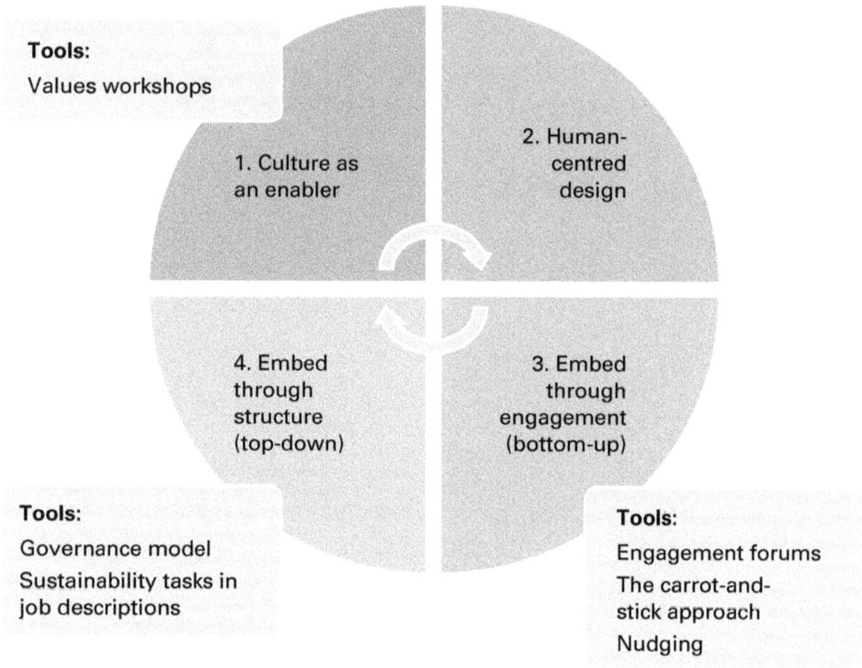

Step 1: Align with your corporate culture

In managing the change needed for a successful sustainability transformation, the organizational culture is central. It serves as the determining factor in how new directions and integrations are perceived and adopted. The cultural fabric of an organization is its unique identifier – something so inherent and bespoke that it may be one of the few things others cannot copy. This cultural identity plays an important role in embedding sustainability and social impact within a company. But is it possible to change or shape a new culture within an organization? Yes, it is. Although it cannot be done overnight, it is possible to influence the organizational culture.

Improving organizational culture requires a strategic and introspective approach, starting with a thorough understanding of the existing cultural landscape. This involves delving into what currently motivates employees and the prevailing norms, values and behaviours that characterize the organization's way of doing things. Once the current culture is mapped out, the next step is to articulate a vision for the desired culture – a culture that embodies openness, transparency, innovation, engagement, empowerment and a strong commitment to ethical behaviour, sustainability and social impact.

With both the present state and the aspirational culture defined, it's crucial to identify the discrepancies between them. This gap analysis is pivotal, as it highlights the specific areas that need to be addressed to facilitate cultural transformation. An action plan can then be developed, detailing concrete steps, timelines and accountabilities to bridge the gap and foster the desired culture. In crafting this plan, it's important to heed Peter Drucker's adage, 'Culture eats strategy for breakfast',[1] which serves as a powerful reminder that cultural alignment is essential for the successful implementation of any strategy. Culture is the soil in which your strategy must grow; without a nurturing cultural environment, even the most well-conceived strategies may fail to take root. Therefore, any plan to shift culture should be considered as fundamental to achieving organizational goals as the strategies devised to reach them.

To foster a culture that naturally gravitates towards sustainable practices, one must consider its various dimensions – narratives, rituals, symbols and the underlying systems that govern behaviour:

1. **Narratives and storytelling:** The stories that are told within an organization shape its identity. Sharing success stories about sustainability, employee initiatives and community engagement can inspire others to follow suit. A great way to do that is through communications updates, newsletters and storytelling through the social ambassadors.
2. **Rituals:** Simple daily acts, such as picking up litter, switching off lights when not in use, being very mindful about food waste or opting for stairs over elevators, reinforce the sustainability ethos when they become routine practices. For sustainability, this could take the form of combining a sustainable culture with health and well-being, for example to encourage people to cycle to work, spend time in nature or eat a more plant-based diet. The key to effecting this change lies in designing and implementing incentives that motivate these environmentally friendly and healthy behaviours.
3. **Symbols:** Tangible symbols, such as recycling bins, branded reusable items (for example branded water bottles) or green spaces within the office, serve as constant reminders of the organization's commitment to sustainability.

4 **Structure and reward systems:** A structure that rewards sustainable actions and ethical behaviours, perhaps through recognition programmes or performance metrics, will encourage employees to take ownership of these values. One could offer benefits like subsidized public transport passes, company support for purchasing electric vehicles or financial incentives for employees who live close to work and walk or cycle. For example, one can do that by actively promoting the participation in various social entrepreneurship programmes. Several consultancy companies offer employees to do pro-bono activities in between assignments. Volunteering can also be promoted as a valuable pathway for personal and professional development. While the reward system isn't necessarily monetary, it should be ensured that such contributions are duly recognized and appreciated.
5 **Control systems and power structures:** Hierarchies and control systems should empower employees at all levels, promoting an open, supportive and transparent environment where mistakes are viewed as learning opportunities. It should be recognized that the journey towards sustainability is uncharted and requires the courage to forge new paths, and that perfection is not immediate. Mistakes are not just inevitable but essential, as they provide potent learning opportunities. In the spirit of hierarchical empowerment, a bottom-up approach should be promoted, empowering employees across all levels to voice their ideas for sustainable practices and ensuring they are heard and considered. To nurture a supportive atmosphere, 'sustainability forums' offer safe spaces to discuss environmental challenges and share knowledge without the concern of negative consequences. It is essential to aim for a learning culture that views sustainability-related mistakes as valuable, one that analyses missteps in a constructive manner and disseminates the lessons learnt throughout the company.

In shaping a culture that champions sustainability, it is crucial to create an ecosystem that is responsible, ethical, curious, innovative and collaborative – a culture that sees equality beyond pay scales and values partnership over competition, solutions over obstacles. Leaders must exemplify the sustainable behaviour expected within the organization. Walking the talk is essential – leaders should visibly engage in sustainable practices and communicate their importance. By thoroughly and consciously working with the organization, it is possible to engrain sustainability into the very essence of its culture, making it a natural and inextricable part of its identity and operations.

Tool: Values workshop[2]

Values are the cornerstone of any organizational culture, serving as the compass that guides behaviour, decision making and strategy. In the context of sustainability, values are particularly critical, as they underpin the commitment an organization makes to its employees, customers and the wider community. When values are embedded within the organizational culture, they create a shared understanding and a collective sense of purpose. This shared ethos becomes a driving force for sustainability, aligning personal motivations with corporate goals and fostering an environment where sustainable practices are not just encouraged but are expected and rewarded.

Values such as integrity, responsibility and respect for the environment act as the lifeblood of sustainable initiatives. They ensure that such initiatives are not seen as mere marketing tactics or compliance obligations but are embraced as fundamental to the identity of the organization. A culture rich in these values will naturally propel sustainability forward, making it a part of every conversation, decision and action. Moreover, when values are authentically integrated into the culture, they help build trust and credibility with all stakeholders. Customers, partners and employees are more likely to engage with and support organizations they believe are genuinely committed to making a positive impact on society and the planet. This trust is invaluable, as it strengthens reputational capital and can provide a competitive edge in the marketplace.

Aligning company values with employee personal values is pivotal for a committed approach to sustainability. When employees resonate with the organization's principles, particularly in sustainability, they become more engaged and enthusiastic, often going above and beyond in their roles. Such alignment attracts and retains talent passionate about sustainability, ensuring a workforce that is motivated and united, especially when faced with challenges. In essence, values act as the seeds from which sustainable behaviours grow. When carefully cultivated and nurtured through continuous engagement and leadership, these values bloom into a culture where sustainability is not just an agenda, but a way of life. It's this cultural transformation that is often the most enduring and impactful result of a genuine commitment to sustainability.

To conduct a values workshop, begin by gathering insights through a survey that explores employees' personal and perceived organizational values. This should involve contributors from every level within the organization, ensuring a comprehensive view of the current culture. During the workshop, which should be a few hours, provide an environment conducive to open dialogue and active participation, with the necessary tools to facilitate the session. Kick off the workshop by clarifying the organization's purpose as a foundation for the values discussion. Encourage an open forum for discussing the values surfaced from the survey, with the aim of fostering a deep conversation to understand various perspectives and form a collective agreement on the core values.

After the discussion, focus on articulating the values clearly and positively. Invite feedback on the drafted values from the team and elaborate based on their input, to form a set of values that truly resonate with the organization's ethos. Following the workshop, introduce the agreed-upon values to the entire team, highlighting their importance and practical application in the company's operations. Ensure these values are ingrained in the organization's practices, from recognition programmes to hiring processes, to create a living culture that consistently reflects these values.

Step 2: Adopt a human-centred approach

Despite myriad negative events and headlines that often dominate our newsfeeds, we, the authors, hold an intriguing belief in the inherent goodness of people. We are convinced that when individuals are presented with a choice, especially under favourable conditions and with a sense of well-being, they will more often than not make decisions that are right and good for the common well-being. To substantiate this optimistic view of human nature, historian and author Rutger Bregman has delved deeply into this topic in his book *Humankind*.[3] Packed with research and data, Bregman illustrates through compelling stories and evidence that, contrary to the often-grim narrative presented by the media, there are numerous instances of human goodness and cooperation, often occurring quietly and without fanfare. Humans are inherently good and, given the right conditions, will typically choose to do the right thing.

One of many notable examples that Bregman provides in the book is a true story that parallels the fictional events in William Golding's *Lord of the Flies*.[4] In 1965, six boys from Tonga got stranded on a deserted island for over a year. Contrary to the chaotic and violent behaviour depicted in Golding's novel, these boys worked together to survive. They set up a small commune with a food garden, hollowed-out tree trunks for storing rainwater, a gymnasium with curious weights, a badminton court, chicken pens and a permanent fire, all from hand-made tools and materials. Despite injuries and disagreements, they managed to maintain peace and cooperation until their rescue. This real-life incident challenges the idea of inherent human savagery and underscores the capacity for cooperation and altruism in difficult situations.

Another example to challenge the commonly held belief that disasters bring out the worst in people concerns Hurricane Katrina, which hit the southern part of the US in 2005. Contrary to the media reports and popular narratives that portrayed widespread looting and violence in the aftermath of the hurricane, Bregman points to evidence that shows a different reality. He highlights how, in the wake of the hurricane, there were numerous instances of people coming together to help each other. Communities organized rescue efforts and provided shelter, food and support to those affected. This communal and cooperative response was far more prevalent than the instances of violence and looting that were widely reported in the media.

Bregman uses this case to argue against the notion that society quickly descends into chaos and selfishness in the face of disaster. Instead, he suggests that such crises often bring out the best in people, fostering a sense of solidarity, empathy and cooperation. This perspective aligns with his broader thesis in the book, which posits that humans are fundamentally good and, given the right circumstances, will act in ways that are beneficial to themselves and others.

Tool: Human-centred design

The philosophy and core belief that humans are inherently good and capable of altruism and cooperation can be seamlessly translated into a human-centred approach in embedding sustainability in an organization. This transition involves recognizing and leveraging the innate tendencies of people towards collaboration, empathy and positive action for sustainable change. That is the essence of this book. HCD can serve as a crucial framework to navigate through this transition, ensuring that sustainability is not merely a strategy but becomes embedded in the organizational culture, guiding every decision and action.[5]

Beginning with empathy, HCD demands an in-depth understanding of the people within the organization: their motivations, their challenges and the barriers they face in adopting sustainable practices. Engaging in dialogues, conducting workshops and utilizing surveys can unravel the complexities and nuances of their daily operations and interactions. This empathetic understanding paves the way towards developing solutions that are inherently attuned to people's needs and capacities, ensuring that they are not merely compliant but instead actively engaged in the sustainability journey.

Consequently, a co-creation process should be initiated involving various stakeholders, including employees, leadership and even customers, to ideate and prototype sustainability initiatives. By involving them in the solution creation process, you not only garner buy-in but also unlock valuable insights and innovations that may otherwise be overlooked. This could involve, for instance, developing new workflows, modifying existing processes or establishing novel partnerships that align with the sustainability goals while respecting and enhancing the work of individuals within the organization.

Moreover, HCD focuses on rapid prototyping and iterative testing, enabling the organization to implement sustainability initiatives in a manner that is adaptable and responsive. Initiatives are tested, feedback is garnered and refinements are made in a continuous loop, ensuring that the initiatives remain relevant and effective in changing internal and external contexts. This flexible approach aids in circumventing resistance and facilitates a smooth, gradual transition towards sustainability, where each iteration is an improvement and a step closer to a more sustainable organizational culture.

In addition, HCD accentuates the importance of communication and storytelling, ensuring that the sustainability journey is not only shared but celebrated across the organization. Narratives of change, successes and learnings should be communicated in a manner that is relatable and inspiring for all. This, in turn, helps in building a shared vision and a collective commitment towards sustainability, fostering an environment where every individual feels valued and becomes a proponent of the sustainability agenda.

In summary, integrating HCD into sustainability strategy embeds empathy, co-creation, iteration and communication into the organizational change process, ensuring that sustainability is not an imposition but a collective, inclusive and adaptive journey towards impactful transformation. This not only ensures the fulfilment of sustainability goals but also fortifies the organization with a resilient, adaptive and deeply embedded sustainability culture, propelling it towards enduring impact and success.

Step 3: Integrate sustainability tasks into all job functions

The content below is based on our collective experiences and not specific to any one role or organization. Our core belief is that most people want to have a purpose in what they do and to contribute to a better world – in both their private and professional lives. Sometimes knowledge is missing, but when a clear pathway is presented and there is not too high investment required, most people want to contribute. More people are looking for a purpose; research shows how important this is to our well-being, contributing to better health outcomes like sharper memory, mood control and longevity.[6]

Inside most companies and organizations, a few people with sustainability roles have climate issues as part of their everyday work. But, according to the organization Project Drawdown, every job must be a climate job if we are to solve this all-encompassing challenge in human history.[7] We would take this statement further and include social and environmental impacts. We all have a role to play, and every job must be a sustainability job.

However, to shift sustainability from being a responsibility solely held by individuals with sustainability in their job titles to a shared duty across the entire organization, we need to explore what this broader ownership looks like in practice. People in management positions have more responsibility and capability to create impact than those working on the floor. But regardless of what position you hold and at what level you are in the organization, you can influence movement in the right direction.

For some organizations, the ultimate goal is the full integration of sustainability, embedding it into every level and function, infusing it into the corporate DNA. This pervasive approach promises a deeply ingrained commitment, but it comes with challenges, requiring a significant cultural and operational transformation. To mitigate risks, such as disruption and dilution of focus, a phased and balanced integration process is essential – one that is responsive to the organization's readiness and unique circumstances.[8] Regardless of the chosen path, embedding sustainability demands commitment across all organizational tiers. It calls for leadership that is dispersed, involving multiple agents of change and fostering collaboration and dialogue. This ensures that sustainability becomes intrinsic to operations and a defining metric of success. Within this ecosystem, CSOs and their teams play a crucial role in orchestrating the shift towards sustainable practices, collaborating with experts across disciplines. Their mission extends

Table 6.1 Governance model for embedded sustainability

Management	Middle management	Individual co-workers
Ensure an ambitious and well-communicated sustainability strategy. Create incentives and a reward system for co-workers and managers to drive the organization correctly.	Establish an open dialogue with co-workers to develop ideas and improvement areas. Translate the sustainability strategy into more concrete action plans and goals towards which each co-worker can contribute.	Even though co-workers might not make strategic decisions independently, plenty of actions stimulate movement (every little drop counts). Co-workers can point out improvement areas to management. They can join or establish local 'impact teams' to drive social and environmental topics. By coming together with others, colleagues or unions, co-workers can build a stronger voice to change things in a positive direction.

beyond strategy development; they must embed sustainability awareness into the fabric of the company's culture through education and engagement. Table 6.1 explores the roles that can be played by management, middle management and individual co-workers.

The rest of this section discusses a few examples of how different functions can gain ownership of sustainability. We believe that although this discussion is of a consumer-facing organization, it can be representative of other organizations and sectors as well. Thus, even though many job functions are not mentioned below, we hope the principles and thinking around how to make each function accountable for their part of the sustainability transition are clear. It is not about changing the nature of the function, but rather about using the position of the function to enable the most sustainable practices. In other words, a teacher should teach about sustainability's challenges and solutions; an engineer should focus on developing more sustainable solutions; and an architect can choose the most sustainable materials.

CEO/C-suite

Imagining a future where business decisions prioritize profit, people and the planet equally hinges on strong leadership, particularly from CEOs and top management. These leaders play a pivotal role in directing the business towards sustainability, fostering a culture that integrates social and environmental considerations into strategies and daily operations. CEOs are tasked with creating the right environment and dedicating sufficient resources for sustainable transitions. Without their commitment, sustainability risks being sidelined. Developing an inclusive culture is also crucial, in order to ensure respect for all employees.

In our experiences, as a former CSO and a country sustainability manager, having the CEO's support – including a seat at the table in executive meetings and adequate resource allocation to sustainability – was key to making sustainability a business priority.

Finance and business steering

The finance department often has a central and leading function in businesses and other organizations. Also, from a sustainability perspective, they have a crucial role in steering the organization towards more sustainable practices. The Deloitte report titled 'Four Faces of the CFO' summarizes the role of the CFO.[9] The four 'faces' include being a catalyst in implementing the strategy and steering operations, being a strategist and setting strategic goals, being a steward to follow up on performance and, finally, being an operator to ensure competence and efficiency in the organization. Thus, sustainability impacts the CFO's role as the company moves towards becoming a more sustainable enterprise.

In our experience, we worked with the finance department and other relevant stakeholders to set up appropriate and ambitious sustainability metrics for the business. We integrated sustainability into the overall follow-up processes and performance frameworks. For example, we included a KPI on store sustainability performance in the recurring store evaluation. We sparked change by simply starting the conversation and keeping sustainability at the forefront of the agenda. We tackled this from all angles – not just ticking boxes for compliance, but also meeting the needs and expectations of our customers and colleagues.

Legal

The evolving landscape of ESG regulations has necessitated a greater emphasis on related legal expertise within organizations. Legal departments play a pivotal role in interpreting and manoeuvring through this intricate environment, ensuring that their organizations not only comply with current regulations but also anticipate and adapt to emerging legal trends. They have the critical task of integrating ethical considerations into contracts, which serve as blueprints for conduct between parties. By infusing these agreements with moral principles, legal teams can foster a culture of responsibility and ensure that business practices align with higher sustainability standards. This proactive approach to legal strategy not only mitigates risk but also positions the company as a leader in ethical business conduct.

Therefore, along with increasing ESG regulations, the demand for in-house sustainability legal expertise within businesses is rising. We experienced this development ten years ago when human rights, product compliance and chemical use requirements were growing. Today, many new policies and laws are being drafted and quickly coming into force. Therefore, having legal expertise and taking action is a pure survival strategy.

Human resources

Putting sustainability high on the agenda within HR has advantages in several aspects. It starts with highlighting sustainability performance and ambitions in employer branding. As Chapter 2 showed, an increasingly large group of employees are interested in working for organizations investing in sustainable practices. New talent can be attracted by leading the way and showing that the organization is committed to social and environmental practices and that future employees can contribute to making the organization and its field more sustainable. Moreover, human resources are central to driving the diversity, equity and inclusion agenda. Employees should feel valued at work by their peers and employer. It is vital to create a thriving workplace founded on the principle that everyone can thrive personally and professionally.

Next to awareness and competence building, we also integrated sustainability into each competence and job description profile, and it became part of the performance evaluation process. This vast and sometimes ungraspable topic became more concrete and tangible for all co-workers in their roles, and changes on different levels of the organization were enabled.

Sales and commercial team

Sales organizations most often face the customer. Since customer awareness and demands on sustainability have increased over the years, the sales organization has an essential role to play in sharing the sustainability performance of both the products or services and the organization as a whole with customers. Although a smaller percentage of customers actively shop based on sustainability (and are willing to pay a higher price), companies must take responsibility to educate customers and make such choices easy. Therefore, the sales team should ensure that information about how the products are produced, what type of material they consist of, what type of packaging is used and how the products are transported – and how the products can enable customers to live more sustainably – is available in all relevant sales channels (for example store, online, customer support and so forth). The sales team can also communicate feedback inputs and customer concerns to the product developers to ensure they are moving in the right direction.

From a sustainability perspective, it is vital to stimulate responsible consumption. A circular economy means a model that reduces material use, redesigns materials to be less resource-intensive and recaptures waste as a resource to manufacture new materials and products.[10] The sales organization has the potential to develop profitable services that enable customers to care for the products longer, to repair them and to resell them to a new owner.

We invested in training so that the sales co-workers could share specific sustainability product features, and we developed in-store communications so that customers could learn about it. We also introduced new products, for example in partnership with social enterprises. One of these examples is provided in Chapter 3 (see the case study of Mireille Geijsen). Based on our design templates, i-did produced a couple of kitchen textile collections made from our pre-consumer textile waste. From unsold textiles, they made aprons, bottle holders and cushions. The products were made by people far away from the labour market. They were produced locally in Utrecht and sold in all our Dutch stores. It was a local and, to some extent, circular product created to improve livelihoods and inclusion.

Communications and marketing

The role of communications and marketing in sustainability involves sharing an organization's ambitions and progress, and the challenges that remain. Authenticity is key, as showing imperfection makes a company relatable. Transparency about sustainability challenges and seeking collaboration are as important as showcasing progress. Additionally, embracing diversity in consumer representation is crucial. This involves not only recognizing different ethnicities, sexual orientations and abilities, but also actively participating in inclusive public debates and reflecting diversity in advertising. Finally, engaging customers in sustainability efforts through marketing initiatives and creating open dialogues with stakeholders, including critical voices, is essential for a comprehensive and inclusive approach.

We were part of launching a sustainability campaign (in 2016) with the purpose to inspire people to live a sustainable life at home. The ambition was to create awareness about products and solutions that help consumers save energy and water, and limit food waste (and also save money). We also wanted to share our progress and ambitions in terms of sustainability. The intention was to create trust among customers and inspire other businesses to follow. Sustainability was the key message in all customer touchpoints for two months. The approach included a TV commercial, in-store communication, a newsletter, social media content and PR events. As a retailer, speaking out about sustainability at that time was not very common. The campaign resulted in increased awareness both internally and externally. One of the retail countries also launched an extensive engagement programme for customers and co-workers in making practical changes in favour of sustainability in their everyday lives.[11]

Customer relations

Customer relations is key to enhancing the customer experience and building loyalty by creating a strong bond and ensuring customers' needs are met sustainably. This includes offering circular services like removal, repairs and resell; ensuring carbon-neutral transport; and adopting an inclusive approach for people with disabilities, the elderly and families with children. It also involves collaborating with social enterprises to reach vulnerable populations, making customer relations an integral part of offering more sustainable and inclusive services. For example, organizations can partner with social enterprises such as Lazarillo to support people with visual impairments. Lazarillo offer a digital seeing aid that can support visitors to navigate more effortlessly in urban areas and building environments.[12]

IT and digital

The IT department can play a role in ensuring that the most sustainable equipment is used and that there are solid processes for e-waste and recycling. They can influence the organization's ways of working around the use of the products, such as turning off computers while not in use, lengthening the product life cycle, offering sharing options and securing responsible sourcing of products.

Moreover, as we increasingly shop online, the digital team has a big role in ensuring that accurate sustainability information is provided in online sales channels. They are also instrumental in ensuring that the right data is being collected and that relevant insights are created. Using AI and algorithms is another way that the digital organization can promote and enable a more sustainable lifestyle by ensuring that the most sustainable solutions are accessible and visible.

Facilities

As a business moves towards more sustainable practices, the facility department has a significant role to play in improving energy efficiency and waste management and incentivizing sustainable use of buildings. For any construction work or new build, there are several sustainability standards to follow to ensure that the most sustainable materials are being used, that there is proper insulation and that there are solid processes for procurement and human rights in construction.

The Shanghai Tower in China and the Bosco Verticale in Milan are two examples of sustainable buildings. The Shanghai Tower uses wind turbines for electricity, collects rainwater and employs energy-saving measures, cutting its carbon footprint significantly. Its design includes natural cooling and sky gardens. The Bosco Verticale, a residential project, features extensive greenery on balconies maintained with recycled water, contributing to urban biodiversity and air quality. These buildings exemplify the integration of sustainable technologies and designs in modern architecture.[13]

Next to the environmental aspect, the facilities department must ensure that the premises are accessible to everyone. Workplaces should provide spaces for wheelchairs, restrooms for mothers to breastfeed and visual aid for visually impaired people.

Design

Designers have a crucial role to play in sustainable development. Whether it is about industrial design, clothing, home products or city planning, a designer has tremendous power to make socially and environmentally conscious decisions. Statistics shows that around 80 per cent of the ecological impacts of a product are determined at the design phase.[14] This includes the entire life cycle of a product, including manufacturing, usage and end-of-life. A creator, or designer, can develop products and solutions that use circular design principles, meaning that they are designed for disassembly, reusability, dematerialization and modularity, and they are long-lasting. Designers can also strive to incentivize sustainable user behaviour, such as making it easy for consumers to repair or reduce overall consumption. In addition, innovation plays a key role in sustainability, enabling designers to leverage new technologies and creative approaches to develop solutions that meet environmental goals without compromising functionality or aesthetic appeal.

The issue of overdosage in laundry detergents is an excellent example of a systemic design problem that can have widespread environmental impacts. Both washing machines and detergent manufacturers have traditionally benefited from consumers using more product than necessary, either through design that encourages overdosing or marketing that suggests more detergent means cleaner clothes. This not only leads to increased costs for consumers but also contributes to environmental pollution, as the excess detergent enters waterways. Leyla Acaroglu, a sustainability-focused designer, actively challenges such design flaws. She draws attention to these and other environmentally detrimental design elements in everyday products. Through her initiative, the Unschool community, she offers educational programmes that aim to disrupt traditional learning methods and cultivate sustainable design thinking.[15]

Design is also crucial from a human rights and social impact point of view. Design thinking can transform the way we develop products, services and strategies. A design thinking approach combines what is desirable from a human point of view with what is technologically feasible and economically viable. Moreover, products and services should be designed with human rights in mind to shed light on important issues faced by vulnerable groups. Human rights and at-risk groups should be considered, from problem statements to prototyping and testing.[16] Finally, to the extent that designers can influence production, they should consider materials and production methods, and working with suppliers to ensure decent working conditions.

Manufacturing

Sustainable manufacturing is the creation of products that minimize negative environmental externalities, conserving energy and natural resources. It is about ensuring human rights and enhancing employee, community and product safety. People involved in manufacturing can apply circular principles to production, aim for zero waste production, lower energy consumption and ensure the best possible working conditions for everyone. Additionally, a significant aspect of sustainable manufacturing involves actively working to reduce carbon emissions. Next to the direct impact of the production, functions involved in manufacturing can review other potential externalities caused by their production. Negative production externalities occur when the production process results in a harmful effect on unrelated third parties. For example, manufacturing plants cause noise and air or water pollution during the manufacturing process. There could also be other negative externalities towards the surrounding communities, such as job losses, human rights abuses and so forth. Working with local NGOs and civil society can enable one to identify and reduce potential externalities.

For a purchasing organization, forging strong relationships with supply partners is paramount. It's essential to establish clear codes of conduct and maintain an open dialogue to address and navigate challenges collaboratively, rather than adopting an adversarial audit-style approach. Engaging with NGOs that bring topic-specific expertise can inform and enhance this process. Acting as a compassionate and proactive participant, rather than a detached buyer, reflects a commitment to ethical practices and human rights within the supply chain.

EXAMPLE Labour migration in production

In the beginning of the 2010s, the issues around labour migration, particularly in South East Asia, started attracting more attention. While labour migration can have beneficial effects for both migrant labourers and the countries employing migrant labour, the widespread global trend also presents several concerns. The legal and cultural context facing the migrant in the receiving country is often challenging in terms of poor working conditions, lack of formal protection, the practice of employers withholding passports, non-payment of wages and inadequate living conditions. Far too often, migrants suffer a denial of freedom of association and workers' rights, discrimination and racism. Thailand has played a significant role in international migration, and it is currently not only a country of origin but also one of transit and a destination. Several Thai industries – such as fishing and seafood processing, construction, agriculture and manufacturing – have become dependent on migrant workers as a fundamental part of their workforce. Migrant workers from Myanmar, Cambodia and Laos make up a considerable portion of the workforce in Thailand, filling positions that Thai workers tend to refuse because of low wages or harsh working conditions. The International Organization for Migration (IOM) estimates that there are around three million workers and accompanying family members in the country.[17]

For Lisen's master thesis, she decided to deep dive into the problem, the various actors and recommended actions. For six months, she conducted research in Thailand and Cambodia. In both countries, Lisen met with human rights organizations, the IOM and the ILO, and she interviewed migrant workers. She mapped the travel routes between common Cambodian communities and workplaces in Thailand and investigated various recruitment agencies. Within production and factory work, the main issues revolved around recruitment. The people interviewed revealed that the recruitment agencies – the intermediaries – had been forcing them into debt. Migrants had to pay almost a year's salary to the intermediaries for arranging the jobs. Because of that, the workers found themselves in a forced labour position, unable to leave due to their high debts.

Purchasing

Two-thirds of the average production-oriented company's ESG footprint lies with suppliers.[18] Therefore, procurement leaders who take bold action can make a decisive difference in sustainability. Many companies are already working to optimize resource consumption within their operations or engage with their local communities. However, taking their responsibility further down the value chain can have an even more significant positive impact. Multinational companies contribute to lifting industry standards when they set requirements on suppliers and business partners. They have the power to influence improvements in energy efficiency, fair trade, responsible sourcing and decent working conditions where employees feel respected and valued.

Purchasers can also support the growth and impact creation of social and other impact enterprises by actively searching for such partnerships. Social enterprises are businesses that are founded with the purpose of solving social and environmental challenges, and they often generate jobs and provide solutions for vulnerable people. Unilever, Microsoft and SAP are examples of corporations partnering with social enterprises.[19] Next to contributing to impact creation, the benefits for the companies include learning from various sectors and smaller agile organizations.

Packaging

Packaging, whether for food, electronics or clothing, has a purpose. The primary purpose of packaging is to protect its contents from damage. During transport, handling and storage, products risk getting broken. However, as packaging is also an element of brand communication, it is often overused. Sustainable packaging refers to sourcing, developing and using packaging solutions with minimal environmental impact and footprint.

People working with packaging have a vital role in ensuring that it is fit for purpose, protects its content, saves resources and minimizes its carbon footprint through energy-efficient production and sustainably sourced raw materials. It is also essential to ensure that the design, level of user-friendliness and materials cycle will contribute to creating the perfect environmentally friendly packaging. Today, most product packaging assumes that all consumers are fully non-disabled. Those with disabilities, injuries and illnesses aren't considered. Inclusive packaging should therefore consider diversities of ability, language, culture, gender, age and other forms of human difference.

Transport/logistics

Sustainable transportation includes walking, cycling, car sharing and green vehicles, and thus has a lower environmental impact that traditional means of transport. In terms of goods transport, there has been development in emission and planning efficiencies. People involved in this sector can positively influence the social and environmental conditions of transportation while reducing costs through efficiency measures. Public transport can be stressful and unsafe for many commuters, including but not limited to women, senior citizens and people with disabilities. We, therefore, need to adopt a gender and inclusiveness lens when developing transport systems for the future. Everyone should be able to access safe and sustainable modes of transport.

EXAMPLE Policies for sustainable transportation

Chelsea Tschoerner-Budde, who has a PhD in sustainable mobility, works as a senior policy officer in Germany's Ministry of Transport and Housing. Her role is pivotal in guiding cities and transportation sectors towards sustainable practices. Chelsea's focus is on crafting policies that encourage and simplify the adoption of eco-friendly transportation methods for businesses. Her expertise lies in clarifying complex regulations, making it easier for companies to embrace and implement green transportation strategies. These policies are crucial in aligning corporate success with environmental responsibility, paving the way for a future where business and sustainability coexist harmoniously.

Chelsea's vision for the future of transport involves a shift towards mobility on demand, transforming how we view and use vehicles. This change will lead to an increase in shared vehicle services and ride-hailing options and enhanced public transportation, creating a well-connected and diverse transport network. Leveraging advanced technologies such as AI and IoT, she aims to improve route optimization and travel efficiency. A key aspect of her work is promoting the adoption of electric and zero-emission vehicles, contributing to the development of a more flexible, efficient and sustainable urban mobility ecosystem.[20]

Step 4: Create engagement (bottom-up)

Creating change in an organization can be approached either top-down, driven by leadership and structural changes, or bottom-up, fueled by employee engagement and grassroots initiatives. Both approaches are necessary for effective and sustainable change. Top-down strategies provide the necessary structure and direction, while bottom-up efforts ensure engagement, creativity and buy-in from the entire organization. A balanced integration of both approaches allows for harmonious and impactful organizational change.

Top-down change is directive and comes from the highest levels of an organization. It involves setting strategic goals, restructuring and implementing new policies. This approach ensures that changes align with organizational objectives and can be quickly enacted. However, it may sometimes lack the input and engagement of those at lower levels. Bottom-up change, on the other hand, emerges from employees and lower-level management. It's characterized by a more participatory approach, where ideas and initiatives are generated from within the workforce. This method can lead to higher employee engagement and innovation, as it allows for diverse perspectives and solutions. However, without adequate support and recognition from the top, these changes might struggle to gain momentum or might not align with broader organizational goals.

Embarking on a sustainability journey often requires balancing high-level strategy with on-the-ground initiatives, such as workplace waste management. To mitigate the potential for overwhelm, it is essential to establish a network of ambassadors and allies early on. Train these allies in sustainability, enabling them to take the reins on tasks like representing green initiatives in meetings, contributing to corporate communications or innovating on workplace sustainability practices. Their early engagement not only aids in distributing the workload but also cultivates a robust community of informed champions for sustainability. By leveraging these allies, you can focus on pivotal leadership roles, securing the success of both individuals' and the organization's sustainability trajectory. As these champions grow in their roles, they perpetuate the culture of sustainability and innovation across the organization.

Tool: Establishing and supporting sustainability forums

A useful approach is to create or support the creation and existence of various sustainability groups and forums. Establishing processes that champion bottom-up innovation is critical for the efficacy of both social ambassadors and sustainability groups, ensuring they are supported and enabled in their endeavours. By allowing every member of the organization to voice ideas and contribute to sustainable solutions, you cultivate an environment ripe for change. Platforms for this exchange – whether digital forums or physical gatherings – must be robust and readily accessible, enabling the sharing of sustainability-centric ideas and success stories. This not only fosters a movement that resonates at every level but also ensures that the collective efforts of social ambassadors and sustainability groups are amplified and integrated into the organization's operations and culture.

To make sustainability a core part of our work, it's important not only to take action but also to recognize and praise those actions, big and small. By highlighting and valuing these efforts, especially the voluntary ones, we show how they contribute to the bigger social and environmental goals. Celebrating these actions encourages participation and helps everyone see how they're part of a larger effort in implementing the sustainability strategy.

Sustainability groups

One way to harness enthusiasm and collective action is through the establishment of sustainability groups. These groups become incubators for innovation, driving sustainability through collaborative action and shared enthusiasm. They are the grassroots from which green initiatives grow, through organizing activities like tree-planting drives and clean-up campaigns. These groups may form organically or, if this does not occur naturally, support can be provided to facilitate their launch in various ways.

Engagement at the community and team levels is not merely about conforming to sustainable practices; it's about initiating a cascade of change that transcends organizational boundaries. A local car-sharing initiative or a second-hand market can spark widespread adoption, leading to profound environmental benefits. Broadcasting these green initiatives serves a dual purpose: it acknowledges the contributions of those involved and inspires further action both within and outside the organization. The narrative of a single successful sustainability project can act as a catalyst, prompting similar endeavours across the globe.

Social ambassadors

Another effective strategy is the appointment of social ambassadors, or sustainability ambassadors, as vital catalysts for change within an organization. Imagine a role within organizations that acts as the heartbeat of sustainability – this is where the idea of social ambassadors comes into play. These are not your average employees; they are the spirited forerunners selected for their passion for sustainability and their innate ability to galvanize their colleagues. It matters little whether they are part of the management echelon or embedded in the operational threads of the company. What is essential is their commitment to the cause and their potent capacity to engage and influence the wider workforce.

In conceptualizing the social ambassador role, envision them as architects of compelling sustainability narratives, crafting communication materials that resonate and motivate. Picture them at the helm of events that capture the imaginations of co-workers and clients alike, expanding the sustainability conversation beyond the confines of the company. Their remit also includes leading workshops that are as educational as they are empowering, tapping into globally recognized events to highlight the organization's social conscience. By training peers, social ambassadors become the stewards of sustainable knowledge dissemination, actively participating in and shaping sustainability reviews to refine the organization's green trajectory.

Allocating a segment of their professional time to these sustainability endeavours – say, 20 per cent – is not just symbolic; it embeds sustainability into the fabric of their daily work life. Through strategic recruitment, these ambassadors are given an official role and the space to have significant impact, thus encapsulating the spirit of engagement with structure that this book advocates. Empowered with resources and a definitive mandate, social ambassadors stand as the vanguards of sustainability, championing the integration of green principles into the cultural and operational tapestry of their organizations.

Tool: Nudging

Making sustainability the path of least resistance can significantly impact an organization's shift towards a greener future. Instead of penalizing non-sustainable actions, incentives should be strategically designed to encourage sustainable behaviour. The principle of nudging is a powerful tool in guiding this transition. By their very nature, people prefer the path of least resistance, opting for the easiest choices in their day-to-day decisions. While many people care about sustainability, the complexities of daily life mean that they often lack the capacity to consider the sustainability aspect of every decision they make. Hence, it is crucial to ensure that sustainable choices are the simplest ones.

The concept of nudging underpins this approach. It entails subtly guiding people towards more sustainable decisions through minor changes in the way options are presented. Rather than overhauling entire systems, nudges alter elements of choice architecture to make the sustainable choice the more attractive or more straightforward option. For instance, consider waste management in a busy retail environment. A residual waste bin that is the first and most prominent option will also be the first and easiest choice for busy co-workers. Placing recycling bins for different waste types – such as glass, plastic and cardboard – further away can make proper waste sorting an effortful task. To nudge co-workers towards sustainable waste management, this arrangement can be rearranged to make sorting waste as simple as throwing it away.[21] In another example, Coca-Cola and McDonald's partnered to encourage healthier beverage choices. By making healthier options the default on ordering screens, customers had to make an additional effort to choose sugary alternatives. This subtle change in choice architecture led more customers to select healthier options, demonstrating the power of nudging in driving more sustainable behaviour.[22]

The beauty of this principle is its broad applicability across different aspects of an organization. Nudges can be used to drive internal change, influence customer behaviour and even shape supplier practices. It's about recognizing and leveraging human behaviour patterns to foster a more sustainable future – making the sustainable choice the easy choice.

EXAMPLE Nudging in practice

A connection between vision and action can be facilitated by the art of nudging – subtly guiding behaviour towards sustainable choices without restricting freedom of choice. A nudge could be as simple as putting up reminders to switch off lights when leaving a room, placing recycling bins in accessible locations or promoting reusable utensils in cafeterias. By breaking down the high-level sustainability strategy into achievable, everyday actions, we can create an inclusive environment where everyone is aware of their contributions to the larger picture. It is in these collective, aligned efforts where the true power of a sustainability-driven organization lies.

Let's consider a practical example from a restaurant setting, focusing on the critical issue of food waste reduction. The dishwashing co-workers and those involved in food serving play pivotal roles in this scenario. By making slight modifications to their regular work habits, such as appropriately sizing meal portions or effectively managing leftovers, they can contribute substantially to reducing food waste. This seemingly simple change in operations can save a significant volume of food from going to waste.

There are good examples of restaurants tackling food waste by integrating food waste scales in their kitchens. The ROI of such scales is very quick, and kitchen staff will be happier not having to throw away perfectly edible food. Thus, tools such as these scales heighten awareness around waste, leading to more efficient food preparation scheduling and better portion control. This type of data-driven approach allows restaurants to dramatically reduce food waste and make a positive environmental and economic impact. It is crucial to not only highlight the positive environmental impact of such actions – like the reduction of carbon emissions associated with food production, packaging and transport – but also emphasize the monetary savings tied to reduced food waste. Linking individual actions to both economic and ecological benefits brings forth a tangible perspective on how everyday operations can contribute significantly to the broader sustainability objectives.

Another example is the practice of turning off appliances when not in use. It's a simple action that can make a substantial difference in energy conservation when practised across the organization. Cultivating conscious habits can lead to significant energy savings, thus benefiting the organization economically and contributing positively to its carbon footprint reduction goals.

Tool: The carrot-and-stick approach

Successfully driving sustainability and operational goals often requires a nuanced balance of incentives and accountability measures. This is where the carrot-and-stick strategy comes into play, fostering both motivation and adherence to standards. The phrase 'carrot and stick' may seem overly reductive, but it underscores a pivotal theme of this book: the drive to foster internal momentum towards sustainability. The goal is to transition from viewing sustainability as a solitary role to embedding it in every facet of the organization. The approach has two elements:

1 The carrot is related to incentivizing excellence:

   (a) **Recognition:** Countries or teams that excel in their sustainability endeavours are rewarded with public acknowledgement. For instance, a stand-out country manager might be invited to present their achievements during business plan weeks. Such platforms not only celebrate successes but also inspire other teams by showcasing exemplary performance.

(b) **Progression and bonus system:** Sustainability achievements aren't just recognized; they're integrated into the professional growth pathway. Whether it's through bonuses, including sustainability milestones in performance reviews, or even factoring these milestones into promotion considerations, sustainability becomes a tangible part of an individual's career progression.

2 The stick is related to ensuring accountability:

(a) **KPIs:** Establishing clear, measurable KPIs ensures that sustainability isn't just a conceptual goal; it has quantifiable benchmarks. Teams and countries have clear targets to work towards, making performance evaluation objective and consistent.

(b) **Performance reviews:** Beyond setting KPIs, regular performance follow-ups ensure that teams remain on track. Those lagging behind or not meeting set standards are quickly identified.

(c) **Regional oversight:** To maintain a consistent standard across the board, regional managers play a pivotal role. They ensure that underperforming countries receive the necessary guidance and resources to improve, fostering a culture of continuous improvement.

In essence, the combination of carrots and sticks creates an environment where excellence in sustainability is not just encouraged but expected. It reinforces the idea that sustainability is not a peripheral objective but central to the organization's broader operational and strategic goals. Integral to this is ensuring that sustainability seamlessly intertwines with business operations. It ought to be ingrained within the company's reward structures, performance evaluations and incentive systems. Furthermore, sustainability considerations should permeate company policies, be a staple in job descriptions and be woven into every functional domain.

Relying solely on the enthusiasm and dedication of a few individuals poses a significant risk. Passion can wane, and champions may move on. To ensure enduring progress, it's imperative to integrate sustainability into the organizational fabric. If your aspiration is to make a lasting impact, anchoring sustainability in the company's core processes is essential.

Step 5: Define a governance structure (top-down)

While fostering a culture of engagement is rewarding, it is equally important to embed these practices into the company's framework to ensure their longevity and impact. For sustainability to become truly established in an organization, it must be an integral part of every facet of the business – product development, packaging, transportation, communications and more. Consequently, it is a shared responsibility that should be shouldered collectively by all members of the organization. While engagement and inspiration are vital drivers of change, they are often transient, subject to the dynamism of human emotions and motivations. To create lasting change, especially in large organizations, it's imperative to institutionalize sustainable practices. This can be achieved by embedding them into the very fabric of the organization – its infrastructure, processes and policies.

By solidifying sustainability principles into formal structures, you create a resilient foundation that isn't solely dependent on individual champions or fleeting moments of enthusiasm. These structural changes become a part of the organization's DNA, ensuring continuity of sustainable practices even in the face of staff turnover or shifts in leadership. Furthermore, by integrating sustainability into core organizational processes and policies, it becomes a non-negotiable aspect of daily operations, rather than an optional or supplementary effort. This not only ensures consistency in sustainable actions but also fosters a culture where sustainability becomes a natural way of operating.

The model that we suggest in Figure 6.2 outlines a holistic framework developed to embed sustainability into key areas of an organization, ensuring thoroughness and long-term integration. It emphasizes the inclusion of sustainability in steering documents such as vision and policies, governance structures (including board responsibilities) and HR processes like job descriptions and trainings. Additionally, the model mandates sustainability as a core consideration in decision-making forums, reporting mechanisms and business planning. By doing so, the model ensures that sustainability is not an afterthought but a fundamental and enduring component of the business strategy and day-to-day operations. The elements of the model are discussed in greater detail in the rest of this section.

Figure 6.2 A governance model for embedding sustainability[23]

Steering documents
Integrate sustainability into existing documents and create new ones, steering the company regarding sustainability.

- Vision/mission
- Values
- Policies
- Guiding principles
- Process map/workflows
- Working methods

People processes
Integrate sustainability into existing documents that steer and guide the HR processes.

- HR idea
- Job descriptions
- Incentive schemes
- Development talks/introduction trainings
- Leadership trainings

Decision-making forums
Integrate specific tasks and responsibilities in the charters of the below forums.

- Board of directors
- Management team
- Committees
- Steering groups

Reporting
Integrate sustainability into existing follow-up and reporting tools, and create new ones where necessary.

- Yearly, monthly, weekly scorecards
- Annual sustainability report
- Functional review

Business Plan
Integrate sustainability into the business plan and budgeting process.

- Business plan
- Budget process

Steering documents

- **Vision/mission:** Your organization's vision and mission are the guiding stars for all activities. Including sustainability in these core documents ensures that all efforts are aligned with sustainable practices.
- **Values:** Corporate values influence the behaviour and decision-making processes of employees. When sustainability becomes a core value, it permeates the corporate culture and everyday actions.

- **Policies:** Policies provide a framework for decision making and behaviour. Sustainable policies ensure that the company's operations are environmentally and socially responsible. For example, a sustainable procurement policy would mandate that the company only sources materials from suppliers who uphold environmental protection standards and fair labour practices. This not only aids in reducing the company's ecological footprint but also fortifies its reputation as a socially conscious entity. Through such policies, sustainability becomes more than an ideal; it becomes a concrete standard of conduct that shapes the company's impact on the world.
- **Guiding principles:** These serve as a compass for the company's strategic direction. Embedding sustainability here ensures the business strategies are developed with long-term environmental and social impacts in mind. For instance, a guiding principle might be to 'operate in a manner that minimizes our environmental footprint while maximizing social benefit'. This principle could lead to strategies such as investing in renewable energy, reducing waste through circular economy practices or implementing fair trade policies in the supply chain. It's these principles that ensure sustainability is not just a side consideration but a core driver of the company's vision for success and its role in the global community.
- **Process maps/workflows:** When sustainability is integrated into processes and workflows, it becomes a part of the day-to-day operations, leading to more eco-friendly and ethical practices. For example, a process map for product development could include steps for assessing environmental impact, such as evaluating the carbon footprint of materials used or ensuring products are designed for recyclability. Similarly, a workflow in the logistics department might incorporate route optimization to reduce fuel consumption or guidelines for partnering with transport companies that use eco-friendly vehicles. By weaving sustainability into these processes and workflows, companies can systematically reduce their environmental impact and enhance their ethical practices, making sustainability an active and consistent part of their operational reality. This is not an easy fix; it will involve extra effort and potential cost conflicts, as sustainable practices are not yet standard across all industries. However, as more organizations adopt these practices, and with stricter environmental legislation, the availability and affordability of sustainable options are expected to improve, making these practices more accessible and cost-effective in the long run.

- **Working methods:** Every organization has working methods, which are the standardized ways tasks are performed to achieve business objectives. These methods encompass the processes, tools and cultural practices that define how work is conducted on a daily basis. When sustainability is integrated into these work methods, it ensures that the organization's operations are consistently aligned with environmental and social governance principles. This integration transforms sustainability from a concept into actionable practices, enabling the organization to operate with a clear conscience and a focus on long-term viability and responsibility.

Decision-making forums

- **Board of directors:** Integrating sustainability into the charters of decision-making bodies, like the board of directors, ensures that sustainability is considered in highest-level strategic decisions.
- **Management teams:** Including sustainability into the charter of the management team, and as a standing item on the team's agenda, underscores its significance as being on a par with sales, brand value, customer care and legal compliance. It embeds ESG into the core responsibilities of leadership, ensuring that strategic decisions and operational oversight are routinely evaluated through the lens of sustainable impact. This approach institutionalizes sustainability, making it a persistent and integrated element in the management team's mandate to guide the company's long-term resilience and ethical footprint.
- **Committees:** In many organizations, decision making is distributed among various forums, including specialized committees focusing on specific areas like HR, commercial operations or finance. While creating a separate sustainability committee can be beneficial, it's equally important to integrate sustainability considerations into the agenda of each existing committee. This approach ensures that sustainable practices are not isolated in a silo but are considered and addressed across all facets of the organization. By embedding relevant sustainability topics within each committee, organizations can ensure that every strategic decision and operational process aligns with their broader sustainability goals, leading to a more comprehensive and cohesive approach to sustainable development.

- **Steering groups:** Steering groups are typically formed to guide and oversee specific projects or initiatives, often temporarily. Their primary role is to provide strategic direction, make key decisions and ensure that the project or initiative aligns with the overall objectives of the organization. These groups can, through a hands-on approach, ensure that sustainability is not an afterthought but a key consideration in project management and operational changes.

People processes

- **HR idea:** The concept of sustainability should be integral to the HR philosophy, attracting talent who are aligned with these values. The HR idea should also link sustainability to employee health and well-being. By promoting a healthy workplace environment and encouraging work–life balance, HR can demonstrate that the company's commitment to sustainability includes the well-being of its employees.
- **Job descriptions:** Including sustainability in job descriptions makes it a part of employee responsibilities, ensuring that everyone contributes to the sustainability goals. As being specific about job descriptions is a central component of embedding sustainability, we have made this a step by itself.
- **Incentive schemes:** When incentives are aligned with sustainable outcomes, it motivates employees to work towards these goals. Recognition and reward systems should be designed to celebrate sustainability achievements. This can take the form of bonuses for teams that reduce energy consumption, awards for innovative sustainability projects or public acknowledgement of employees who lead community engagement efforts. This may also involve clear career paths that reward and advance employees who contribute to sustainability goals. This ensures that employees see a future in which their commitment to sustainability is a key component of their professional growth within the organization.
- **Development talks/introduction trainings:** These training sessions can educate and inspire employees about the importance of sustainability in their roles. This includes training programmes that educate employees about sustainable practices and how to implement them in their work.
- **Leadership trainings:** Leaders set the tone for the organization. Training them in sustainability ensures they can lead by example and steer their teams towards sustainable practices.

Reporting

- **Yearly, monthly and weekly scorecards:** Regular reporting on sustainability keeps it front and centre, allowing for continuous monitoring and improvement. Sustainability metrics should be integrated into all relevant scorecards and KPI dashboards, not merely as a separate legal requirement but as a core aspect of business analytics. This means evaluating material sustainability KPIs alongside traditional financial metrics like sales, customer visitation and costs, ensuring that business decisions are made with a comprehensive view of sustainability as an integral part of the company's performance and strategic direction. By doing so, organizations commit to steering their business with sustainability as an essential and inseparable factor in their operational and strategic success.
- **Annual sustainability report:** This document communicates the company's sustainability performance to stakeholders, reinforcing the company's commitment to sustainable practices.

See Chapter 8 for more on reporting.

Business plan

- **Business plan:** Different organizations approach their planning processes at different levels of detail, reflecting their size, context and purpose. While some might develop extensive, multi-year plans, others may opt for concise, one-page documents outlining their strategy for the upcoming year. Regardless of the format or time frame, the business plan is a crucial tool that guides the organization's activities and priorities for the designated period. Consequently, organizations should strive to embed sustainability within this planning process and documentation. This integration ensures that sustainability is not an afterthought or a peripheral consideration, but a fundamental and driving force in the organization's strategy and operations, guiding decision making and actions throughout the planning period.
- **Budget process:** The budgeting process varies across organizations, with each adopting workflows that suit its unique operational needs. However, incorporating sustainability into the budget process is a critical and challenging task that holds significant importance. To enact meaningful changes aligned with sustainability goals, adequate funding is crucial. Therefore, organizations should endeavour to integrate sustainability considerations into the core of their budgeting process. This integration

ensures that sustainability is not relegated to an additional project or an afterthought tacked on at the end of the budgeting cycle. Instead, it becomes a fundamental component of financial planning, intricately connected with the overall business model. By allocating resources to sustainability initiatives right from the start of the budgeting process, organizations can ensure that these important objectives are adequately funded and prioritized, reflecting their commitment to sustainable operations and growth.

Each of these components should be succinctly addressed and interconnected to ensure sustainability is not peripheral but central to the business's identity and operations. When setting up these infrastructures, it's vital to ensure they are adaptable. The sustainability landscape is continually evolving, and what's deemed best practice today might change tomorrow. Hence, built-in flexibility allows the organization to pivot and adapt to new sustainability insights or challenges.

Ultimately, the goal is to create a durable framework for sustainability that is interwoven into the organization's structure, processes and culture. This ensures that sustainable practices and improvements are deeply ingrained and not contingent on the tenure of current leaders or employees. Such an approach ensures that the advancements in sustainability become an enduring component of the organization, maintaining their influence and driving continued positive impact well into the future, independent of individual contributions.

Align the internal reward systems with the desired achievements and results

Shaping your organization's reward systems to reflect your sustainability objectives is another crucial step in embedding sustainability. Consider the instance of introducing e-commerce into the retail sector. Store managers are asked to encourage online sales, which risks diverting customers from their physical stores to an alternate sales channel. This shift can lead to a reduction in store visits and, potentially, in-store sales. Under these circumstances, why would a store manager willingly support this transition? The answer lies in aligning the reward system with the intended change. If store managers' incentives are tied solely to physical store performance, they may resist promoting e-commerce. However, if their reward system is adjusted to encompass both online and in-store sales, managers will be motivated to encourage the new sales channel.[24]

It is similar with all sustainability initiatives. For example, often store managers manage and decide on their operational budget. If a store manages to become more energy-efficient, energy-related costs will go down, and the operational budget would thus be reduced for the following year. However, if the local budget is not designed to be earmarked for specific costs, and the store manager can decide how to allocate the budget, then the incentive to reduce energy costs is small, as the store manager's total budget will be reduced.

The key take-away here is that when implementing significant changes, it's essential to ensure that reward systems are aligned with the desired outcomes. This alignment fosters a supportive environment for change and mitigates resistance that may arise due to perceived threats to personal performance metrics. Aligning incentives with desired sustainability outcomes sends a clear message about your organization's commitment, serving as both a motivator and a measure of progress towards these goals.

Furthermore, understanding your company culture and what genuinely motivates your employees is fundamental. Monetary incentives might not always be the most effective driver for all employees. For some, aligning their work with their personal values and seeing their contributions to a greater cause could be a powerful motivator. Recognition schemes like 'Employee of the Year' for outstanding contributions to sustainability can also act as strong incentives. Additionally, consider the frequency and timeline of your performance assessments. A focus on short-term, quarterly reporting often prioritizes immediate financial gains over long-term sustainability goals.

In essence, embedding sustainability involves aligning your internal reward systems, recognitions and performance evaluations with your sustainability objectives. By doing this, you can motivate employees to contribute to these goals, thereby ensuring sustainability becomes a shared responsibility and an integral part of your organization's culture and values.

Summary and key take-aways

This chapter serves as an essential guide to decentralizing sustainability within organizations, emphasizing that the task is too expansive to be relegated to a single person or a small central team. Through real-world examples, the chapter has brought to light how different business functions and units can play a part in sustainability, making it an organization-wide endeavour rather than the purview of a few.

The age of siloed sustainability management is over. Sustainability is everyone's job, and it must be woven into the very fabric of the organization, from the executive suite to the mailroom. It is only when each member of the organization embraces their role in promoting sustainability that we can create truly resilient, sustainable businesses ready for the challenges and opportunities of the twenty-first century. The chapter has also stressed the importance of securing both a soft (engagement and bottom-up) and hard (governance and metrics) transformation. The core message is clear: embedding sustainability effectively necessitates a collective effort, one that brings together diverse skills and perspectives from across the organization. Moreover, we stress the importance of different functions and levels of the organization contributing and being aligned, as lack of internal co-ordination and conflicting goals can be real barriers. By embracing this approach, companies are better positioned to meet the multifaceted challenges and opportunities presented by sustainability.

In conclusion, to fully enact change, recognizing the pivotal role of culture is indispensable. The human-centred approach that we advocate underscores the importance of engagement and leveraging early adopters. However, for meaningful and enduring transformation, these elements must be integrated into the organization's structures. It's through this integration that behaviour is shaped and new norms are established, ensuring sustainability becomes second nature to every employee's daily routine.

Endnotes

1. Jacob Engel. Why does culture 'eat strategy for breakfast?', *Forbes*, 20 November 2018. www.forbes.com/sites/forbescoachescouncil/2018/11/20/why-does-culture-eat-strategy-for-breakfast/ (archived at https://perma.cc/9AMX-MJ75)
2. How to run a successful values workshop, Fabric Academy. www.fabric-academy.com/insights-tools/how-to-run-a-successful-values-workshop (archived at https://perma.cc/L9GR-SCDD)
3. Rutger Bregman (2021) *Humankind: A hopeful history*, Bloomsbury, London
4. William Golding (1954) *Lord of the Flies*, Faber and Faber, London
5. Lauren Landry. What is human-centred design? Harvard Business School Online, 15 December 2020. online.hbs.edu/blog/post/what-is-human-centered-design (archived at https://perma.cc/4WX5-W7QP); What's the difference between human-centered design and design thinking? IDEO Design Thinking. designthinking.ideo.com/faq/whats-the-difference-between-human-centered-design-and-design-thinking (archived at https://perma.cc/9W3U-PUT4)

6 Nick Craig and Scott A Snook. From purpose to impact, Harvard Business Review, May 2014. hbr.org/2014/05/from-purpose-to-impact (archived at https://perma.cc/65XP-7VS9)
7 Climate solutions at work: Unleashing your employee power, Project Drawdown, September 2021. www.drawdown.org/sites/default/files/210920_Drawdown_AtWork_06.pdf (archived at https://perma.cc/89K4-JP33)
8 How to make sustainability a part of your company DNA, UN Global Compact. unglobalcompact.org/take-action/20th-anniversary-campaign/how-to-make-sustainability-a-part-of-your-company-dna (archived at https://perma.cc/KW26-9VL3)
9 Deloitte. Four Faces of the CFO. www2.deloitte.com/us/en/pages/finance/articles/gx-cfo-role-responsibilities-organization-steward-operator-catalyst-strategist.html (archived at https://perma.cc/F72X-TUZZ)
10 What is a circular economy? Ellen MacArthur Foundation. ellenmacarthurfoundation.org/topics/circular-economy-introduction/overview (archived at https://perma.cc/5Y9B-DVWY)
11 Patrick Elf, Amy Isham and Birgitta Gatersleben. Above and beyond? How businesses can drive sustainable development by promoting lasting pro-environmental behaviour change: An examination of the IKEA Live Lagom project, Business Strategy and the Environment, October 2020. cusp.ac.uk/themes/aetw/journal-paper-lagom/ (archived at https://perma.cc/MJT2-VRD3)
12 See lazarillo.app (archived at https://perma.cc/B867-4Z4D)
13 Helen Roxburgh. Inside Shanghai Tower: China's tallest skyscraper claims to be world's greenest, *The Guardian*, 23 August 2016. www.theguardian.com/cities/2016/aug/23/inside-shanghai-tower-china-tallest-building-green-skyscrapers (archived at https://perma.cc/F8US-GUBB)
14 An introduction to circular design, Ellen MacArthur Foundation, 7 June 2022. www.ellenmacarthurfoundation.org/news/an-introduction-to-circular-design (archived at https://perma.cc/5QSN-N2RJ)
15 See www.leylaacaroglu.com (archived at https://perma.cc/S3V6-CAA3)
16 Caroline Sinders. We need human rights centered design, XD Ideas, 21 February 2020. xd.adobe.com/ideas/perspectives/social-impact/human-rights-centered-design/ (archived at https://perma.cc/ZQ85-AF35); The Human Rights Centered Design Curriculum. www.humanrightscentered.design (archived at https://perma.cc/QKL5-N5KC)
17 IOM, Ministry of Foreign Affairs to Promote Evidence-Based Migration Discourse and Media Reporting in Thailand, IOM, 1 September 2023. https://thailand.iom.int/news/iom-ministry-foreign-affairs-promote-evidence-based-migration-discourse-and-media-reporting-thailand (archived at https://perma.cc/H25K-RRMX)

18 Celine Cherel-Bonnemaison, Gustav Erlandsson, Ben Ibach and Peter Spiller. Buying into a more sustainable value chain, McKinsey, 22 September 2021. www.mckinsey.com/capabilities/operations/our-insights/buying-into-a-more-sustainable-value-chain (archived at https://perma.cc/3U9N-UMC7)

19 See, for instance, Francis Ahene-Affoh. Social impact and partnerships, SAP, 2017. www.sap.com/dmc/exp/2017_03_46558/enUS/stories/social-impact-and-partnerships (archived at https://perma.cc/8BRF-YPX8)

20 Interview conducted December 2021

21 Bryann DaSilva, Julia Dhar, Sana Rafiq and David Young. Nudging consumers toward sustainability, BCG, 20 May 2022. www.bcg.com/publications/2022/nudging-consumers-to-make-sustainable-choices (archived at https://perma.cc/98UD-CYDS)

22 Interview conducted February 2021

23 Model developed by the authors of this book. Inspiration: Anne Kwan, Maximilan Schroeck and Jon Kawamura. Architecting an operating model: A platform for accelerating digital transformation, Deloitte Insights. www2.deloitte.com/content/dam/insights/us/articles/5078_architecting-an-operating-model/DI_architecting-an-operating-model.pdf (archived at https://perma.cc/2J6N-ZY9C)

24 Sudheer Chava, Alexander Oettl, Manpreet Singh and Linghang Zeng. The effect of e-commerce expansion on local retail, Summary of NBER Working Paper 30077. www.nber.org/digest/202208/effect-e-commerce-expansion-local-retail (archived at https://perma.cc/G83P-C952)

Stakeholder and change management 07

The transition to a sustainable business model requires the engagement of a diverse set of stakeholders, both within and outside the organization. By understanding and addressing these stakeholders' needs, expectations and concerns, organizations can build the foundation for a more sustainable and resilient future.

Fundamentally, becoming an organization that operates within the planetary boundaries and in alignment with society's social contract requires change management – not only within the organization but often in terms of interacting with the wider stakeholder community. As with all change, it is about being clear on the purpose of the change, what you want to achieve, the benefits and drawbacks of the change and the timeline of the change. Fundamentally, it boils down to 'what's in it for me', no matter if you are an NGO with a long-term partnership with the organization, an employee who needs to adjust their day-to-day tasks or a shareholder wondering about the implications for the company's bottom line and long-term value creation.

This chapter will introduce the key stakeholders, outline effective change management tools and detail strategies for executing change throughout the organization, as shown in Figure 7.1.

Step 1: Map and understand your stakeholders

The engagement and cooperation of stakeholders within and outside an organization is crucial for the successful implementation of sustainability-related initiatives. These stakeholders can drive, influence or impede the

Figure 7.1 Steps in stakeholder and change management

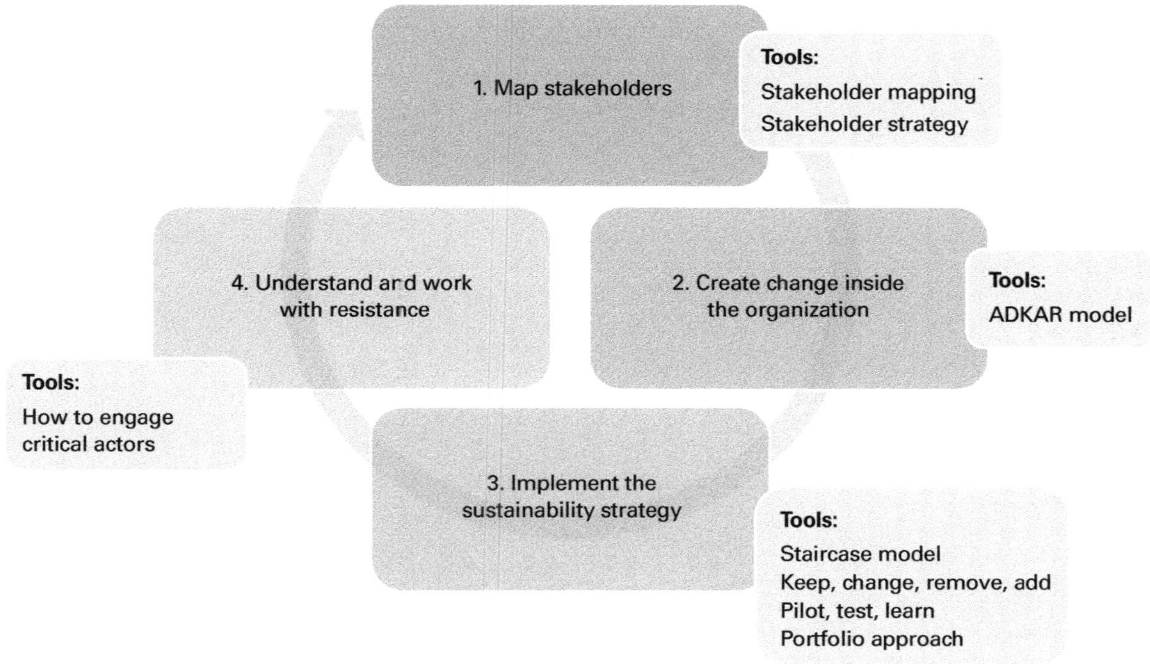

transition towards a more sustainable business model. Some of the most relevant stakeholders in sustainability are outlined below:

1. **Shareholders:** As the owners of the company, shareholders' perspectives and demands are crucial. Today's investors increasingly prioritize organizations that work with sustainability, given their potential to mitigate risk and generate long-term value. Investing in sustainability or ESG issues is on the rise, despite regional differences, underscoring the growing demand for sustainable business practices among the investment community. Family offices being passed on to the younger generation has led to an increasing focus on sustainability-related investments.[1]
2. **Board members:** The board of directors governs the strategic direction of the organization and has a fiduciary duty towards the company and its shareholders. They have a responsibility to consider the long-term viability of the company, making them crucial stakeholders in sustainability. Board members have a primary duty to the company and the shareholders that they serve, ensuring the company's management is taking the right value-creating steps, both in the present and for the future.[2] This is vital, because shareholders often aren't privy to the daily workings of the company. As such, a significant portion of a board's time goes into examining past financials and forecasting future scenarios.[3] A board that understands and embraces sustainability can effectively integrate these concepts into the company's overall strategy, setting the tone from the top. Pia has gathered experience from her roles on various boards, driving sustainability agendas in companies spanning different sectors and regions: 'We evaluate the sustainability impact of our organization, assessing how we're advancing towards our sustainability objectives while reflecting on our business strategies and exploring emerging business models.'
3. **Employees:** Co-workers are an organization's most valuable asset, and their engagement in sustainability efforts is critical. As outlined in Chapter 2, many employees today seek out employers that align with their values, making sustainability a key differentiator in talent acquisition and retention. Moreover, employees can act as change agents, driving sustainability initiatives at all levels of the company. You can, for example, engage co-workers in sustainability by promoting inclusivity and ownership. Encourage them to help craft the strategy, which increases commitment. Utilize employee surveys and workshops for feedback and

education to refine sustainability initiatives. Launching the strategy as a major event can boost enthusiasm and participation, transforming sustainability into a shared corporate culture.

4 **Customers:** The market demand for sustainable products and services is growing. Consumers are increasingly making purchase decisions based on a company's environmental and social performance. Thus, meeting these consumer demands is not only a matter of good corporate citizenship but also a business imperative. Younger consumers, especially millennials and Gen Z, are becoming increasingly aware and demanding in their purchasing decisions, thanks to greater access to information and heightened understanding of global issues. Their strong desire for transparency has led them to favour companies that demonstrate responsible and sustainable practices. This growing demand is driving a significant shift towards sustainability in various industries.

5 **Suppliers and business partners:** An organization's sustainability efforts extend to its supply chain. Suppliers and business partners play a significant role in the environmental and social impacts of a company. It is, therefore, important to engage with these stakeholders to ensure they also follow sustainable practices.

6 **Government and regulators:** Laws, regulations and policy incentives play a major role in promoting or limiting sustainable practices. Government bodies and regulators can impose standards and create conditions that foster sustainable business. Understanding the regulatory landscape and engaging proactively with these entities can help a company navigate towards sustainability.

7 **NGOs and critics:** NGOs, activists and critics can put pressure on companies to improve their sustainability performance. NGOs, moreover, often act as proxies (or voices) for nature or vulnerable groups. While it may be tempting to view these stakeholders as adversaries, they can provide valuable external perspectives and highlight areas for improvement. Engaging constructively with these stakeholders can improve a company's reputation and help it avoid potential pitfalls.

8 **Communities:** Local communities affected by a company's operations are crucial stakeholders. They can support or resist projects based on their perceived impact on the community's well-being. Building relationships with these communities, addressing their concerns and providing benefits can create a supportive environment for the company's operations.

Understanding various stakeholders and their perspectives

Behaviour change is a critical component of embedding sustainability within an organization. It involves influencing attitudes and actions at every level, from top management to frontline staff, and among all stakeholders, from suppliers and partners to customers and communities. The complexity of behaviour change lies in the diversity of motivations and trigger points that exist across these different groups.

People are motivated by a range of factors. For some, the prospect of financial gains or cost savings could be a strong motivator, while for others the desire to create a positive social impact might be a driving force. Some might be motivated by the opportunity to learn new skills or by earning recognition among their peers. Understanding these different motivations is key to designing effective engagement strategies and tools. For example, to engage employees in a company-wide energy-saving initiative, a combination of strategies could be used. This could include providing training on energy-efficient practices, setting up a rewards system for departments that achieve the highest energy savings and celebrating success stories in company communications. To engage suppliers in sustainability efforts, the company could offer incentives such as preferential contracts to suppliers who meet certain sustainability standards.

Trigger points refer to the moments or events that prompt people to change their behaviour. These could be personal experiences, like witnessing the impacts of climate change, or external events, like new regulations or market trends. Trigger points could also be created intentionally, such as by setting clear targets and deadlines or by launching campaigns that raise awareness and urgency around sustainability issues. Engagement tools are the methods and channels used to communicate with and influence different stakeholders. These could range from face-to-face meetings and workshops to digital platforms and social media campaigns. When choosing tools, one should consider the preferences and habits of the target groups. For example, younger employees might respond well to interactive online learning platforms, while older employees might prefer more traditional training sessions.

Lastly, to create win-win solutions, it is crucial to put oneself in the shoes of others, to understand their perspectives, interests and constraints. This involves active listening, empathy and dialogue. It also involves looking for opportunities where sustainability can enhance value for different stakeholders, whether it's improving operational efficiency, enhancing brand reputation or delivering innovative products and services that meet the growing demand for sustainability. Empathy, or the ability to understand and share the feelings of another, is an essential skill in this process. It is not merely about comprehending another's point of view; rather, it is about truly feeling it, walking in their shoes. Practising empathy helps us to bridge gaps between different stakeholders, enabling us to tailor our approach to meet them where they are and to address their unique concerns and aspirations. For instance, empathizing with a supplier might involve understanding the pressures they face, their capacity constraints and their motivations; this can, in turn, inform a more collaborative and effective sustainability partnership.

Additionally, empathy helps to foster an inclusive and supportive culture within an organization, making it easier for people to adopt new behaviour and embrace change. When employees feel heard and understood, they are more likely to contribute their ideas, take ownership of their actions and support organizational goals. Moreover, empathetic leaders can inspire and engage their teams more effectively. By acknowledging the challenges and appreciating the efforts of their team members, leaders can build trust and motivate their teams towards the shared vision of sustainability. Thus, empathy is not only a valuable interpersonal skill, but also a strategic tool for driving sustainable change.

CASE STUDY Everyone may not care about trees, but they do care about their children

Encouraging stakeholders to actively participate in sustainability can be particularly effective when the focus is on how climate change directly affects the future of children, making the well-being of future generations a persuasive approach for addressing certain stakeholders.

Our Kids' Climate is a global coalition connecting climate parent organizations and groups in more than 40 countries. The coalition was initiated in 2015 by Frida Berry Eklund and the Swedish organization Våra barns klimat (previously Föräldravrålet). Our Kids' Climate became influential by working with international groups and participating in major events, like the 2015 Paris Climate Summit, and by spreading a message that appealed to people beyond political or ideological lines – centred around the love and protection of children today, and generations to come.

Frida uses her communication skills to push for immediate action to protect future generations from the worsening climate crisis. Inspired by concerns for her children's future, she works to create change at a deeper level. She stresses the need for climate education for people of all ages, including training for teachers, and advocates open discussions about the climate crisis with kids.

She is also the co-founder of another public participation project, Klimatkollen (Climate Checker), which makes climate data easy to understand and encourages political action. Frida balances the urgency of climate issues with daily life, turning her emotions into positive actions like supporting environmental groups and dedicating her work life to creating systemic change. Her story shows that everyone can make a difference in promoting sustainability through their unique abilities and actions.[4]

Similarly, in the documentary *Decade of Action*, leaders from various fields pen heartfelt letters to their grandchildren, offering a powerful and personal glimpse into their hopes, fears and aspirations for the future.[5] These letters, filled with wisdom and emotion, not only articulate their visions for a more sustainable and equitable world but also serve as a touching legacy and a call to action for the coming generations, emphasizing the urgency and importance of the present decade in shaping the future of our planet.

To conclude, behaviour change is not a one-off event but a continuous process. It requires patience, creativity and a deep understanding of people and their contexts. It is at the heart of transforming an organization towards sustainability.

Tool: Forming a stakeholder strategy

Crafting an effective stakeholder strategy hinges on understanding what stakeholders need to know and ensuring they are equipped to take action. This involves speaking their language and meeting them where they are in their sustainability journey. Thus, the language and semantics around sustainability play a crucial role in engaging stakeholders effectively. It's important to frame discussions in a way that resonates with stakeholders' values and concerns. For instance, rather than narrowly focusing on environmental sustainability, we can broaden the conversation to encompass aspects such as public health, well-being and security issues. These terms strike a chord with fundamental human desires for health, quality of life and safety.

For example, discussing sustainability in the context of public health emphasizes a universally relevant issue, connecting environmental actions with the well-being of individuals and communities. Similarly, talking about sustainability in terms of well-being highlights its impact on our daily lives, while framing it as a security issue underscores the stability and safety challenges posed by environmental degradation. By highlighting the immediate, tangible impacts of climate change and biodiversity loss, such as the quality of the air we breathe, the water we drink and the food we eat, we bridge the gap between high-level concepts and personal experience. This approach makes sustainability an intimate and urgent matter, extending beyond environmental concerns to our collective survival and quality of life.

Therefore, a well-designed stakeholder strategy is tactical and intentional with communication, utilizing appropriate framing and messaging to transition sustainability from a specialized interest into a shared, imperative goal. It's about conveying that sustainability is not just about the environment; it's about safeguarding our common future.

Step 2: Create change inside the organization

So, how do we start bringing the various stakeholders into action? Embedding sustainability in an organization requires change management. The ADKAR model is perhaps the most established version.

Tool: the ADKAR model[6]

1 **Awareness:** Understand the need for change. This involves communicating with stakeholders about why the change is necessary and what the consequences of not changing may be.

2 **Desire:** Build a desire to support and participate in the change. This phase involves fostering a positive perception of the change among those affected, which can be done through effective communication and involvement in the decision-making process.

3 **Knowledge:** Know how to change. This involves training and education on the new processes, behaviour or technologies that are being implemented.

4 **Ability:** Be able to implement the change at the required performance level. This phase often involves hands-on work, coaching and problem solving to help individuals put their knowledge into action.

5 **Reinforcement:** Sustain the change over the long term. This involves rewarding and recognizing those who have adopted the new behaviour or processes and continuously analysing the effectiveness of the change.

These steps aren't always linear, and some may need to be revisited as the change process unfolds. However, this model provides a solid framework for understanding and managing change in an organization. For each of the change management stages, there are different tools and exercises to use to bring your stakeholders with you.

Awareness stage

The focus is on making a compelling case for change by understanding stakeholders' perspectives and clearly communicating the necessity and benefits of a sustainable shift. Key steps include listening to stakeholders to grasp their priorities and knowledge, articulating the reasons for sustainability from various angles (values, cost savings, customer expectations) and presenting current sustainability levels to highlight the need for change. It's crucial to acknowledge potential resistance, providing reassurance and fostering an environment of open dialogue. Leaders should illustrate the positive outcomes of sustainability, demonstrating their commitment through actions and leveraging influential team members to champion the sustainability cause.

Desire stage

The focus here is on building a positive outlook and motivation towards sustainable change. Leaders play a crucial role by clearly communicating the benefits of sustainability for the organization and individuals, addressing concerns and encouraging active participation. Key strategies include highlighting the advantages, such as cost savings, improved reputation and personal growth, alongside showcasing success stories and early adopters as inspirations. Persuasive messaging that connects emotionally and aligns with the company's values is essential to generate enthusiasm and commitment to sustainability. Involving employees in the change process and demonstrating the alignment of sustainability with the organization's mission further cultivates a collective desire to embrace and drive sustainable practices.

Knowledge stage

Here the focus is on equipping employees with the necessary sustainability understanding and skills. Offer diverse, engaging learning formats tailored to roles, blending theoretical insights with practical applications. Highlight each person's contribution to sustainability goals, promoting ongoing education and open dialogue. Leaders should model commitment and recognize progress, fostering a culture where continuous learning and the application of sustainable practices are valued and encouraged.

Ability stage

In this phase, the goal is to ensure that employees can effectively implement sustainable practices. Leaders should facilitate practical application opportunities, equip teams with necessary resources, offer guidance and align job roles and metrics with sustainability goals. Monitoring progress and being adaptable, demonstrating commitment and celebrating successes are also key. This approach ensures that knowledge about sustainability translates into tangible actions and results within the organization.

Reinforcement stage

Sustaining the integration of sustainability into organizational culture is key. Leaders should keep communicating the value and progress of sustainability efforts, celebrate achievements, provide ongoing support for challenges, update organizational frameworks to embed sustainable practices, conduct regular evaluations to ensure consistency, encourage open feedback and lead by example in prioritizing sustainability. These steps help solidify the changes, ensuring they become a lasting part of the organization's operations and culture.

CASE STUDY Art as a tool for change

As a perhaps unorthodox method within the business landscape, Laura Betancur suggests using art as a tool for change. Growing up during the Colombian armed conflict in the tumultuous 1990s, she found herself in the world of art. For Laura, art offered a sanctuary, an alternate universe where pain could be transmuted into expression, providing a silent yet profound dialogue between trauma and healing. Whether through theatre, music or visual art, she found solace and a mechanism to navigate through her traumatic memories without the necessity of verbal articulation. This early interaction with the expressive arts, not just as a coping mechanism but also as a subtle form of rebellion against violence, solidified her resolve to harness art as a tool for social transformation.

Today Laura works with communities, hospitals and schools as an expressive arts therapist, to forge spaces for dialogue, reflection and actionable change. The medium of art becomes a vessel through which participants, of different ages and societal roles, can engage in a therapeutic process, navigating their pain, healing and growth in a manner that is intrinsically connected yet individually expressive.

Through structured programmes, which feature methods such as sewing, painting, acting, writing and music, Laura guides participants on journeys of self-exploration and collective sharing. For instance, her programme aimed at women not only provides a safe space for sharing experiences but also serves to educate and empower participants through human rights education and emotional health awareness. Through exposure to female artists and activists who use art to challenge gender violence and social injustices, the participants are emboldened to leverage their own experiences for solution-oriented discussions and actions. Laura shows that art is not merely a tool for after-the-fact intervention, but possesses the latent potential to pre-emptively mitigate issues tied to racism, oppression and poverty by fostering an environment of expressive dialogue and empathetic understanding.

Her approach exemplifies sustainability as a concept tied not just to environmental and economic issues, but also to social justice, mental health and community empowerment. Art, transcending linguistic and cultural barriers, serves as a universal medium to communicate complex sustainability topics, fostering public engagement. In organizations, art enables employees to express and explore their perspectives on sustainability, fostering a shared understanding and collaborative approach to sustainability goals. Laura's work illustrates art's dual role as a tool for personal expression and a mechanism for collective action in sustainability.[7]

Step 3: Implement your sustainability strategy

Change management is a critical component in achieving the strategy. Implementing sustainability changes necessitates behavioural modifications at every level of the organization. This requires strong leadership, effective communication and an understanding of the cultural nuances that influence how change is perceived and enacted. It is essential to highlight the benefits of the change, align it with the company's core values and consistently reinforce the importance of sustainability through training and development programmes.

Translation of the strategy to action plans

Once you've formulated a high-level sustainability strategy, the immediate next step is its implementation across the organization. This overarching vision needs to be distilled into actionable plans tailored for various business sectors and hierarchical levels. To ensure ownership and buy-in from the organization, the process should be spearheaded by the respective owners of the specific action plans. As a sustainability advocate, your role is to provide guidance and support, reinforcing the significance of their contributions.

Ultimately, all employees should have an understanding of their unique role within this strategy. The connection between an individual's actions and the larger sustainability objectives should be unmistakable, tracing a clear line through sub-plans, unit plans, regional strategies and other organizational frameworks, culminating in the realization of the broader sustainability goals.

Change management, particularly when it involves embedding sustainability into an organization, is not a linear process but a dynamic, iterative cycle of continuous learning and improvement. This non-linear progression can be understood and leveraged through the concept of learning loops. Learning loops, whether they are single, double or triple, are fundamental to understanding how organizations learn, adapt and evolve. They represent a system of learning and relearning, as the organization navigates through the process of change, gathering data, learning from it and implementing changes based on those learnings. In single-loop learning, the organization makes adjustments based on what's working and what's not, while still staying within established systems and norms. Double-loop learning encourages us to question and challenge these norms and systems themselves, leading to more transformative changes. Triple-loop learning goes a step further by reflecting on how learning occurs, which can lead to changes in the organization's core values and beliefs.

During the process of change management, an organization should ideally be striving for triple-loop learning, seeking not only to improve and adapt but to continually reflect on and evolve the way it learns and changes. This approach is critical in managing complex issues like sustainability, where the situation continually evolves and the challenges are systemic. Moreover, embracing this cyclical perspective on change management allows organizations to view any setbacks or 'failures' not as a roadblock, but as a valuable source of learning. This iterative process is a fundamental part of resilience, adaptability and, ultimately, long-term success in an organization's journey towards sustainability. It cultivates a culture of continuous improvement, where learning and development are seen as collective, ongoing processes rather than one-off events.

Utilizing learning loops in change management involves a few key steps. First, establish clear, measurable objectives and regularly measure progress against these. Second, create a culture of openness and critical reflection, where assumptions can be questioned and new ideas can be tested. Third, ensure that there are mechanisms in place to feed learning back into the organization's strategy and operations, and to adjust goals and plans as necessary. Finally, communicate this process widely, emphasizing the value of learning and continuous improvement. This continuous learning approach, coupled with a genuine commitment to transparency and inclusivity, will enable organizations to more effectively embed sustainability into their ethos and operations, paving the way for lasting, meaningful change.

In your role as a leader, it's essential to understand that the fruits of your labour might not be visible immediately, especially when it comes to implementing sustainable practices. The transformation might seem slow, with many efforts seemingly not providing immediate returns. This is quite akin to shaking a ketchup bottle. You know the contents are in there, but despite your repeated attempts, they don't pour out instantly. However, like the ketchup effect, the change suddenly happens all at once. Your persistent efforts, investment and patience eventually converge, resulting in a rapid acceleration of change that may surprise you with its intensity and speed. This phenomenon reaffirms the significance of perseverance and strategic consistency. It is the validation of your long-term commitment to sustainability, often giving rise to a sudden cascade of benefits that further propels your organization towards its sustainability goals. In this process, every shake of the bottle – every little change you make – is important. Because even if it doesn't produce results right away, it is accumulating force, building towards that moment of breakthrough.

Tool: The staircase model – to set ambition level

In our pursuit of sustainability, it's crucial to recognize the varying contexts in which companies operate. A global strategy, while unified, must be acutely aware of regional nuances. To address this, one can use the staircase model, categorizing sustainability actions into three distinctive tiers: Must, Exceed and Excel. Each level is tailored to different contexts and stages of progress. Each unit, based on its capabilities and prevailing conditions, can opt to maintain a baseline level, push beyond or even excel. It's crucial to recognize that today's minimum standards may not suffice tomorrow. As the organization evolves, so too will the expectations.

1. **The Must level:** This foundational tier encompasses essential sustainability requisites that all units must achieve. It's especially pertinent to regions where practices like landfill waste disposal are still prevalent. While environmental concerns such as waste reduction and recycling are paramount, it's equally crucial to address socio-economic issues like corruption and human rights. Here, sustainability transcends just the environment, integrating ethical business operations and social responsibilities, from ensuring fair employment to fostering community development.
2. **The Exceed level:** This level propels organizations to transcend foundational sustainability benchmarks. Suited for regions with established sustainability norms, it encourages companies to challenge conventional standards. Initiatives might include advanced waste management, renewable energy adoption or championing industry-wide policy reforms.
3. **The Excel level:** Representing the zenith of sustainability endeavours, this level is tailored for regions where sustainability is a given, not an exception. To differentiate themselves, companies must be trailblazers. Whether it's by innovating sustainable technologies or catalysing systemic societal shifts, the mandate is clear: innovate, collaborate and lead.

Effective navigation through these tiers demands robust change management. Introducing sustainability shifts means evolving behaviour across the organizational spectrum. It calls for visionary leadership, adept communication and a nuanced understanding of cultural variables impacting change reception and execution. Ensuring these changes resonate with core values, coupled with continuous sustainability reinforcement via training, is essential. While the staircase model provides a systematic blueprint, the journey to sustainability isn't always straightforward. Setbacks, recalibrations or even ground-breaking advancements might change the course. Such dynamics are inherent in the sustainability voyage, and recognizing them is crucial.

Tool: Keep, Change, Remove, Add model – to evaluate and improve

The Keep, Change, Remove, Add model is a powerful tool in strategic work and engaging people in the process of change. It embodies the idea of incremental, ongoing positive change. This model allows organizations to systematically review and improve their strategies while involving people at all levels in the process. It supports the creation of a culture that values thoughtful change and continuous improvement, which is essential for sustainable growth and success. Here's how it integrates into strategic planning and execution:

- **Keep:** This step involves identifying what is currently working well within the organization. These are the processes, practices or strategies that have proven effective and should be maintained. Recognizing these elements provides stability and continuity, which are crucial for any change management process.
- **Change:** Here, the focus shifts to what could be improved. These are areas where current strategies or processes are not performing optimally and could be tweaked. The change aspect encourages the organization to evolve and adapt to new challenges or opportunities.
- **Remove:** This involves eliminating processes or strategies that no longer serve the organization's goals or have been identified as wasteful or inefficient. By removing these elements, the organization can streamline operations and focus more closely on its core objectives.
- **Add:** Finally, this stage is about introducing new processes, strategies or initiatives that the organization has not tried before but that could potentially bring value. This is where innovation comes into play, allowing for fresh ideas to be implemented in the quest for enhanced performance.

Tool: Pilot, Test, Learn – for iterative implementation

It's essential to create systems and initiate pilot projects that are inherently agile, meaning they should have concise feedback loops that facilitate rapid learning and adaptation. By ensuring these loops are short and direct, the system or pilot can adapt, refine and even unlearn processes that aren't yielding the desired outcomes. In a constantly evolving landscape like sustainability, the ability to swiftly course-correct based on feedback is invaluable. Furthermore, by managing roll-outs across different countries in staggered phases, the organization can maintain a level of agility. This staggered approach allows for the continuous incorporation of feedback, ensuring that each phase benefits from the lessons learnt in the previous ones. This systematic and phased methodology underscores a commitment to excellence and adaptability, ensuring that only the most effective and refined initiatives achieve global implementation.

The process typically begins on a small scale, ensuring that new initiatives are viable before expanding them further. This test-and-learn methodology allows for real-world examination of potential obstacles and benefits. Starting with a *pilot phase*, an initiative is introduced in a single store or perhaps on a country level. This pilot acts as a microcosm of the broader ecosystem, allowing the team to gauge initial responses, identify areas of improvement and understand the potential impacts of a larger roll-out. Upon a successful pilot, the initiative moves to a *test phase*. During this stage, it is introduced to multiple units or even several countries. This multi-market testing offers diverse feedback, catering to varied demographics and operational conditions. It's crucial in understanding the nuances of different regions and ensuring that the initiative is adaptable. Once the testing phase yields positive results and any necessary refinements are made, the initiative transitions to the *full roll-out phase*. At this juncture, the concept is introduced globally. This phased approach ensures that by the time the initiative reaches a global audience, most potential challenges have been addressed and the likelihood of success is maximized.

Tool: Portfolio approach

The portfolio approach presents a strategic alternative to the pilot approach.[8] This methodology stands out due to its emphasis on diversification and risk spreading, a stark contrast to the more focused and singular nature of the pilot approach. At its core, the portfolio approach involves simultaneously launching multiple projects or solutions. This multiplicity is crucial, as it allows an organization to distribute its risks across various initiatives. Unlike the pilot approach, which concentrates resources and efforts on a single solution, the portfolio method spreads investments and attention, reducing the impact of the failure of any one initiative. For example, a business aiming to create a circular business model might test multiple projects simultaneously. It could test one repair service, one buy-back service and one service focused on renting out products. By launching several smaller pilots concurrently, the business diversifies its risk and enhances its learning capacity.

This variety can be particularly advantageous in the field of sustainability, where solutions often need to address complex and multifaceted issues. Another significant aspect of the portfolio approach is its inherent flexibility. Organizations can dynamically shift resources and focus between projects based on their performance and feedback. This adaptability is crucial in rapidly responding to changing environmental and market conditions, which are common in sustainability endeavours. However, this approach does come with its challenges. It is inherently more resource-intensive, requiring significant management oversight and coordination. Balancing multiple projects, each with its own set of variables and outcomes, can be a complex task. Despite this, the potential benefits of uncovering multiple viable solutions can outweigh these challenges, especially for organizations with the capacity to manage such a diverse range of initiatives.

Step 4: Understand and work with resistance

Addressing resistance is key in sustainability efforts, as change often meets opposition from stakeholders due to various reasons. This resistance isn't always about unwillingness; it can stem from fear, insecurity or discomfort with the unknown. People may fear loss of control or failure in breaking away from comfortable routines. Sociocultural resistance might arise from social pressures or norms that discourage deviation. Systemically, organizations and structures often resist change due to entrenched practices, rigid hierarchies and bureaucratic challenges. Understanding these underlying causes is crucial for navigating and mitigating resistance in pursuit of sustainability.[9]

Within organizations there might be structural obstacles to change, like inflexible processes and procedures, or there might be a lack of effective leadership to facilitate the change. Power dynamics also play a key role in resistance to change, as those in power may perceive the change as a threat to their position or status. Systemic resistance to change can also be fuelled by the collective behaviour of individuals within the system. If the majority of individuals are resistant to change due to personal fears and insecurities, this collective resistance can permeate the entire system and make change even more difficult.

Concentrating efforts on early adopters in change management fosters an atmosphere of optimism, as their positivity can be infectious. Their immediate action allows for swift progress, establishing quick wins that can bolster morale. They serve as effective ambassadors for change, influencing peers with their experiences, and their proactive stance often provides insightful feedback for initiative refinement. Engaging those already supportive of the change promotes efficient resource utilization. Finally, as the initiative gains traction and its benefits become clear, general resistance in the organization tends to wane. However, it remains crucial to engage sceptics constructively, addressing their concerns to gradually usher them into acceptance of the change.

Tool: How to engage critical actors

Engaging critical actors within an organization is crucial to the success of sustainability initiatives. These individuals can be leaders, influencers or even sceptics who, once won over, can become some of your strongest allies. They have influence over their peers and can help to disseminate and reinforce sustainability values throughout the organization.

- **Identify key actors:** To start with, you must identify who these critical actors are. They could be department heads, team leaders or influential members who have a significant impact on their peers. Once identified, invest time in understanding their views and concerns, and what motivates them.
- **Build personal relationships:** Building personal relationships with these individuals can create a platform for open and constructive dialogue. Regular, casual conversations can help you understand their reservations and potentially uncover the root causes of their scepticism.
- **Provide relevant information:** Arm them with relevant, easy-to-understand information about sustainability and its benefits. This could involve demonstrating the positive impact of sustainability on the organization's bottom line and reputation, or even the personal benefits they stand to gain, such as skills development or job satisfaction.
- **Align sustainability with organizational goals:** Help these individuals understand how sustainability aligns with and can enhance the achievement of their own goals and those of the organization. The connection between sustainability and business success is a compelling argument for sceptics.
- **Showcase success stories:** Sharing success stories, both within and outside the organization, can help to illustrate the potential benefits and feasibil-

ity of sustainability initiatives. It's important to present case studies that are relatable and reflect the realities and aspirations of your organization. For instance, a CEO should understand how the initiative contributes to the business's long-term growth, while a marketing manager should see its benefits in terms of enhancing brand positioning and market presence. This tailored approach ensures that each decision maker perceives the direct relevance and value of the initiative to their specific domain.

- **Involve them in decision making:** Involving critical actors in the decision-making process can foster a sense of ownership and personal investment in sustainability initiatives. When people feel that their opinions are valued and that they can make a difference, they are more likely to buy into the process.

As for sceptics, while it can be challenging to engage them, it's not always advisable to invest heavily in converting the hardest sceptics initially. The energy and resources spent could yield higher returns if directed towards engaging individuals who are more open to the sustainability agenda. However, if there are sceptics who hold key positions, working constructively with them becomes essential. The goal should not necessarily be to convert them into believers immediately, but rather to foster an environment where they feel comfortable expressing their concerns and where their input is valued and considered. Over time, this approach may help to shift their perspective.

In conclusion, it is important to recognize that resistance to change is complex and multidimensional. It involves interrelated individual and systemic factors. Understanding these factors can help in addressing resistance effectively and facilitating positive change.

Summary and key take-aways

In conclusion, this chapter has mapped out the landscape of stakeholder engagement, providing valuable insights into the identification and management of key stakeholders. By offering practical examples, it has elucidated the dynamics of effective stakeholder relationships.

Moreover, the chapter has meticulously detailed the essential steps of change management, delving into the nuances of the ADKAR model. Each stage of this model has been explored, offering guidance on what leaders should be mindful of as they navigate the complexities of organizational change. Additionally, the chapter has laid out a comprehensive framework for embedding sustainability into the core strategy of an organization. By introducing a variety of tools and methodologies, it aims to equip leaders with the necessary resources to drive the sustainability agenda forward. The intent has been not just to inform but to empower leaders on this transformative journey, aiding them in orchestrating change that aligns with the greater goals of sustainability and responsibility.

Endnotes

1 Matthew Millard-Beer. The next generation bringing sustainability to the forefront of family office transitions, Itriom. 6 March 2023. itriom.com/staging-site/the-next-generation-bringing-sustainability-to-the-forefront-of-family-office-transitions/ (archived at https://perma.cc/5PCF-B7XJ)

2 Stephen Conmy. What does fiduciary duty mean? Corporate Governance Institute, 2024. www.thecorporategovernanceinstitute.com/insights/lexicon/what-does-fiduciary-duty-mean/ (archived at https://perma.cc/EU83-98PK)

3 Robert G Eccles, Mary Johnstone-Louis, Colin Mayer and Judith C Stroehle. The board's role in sustainability. Harvard Business Review, September–October 2020. hbr.org/2020/09/the-boards-role-in-sustainability (archived at https://perma.cc/T5FY-HE5M)

4 Interview conducted March 2021

5 Wim Vermeulen and Bart Lombaerts. *Decade of Action*, documentary, 2020. www.youtube.com/channel/UCVFWazDmG5mvMcNQwJX5gaw/channels (archived at https://perma.cc/2XNY-K4U5)

6 ADKAR change model, Think Insights. thinkinsights.net/consulting/adkar-change-model/ (archived at https://perma.cc/K2BK-JVJQ)

7 Interview conducted January 2022

8 See www.climate-kic.org (archived at https://perma.cc/8YKU-MRWF)

9 Brianna Herman. System factors for managing resistance to change, Acuity Institute, 19 November 2023. acuityinstitute.com/blog/system-factors-for-managing-resistance-to-change/ (archived at https://perma.cc/7R2J-LPH4)

Reporting 08

In this chapter, we turn our focus to the bedrock of effective sustainability strategy: reporting – or monitoring, evaluation and learning (MEL). The painstaking process of gathering data lays the groundwork for a robust monitoring and follow-up framework, which is an indispensable precursor for continual evaluation and learning. This iterative process is pivotal for adapting and refining your strategies over time.

While monitoring and reporting might not quicken the pulse for everyone, their role in catalysing transformation is unambiguous. The axiom 'What gets measured gets managed' aptly highlights the significance of this process. To kindle progress and propel change, it is crucial to establish a baseline and chart the journey transparently for all stakeholders. The initial stage applies irrespective of where you stand on the sustainability spectrum: what is vital is to capture an accurate snapshot of your current state by conducting an exhaustive assessment. This involves identifying the most vulnerable areas and pivotal issues through a materiality assessment, setting the stage for prioritized and focused action.

This chapter emphasizes the need to set up robust systems for tracking the efficacy of your change strategies, whether by employing KPIs, logical frameworks (logframes) or outcome harvesting techniques. We will explore how a pragmatic approach to sustainability is predicated on the availability of relevant data. By equipping sustainability champions with the data they need, individuals and businesses are better positioned to make informed, environmentally sound decisions. This empowerment through data can engender significant shifts. When organizations commit to sustainability and communicate their journey through transparent, real-time dashboards and regular reviews, they magnify their impact on the sustainability front. We suggest using this circular process for a reporting system in an organization, which involves a continuous loop of five critical steps:

1 **Understand the reporting landscape:** Begin by gaining a comprehensive understanding of the fast-evolving reporting landscape at local, regional

and global levels. This step ensures that the organization is up to date with the latest reporting standards and practices.

2 **Assess where you are:** Evaluate the organization's current reporting position. This involves reviewing existing data collection, reporting processes and compliance with relevant standards, which provides a baseline for improvement.

3 **Create a MEL framework:** Develop an MEL framework that outlines KPIs, data collection methods and learning objectives to guide the organization's reporting activities.

4 **Collect and handle data:** Implement the MEL framework by collecting and managing data. Ensure that data collection methods are robust and that the data handling processes uphold data integrity and security.

5 **Evaluation and learning:** Analyse the collected data to evaluate the organization's performance against its objectives. Use the insights gained for learning and improvement, feeding this back into the reporting landscape to understand the impact and progress.

Throughout this process, aim to actively utilize data within the organization for key decision making and ensure that the data is communicated transparently to all stakeholders. This transparency not only helps in maintaining accountability but also fosters a culture of continuous improvement and evidence-based decision making.

Step 1: Understand the reporting landscape

While reporting may initially appear daunting, it's essential to perceive it simply as a tool and process designed to organize your work systematically. Furthermore, it's imperative not to navigate this process solo; ensure you involve the pertinent stakeholders at each phase. Establishing this correctly from the outset will not only facilitate reporting but also enhance both internal and external communications. Below is an overview of how to approach MEL when embedding sustainability in your organization. Although our journey began in the assessment chapter, where we introduced the theory of change, and continued in the strategy chapter, with the delineation of the KPIs, what follows is a more comprehensive overview, exploring the entire reporting and learning agenda from A to Z.

MEL is essential for embedding sustainability in business by ensuring oversight, assessment and iterative learning to amplify impact. MEL not only safeguards and maximizes the impact of sustainability efforts, but also promotes accountability and transparently shares results. MEL is more than its components; it's key to aligning with and advancing sustainability and business goals through continuous improvement and data-informed decisions. Integrating MEL with sustainability ensures inclusivity and adaptability by involving stakeholders and staying resilient amid global changes. In application, MEL has been proven to shape the paths of sustainability projects by avoiding pitfalls like misaligned goals or lack of stakeholder engagement. Implementing MEL requires clear objectives, thorough stakeholder buy-in and adequate resources to lay a strong foundation for future strategies.[1]

When MEL and sustainability work together, they create a future that's not only sustainable but also resilient and inclusive. Further discussions will unfold how to effectively execute and refine MEL in sustainability, providing a theoretically and pragmatically sound road map. Keeping everyone in the loop about your sustainability efforts is like sharing the chapters of an exciting book, where your organization is the main character on a journey towards a more sustainable future. It's important to share the story – the highs, the lows and everything in between – with everyone involved.

An exciting road trip

Imagine you're on a road trip. Your stakeholders, like your team, customers and partners, are your travel buddies. They'll want to know how far you've come, the milestones you've hit and even the bumps on the road. Regular updates, whether they're big annual summaries or little check-ins along the way, are your postcards from the journey, keeping everyone engaged and excited about what's next. When your team sees how their hard work directly contributes to reaching those important milestones, it's like giving them a shoutout in your travel blog. It shows them their efforts aren't going unnoticed and keeps the energy high for the next leg of the journey. Setting clear markers of success and giving everyone a peek at the progress, through straightforward and open reporting, simply ensures that the journey remains enjoyable, inclusive and headed in the right direction. So, sharing the story – the data, the achievements and even the challenges – ensures your sustainability journey is a collective adventure, where everyone's on board, cheering for every step forward.

Tool: Working with globally agreed reporting frameworks

Navigating through the expanding sea of global sustainability legislation can be complex and ever shifting. While a detailed exploration of specific regulations might render this content quickly outdated, it's pertinent to highlight certain key aspects as illustrative examples. The imperative point to digest here is that the global legislative landscape is progressively steering towards intensified and more stringent sustainability reporting and practices. And it's not just Europe. From Asia to the Americas, legal requirements around sustainability reporting and practices are on the ascent.

Therefore, it's pivotal for businesses to not only comply with current laws, like the Corporate Sustainability Reporting Directive (CSRD), but also anticipate and prepare for future legislation by solidifying their sustainability practices and reporting processes as soon as possible. Why is this urgency crucial? Simply put, by establishing robust processes sooner, you're not just aligning with current legislation; you're also creating a resilient framework that can more easily adapt to future regulations, thereby safeguarding your business against potential future compliance challenges and enabling it to navigate through the evolving legal seascape with agility and assurance.

Embedding systematic, well-structured MEL processes into your sustainability initiatives is not merely about compliance. It's also about being prepared, being a step ahead and ensuring that your sustainability strategy is not only robust but also flexible and adaptable to changes in the legislative tides. With the established MEL frameworks and processes, your journey through the sustainability seascape will be navigated with foresight, adaptability and a keen eye towards the horizons of future sustainability legislations and trends.

Important reporting frameworks

The Global Reporting Initiative (GRI) is the framework of choice for many companies around the world when it comes to sustainability reporting. It offers a comprehensive set of standards that enable organizations to report their ESG performance with the same diligence applied to financial reporting. This widespread and internationally recognized framework is instrumental in helping businesses measure and communicate their sustainability impact, fostering a greater level of transparency and accountability in the corporate sector.

The Transition Pathway Initiative (TPI) is a global, asset-owner-led initiative that evaluates companies' readiness for the transition to a low-carbon economy, offering open-access assessments to the investment community.[2]

The CSRD is a new European Union (EU) directive that requires companies to disclose extensive information about their sustainability performance.[3] Companies have to follow the European Sustainability Reporting Standards (ESRS) for these disclosures.[4] Given the wide-reaching implications of the CSRD, it is necessary for companies to transition towards a more transparent and sustainability-focused business strategy. The CSRD's guidelines apply not just to European companies but also to those in Asia and the Americas, making it a globally significant directive. In summary, the CSRD is pushing companies to integrate sustainability deeply into their business strategies and to consider not just how the world affects them but also how they affect the world. It calls for a more comprehensive, strategic approach to sustainability, with close oversight from top-level management:

1. **Shift 1 – Integrating sustainability into business strategy:** The CSRD aims to integrate sustainability into the core business strategy. While executives often treat sustainability as a matter of legal compliance, the CSRD requires a more strategic approach. Companies must show how they have assessed business opportunities and risks related to sustainability. They need to detail their strategies for improving sustainability performance, and all this information must be included in a single report.
2. **Shift 2 – The company's impact on the world:** The CSRD also focuses on the inside-out view of a company's impact on society and the environment, termed 'double materiality'. While companies often look at how environmental or social issues could affect them (the outside-in view), the directive mandates that they also consider how they impact the world. This is expected to evolve management practice. For instance, a company might have to consider the effects of producing and using microplastics, not just how using such materials might affect the company itself.
3. **Shift 3 – Decision making based on performance drivers:** The CSRD aims to integrate sustainability considerations into corporate decision making processes. While non-financial performance indicators, such as employee retention, have been considered in decision making before, the CSRD mandates a more structured approach to include sustainability factors. Companies will have to articulate the methods they use to

allocate resources across different projects and investments that balance both financial and sustainability outcomes. This will involve the use of frameworks that can translate sustainability impacts into economic terms to facilitate more informed decisions.

4 **Shift 4 – Reliable sustainability data:** Data integrity is crucial for effective decision making. The CSRD requires companies to ensure their sustainability data is as reliable as their financial data. This is a response to the general scepticism around greenwashing, as highlighted by a 2023 PwC survey in which 94 per cent of investors expressed doubt over the veracity of corporate sustainability reports.[5] The directive mandates that an external party must assure a company's sustainability disclosures. This will necessitate improvements in the systems and controls used to collect and manage this data. Companies have a short time frame to upgrade their data systems, with the requirements coming into effect for the 2024 fiscal year.

Step 2: Assess where the organization is

As we have dedicated a whole chapter (Chapter 4) to the assessment stage, we here refer back to that discussion. However, remember that using careful and well-planned evaluations as part of your business strategy helps you keep an eye on, assess and improve your efforts in sustainability. In this way, your business can remain effective at dealing with the changing ways of doing sustainable business. Below we provide an example of how you can develop tools that continually assess your organization's performance.

Tool: Operational excellence audit

A useful tool to continuously and regularly assess where the organization stands, especially in companies with many widespread sales units (such as stores), is the operational excellence audit, which is a robust tool for assessing various operational aspects of an organization's stores. Overall, this tailored assessment tool serves as an invaluable asset for organizations aiming to achieve excellence. By covering a wide range of areas, offering customization and focusing on continuous improvement, it helps organizations stay competitive and responsive in an ever-changing business environment.

Often there are several different audit tools, focusing on different functions, while securing that interdependency between functions is also highlighted and assessed. Often, a specific function is unable to run optimally if it is not also engaging and working well with other functions of the store. There is, for example, the commercial audit, which focuses on the customer journey, exploring details like product pricing, availability, display and ease of purchasing. This section of the audit is designed to ensure that every aspect of the customer experience is optimized for satisfaction and efficiency. The customer audit, on the other hand, assesses how the store engages with customers and the local community. It explores practices like encouraging public transport usage, providing sustainability workshops and offering product return and repair options. The audit also examines the store's role in supporting social projects and collaborating with social enterprises. Finally, the sustainability audit addresses sustainability within the store's influence. It includes detailed examinations of environmental performance indicators such as energy and water usage, with a special focus on elements like lighting and waste management. This audit also looks into the integration of renewable energy sources and ongoing efforts for improvement.

Operational excellence audits involve in-depth, in-person evaluations that are not just about reviewing documents but also include physical inspections of the store to ensure that operational practices align with strategic plans. The frequency could vary, based on what each organization needs and how it is set up. Audits could happen as often as twice a year or as rarely as every other year. The people performing these audits should come from different parts of the organization to add cross-functional learnings. This includes staff from important functions, from the headquarters and also from different units. For example, staff from one store might help with audits at another store. This is a good way to share what's been learnt in different places.

During the audit or evaluation meeting, stores are encouraged to showcase their achievements. Specialists in various areas lead discussions, fostering a sense of shared learning and community among stores. The audit system incorporates incentives and competitions to motivate stores to surpass benchmarks. It aims to create a culture that values continuous improvement and aspires to outstanding performance in sustainability. Stores receive an overall score post audit and if improvements are needed, they are encouraged to develop and implement action plans.

Step 3: Craft a robust MEL framework

Crafting a solid MEL framework requires a particular and systematic approach in which the Theory of Change (ToC), introduced in Chapter 4, plays a pivotal role. Starting with the ToC provides a structured visualization of how and why a desired change is expected to happen in a particular context, linking outcomes and activities to explain how the desired change will come about.

Next, KPIs are set, coming directly from the ToC; they should be both relevant and purposeful. These KPIs serve as critical metrics for monitoring progress, while the evaluation component revolves around analysing data to separate the effectiveness and impact of interventions. Lastly, the learning aspect is integrated, which involves utilizing insights and data gathered to inform and enhance ongoing and future strategies and actions, thereby closing the MEL loop and ensuring continual improvement and adaptation throughout the project life cycle. In essence, the entwinement of the ToC, strategic KPIs and a diligent evaluation of insights collectively forge a robust MEL framework, guiding projects towards impactful and sustainable outcomes.

We believe that, just as organizations should aim for an integrated sustainability strategy, reporting and KPIs should also be seamlessly incorporated into the business performance framework. ESG data shouldn't be viewed merely as non-financial information; it is vital business data. Advise your team that if they don't observe an impact on the business from certain ESG KPIs over a span of a few years, those KPIs may be removed from the business framework. Metrics like diversity indexes and energy consumption are not just numbers; they are critical business data that can impact the profit and loss (P&L), perhaps not immediately, but certainly over time.

Tool: KPI selection process

Setting the right KPIs for your sustainability strategy is like laying the foundation for a building. It determines the strength and direction of your entire effort. As you weave them into your ToC and MEL framework, a few guiding principles can help ensure they effectively track and communicate your progress.

Firstly, always prioritize relevance. KPIs should be closely tied to your sustainability objectives, echoing the outcomes you're striving for. They should also resonate with your stakeholders, encapsulating the aspects of your strategy that truly matter to them. Ambition is key, but it must be balanced with realism. While your KPIs should challenge and inspire your organization to reach new heights, they should also be grounded, taking into account the resources at hand and the environment you operate in.

The ability to measure your KPIs is crucial. Choose indicators based on data that's both accessible and consistent. Setting a clear baseline for each KPI will also help in tracking progress. If you can't measure it, you might need to rethink if it's the right KPI. It's also essential to ensure that the progress on these KPIs is transparent to your team. Use tools or dashboards to visually represent this data, and regularly communicate updates. This keeps everyone aligned and fosters a sense of collective achievement. When crafting KPIs, remember the SMART criteria:

- **Specific:** Your KPIs should be clear and focused. To give an example, 'Make the company greener' is not a specific goal. 'Reduce greenhouse gas emissions from corporate operations by 75 per cent by 2028, compared to a 2023 baseline' is specific and measurable.
- **Measurable:** Progress should be quantifiable. 'Improve the company's impact on the environment' is not measurable, but 'Implement a recycling programme to decrease waste to landfills by 50 tons in the first quarter of operation' is.
- **Achievable:** Be realistic given your resources and constraints. An example of a non-achievable KPI is 'End all forms of pollution coming from the company immediately'. In contrast, an achievable goal might be 'Switch to 100 per cent renewable energy sources for all manufacturing plants by the end of 2024'.
- **Relevant:** KPIs should align with your objectives and stakeholder expectations. An example of a non-relevant KPI is 'Invest in an array of unrelated, small-scale community projects without a clear link to the company's core sustainability strategy'. A relevant KPI might be 'Invest in local community health programmes, aiming to reach at least 1,000 individuals each year with preventive health workshops and check-ups'.
- **Time-bound:** Set clear time frames for achieving the KPIs. An example of a non-timebound KPI is 'Aim to become more sustainable at some point in the future without setting a clear deadline'. And here is one with a clear time frame: 'Achieve zero net deforestation in supply chains by 2030 through sustainable sourcing and conservation efforts.'

These goals can span a variety of sustainability aspects, such as reducing carbon emissions, minimizing waste generation, enhancing energy efficiency, promoting responsible sourcing and prioritizing social responsibility initiatives. For instance, a manufacturing company might aim to eliminate its greenhouse gas emissions within five years. This overarching goal can then be broken down into smaller, more immediate targets, like implementing energy-efficient machinery within two years or switching to renewable energy sources for at least 25 per cent of its operations within five years. Concurrently, the company might set goals around waste management, such as reducing production waste by 30 per cent in three years, which can be achieved through measures like optimizing production processes and recycling or reusing manufacturing by-products. Including social responsibility in the sustainability goals is also critical. A company could commit to improving community engagement or worker welfare. This might mean setting a target to invest a certain percentage of profits back into local communities or aiming to achieve zero workplace accidents by improving safety standards and training. In a retail organization, sustainability goals might revolve around responsible sourcing. This could involve ensuring that 75 per cent of the products are sourced from suppliers that meet specific environmental and social standards within a set time frame. Such a goal could be broken down into actions like updating supplier selection criteria to include sustainability benchmarks and regularly auditing suppliers for compliance.

Discussing reporting in sustainability reveals that certain objectives are more straightforward to quantify than others. Let's consider energy consumption as an example. It's relatively uncomplicated to measure, thanks to available tools and its direct correlation with costs: reducing energy use concurrently trims expenses. Investing in renewable sources like solar or offshore wind often yields commendable returns on investment. Conversely, when we navigate through social metrics, complexities arise. Posing a goal like 'a better life for people' demands definition and specificity. What does it encompass? Using a company like Unilever as an example, their approach might involve creating products that foster sustainable living or partnering with suppliers and social enterprises that employ vulnerable individuals. Offering training and income opportunities does make a tangible difference. Here, measurements might involve the number of people reached or days of training provided.

If the focus shifts towards community engagement aiming for long-term change – perhaps aiding farmers to adopt sustainable practices that enhance yield and income – employing in-depth interviews could offer insights into the impact of your interventions. For exploring well-being among your workforce, detailed surveys might be the tool of choice, unravelling the nuances of the impacts of your actions. Always bear in mind that actions may usher in unintended consequences. Therefore, ensuring that your data captures all facets and formulating a responsive plan is crucial for steering towards intended goals while mitigating unforeseen setbacks.

All these goals, though diverse, are interlinked and contribute to a holistic sustainability strategy. Each goal supports and reinforces the others and, together, they guide the organization towards a sustainable future. The value of bringing in a third-party reviewer or auditor in this process cannot be understated. An external audit brings an unbiased perspective and can critically assess the targets' relevance, feasibility and alignment with overall sustainability strategy. Such external verification boosts credibility and trust in the organization's commitment to sustainability. It also offers an opportunity to learn from external expertise and incorporate best practices. Furthermore, in instances where certain targets are not met, an external auditor can provide a transparent assessment of the challenges encountered, lending credibility to the organization's communications about these setbacks. This transparency is key in maintaining stakeholder trust and demonstrating the organization's genuine commitment to its sustainability journey.

Finally, a couple of additional pointers: don't drown in too many KPIs. A few vital, well-chosen ones can be more impactful than a sea of less relevant indicators. Also, be ready to adapt. As your strategy evolves or as you face new insights, be prepared to tweak your KPIs. Engaging diverse stakeholders in the process of setting these KPIs can also offer varied perspectives and ensure broader buy-in. In summary, KPIs are the compass of your sustainability strategy. While they guide internal decisions, they also shine a light on your external commitment, progress and impact in the world of sustainability. By focusing on relevance, balance and measurability, and by adhering to the SMART criteria, you'll set the stage for a strategy that's both effective and communicative.

Step 4: Collect and handle data

Navigating MEL's complex landscape often presents challenges for organizations as regards data management. Data collection is crucial for monitoring and follow-up, with constant evaluation and learning essential for strategy improvement. Ensuring data quality is vital for effective sustainability strategies, as inaccuracies can lead to misguided actions. Resource constraints, especially in smaller entities, can hinder data collection efforts. Once collected, analysing this complex, multi-source data requires specialized skills, with organizations sometimes struggling to derive meaningful insights due to expertise gaps or data complexity. Moreover, it's critical that data not just fills reports but actively informs decision making, presenting a challenge in making data understandable and compelling for various stakeholders. Recognizing the difficulty in collecting perfectly accurate data, we recommend collecting 'good enough' data to support informed decisions, balancing precision with practicality.

To overcome these challenges, organizations can adopt data management tools to streamline processes, invest in capacity building to enhance data analysis capabilities, and ensure data collection aligns with sustainability goals to maintain relevance. Initiating pilot projects to refine data strategies and fostering a data-driven culture can embed effective data management practices. An iterative approach to data management, adjusted based on feedback and evolving needs, supports continuous improvement and alignment with sustainability objectives. This strategic approach addresses the critical challenge of data management in MEL, driving sustainability initiatives founded on insights and optimized through learning.

To drive change, establish a clear baseline and transparently share progress with stakeholders. The initial status, whether new to sustainability or already on the path, is less important than setting up systems to track change strategy progress, using KPIs, logframes or outcome harvesting. Imagine compiling a puzzle of data to depict your company's sustainability performance clearly. This marks the beginning of your journey in data management within the MEL framework.

1. **Using the right tools:** Think of using easy tools you already have to gather your data – like how you might use a handy scoop to collect puzzle pieces. Ensure the tools can help you see the data easily, maybe through simple charts or dashboards.
2. **Setting up smooth processes:** Map out a simple plan for how and when to collect your data pieces, ensuring you're not missing any and that they're fitting in the right places. Regularly check to make sure the pieces (data) are correct, and store them safely, but in a spot where you can easily grab them when needed.
3. **Involving your team:** Make sure someone in your team who knows the ins and outs of these tools and processes is in charge of managing these puzzle pieces. Ensure they know what to do through proper training and guidance.

4 **Making the most of your data:** Now, don't let those gathered pieces just sit there! Use them to create different pictures (reports, dashboards and so forth) that can tell everyone how well you're doing on your sustainability journey. Be open and clear about your successes and the places where the puzzle isn't fitting together just right.

Step 5: Evaluate progress and learnings

Think of assessing your data as somewhat like reviewing a novel chapter. Each piece of information tells a part of the story, and together they form a narrative about your sustainability initiatives: engaging, yet substantial.

1 **Analysing the narrative (assessing data):** Carefully read through the data, like you would explore the plot in a chapter. Look for key events (data points) that stand out. Are there surprising twists (unexpected results) or steady progressions (consistent data trends)? Your role is to sift through these pages (data sets) and understand the unfolding storyline (overall impact and progress).

2 **Explaining the themes (interpreting results):** Once you have a grasp of the story (understood the data), it's crucial to convey these insights to your colleagues or stakeholders in a manner that is succinct yet comprehensive. Utilize visual aids like simple graphs or charts to depict the trends and results, ensuring the critical messages are both clear and accurate.

3 **Discussing the book (communicating insights):** Share your findings with others, crafting a dialogue that is both informative and accessible. Keep in mind that different audiences may require various levels of detail and technicality. Whether you're addressing your internal team or external stakeholders, ensure that your communication is tailored to their familiarity with and level of interest in the data.

When evaluating and interpreting your data, always keep the end user at the forefront of your considerations. Ask yourself: how will this data be most relevant to them? What insights will they derive most value from? How can I present the data in a way that is most comprehensible and actionable for them? Tailoring your analysis and communication to the specific needs and preferences of your users not only enhances clarity but also ensures that the insights provided are truly impactful and actionable.

When embedding sustainability in an organization, think of the data as your guiding star, helping you steer, engage and motivate all involved. Let's say you've rolled up your sleeves and revamped waste management. If the data doesn't show improvement, it's like a plant not blooming: it prompts you to dig deeper and find out why. Are the steps clear to your team? Maybe the flow of work around waste needs a tweak? Or perhaps the change wasn't communicated in a way that everyone could grasp and get behind? Picture launching a pilot programme, maybe one aiming to bring closer those who are distanced from the job market. If data indicates people aren't eager to return, it sparks questions. Were there cultural barriers that were overlooked? Was the 'why' behind the programme not communicated effectively, or were individuals not involved from the get-go? Did existing team members feel their roles were being overshadowed? Each of these queries unveils a learning moment from your efforts.

The key is to weave learning loops into your practices. Picture a circular path where your actions lead to results, which you then analyse and learn from, feeding that understanding back into your next actions. Moreover, empower your team with a platform to voice their joys and concerns. It's like providing a space where they can share what plants are blooming brilliantly and which might need a little extra care. That way, every piece of data, every voice, becomes a stepping stone towards nurturing and refining your sustainability initiatives, ensuring they are robust, inclusive and truly making a difference.

Step 6: Share the collected data

Once we have collected this essential data, our next priority is to make it accessible to the entire organization. Transparency is key; it will enable every team member to track our progress, understand our successes, and also be aware of any setbacks. This visibility isn't only about information sharing; it's about fostering an environment where every individual feels personally invested in our sustainable growth.

One way to make this clear is to put together a dashboard (think of it as our puzzle picture) portraying important KPIs for each relevant unit. Such a dashboard helps to quickly and clearly show how each unit is performing, enabling management and other stakeholders to make immediate, informed decisions on the spot. In summary, think of data as pieces of a bigger picture. Managing it should be like gently gathering, checking and using those pieces to create a clear, full picture of your sustainability efforts. Your data tells the story of your journey, showcasing your wins and learning points, and the paths that will guide your next steps. So, keep it light, simple and enjoyable as you piece together your sustainability story!

EXAMPLE Solar panels for household use

Let's illustrate this with a clear, relatable example: solar panels for household use. The simple technology of solar panels transforms sunlight into electricity, providing a household with clean, renewable energy. Most contemporary solar power systems are equipped with real-time tracking devices, allowing homeowners to view their energy production data instantly and accurately. Just imagine how motivating it would be to see the immediate impact of using solar panels on your energy bills, as well as on the environment. You can watch the numbers go up as more and more clean energy is produced, reducing reliance on fossil fuels. This is exactly the sort of enthusiasm and proactive engagement sustainability leaders should aim for.

Summary and key take-aways

In conclusion, MEL needs to be woven into the entire sustainability journey, not appended as an afterthought. It's vital to embed these processes from the onset, ensuring alignment with overall strategy and keeping relevant stakeholders engaged throughout the journey. Starting might seem daunting, but remember that subdividing larger goals into smaller, manageable steps and collaborating with others can simplify the process. A culture of experimentation – testing and learning as you go – can foster a vibrant, adaptable strategy. Moreover, embracing a methodology that includes consistent learning and feedback loops not only fortifies the strategy but also ensures it remains relevant and flexible in changing circumstances. At every organizational level, communications and MEL should be directly relevant; all team members should be able to comprehend and articulate what the higher-level goals mean for them in their specific roles.

Thus, creating an environment where sustainability objectives are clear, tangible and interwoven into every facet of the organization ensures that the journey, though progressive, is coherent, inclusive and impactful. In other words, taking a step back, let's solidify our understanding with three key take-aways:

1 **Embed from the outset:** MEL and communications are not final steps, but foundational elements that need to be integrated from the start of your sustainability strategy. Their implementation should be apparent in every phase of the journey, ensuring actions and messages are aligned and purposeful.

2 **Collaboration and continuous learning:** Approaching MEL and communications should be a collaborative and iterative process. Embrace a mindset that allows for testing, learning and adjusting strategies based on feedback and findings, ensuring that your approaches are always evolving and adapting to maintain relevance and efficacy.

3 **Relevance at every level:** Ensure that high-level goals and strategies are broken down in a manner that makes them pertinent and actionable at every layer of the organization. This approach ensures that all team members, regardless of their roles, understand and can articulate how they contribute to the sustainability journey, fostering a cohesive and company-wide commitment to sustainability objectives.

Endnotes

1 The purpose and benefits of a Theory of Change model, The Open University. www.open.edu/openlearncreate/mod/oucontent/view.php?id=80572&section=2 (archived at https://perma.cc/GX88-HMYT)

2 FAQ, The Transition Pathway Initiative. www.transitionpathwayinitiative.org/faq (archived at https://perma.cc/W422-CYHV)

3 Take your sustainability transformation to the next level, EY. www.ey.com/en_dk/sustainability/sustainability-next-level?gclid=Cj0KCQiA67CrBhC1ARIsACKAa8QxtRVIrNM_YLCZoMxpd_ZMOoNz6sS_WzzsfjYo57_BJhMxPI3ro5caAmV0EALw_wcB (archived at https://perma.cc/XQ9U-NVUC)

4 KPMG. Get ready for European Sustainability Reporting Standards: Understanding the first set of ESRSs, November 2023. assets.kpmg.com/content/dam/kpmg/xx/pdf/2022/07/talkbook-get-ready-for-esrs.pdf (archived at https://perma.cc/NL82-EZM2)

5 94% of investors believe corporate reporting on sustainability performance contains unsupported claims: PwC 2023 Global Investor Survey, PwC, 15 November 2023. www.pwc.com/gx/en/news-room/press-releases/2023/pwc-2023-global-investor-survey.html (archived at https://perma.cc/4FA5-9Z6T)

Communication and advocacy 09

In placing this chapter towards the latter part of the book, we don't intend to imply that it's of lesser importance or that it should be the final step in your sustainability journey. On the contrary, effective communication is a foundational element that should be incorporated from the very beginning. Prioritizing communication in sustainability is essential, because it serves as the vital bridge that connects your sustainability initiatives with stakeholders, transforming passive awareness into active participation. A well-crafted communication strategy does more than just showcase your sustainability efforts and triumphs; it also narrates your organization's journey, including the lessons learnt from challenges faced. This approach allows your organization to articulate its story, emphasizing its mission, objectives and progress, thereby deepening bonds with all stakeholders. Internally, effective communication ensures that employees are informed and engaged with the company's sustainability goals, fostering a shared mission. Externally, it's instrumental in building credibility, shaping your market presence, satisfying regulatory requirements and presenting an authentic image of your sustainability endeavours to consumers and stakeholders.

This holistic approach to communication is not merely an operational task but also a reflection of your core values, forming the crucial conduit for fostering awareness, engagement and participation in your sustainability journey. At the heart of sustainable communication is authenticity and engagement. It involves sharing genuine messages and fostering active dialogue. Customizing your message for different audiences enhances its relevance and impact. Whether it's through compelling storytelling, data analytics or visual strategies, your aim is to create an accessible and engaging narrative about sustainability. Navigating challenges like message consistency and tone is part of the process, but the commitment to transparent and continuous reporting of both achievements and setbacks is essential.

Communication is an integral part of the sustainability process, which is about crafting an image and a message that resonate with your goals from the very start and weaving this narrative consistently through every step. Through communication, we bring to life the metrics and data discussed in relation to monitoring, evaluation and learning (MEL) (Chapter 8), translating them into a narrative that illustrates your journey, celebrates your successes and honestly conveys the challenges faced along the way. This open dialogue builds trust and encourages stakeholder engagement. In today's climate of heightened scrutiny, transparent and compelling communication is paramount. Effective communication ensures that sustainability initiatives are understood, embraced and valued not just within the company, but also in the broader community.

This chapter will guide you in developing a comprehensive communications plan that addresses both internal dialogue and public discourse. We'll provide practical tools and examples to help shape your messaging and explore how to manage communication during crises. Furthermore, we will delve into advocacy and partnerships and how your company can champion causes that align with your values and make a real-world impact. We suggest the following steps in order to enhance sustainability communications:

1. The process begins with an assessment of the organization's current sustainability positioning, in order to understand how it is perceived in terms of its environmental and social initiatives.
2. Next, the model guides you to define the goal positioning, helping to envision whether the aim is to emerge as a leader, an inspirational figure or a trusted brand in sustainability.
3. Following goal setting, the model advises mapping stakeholders, establishing the tone of voice and selecting the most effective communication channels, distinguishing carefully between internal and external communications.
4. The subsequent stage involves crafting tailored messages, stories, proof points and activities that resonate with the identified audiences and communication channels.
5. Finally, the model emphasizes the importance of advocacy and active participation in sustainability dialogues, as well as partnerships, reinforcing the organization's commitment to sustainable practices.

The process is circular, promoting constant learning and adaptation. After executing the communication plan, the process loops back to reassessment of the organization's positioning, ensuring that the communications strategy is dynamically evolving and responsive to the outcomes of the previous cycle. Each of these steps will be expanded upon in this chapter, providing a comprehensive guide to implementing a successful sustainability communications strategy.

Step 1: Understand your current position

An organization's current positioning in sustainability is a complex mosaic, reflecting how various stakeholders perceive the company's actions and commitments. To understand this positioning, the organization must engage in a holistic assessment that captures shareholder expectations, customer experiences, media representations and broader market dynamics.

As mentioned in the assessment chapter, the process begins with gathering intelligence. This involves evaluating the feedback from shareholders and discerning customers' attitudes, as they often hold up a mirror to the company's public sustainability image. The media's portrayal, too, is a barometer of public perception, offering insights into how the company's sustainability narrative is crafted and received. Beyond direct feedback, understanding market dynamics plays a critical role. An analysis of who buys the products, whether the offerings resonate with a younger or older demographic, and how the quality is perceived will contribute to the sustainability image. This narrative is further coloured by the company's voice in public discourse: does it speak out on relevant issues? Is it seen as a responsible actor? Are the messages authentic?

This initial exploration is more than just data gathering; it's a strategic exercise in self-reflection, setting the stage for the organization to align its sustainability ambitions with stakeholder values. By weaving together these diverse perceptions, a comprehensive picture emerges, serving as the baseline from which a forward-looking sustainability strategy can be developed – one that aims not just for incremental improvement but for transformational change.

Step 2: Define the goal of your positioning

The aspirations for your organization's public image have been articulated in the strategy chapter, where the broad objectives are set. In the realm of communications, these ambitions become focused on shaping perceptions across all stakeholder groups. It's about carefully crafting an identity that resonates with your values and goals.

Do you aspire to be recognized as a frontrunner in sustainability, setting the standards for others to follow? Is your aim to be known for providing the most sustainable products and services in the market? Or perhaps you seek to position your organization as a thought leader, influencing discourse and driving innovation in sustainability practices? This phase of communication strategy is where you refine how these strategic objectives translate into a public persona that aligns with your desired reputation and brand identity.

Step 3: Map your stakeholders – internal and external communications

As this step has been covered in Chapter 7 (on stakeholders), in this chapter we thus focus on the communications strategies for internal and external communications. One can use communications to explain three different aspects of a product: a product's 'footprint' (its sustainability credentials in terms of how and where it was produced), 'handprint' (what the product allows you to do) and 'brainprint' (the impact of marketing and media on people's values, mindsets and aspirations, enabling a sustainable and healthy lifestyle).[1] Using all three is a key lever in creating a link between purpose, innovation and customer engagement.

Internal communications: Empowering employees and fostering ambassadorship

Empowering employees to be the torchbearers of sustainability within an organization isn't just beneficial; it's essential for embedding a culture of environmental stewardship and social responsibility. An effective internal communications strategy is the lifeblood of this empowerment, facilitating a clear understanding of the organization's sustainability initiatives and enabling every employee to act as an ambassador for these values.

At the heart of effective internal sustainability communications is a well-defined approach that specifies the essential messages, channels and desired outcomes. This approach should clearly delineate the organization's sustainability goals and illustrate how they integrate with the broader business objectives. Effectively conveying this integration is key to demonstrating how sustainability is an intrinsic part of the company's ethos.

While this section primarily focuses on internal communications, it's important to recognize that employee ambassadorship also extends to external narratives. Employees who are engaged and informed are more likely to convey consistent and compelling sustainability messages to the outside world. An external communications strategy should, therefore, consider how employees represent the company's sustainability initiatives in wider conversations – from industry conferences to casual social interactions.

By intertwining an internal communications strategy with engagement, education, recognition and feedback, organizations can foster a culture where every employee feels empowered to lead and advocate for sustainability. This culture not only enhances the organization's internal operations but also strengthens its external standing in the global marketplace as a leader in sustainability. The collective voice of a workforce aligned with sustainability values is a powerful amplifier in the push towards a more responsible future.

Tools for internal communication

Communication channels and feedback loops

Diverse communication channels such as intranets, newsletters, webinars and town halls ensure that messages reach everyone. Feedback loops are equally important; they can be established through surveys, suggestion boxes and forums. These feedback mechanisms offer insights into how well sustainability initiatives are understood and embraced by the workforce.

Engaging employees in sustainability initiatives

Engagement is about creating a sense of ownership and participation. Employees are more likely to advocate for sustainability initiatives if they feel they have a stake in the outcomes. Organizations can engage employees through regular updates and interactive sessions and by inviting them to be part of sustainability committees or working groups. These initiatives allow employees to become active participants rather than passive receivers of information.

Education and training programmes for sustainability

Knowledge is power and, in the context of sustainability, it is the catalyst for change. Offering educational workshops, e-learning modules and speaker sessions can raise awareness and understanding of sustainability issues and the organization's response to these challenges. Training programmes should be designed to equip employees with the skills they need to implement sustainable practices in their roles.

Celebrating sustainability milestones

Recognition is a powerful motivator. Celebrating milestones and achievements in sustainability can reinforce positive behaviour and encourage continuous improvement. Recognition can be as formal as awards for sustainability champions or as informal as shout-outs in internal communications. Jody Michael, in her article 'Why we need to celebrate minor milestones,' emphasizes the importance of acknowledging and celebrating small achievements in our personal and professional lives.[2] She argues that while major goals are rare, the journey towards them is marked by numerous small victories that deserve recognition. Celebrating these moments can boost morale, inspire creativity and foster a positive mindset. The article highlights the psychological and physiological benefits of gratitude and underscores the 'progress principle', which suggests that making progress in meaningful work is the most significant motivator. It advises breaking goals into smaller, manageable milestones, tracking progress, giving credit and celebrating achievements as a team.

The external communications plan

External communications involve the strategies and actions a company uses to engage and inform individuals and organizations outside of its internal structure. This plan ensures that all stakeholders – from customers to partners – are informed, engaged and motivated by the organization's commitment to sustainability.

External communications are essential in advancing an organization's sustainability, playing a multifaceted role in both organizational development and societal impact. These communications enhance transparency and accountability, as openly sharing sustainability goals and progress invites external scrutiny, builds trust and demonstrates commitment to real-world impact. Publicly declaring sustainability goals also drives internal commitment, setting clear expectations and motivating employees and stakeholders to actively engage with these objectives. External communications strategies are vital in building consumer trust and loyalty in an environmentally conscious market, attracting customers who value environmental and social responsibility. By openly addressing both the successes and challenges in sustainability efforts, organizations display a proactive stance and dedication to continuous improvement, managing reputational risk effectively.

A robust external communications strategy for sustainability encompasses storytelling and dialogue with stakeholders, going beyond traditional sustainability reporting. This contributes to enhancing the business's sustainability strategy, bolstering talent equity, brand equity and reputation equity. It involves connecting different elements – such as purpose, strategy, reporting, engagement, partnering and advocacy – with steps, including framing the narrative, identifying sustainability stories, effective branding, getting the message and tone right, and being adaptable to the fast-moving nature of sustainability. Effective sustainability communications should be clear, credible, complete, compelling and customized to the audience, with a tone that is honest and appreciative.

Tools for external communications

Crafting the sustainability message for public release

The public sustainability message should be more than a statement; it's a narrative about the organization's journey. To craft this message, organizations must intertwine their sustainability achievements and aspirations with compelling storytelling that appeals to a broad audience. This message must be clear, transparent and honest, reflecting true actions and commitments and avoiding greenwashing at all costs. It should address the 'why' behind sustainability efforts, outline the 'how' in terms of concrete steps taken and illustrate the 'what' regarding the outcomes achieved and sought.

Media relations and press engagement

Media relations play a crucial role in amplifying your sustainability message. Engaging with the press involves more than just sending out press releases; it's about building relationships with journalists and influencers within the sustainability space. By positioning the organization as a thought leader and reliable source of information on sustainability issues, a business can secure meaningful coverage that not only informs but also shapes public opinion. Prepare media kits, arrange press conferences and be available for interviews to keep the conversation around sustainability dynamic and ongoing. Press engagements might include curated events, sustainability report releases or exclusive interviews about the company's initiatives. It's essential to provide the media with rich content such as case studies, infographics and compelling narratives that can be easily shared with their audiences.

Customer engagement and education

Educating customers is key to fostering a sustainable culture. Organizations should use every touchpoint – from packaging to digital platforms – to communicate the importance of sustainability and how customers can contribute. Initiatives can include incorporating educational messages into product design, offering workshops or webinars on sustainable living or creating interactive platforms where customers can track the environmental impact of their purchases. It is about creating an experience where the customers not only understand the company's sustainable efforts but are also empowered to make sustainable choices themselves.

Marketing for a better future

Marketing plays a critical role in promoting a sustainable future. It must go beyond selling products or services and focus on shaping consumer behaviour and mindsets towards sustainability. This can be achieved through campaigns that highlight the environmental and social benefits of products or services and encourage customers to take part in a shared mission for a better future. Sustainability marketing strategies can leverage digital channels to create targeted, engaging content that resonates with environmentally conscious consumers. Influencers should be employed to broaden the reach and sustainability metrics should be included in marketing performance indicators, to ensure that campaigns contribute positively to the company's sustainability goals.

Collaborating with partners and stakeholders

A comprehensive sustainability strategy involves collaboration with a network of partners and stakeholders. It's about joining forces with suppliers, NGOs, industry groups and even competitors to achieve broader sustainability goals. Communication efforts should highlight these partnerships and the mutual benefits derived, such as shared resources, collective impact initiatives or co-developed innovations. Stakeholders should be regularly updated on collaborative efforts through reports, newsletters or joint events that showcase the value of partnership in driving sustainable change.

Sustainability reporting and communication

View sustainability reporting as chronicling your organization's journey towards its sustainability goals. It's akin to crafting a detailed travelogue, where every step, challenge and success story is documented with clarity and precision. Not just a statutory requirement, it's a testament of your commitment, showcasing tangible proofs of your initiatives, impacts and learnings in the sustainability realm. Here's where the art of storytelling intertwines with data and facts:

- **Crafting and sharing stories:** Your sustainability story is unique and deserves to be told in a manner that resonates with the audience. Integrating both data (the what and how much) and narratives (the why and how) creates a compelling story that conveys not only the impacts and outcomes but also the ethos and efforts behind them.
- **Engaging with stakeholders:** Stakeholder engagement is about building relationships and fostering trust. Be it employees, customers or the wider community, ensuring they are informed, heard and valued is pivotal. Craft messages that speak to them, involve them in the journey and showcase how their involvement makes a tangible difference.
- **Utilizing various channels:** Different stories may find their best audience through different platforms. Newsletters might work best for in-depth insights, blogs for showcasing the behind-the-scenes development of your initiatives, and social media for engaging a wider, perhaps younger, audience with visuals and bite-sized content. Choose the medium that best amplifies your message and resonates with your audience.

And let's underscore two vital underpinnings of reporting and communication: transparency and authenticity. Transparency implies presenting a clear, unobstructed view of your activities, be they successes or lessons learnt from failures. It's about being open with your data, methodologies and outcomes, allowing stakeholders to see and understand your journey with all its ups and downs. Authenticity, on the other hand, is about being true to your organizational values and promises. It's reflected in how genuinely your sustainability efforts align with your stated goals and mission and how faithfully your communications depict your actual endeavours and achievements.

In essence, sustainability reporting and communication, when interwoven with transparency and authenticity, not only fulfil statutory obligations but also become powerful tools in engaging stakeholders and amplifying the impact of your sustainability initiatives. So, as we delve deeper into communications in the rest of this chapter, keep these foundational elements in mind, ensuring your messages are not just heard but also believed and acted upon.

Step 4: Deploy communications activities

In the realm of communications, particularly when navigating the complexities of sustainability messaging, having the right tools at your disposal is not just beneficial; it's imperative. The landscape is rich with resources, each offering unique advantages to streamline your efforts and optimize your impact. We've curated a selection of tools that stand out for their efficacy. Some are versatile enough to be integrated into a broader strategy, while others serve specific functions that shine in isolation. The context of your message and the outcomes you seek will determine whether you combine these tools or employ them individually. This flexibility ensures that, regardless of the situation, you're well equipped to communicate with clarity, persuasion and purpose.

The journey of strategy crafting begins with the crucial step of positioning, as delineated in Chapter 5. Here, a fundamental question surfaces: what do you want to be known for? The positioning becomes a cornerstone upon which your entire communication strategy will lean, ensuring that your sustainable actions and narrative are not only coherent but also project a clear, unified image of your organizational identity and aspirations.

Within the scaffolding of communications, several key components act as the building blocks that structure your messaging and engagement strategy. At a high level, communications generally encapsulate aspects such as targeting the message, which hones in on the specificity of what your intended audience should know, feel, do and remember. It's pivotal to have a crystal-clear understanding of these facets, because they underline the essence of your message and influence how it will be shaped and conveyed. Essentially, they answer the questions: what information do you wish to convey? How should it resonate emotionally with the audience? What actions do you hope it will inspire? And, importantly, what key take-aways should linger in the minds of your audience? In crafting your sustainability communications plan, strive for a balance between information and inspiration, between the practical and the visionary. Engage your audiences not just with the 'what' and the 'why', but, most importantly, with 'how' they can be part of the sustainable transformation.

As discussed previously, stakeholder engagement is key in embedding sustainability. As a leader you must identify and tailor messages for varied internal and external stakeholders. You also need to utilize suitable platforms and mediums to reach and resonate with each group. Developing a sustainability narrative involves more than planning activities; it's about shaping a story that resonates authentically with your stakeholders and strengthens your brand identity. This narrative isn't just an invitation to observe your sustainability journey; it integrates your sustainable ambitions into the very fabric of your corporate identity and strategic vision.

In essence, each tool and strategy in your communications arsenal should serve to fortify your positioning, enabling you to carve out a space in the minds of your stakeholders. This will ensure that your organization is not just known but also respected and valued for its sincerity, consistency and commitment towards sustainability. It's through these strategic communications, authentically and thoughtfully crafted, that an organization can genuinely resonate with and mobilize its audience in its sustainability journey.

Tools

Key messages

Key messages distill the core of what you wish to communicate into clear, concise statements that permeate all your communication mediums. To maximize reach and impact, your communications plan should outline the key messages for each stakeholder group, the proof points that will support these messages and the most effective channels for dissemination. Whether through social media, reports, presentations or direct dialogue, each channel offers distinct advantages for engaging your audience.

Tailoring your message is crucial, as it should reflect the diverse contributions individuals and groups can make towards sustainability. While acknowledging the challenges is important, the emphasis should be on practical solutions and collective action – 'how' we can all contribute to making a difference. To ensure your messaging hits the mark, remember the five Cs:[3]

1 **Clear:** Your message should be easy to understand, and free of jargon and technical terms that could alienate your audience.
2 **Credible:** Support your claims with data and evidence. Authenticity in your communications builds trust.
3 **Complete:** Provide a full picture, addressing potential questions and concerns proactively.
4 **Compelling:** Craft a narrative that captures attention and inspires action.
5 **Customized:** Adjust your message to suit different stakeholder groups. Each segment, whether it be investors, customers or NGOs, has unique concerns and interests.

Tone of voice

Additionally, maintaining an authentic and consistent tone of voice is pivotal. It's not just about what you say, but how you say it. Ensuring that your tone is a genuine reflection of your organizational values and remains consistent across all communication channels enhances credibility and fosters trust among your stakeholders. This tone becomes a recognizable and relatable voice that your audience comes to associate with your organization, further solidifying your positioning and identity in their perception. An authentic and optimistic voice, supported by evidence, creates an inviting and convincing narrative. Embrace an expansive tone that opens up possibilities and encourages stakeholder engagement.

The message house

The message house tool further builds upon this.[4] It provides a structured framework that encapsulates your key messages, supporting arguments and overarching communication objectives, ensuring a coherent and consistent narrative throughout. The Pyramid Principle, developed by Barbara Minto in 1973 and fundamental to McKinsey's communication training, is an effective framework for organizing information and arguments to enhance clarity and impact in corporate communications. This structured approach, guiding everything from routine emails to strategic storytelling, involves distilling information into a hierarchical format with a single overriding communications objective. The language used should resonate with your audience, employing a tone of voice that aligns with your organization's vision and values. It's essential to communicate not just the vision, but also the positive role that stakeholders can play.

Storytelling for a brighter future

Reflecting on the state of the world can sometimes cast a shadow on our spirits, especially as we face myriad challenges that seem insurmountable. It's easy to fall into a chasm of despair, but we must remind ourselves of the journey of progress humanity has made, as highlighted in Chapter 1. Maintaining a sense of optimism is vital – it's the kindling that sparks movement and powers the engines of change. Optimism fuels our resilience and directs our focus towards the progress that can, and must, be made. In this pivotal role, communications become more than a mere transmission of information; it's the craft of constructing a new narrative. Creating a positive story is an essential component of this craft. It's about showcasing the milestones of progress and the potential for more – a story that captures imaginations, uplifts spirits and rallies collective action. It's about demonstrating, through our words and actions, that each step forward, no matter how small, contributes to a momentum that can lead to transformative change. By committing to this optimistic but realistic storytelling, we do not disregard the gravity of our challenges. Instead, we choose to approach them with the belief that with concerted effort and collective will, we can continue to write a story of hope, progress and human ingenuity.[5]

Avoid greenwashing and green hushing

In the pursuit of genuine sustainability, corporations face the dual dilemmas of greenwashing and green hushing, each undermining trust in different ways.[6] Michelin's well-intentioned pledge in 2015 to reforest 90,000 hectares in Indonesia is a stark example of greenwashing, where aspirations were not matched by sustainable practice. The Volkswagen emissions scandal serves as another notorious case of greenwashing, where the company manipulated data to falsely present their vehicles as more environmentally friendly than they really were. This deceit not only resulted in massive financial and reputational damage for the company, but also significantly eroded public trust, emphasizing the catastrophic impact that greenwashing can have on stakeholders' faith and a company's credibility. This sort of disingenuous claim can degrade consumer trust and potentially lead to regulatory penalties.

An equally pernicious practice is green hushing, characterized by organizations under-reporting or entirely omitting their sustainable achievements. This tendency, possibly rooted in the fear of scepticism or critique, leads to a diminished public awareness of the positive steps taken towards environmental stewardship. In a survey by South Pole, about 25 per cent of 1,200 companies with robust sustainability agendas chose not to promote their sustainable strides. Green hushing often stems from the fear that these communications might be labelled as greenwashing. An article in the journal *Environmental Sciences Europe* from 2020 suggests that when greenwashing becomes more prevalent, green scepticism also increases.[7] This scepticism casts doubt on even legitimate green claims, making it harder for consumers to discern the credibility of environmental marketing efforts.

The phenomenon of green hushing carries significant, often overlooked, risks. When companies choose to remain silent about their environmental efforts, the consequences can be surprisingly counterproductive. The absence of public engagement leads to diminished accountability, where internal sustainability goals are at risk of being sidelined or forgotten. Moreover, this silence can be misconstrued as an indication that financial performance is prioritized over environmental stewardship, casting doubt on the company's commitment to sustainability. By not sharing their green practices and milestones, companies also miss out on the opportunity to inspire others and to position themselves as leaders in the fight against environmental degradation. Furthermore, the competitive spirit, which is a potent driver of innovation and progress in sustainability, can be severely dampened if achievements and ambitions in this realm are kept under wraps.

As a response, the Directive on Empowering Consumers for the Green Transition (ECGT), a new law designed to stop unfair corporate practices that hinder sustainable consumer choices, has been issued.[8] Set to be integrated into national legislation across the European Union (EU), the Directive will specifically outlaw various greenwashing tactics, such as misleading climate-neutral claims, to promote more honest and environmentally conscious marketing.

CASE STUDY Embedding sustainability in the creative industry

In the realm of marketing and the creative industry, Lemz and, later, HavasLemz have set a powerful example of how brands can drive societal change. Co-founded by Peter de Lange, this agency has shown that the role of marketing extends far beyond selling products; it's about building strong brands that embody sustainability and social responsibility.

By focusing on a brand's deeper purpose and its potential to contribute positively to society, Lemz and HavasLemz have demonstrated how marketing can be a tool for significant social impact. Take, for instance, their collaboration with a Dutch coffee brand. Instead of a conventional marketing campaign, they initiated Neighbour Day, a concept that fostered community connections, showcasing the brand's commitment to societal values in addition to its products. Similarly, they transformed a laundry detergent brand's message – from a focus on stain removal to celebrating the joys of children playing outdoors, leading to the creation of the Omo Buitenspeel Bond [Omo Outside Playing Foundation]. These campaigns did more than just promote products; they shifted public perception and influenced societal norms. By aligning brand values with societal needs, they created awareness and encouraged positive behaviour change among consumers. Another profound impact was seen in the agency's partnership with Terre des Hommes to combat online child trafficking. By creating Sweetie, a virtual child designed to catch predators, Lemz utilized its creative expertise to address a critical social issue, proving that creative strategies can be effectively employed to solve complex societal problems.

By deeply integrating purpose and societal value into their operations, HavasLemz shows that companies can indeed be successful while contributing positively to the world, setting a new standard for how brands can impact society.[9]

Step 5: Advocate and partner for change

Finally, let's discuss advocacy and partnerships. These concepts have the potential to enable organizations to create lasting, systemic change that reaches beyond their immediate sphere of influence. The way businesses engage in advocacy and partnerships can shape public discourse, influence policy-making and decision making, and bring about transformative change in society.[10] This two-pronged impact framework is a powerful tool for engendering positive change.

Internally, a leader can amplify sustainability by actively engaging with team members, cultivating a culture wherein sustainability is not just a peripheral objective but integrated into the very ethos of the organization. This involves illuminating the intrinsic and extrinsic value of sustainable practices, facilitating educational initiatives and embodying the advocated practices; the leader thus becomes a living testament to the sustainable change their team and the organization at large wish to witness. All of us, as individuals, and each organization and each country, have the potential to make a difference – both directly and indirectly. The direct impact we have is crucial, but the influence we exert on others can have a ripple effect that is significantly larger and more enduring. In essence, our actions today are creating the world of tomorrow. By taking the lead, by setting new and more sustainable standards and by helping our customers live more sustainably, we can bring about a change that is not just limited to our immediate environment, but that can resonate globally.

On the external front, rather than merely conforming to the prevailing system, sustainability leaders can strive to exert a tangible impact upon the ecosystem they operate within. Engaging in advocacy, they could influence legislative processes, for instance, ensuring that policy frameworks are conducive to, and supportive of, sustainable practices and ethical business operations. Being an active participant in global platforms, such as the UN Global Compact, not only amplifies a company's commitment to principled business but also aids in pushing the envelope to establish stringent and constructive preconditions in areas such as circular economy principles or biodiversity conservation. Moreover, external advocacy, particularly when it springs from a genuine place of wanting to elevate industry-wide sustainability standards, helps position the leader – and, by extension, their organization – as a pioneering force in the sustainability realm. It garners respect, facilitates the formation of valuable alliances and enhances the potential to mould a more sustainable business landscape.

However, it's pivotal to note that these efforts in advocacy should not be solitary endeavours. Leaders, while playing a crucial role, should leverage the collective expertise and skills within their teams, collaborating closely with departments like communications, PR and other experts within the business. The CEO and other high-ranking officials can also play a critical role, ensuring that advocacy efforts are robust and aligned and that they permeate every tier of the organization. It's about fashioning a united front, wherein every stakeholder, both internal and external, is on board, propelling the sustainability agenda forward cohesively and effectively. This collaborative approach not only disperses the workload but also amalgamates diverse perspectives and skills, enriching the advocacy and enhancing its impact and reach, thereby meticulously weaving sustainability into the organizational and external operational tapestry.

Tool: Create an advocacy strategy

Advocacy in the context of sustainability is the act of actively supporting and promoting policies, practices and actions that contribute to a more sustainable and equitable world. It involves leveraging influence and resources to drive change and advance a sustainability agenda that aligns with the health of our planet and the well-being of its inhabitants.[11] Effective advocacy in sustainability is not merely about raising your voice; it's about ensuring that when you do, it resonates with authenticity and aligns with your core values and strategic vision.

- **Authentic advocacy:** Your advocacy efforts should stem from a place of genuine commitment. They must be consistently practised, reflecting a true representation of what your organization stands for. When stakeholders see that your words match your actions, your influence grows.
- **Alignment with values and strategy:** Every statement, campaign or initiative must be coherent with the broader strategy and the values that define your organization. This alignment reinforces credibility and positions your company as a leader in sustainability, one that speaks with knowledge and conviction.
- **Radical openness:** Embrace transparency by being radically open about your sustainability efforts, successes and even failures. This approach not only reinforces trust but also invites others to join the conversation, leading to shared learning and progress.
- **Practising what you preach:** It's essential that the values you advocate publicly are mirrored in your business operations and organizational culture. When there's a direct correlation between your advocacy and your business model, the message is powerful and persuasive.
- **Humility – the path to continuous improvement:** While advocating change, it's important to maintain humility. Listen to stakeholders, learn from diverse perspectives, and be willing to adapt. This posture not only fosters collaboration but also signifies a commitment to ongoing improvement.

In essence, advocacy is about championing the causes that matter most to sustainability. By speaking out with clarity and living out your values with integrity, your organization can lead by example and inspire change on a broader scale. Furthermore, by sharing your aspirations and the journey towards them, you open doors to collaborations with other actors in the ecosystem. These potential partnerships can lead to vital systemic changes, further propelling your sustainability efforts. Lastly, your open advocacy can inspire other players, even competitors, to embark on their own sustainability journeys. This ripple effect can then contribute significantly to global sustainability efforts, reinforcing the importance of your role as a sustainability leader.

EXAMPLE The cascading effect of indirect impact

Consider, for example, a small tech start-up. Its direct business impact is the software or product it develops, which can directly enhance the lives of its employees and consumers. But the other leg, the indirect impact, is perhaps more profound. By pioneering a unique, efficient approach to problem solving, this start-up can inspire other businesses in the tech industry to adopt similar practices, revolutionizing the way the sector operates. This cascading effect can ultimately lead to industry-wide improvements in productivity, innovation and sustainability.

We can see this two-legged impact in play on larger scales too. Look at a nation such as Denmark, known for its renewable energy initiatives. Its direct impact comes from reducing its own carbon footprint, but its influence extends far beyond its borders. By showcasing the feasibility and benefits of clean energy, Denmark is influencing other countries to move towards more sustainable energy solutions, effectively changing the global narrative on environmental preservation.

Patagonia, a US-based outdoor clothing company, is renowned for its sustainability advocacy. The company is committed to environmental causes, using sustainable materials in its products and donating a portion of its profits to environmental organizations. Patagonia's initiatives also extend to supporting grassroots movements, engaging in environmental campaigns and implementing practices to reduce its carbon footprint. Their dedication to sustainability goes beyond mere corporate responsibility, influencing their business decisions, product design and overall company ethos.[12]

Infosys, a multinational corporation based in India, is another example of sustainability advocacy. Infosys is highly committed to sustainability and has made significant strides in renewable energy usage, water conservation and reducing carbon emissions. The company has invested in energy-efficient buildings and green infrastructure across its campuses. Infosys also actively promotes sustainability through its CSR initiatives, focusing on environmental stewardship and sustainable practices. Their efforts in integrating sustainability into their business operations have set a benchmark for other companies in Asia and globally.

Partnerships

Regardless of its scale or industry, an organization cannot navigate the complexities of sustainability alone. Collaborative efforts with NGOs, fellow corporations and cross-sector alliances serve to bridge the gaps in expertise, resources and influence. For instance, NGOs bring to the table their grassroots insights and advocacy prowess, while businesses contribute scalability and executional expertise. When these diverse strengths are aligned towards a common goal, the resulting synergy can elevate the sustainability conversation to new heights.[13]

A prime example of such collaboration is the intersection of innovation and the future of food. Partnerships that combine the nimble innovation of start-ups with the scalability of established food companies can result in groundbreaking sustainable food solutions. These collaborations might explore alternative proteins, reduce food waste through supply chain innovations or enhance agricultural practices to be more eco-friendly. Integrating external innovation through partnerships can enable businesses to not only contribute to a more sustainable food system but also position themselves as leaders in the emergent green economy.

EXAMPLE The Rainforest Alliance certification

The Rainforest Alliance certification is an example of cross-industry collaboration. This initiative focuses on promoting environmentally responsible practices in various sectors, including agriculture, forestry and tourism. The Rainforest Alliance works by setting comprehensive sustainability standards, which include criteria for environmental protection, social equity and economic viability. Businesses in the relevant industries that meet these standards are allowed to display the Rainforest Alliance Certified seal on their products and services. This certification is recognized globally and helps consumers make informed choices about supporting sustainable practices.

Major companies across different sectors have partnered with the Rainforest Alliance to certify their products. For example, in the coffee and chocolate industries, several well-known brands have committed to sourcing Rainforest Alliance Certified ingredients. This not only ensures that their products are produced in an environmentally and socially responsible manner, but also addresses consumer demand for ethically sourced products. These collaborations and partnerships show how industries can come together to make a meaningful impact on global sustainability efforts.[14]

In essence, partnerships are not just a strategic choice but a necessity in today's interconnected world, where the sustainability challenges we face are too intricate and expansive for any single entity to solve alone. Through collective efforts, shared values and combined strengths, partnerships hold the key to unlocking a sustainable future for all.

Advocacy and influencing

Organizations can leverage influencers to boost their sustainability efforts, tapping into their ability to engage and influence followers, especially younger demographics. Influencers can effectively communicate sustainability initiatives, making them more relatable and understandable to a broad audience. These collaborations can enhance an organization's reach, diversify its supporter base and drive participatory action through viral campaigns. By partnering with trusted influencers, sustainability leaders can amplify their message and credibility, fostering greater engagement and impact in their sustainability endeavours.

Advocacy and activism

Activism has shaped societal progress across areas like environmental conservation, gender equality and civil rights, with figures from Rosa Parks to Greta Thunberg demonstrating the power of advocacy. For CSOs, activism offers a complex landscape: while it can challenge business practices, it also presents opportunities to align with stakeholder values. By engaging with activism constructively, businesses can foster dialogue, learn from external perspectives and collaborate on initiatives that resonate with their audience and enhance their sustainability efforts.

CSOs play a key role in integrating activism into the corporate strategy, facilitating internal inclusivity and ensuring that engagement is authentic in order to avoid perceptions of opportunism. Transparent communication about the company's activist engagements can bolster credibility and align the organization more closely with societal values. Effectively, embracing activism not only advances a company's sustainability agenda but also strengthens its role as a socially responsible entity.

Summary and key take-aways

We have emphasized that sustainability must evolve into a core element of organizational culture, driven by effective internal communication that empowers employees to become sustainability advocates. Education is essential, as it serves as the foundation for a sustainable mindset across the company. Externally, the emphasis on crafting engaging sustainability narratives highlights the role of storytelling in connecting with audiences and integrating sustainability with the brand's values. Through viewing customers as partners and educating them, an organization can foster a community invested in a sustainable future. Collaboration with stakeholders amplifies impact, enabling larger-scale sustainability projects.

This chapter has underscored the importance of accurate measurement and transparent reporting to avoid the pitfalls of greenwashing or green hushing. Authentic sustainability requires transparency, collaboration and strategic integration. Effective communication ensures credibility and engagement, leading towards a sustainable future.

This journey is ongoing, requiring continuous adaptation and openness to new trends and innovations in sustainable communications.

Endnotes

1 Based on e-mail communication with Ben Kellard, Director Business Strategy, CISL

2 Jody Michael. Why we need to celebrate minor milestones, *Forbes*, 20 September 2021. www.forbes.com/sites/forbescoachescouncil/2021/09/20/why-we-need-to-celebrate-minor-milestones/ (archived at https://perma.cc/387G-U99H)

3 Cheryl Keates. The five C's of effective communication, *Forbes*, 10 September 2018. www.forbes.com/sites/forbescoachescouncil/2018/09/10/the-five-cs-of-effective-communication/ (archived at https://perma.cc/TVK7-BDSA)
4 Adrian Dearnell. Use the 'pyramid principle' to build your 'message house', *Forbes*, 13 October 2022. www.forbes.com/sites/adriandearnell/2022/10/13/use-the-pyramid-principle-to-build-your-message-house/ (archived at https://perma.cc/Y3CS-YGL9)
5 Chris Nolan. How storytelling can change the future: What's wrong and how to fix it, Warp News, 16 January 2023. www.warpnews.org/essays/how-storytelling-can-change-the-future-whats-wrong-and-how-to-fix-it/ (archived at https://perma.cc/W8HP-3WF3)
6 Aisha Ayoade. What is greenhushing and is it worse than greenwashing? Futerra, 20 June 2023. www.wearefuterra.com/blog/what-is-greenhushing-and-is-it-worse-than-greenwashing (archived at https://perma.cc/X5ER-XPV8)
7 Sebastião Vieira de Freitas Netto, Marcos Felipe Falcão Sobral, Ana Regina Bezerra Ribeiro and Gleibson Robert da Luz Soares. Concepts and forms of greenwashing: A systematic review, Environmental Science Europe, 2020, 32 (19). enveurope.springeropen.com/articles/10.1186/s12302-020-0300-3 (archived at https://perma.cc/TQJ5-2QUD)
8 New EU law empowers consumers against corporate greenwashing, European Environmental Bureau, 17 January 2024. eeb.org/new-eu-law-empowers-consumers-against-corporate-greenwashing/ (archived at https://perma.cc/KTB2-J2DY)
9 Interview conducted December 2021
10 Practical sustainability, Infosys. www.infosys.com/services/engineering-services/service-offerings/sustainability-practice.html (archived at https://perma.cc/MX4X-YLVJ)
11 Advocacy strategy best practices: 13 advocacy strategies for running a successful campaign, Votervoice. info.votervoice.net/resources/13-advocacy-strategies-for-running-a-successful-campaign (archived at https://perma.cc/C4GR-BGCB)
12 See www.patagonia.com/activism/ (archived at https://perma.cc/W29T-KGJD)
13 Jonathan Doh. Partnering with NGOs: The 4 keys to success, Network for Business Sustainability, 26 October 2020. nbs.net/partnering-with-ngos-the-4-keys-to-success/ (archived at https://perma.cc/3H2J-X825)
14 See www.rainforest-alliance.org (archived at https://perma.cc/GZ66-RT93)

PART 3
Leadership and self-care in sustainability

Having explored the expansive landscape of sustainability in Part 1 and then gone into the practicalities and different steps of embedding sustainability in the organization in Part 2, we now turn to Part 3, the concluding segment of our explorative journey on how to succeed with a sustainability transformation.

We begin this part by delving into a crucial aspect that binds everything together: leadership, self-care and resilience, where we focus on the pivotal role of human-centred leadership. We emphasize the importance of self-leadership as a cornerstone for effective and sustainable leadership in any organization. It's about understanding and harnessing your inner strengths, values and motivations as a leader. Throughout this chapter, and other parts of the book, we have incorporated interviews with seasoned leaders and pioneers in the field of sustainability, as well as personal reflections and learnings from our journeys as CSO and sustainability manager.

We continue with a chapter on reflections and learnings taken from the implementation steps described in Part 2 and the learnings on leadership and self-care. This is more than just a summary; it's an invitation for you to pause, ponder and personalize the insights and knowledge you've gathered throughout this book. It's a space for you to contemplate your own leadership journey in sustainability, drawing inspiration and guidance from myriad experiences shared in the preceding chapters.

We end the book with some short concluding remarks. In essence, Part 3 is about enriching your leadership toolkit, nurturing your inner leader and preparing you to not only lead others but also take care of yourself in this challenging, yet rewarding, endeavour of driving sustainable transformations. Remember, driving a sustainability transformation is a marathon, not a sprint.

Leading yourself and others in the sustainability transition

10

In a world increasingly defined by climate change, resource scarcity and social inequity, the role of the CSO or sustainability leader has evolved from a peripheral specialty to a central force that drives corporate innovation and long-term viability and relevance. As guardians of corporate sustainability, CSOs are uniquely positioned to influence the ethical compass and strategic direction of their organizations.

However, leading in this domain is as much about personal transformation as it is about professional responsibilities. The imperative of sustainability leadership cannot be overstated. As a sustainability leader, you carry the weighty responsibility of integrating environmental stewardship, social value and (long-term) economic performance into the DNA of your organization. Beyond the strategy charts and impact reports lies the core of all influential leadership: the self. Understanding your role is not just about the functional job description – it's about discovering the purpose, the passion and the personal values that propel you to inspire change. Inspiring change in others is critical, as sustainability is not, and cannot be, a one-person show. A sustainability transformation will fundamentally only happen when everyone, no matter which job they hold, in an organization understands and takes responsibility for their part.

As we embark on the final part of our book, we go deeper into a crucial aspect of sustainability implementation: leadership. The journey towards sustainable practices and policies is complex and multifaceted, requiring a leadership approach that is human-centric, inclusive and innovative. We'll dive deep into the art of personal leadership in sustainability, and the power of reflection, self-care and the necessary self-compassion that underpins longevity in this field. In a vocation that is as much about leading others as it is about managing oneself, these are the tools that ensure not only success but also well-being.

We begin by delving into the essence of your role, guiding you through the journey of finding purpose and understanding the profound impact of personal leadership intertwined with the Japanese concept of Ikigai – finding joy, fulfilment and balance in the work that you do. We examine the inner development goals that form the backbone of not just successful, but meaningful, leadership. We acknowledge the challenges – staying resilient and upbeat in a field that's as demanding as it is rewarding. You'll find out why being a CSO can be considered the most exciting job in the world, and we'll tackle the top questions that define and shape the world of CSOs.

The chapter's structure is based on a circular model of growth and development for the role of a leader, including CSOs:

1. **Personal leadership:** Utilizing tools such as Ikigai and the Individual Development Goals (IDG), this phase is crucial for individuals to uncover and align with their core values, strengths and purpose. This foundational understanding of oneself is vital for effective leadership.
2. **Leading yourself and others:** Building upon personal leadership, this step extends the focus to include leadership skills that are essential for both self-management and guiding others. It emphasizes the importance of understanding how to effectively lead oneself before extending these skills to lead teams and influence others positively.
3. **The role of the CSO:** This section provides insights into what the position entails, including the strategic thinking, decision making and leadership qualities necessary to fulfil this role successfully. It builds on the more extensive overview of the tasks of the CSO outlined in Chapter 2.
4. **Self-care:** Recognizing the importance of maintaining personal well-being, this phase introduces various self-care tools and practices. It underscores the idea that effective leadership and personal health are interconnected and that taking care of oneself is essential for sustainable professional growth and leadership effectiveness.
5. **Growing in the role:** The final step in the circular model focuses on continuous development and growth within one's role. This stage explores various opportunities and strategies for professional development,

aiming to foster ongoing learning, adaptability and advancement in leadership capabilities.

As you turn the page, embark on this transformative journey with a clear understanding of your role and a heart full of commitment. The road ahead for sustainability leaders is not a solitary one – it is a path forged by the collective strides of dedicated professionals like you, who continuously seek improvement, learning and, above all, ways to make a difference in our world. Welcome to the chapter that speaks not just to the head, but also to the heart of sustainability leadership.

Purpose and personal leadership

Imagine suddenly finding yourself on a bus filled with people, all absorbed in their activities. You don't remember boarding, nor do you have any idea of the destination. Confused, you ask others around you where you're all heading, but they seem just as clueless, content to engage in distractions like sharing a meal, watching a movie or gazing at the scenery rolling by. This scenario isn't far from life itself. We often get caught up in our routines, the ebb and flow of daily tasks, until a moment of clarity strikes and we begin to question our journey. Where is this path leading us? Why are we on this route in the first place? What part do we play in this collective voyage?[1]

Recognizing your direction and purpose is vital, not just on a personal level but also within a team, an organization and society at large. It's about finding your own compass, setting a course that aligns with your values and understanding how that journey contributes to the larger picture. It's these moments of reflection that can bring meaning to our actions and clarity to our destinations. Understanding your role is about recognizing the multidimensional impact of your actions and the strategic integration of sustainability goals with business objectives. It's about leading change, challenging the status quo and being a catalyst for transformation.

Aligning your personal purpose with your work

Reflecting on your personal purpose is a critical aspect of self-development and an important tool for achieving satisfaction and fulfilment in life, both personally and professionally. Your personal purpose defines what you stand for, what you value, and what inspires and drives you to contribute positively to the world. It sets your life's direction, helps to guide your decisions and serves as a constant reminder of why your work matters.

The concept of 'purpose' is often associated with organizations or companies, which typically have clear visions and missions. However, individuals also need a defined purpose. According to an article in the *Harvard Business Review*, your personal purpose goes beyond your occupation or qualifications; it encapsulates who you are as a person, what you bring to the table and how you do it.[2] It's about understanding your unique talents, strengths and passions, and how you can use them to make a meaningful difference. We have already mentioned the book *Start with the Why*, in which Simon Sinek emphasizes the power of understanding your purpose.[3] Sinek asserts that while most people know what they do and how they do it, few genuinely understand why they do it. This 'why', or purpose, is what inspires and motivates action. Whether your purpose is to be a catalyst for positive change, to help organizations transform towards more sustainable practices or to create innovative solutions for a better world, identifying your 'why' can help to keep you motivated and focused, enhancing your potential to make a positive impact on the world.

Tool: Ikigai – the philosophy of purpose

A meaningful framework for self-discovery and expressing one's purpose can be found in the ancient Japanese concept of Ikigai.[4] Derived from two Japanese words, 'Iki', meaning 'life', and 'gai', translating to 'value or worth', Ikigai is the profound intersection of passion, talent, market demand and, importantly, the world's needs. It serves as your 'reason for being' or, in simpler terms, the driving force that gets you up every morning and propels you forward.

At its core, Ikigai revolves around the harmonious alignment of four distinct, yet interconnected, spheres of your life. These are the passion you exude for what you love, the professional proficiency you hold, the economic sustainability of your livelihood and the beneficial impact you make on the world. Interestingly, the element of making a positive global contribution is what sets Ikigai apart from other purpose models. Recognizing and acting upon this planetary need offers an elevated sense of purpose and fulfilment. In today's world, this awareness is more crucial than ever. We must place the needs of the planet and humanity as our guiding star and then navigate the best ways to contribute, leveraging our unique skills and passions. Unearthing your Ikigai involves deep introspection and self-questioning across the four facets: passion, mission, profession and vocation, as shown in Table 10.1. It's about delving into what you love, what you excel at, what provides your

Table 10.1 Questions and reflections for finding your purpose with Ikigai

Main questions	Reflections
What does the world need?	• Doing something to improve the world is what this book is all about. Therefore, reflect on whether you, through the role, are solving a social, economic or environmental problem.Is the sector, organization or function contributing to the SDGs? • Are there other ways to strengthen the contribution and to focus on sustainability and social impact?
What do I love doing?	• In order to do an excellent job, it helps to have passion for the work and the cause. If you don't enjoy it or believe in it, perhaps looking for something more aligned with your interests would be better. Ask yourself if the organization you are working for is the place where you can have the most positive impact.
What am I good at?	• To create impact, you should, of course, work with something that you are good at. As this book has proven, to contribute to sustainability this could be almost any area, including marketing, engineering, finance, tourism and art. • It can also be helpful to think about broader skills, such as networking, debating, negotiating, researching, crafting, coding and so forth. When you are looking for what to study or have just graduated, it is hard to know if you are good at a given field or profession, but you know you are good at specific skills and you know which environments you thrive in. • The work of sustainability will require all sorts of competencies, so sharpening and improving your skill set will help to achieve the larger goal of contributing to a better world.
Can I also make a living out of this?	• Finally, according to Ikigai, you need to be able to make a living out of your profession.

living and what the world is calling for. Upon successfully aligning these areas, you awaken to your Ikigai – your unique purpose that not only fuels your existence but also impacts the world positively.

Tool: The Inner Development Goals (IDGs)

The technical skills and knowledge required for the role as CSO or sustainability manager are essential, but it's the inner qualities of leadership – emotional resilience, ethical clarity and the ability to inspire – that truly empower a CSO to drive change. These qualities are cultivated through a commitment to IDGs.[5]

These are personal benchmarks that focus on the emotional, cognitive and ethical aspects of a leader's persona. They underpin the effectiveness of sustainability initiatives by ensuring that those who lead them are grounded, clear-headed and empathetic. The IDGs are a powerful tool, fostering the qualities needed to navigate the complex web of sustainability challenges. Here's how the IDGs support CSOs in their work:

1. **Being – relationship to self:** CSOs must exhibit a profound sense of self-awareness and self-regulation. By setting goals around mindfulness and introspection, leaders can maintain their inner equilibrium amid the high-pressure demands of their role.
2. **Thinking – cognitive skills:** Critical thinking, systems thinking and creative problem solving are cognitive skills essential for a CSO. IDGs focused on cognitive development help in dissecting complex sustainability issues and forging innovative solutions.
3. **Relating – caring for others and the world:** Empathy and compassion are at the heart of sustainability. CSOs must lead with a sense of duty towards others and the environment. IDGs promote an understanding and caring attitude, which is crucial for fostering a culture of sustainability.
4. **Collaborating – social skills:** The ability to collaborate across departments, organizations and even industries is vital for a CSO. IDGs that build communication, teamwork and negotiation skills enable CSOs to create synergies and build effective partnerships.
5. **Acting – driving change:** Finally, the capacity to act decisively and inspire action in others is what sets great leaders apart. IDGs focusing on initiative, adaptability and leadership ensure that CSOs are able to not only strategize but also mobilize their organizations towards sustainable outcomes.

Leading yourself

The concept of Ikigai presents a profound opportunity for sustainability leaders to intertwine their personal and professional purposes, ultimately bolstering their leadership capabilities. When these leaders apply Ikigai to their lives, they are not only aligning their career with their passion but also making sure it serves a larger purpose – addressing the needs of our planet and humanity. Through Ikigai, sustainability leaders can derive a sense of fulfilment and resilience, as their work becomes an extension of their personal purpose. Their professional endeavours cease to be merely tasks to accomplish, transforming instead into avenues for expressing their deepest passions and making a positive impact. This deep-rooted alignment can foster greater endurance, conviction and motivation in the face of the complex challenges of sustainability leadership. Ikigai thus serves as a compass that directs sustainability leaders towards not just a career, but a vocation that encapsulates their whole self. It's a journey of discovering and implementing a purpose-driven life that's inherently sustainable, gratifying and influential in making the world a better place.

Working towards a sustainable future and creating a positive impact are noble, albeit challenging, goals. Such aspirations often require significant personal investment and alignment with an organization that shares these values. However, there may be instances where you find yourself working in an environment where sustainability and impact are not prioritized or where the strides towards these goals are not as bold or as decisive as you believe they should be. You might find that despite your best efforts, your attempts to instigate change are met with resistance, or you lack the necessary resources, authority or mobilization capacity to bring about significant progress. Changing an organization's course, or influencing an industry's trajectory, can be a slow, arduous process, requiring patience and resilience. However, if after continuous effort and soul-searching, you find yourself still feeling unable to make headway, it may be time to take care of yourself and explore new avenues. It's not a failure, but rather a realization that your talents, passion and drive might be better utilized elsewhere. In such situations, it is thus essential to acknowledge your feelings and assess your position critically. If you've tried persistently to effect change and faced continuous obstacles, you might need to consider whether your current organization is the right platform for you to make the difference you aim for. It's a brave decision to make, but remember, aligning yourself with an organization that shares your purpose and values is crucial for making meaningful contributions and maintaining your professional satisfaction and personal well-being. You could, for example, move to another function within the same organization, where you might have a higher mandate to make changes. You might look for another, more dedicated, organization within the same sector. Or you might find your purpose in a new field or sector all together.

Leading others

Bear in mind that your colleagues, like you, are on their own quest for meaning and purpose within the workplace. And remember that creating a sustainable impact does not confine you to a specific sector, type of organization or role. You don't have to be a CSO or work for an NGO to effect change. You can make a significant impact from any position, in any organization, within any sector. It's about finding a place where your skills, passion and purpose can flourish and contribute to a sustainable future. The breadth and scale of the change required mean that there is room for everyone to contribute. We need every person on board this transformational journey towards a sustainable future. Each effort counts, no matter how small, and your unique contribution could be the tipping point for substantial, lasting change.

Amid the hustle of daily responsibilities, performance metrics and financial rewards, there lies a shared human aspiration among your peers to connect their efforts to a larger, more impactful narrative. It's easy to feel isolated in your efforts, especially when facing resistance to sustainability and social impact initiatives. However, it's crucial to recognize that such opposition is not personal; it often stems from entrenched systems within organizations and society that prioritize different values.[6] Yet, as the former Buddhist monk Björn Natthiko Lindeblad poignantly shares in his book *I May Be Wrong*, even those who seem to have reached the pinnacle of career success may find themselves unfulfilled. Lindeblad himself, once on a promising corporate trajectory, chose a path less trodden to seek contentment and purpose. He left behind a burgeoning career to embark on a spiritual journey as a Buddhist monk, a testament to the profound human desire for a meaningful existence that aligns with one's inner values and happiness.[7]

Programmes centred around the IDGs – be it through mindfulness exercises, leadership coaching or cognitive skills workshops – serve as vital instruments in a CSO's toolkit. By embedding these inner development practices into the culture of the organization, a CSO can enhance their own leadership capacity and foster an environment where sustainability can thrive. By emphasizing these IDGs, a CSO can transcend the traditional constraints of their role, leading not just with policies and strategies but with heart, inspiration and transformative vision. The result is a leadership style that is as sustainable as the goals it seeks to achieve, fostering an organizational culture capable of making a positive impact on the world.

As a leader, it's important to weave this understanding into your work. Strive to align individual purposes and motivations with the broader missions and visions of the organization. Foster an environment where the search for meaning is acknowledged and supported, and where every team member feels that their contributions are valued not just for their immediate impact but also for their deeper significance. This approach can transform routine tasks into stepping stones towards fulfilling not just organizational goals, but personal aspirations as well.

The most rewarding job in the world

The role of a CSO is more than a job; it's a calling that resonates with the most pressing needs of our time. It is a role that is inherently rewarding, both professionally and personally, for several compelling reasons. In our experiences, we have found immense joy and fulfilment in the role. For us, it wasn't just a position to fill; it was an exciting and dynamic journey filled with fun, intrigue and an incredible depth of variety. No two days were ever the same, each one presenting new challenges to tackle and complex problems to solve. The work constantly engaged us with a diverse array of fields, people and experts, both internally within our organizations and externally in the wider sustainability community. But beyond the variety and the constant intellectual stimulation, what truly resonated with us was the profound sense of meaning our roles provided. The chance to make a tangible impact on our planet and society made every effort worthwhile, rendering the CSO role not just a job, but a deeply rewarding life experience:

- **Driving meaningful change:** A CSO is positioned at the forefront of driving meaningful change within an organization and, by extension, in society and the environment. This role offers the unique opportunity to lead initiatives that directly contribute to a healthier planet and a more equitable world. CSOs are able to see the tangible results of their efforts, whether it's in reduced carbon footprints, improved labour practices or enhanced CSR. The knowledge that one's work contributes positively to the global good is profoundly fulfilling.

- **Innovating for the future:** Sustainability is a field ripe for innovation. As a CSO, one gets to push the boundaries of 'business as usual' and develop new ways to integrate sustainable practices into every level of a company's operations. This is not just about risk management; it's about reimagining products, processes and business models. The challenge of thinking creatively and the joy of pioneering sustainable solutions is an exciting and intellectually stimulating aspect of the job.
- **Building a legacy:** Sustainability leadership is legacy work. CSOs have the chance to leave a lasting impact that goes beyond quarterly profits. The policies, systems and cultural changes they help to implement will resonate through time, defining a responsible path forward for the organization. It's an opportunity to build something enduring and meaningful – a true legacy of stewardship and foresight.
- **Leading cultural transformation:** CSOs are not just managers; they are culture creators. They have the chance to transform the heart of the company by embedding sustainability into the corporate DNA. This is a profound responsibility – shaping corporate culture, influencing employee values and steering the organization towards a purpose that transcends traditional business objectives. It's a role that has the power to change mindsets and create a collective sense of purpose and pride within the workplace.
- **Engaging with diverse stakeholders:** Being a CSO involves engaging with a wide array of stakeholders – investors, employees, customers, suppliers, communities and regulators. This engagement allows for a rich diversity of perspectives and the chance to build coalitions and consensus around sustainability goals. There is significant reward in bringing together varied interests to achieve common goals that benefit all parties and the planet.
- **Personal and professional growth:** The nature of the role demands constant learning and adaptation. CSOs must stay abreast of global sustainability trends, regulatory changes and emerging technologies. This continuous learning curve ensures that one is always growing both personally and professionally, keeping the work dynamic and CSOs at the cutting edge of their field.
- **Financial and strategic impact:** While the intrinsic rewards are substantial, the role of a CSO also carries significant strategic and financial impact. By mitigating risks, identifying efficiencies and opening up new markets, a CSO can drive profitability and long-term financial health for

their organization. There's a deep sense of achievement in showing that sustainability and profitability are not mutually exclusive but are, in fact, mutually reinforcing.

- **Alignment of personal and professional values:** Perhaps most fulfilling of all is the alignment of one's personal values with their professional work. For many CSOs, their role is a reflection of their beliefs about environmental stewardship, social responsibility and ethical business practices. To go to work each day knowing you are acting on your values is a reward that resonates deeply and brings a sense of coherence and integrity to one's life.

To summarize, the role as a CSO represents the convergence of passion, purpose and profession. It offers the opportunity to make a difference, the excitement of innovation, the satisfaction of leading change and the joy of living one's values. For those who take on this mantle, the work is as challenging as it is rewarding and the impact is as broad as it is deep. It is a role that not only shapes careers but also contributes to shaping a better world.

However, it's paramount to understand that a CSO cannot shoulder the entirety of these expectations alone. For true impact, sustainability must be integrated and embedded throughout the organization, with every department and individual playing a part, as outlined in Chapter 6. Only through such collective effort can the goals be genuinely realized.

Challenges at work: Being a CSO or sustainability leader

However, all jobs come with its challenges, and not the least within sustainability. The role of a CSO or sustainability leader is inherently challenging. As just one individual, the weight of the vast responsibilities and tasks can seem like an impossible equation to balance. Numerous challenges emerge both internally and externally. In our experience, a key challenge was juggling various priorities while ensuring sustainability remained a focal point or was seamlessly integrated into primary business objectives. Additionally, reconciling the short-term demands of businesses with the longer-term view of sustainability posed its own set of difficulties. The shifting landscape of external (and internal) expectations was a continuous challenge. Striking the right balance between over-promoting sustainability (greenwashing) and under-communicating (green hushing) is yet another. The question remained: what should be communicated, how and to what extent? And, finally, fostering collective alignment – ensuring every member understood our objectives, their significance and their specific roles (especially concerning how each function or country could participate and contribute) – was always on the radar.

Some other recurring themes revolved around the contrast between ambition and execution. In essence, while the aspiration to achieve sustainability goals was clear and evident, the practical constraints, especially from a financial perspective, often posed challenges in the path to broader implementation and impact. Those executing sustainability often express frustrations over the disparity between the company's stated sustainability ambitions and the financial constraints within the budgeting process. These limitations often impeded the full realization of these ambitions. And, similarly, while initial pilot projects and tests for sustainability initiatives were generally feasible and often greenlit, the challenge arose when attempting to scale these pilots to a broader, company-wide level. The transition from a successful small-scale initiative to full-scale implementation proved to be a consistent hurdle.

Thus, in short, the following are the most common challenges that we've experienced and that were shared with us by people in our sustainability network, are as also further echoed in Chrissa Pagitsas' book *Chief Sustainability Officers at Work*:[8]

- **Budgetary constraints:** A CSO often has to be an advocate for the financial benefits of sustainability, demonstrating how sustainable practices can lead to cost savings and new business opportunities in the face of budget cuts or constraints.
- **Organizational buy-in:** It can be challenging to convince every level of the organization to commit to sustainability practices, especially if they are seen as costly or disruptive in the short term. Continuous engagement and demonstrating the value of sustainability initiatives are vital.
- **Rapidly changing landscape:** The field of sustainability is one of constant evolution, with new technologies, policies and societal expectations emerging regularly. Staying educated and adaptable is a must.
- **Balancing company goals:** The CSO must juggle the immediate demands of a business, such as profitability and growth, with the longer-term imperative to reduce environmental impact and be socially responsible.
- **Incentive structures:** Aligning the company's incentive structures with long-term sustainability goals is often a difficult task, as traditional bonus systems focus on short-term results.

- **Time management:** With such a vast scope of responsibilities, effectively managing time is a persistent challenge for CSOs.
- **Knowledge gaps:** Addressing the lack of understanding about sustainability issues within the company is critical. This requires the CSO to be an educator and advocate for change, often starting from the ground up.

Self-care for sustainability professionals

Climate change, injustice, poverty, biodiversity and water scarcity are some of the global challenges highlighted throughout this book. Being aware of, and working with, sustainability and social impact means thinking and being aware of serious topics and challenges every day. You cannot turn a blind eye to these issues, as it is your job to be aware and make others aware, to enable action and change. This can at times be exhausting and depressing. Although we are working to make the world a better place and changing the direction of the negative curves, it sometimes feels heavy. The question 'Am I doing the right thing, or doing enough?' is constantly there, as is the frustration of the slow development of progress. Working to make things better takes time, time we do not really have, and progress is sometimes slow. The lack of perceived impact can make us lose motivation and hope.

In light of these global issues, sustainability teams are under immense pressure to make a difference. The pressures are growing, with professionals facing increased demands for impactful results, often with limited resources and the added strain of post-pandemic recovery. Many report working longer hours and feeling burnt out, and some are even dealing with mental health challenges.[9] Despite these difficulties, there's a silver lining, with a noticeable increase in employee volunteerism. This shows that employees are eager to contribute to meaningful causes, which can help boost morale and align company values with personal convictions. Moreover, while budgets have often been tight, with many companies previously reporting stagnant or reduced sustainability funds, it seems as if a significant shift is on the horizon. According to Honeywell, in 2022, over 90 per cent of companies were planning to increase their environmental sustainability budget in the following year, indicating a growing commitment to sustainability despite past financial constraints.[10] Continued strong support and proper funding are crucial in sustaining this momentum.

Thus, in order to not only survive, but thrive, in our jobs, it is crucial to take care of ourselves and be attuned to the impact of this work on our own well-being. We cannot always be absorbed by the problems. We must seek out healthy and inspiring work environments. While the weight of the problems may often seem immense, it's crucial to remember that leading change requires strength, resilience and, most importantly, self-leadership.

> Whoever you are, and whatever you do, the world needs you to lead. There will be times when happiness may feel elusive and the horizon impossible to reach. But remember that each day, we wake up to another chance to renew the world. Daily, we have a choice to recommit to the work we came to do. Daily, we can reconstitute the promise of hard-edged hope.[11]

In light of this, it's crucial for us as sustainability leaders to build robust support networks, engage in self-care practices and maintain a balanced approach to our work, even as we push to make impactful changes. Just as a sturdy ship cannot be steered by a faltering captain, sustainable change cannot be driven by a leader who is depleted. To lead others effectively, it's imperative that we first learn to lead ourselves. This means taking time for self-care, ensuring we remain resilient amid the intensity of our mission.

Beneficial habits for personal well-being and long-lasting leadership

In both our own experiences, and in conversations with friends and colleagues in the sustainability space, we have observed a common thread that unites those of us who have chosen to be sustainability leaders. We are often the ones tirelessly working towards wide-reaching and consequential goals, shouldering the weighty responsibility of protecting our planet. The scale of the tasks before us can be immense, and the burden can sometimes feel overwhelming. We are frequently the ones catalysing change within our organizations, standing at the frontlines of sustainability efforts. However, this position can also lead to a sense of isolation as we grapple with the challenges largely on our own. This mixture of high stakes, personal commitment and feelings of isolation increases our vulnerability to burnout.

While neuroscientist Andrew Huberman acknowledges that there isn't a one-size-fits-all approach to well-being, he identifies several universal strategies that can enhance overall health.[12] Developing good habits is a cornerstone of effective leadership and self-care, especially when working in demanding fields such as sustainability. The habits we cultivate profoundly affect our mental, emotional and physical well-being, our resilience and, ultimately, our ability to perform at our best. Huberman emphasizes five fundamental daily habits for optimal mental and physical health: sleep, sunlight, movement, nutrition and social connection. Adequate sleep is crucial for stress relief, emotional stability and overall health. Exposure to morning sunlight helps regulate the body's circadian rhythm and is essential for vitamin D absorption. Regular exercise, incorporating resistance, mobility and cardio is vital for brain and cardiovascular health. A balanced diet, potentially including intermittent fasting, supports the gut microbiome and overall well-being. Lastly, maintaining social connections is critical to combat loneliness and its associated health risks, contributing significantly to happiness and longevity. These practices form a strong foundation for health, accessible to most individuals.

EXAMPLE Some beneficial habits for leaders[13]

- **Prioritize self-care:** Self-care goes beyond merely taking breaks. It involves intentional actions to take care of your physical, mental and emotional health. This can include regular exercise, balanced nutrition, sufficient sleep and activities that you enjoy and that help you relax and de-stress.
- **Consistent sleep schedule:** A good night's sleep is crucial for cognitive functioning, emotional well-being and overall health. Aim for consistent bedtimes and wake-up times to regulate your body's clock and improve the quality of your sleep.
- **Nutritious food:** A well-balanced diet is important for maintaining energy and focus. Include a variety of fruits, vegetables, whole grains, lean proteins and healthy fats in your diet. Stay hydrated and avoid excessive caffeine and alcohol.
- **Regular exercise:** Physical activity improves mental clarity, mood, energy levels and stress management. Find a form of exercise you enjoy and can incorporate into your routine, whether it's a morning jog, an evening yoga class or a midday walk.
- **Mindfulness practices:** Mindfulness can help you stay centred in the midst of stress and chaos. Practices like meditation, deep breathing exercises or even mindful walking can help you cultivate mindfulness.
- **Continuous learning:** Great leaders are always learning. Keep up to date with the latest sustainability trends and strategies, and always seek opportunities to expand your knowledge and skills.

- **Networking:** Building relationships with other leaders in your field can provide invaluable support, insights and opportunities. Attend events, join relevant forums and reach out to peers and mentors.
- **Boundaries:** Learn to say no when necessary. Overcommitting can lead to burnout, so it's important to set boundaries to protect your time and energy.
- **Regular breaks:** Take short breaks throughout the day to rest and rejuvenate. This can improve productivity and prevent burnout.
- **Reflective practices:** Regular reflection can help you gain perspective, learn from experiences and make better decisions. This can be as simple as journaling or taking a few minutes at the end of each day to contemplate.

Remember, these habits are not one-size-fits-all, and what works for one person may not work for another. Experiment with different strategies and find what works best for you. Start small, focus on consistency and remember that small, regular actions can lead to significant changes over time. In summary, the world needs you to lead, but to do that effectively, you need to lead yourself first. Be compassionate with yourself, take time to recharge and remain focused on your unique contributions to the cause. Remember, the world is waiting for you, and each day brings with it a renewed opportunity to create meaningful change. Embrace it with strength, resilience and a renewed sense of purpose. The following sections discuss a few other ways to stay resilient and maintain your well-being that we have found useful.

Refocus your thinking

As a leader, if you find yourself clinging to unhelpful thoughts, here is an exercise recommended by the former Buddhist monk Björn Natthiko Lindeblad:[14] Shift your focus to something else, acknowledging that thoughts are nourished by attention. Imagine the process of holding on to thoughts as gripping with a clenched fist. Now visualize releasing that grip, allowing your hand to open, signifying the release of those thoughts. Allow them to pass without engaging further. This simple gesture of momentarily letting go can have profound effects. Consciously direct your attention towards more constructive matters, fostering a clearer mind for decision making.

Find ways to re-energize through knowledge sharing

Sustainability is not a sprint, but rather a marathon. During tough times, self-motivation becomes the torchbearer, illuminating the path forward.

When loneliness seeps in and everything feels overwhelming, it's crucial to connect with others who are navigating a similar path. Look for online forums, communities or social networks where sustainability leaders gather, exchange experiences and provide mutual support. Being part of such a community can help validate your experiences, provide comfort and generate innovative solutions to shared challenges. Pia had the luxury of having a large sustainability team working with her, and when she needed re-energizing she often sat down with some of her inspirational team members to dig into a specialty topic and get energy from learning about new developments and projects – and just absorbing the shared inspiration of working with people who love what they do.

Practise news detox

While it's important to stay informed, the onslaught of negative news can be overwhelming and disheartening. Headlines often highlight disasters, conflicts and negative events, creating a skewed perception of the world. News, by definition, signifies noteworthy or unexpected events, and, unfortunately, it's often the negative or dramatic incidents that tend to be unexpected or grab our attention. This phenomenon, sometimes called negativity bias, is not just a media practice, but a reflection of human psychology; we are evolutionarily wired to pay more attention to threats or bad news. However, this approach often results in a skewed representation of reality. The continuous stream of negative news can lead to what is known as mean world syndrome (a term coined by the media researcher George Gerbner), where people perceive the world to be worse than it actually is.[15]

It's important to remember that news is not a comprehensive representation of everyday life, but rather a spotlight on specific, often extraordinary, events. Positive developments and gradual improvements – be it in the field of sustainability, public health or social issues – often go underreported, simply because they don't have the same shock value or immediacy as negative news.[16] Therefore, while staying informed is important, it is as important to stay energized and not get stuck in all the negative news. Here are some simple things you can do:

- Take a break or stop following and reading all negative news. Simply do a news detox every now and then. Give yourself a break and focus on the promising developments. It is essential to understand the complexity of sustainability, but one must not get lost in it.
- Balance the consumption of news with positive narratives and success stories to maintain a more rounded perspective on the world. It is thus

crucial to balance the negative with the positive – to remember that progress is happening, even if it's not in the limelight. There are various outlets dedicated to reporting positive news, like the Good News Network or Positive News. These platforms offer a refreshing perspective, showcasing how humanity is constantly striving to make the world better.

- Engage with thought-provoking literature to keep your spirits high. Books like *Drawdown: The Most Comprehensive Plan Ever Proposed to Reverse Global Warming* by Paul Hawken offer insights into the challenges and potential solutions in our fight against climate change.[17]

Be nice to yourself

For Pia, effective leadership is a blend of self-awareness and empowerment. She emphasized the importance of mastering her domain while acknowledging the areas she might not be well versed in. This candid recognition of strengths and weaknesses isn't confined to personal introspection; it extends to her team and the larger organization. Pia believes that true leadership isn't about getting entrenched in minutiae, but about empowering others to take the lead, driving the agenda forward. By doing so, she fosters an environment where her team feels equipped and motivated to execute the vision, free from micromanagement.

Like any leader, Pia acknowledges having made several mistakes along her journey. One major pitfall was getting ensnared in frustrations and sometimes finding it challenging to rejuvenate and regain focus. Another oversight was underestimating the apprehensions of her team and stakeholders during transformative phases. She realized, in retrospect, that she often didn't fully grasp the perspectives and backgrounds of those she was communicating with, which led to missed opportunities in effectively conveying the potential advantages of the changes she was proposing. This taught her the importance of empathetic communication and the need to address and allay fears when leading change.

Stay focused

Self-leadership extends beyond merely looking after our physical and mental health. It also involves maintaining a sense of perspective, focusing on areas where we can have the most significant impact rather than striving for unattainable perfection. This pragmatic, solution-oriented approach can serve as an effective strategy for managing the complexity of sustainability, without becoming lost within it. Don't try to be perfect in everything you do. Think about the impact arrow presented by psychologist Kali Andersson. Focus on what you are good at and where you can make significant changes.

Avoid the pressure of being a 'saint'

Navigating the world of sustainability leadership often comes with an implicit expectation of personal perfection, an image of someone who is an absolute paragon of sustainable living. Individuals working in sustainability are often expected to lead lives completely devoid of any carbon footprint, subsisting on a vegan diet, eschewing all forms of transportation that contribute to carbon emissions and abstaining from buying anything new. This can manifest as an unspoken pressure to embody the ideals one advocates, in every aspect of one's life. While it is commendable and often inspiring to 'walk the talk', this expectation can also inadvertently create a burdensome ideal that is almost impossible to fulfil entirely.

While embodying the values you advocate is fundamental to sustainability leadership, it's crucial to strike a balance. It's important not to let the pressure to be a 'saint' eclipse the broader goal of achieving systemic change. We are all human, and it's natural to have inconsistencies. Rather than striving for individual perfection, the focus should be on driving a larger, systemic shift towards sustainability. This is, however, not intended to undermine the importance of personal actions in line with sustainable principles, but rather to emphasize the pragmatic approach. Your greatest impact may lie beyond perfecting your lifestyle. It might be more fruitful to engage with partners, influence policies, create sustainable solutions or raise awareness. Each individual has unique strengths, and recognizing where you can contribute most effectively can be a more empowering strategy.

Moreover, over-emphasizing personal perfection can lead to frustration and exhaustion, leaving one with little energy for broader change efforts. Instead of solely focusing on personal actions, channeling your energy towards larger, systemic shifts can be more impactful. So, do not chastise yourself for not achieving absolute perfection in sustainable living. It's about making conscious choices and identifying where you can create the most significant positive change.

Remember to laugh!

Being open to joy, laughter and pleasure is not a dereliction of duty, but rather a necessary part of the journey towards a more sustainable world. Happiness can act as a powerful motivator, encouraging us to strive harder and reach further. When we are well rested, content and fulfilled, we are better equipped to inspire those around us, spreading positivity and progress. When we are happy and well, we are more likely to spread good energy and impact the world.

Embrace your space, politely yet boldly

Lisen stepped into the role of a sustainability manager within a management team leading an organization of 5,000 co-workers. At the age of 27, she was the youngest and female. She had been brought up in the Swedish tradition of listening intently and speaking only when a conversational gap presented itself. This cultural habit made it tough for her to break into discussions. She spent months in the background, waiting in vain for an opening to voice her thoughts. But then it dawned on Lisen that her politeness wasn't getting her anywhere. She realized it was actually not about her personal journey; it was about her mission. She was there to enact change, to guide the organization towards more sustainable and inclusive practices – a task of undeniable importance.

By remaining silent, she wasn't doing anyone any favours. While she still valued listening as a key societal and interpersonal skill, she knew it was time for her to assert herself. To align with the forthright Dutch business culture and to elevate sustainability in the company's priorities, she began to speak up. Claiming her space in the room, Lisen saw herself as making a contribution, not imposing on others. The purpose was clear: to contribute to creating a work environment that was not only better and more sustainable but also more inclusive, bringing benefits to both the organization and the wider world. Similar to this example, other sustainability leaders should be encouraged to step up to claim their space, break existing structures and forge new pathways and opportunities for progress.

Taking breaks is not just acceptable – it's necessary

Sustainability work, while crucially important, can be incredibly demanding, often requiring an intense level of focus, commitment and resilience. Balancing this workload with the necessity for rest and recovery is a fundamental aspect of maintaining longevity and productivity in the role. To do this, identify the means of recovery that work best for you on a personal level, and intentionally create space for these activities in your routine.

Moments of respite and renewal are not a sign of weakness, but of strength and resilience. In these moments, engage in activities that bring you joy and relaxation. Different people rejuvenate in different ways. For some, meditation provides a serene and introspective opportunity to reconnect with their thoughts and feelings, reducing stress and bolstering mindfulness. Physical activity, such as exercising or taking a walk in nature, can be another powerful way to promote relaxation and rejuvenation, as it can help to reduce mental fatigue, improve mood and enhance overall well-being. For some people, a 15-minute run can resolve the most challenging problems. Sleep, often overlooked in our busy schedules, is a cornerstone of recovery. Quality sleep gives your body and mind the opportunity to repair, rejuvenate and refresh, boosting your ability to handle stress and maintain a positive perspective. Screen-free time is another essential recovery strategy in today's technology-driven world. Disconnecting from digital devices can help reduce cognitive overload, giving your mind a chance to rest and recuperate. Similarly, enjoying time with friends, going camping or embarking on an adventure can serve as valuable means of escape, offering a change of pace and environment which can help to recharge your batteries.

These experiences can re-energize you and rekindle your passion for your work. Identifying your unique combination of restorative practices is a process of self-discovery. Pay attention to which activities leave you feeling refreshed and invigorated, and intentionally incorporate these into your routine.

Meet a professional coach

Sometimes, however, rest and relaxation activities might not be enough, and you may find it beneficial to seek support from outside. This could be in the form of a mentor or a coach, someone who can provide guidance, perspective and encouragement. Participating in retreats or workshops can also be beneficial, offering the opportunity to connect with others facing similar challenges, learn new strategies for dealing with stress and gain inspiration and motivation.

CASE STUDY The role of a coach

In the context of driving change and ensuring that people's voices are heard, coaching assists leaders in navigating through the multifaceted challenges and opportunities that sustainability initiatives present. A coach, metaphorically helping transport a leader from point A to B, employs principles like active listening, trust building and encouraging potential to pave the way for transformative change. In light of well-being and the IDGs, coaching underpins the imperative of aligning one's inner state with outward actions and decisions, which is particularly critical when the objective is to embed sustainability into an organization's ethos. Coaching, in this context, is not just about performance but also about fostering a sense of purpose and well-being among leaders and teams. Simultaneously, leaders who are themselves in a stable state of well-being and whose actions resonate with their values are better positioned to inspire and drive change. This alignment, facilitated through coaching, not only enhances personal well-being but also catalyses a positive ripple effect across the organization, ensuring that sustainability is not just embedded but also practised authentically. In summary, coaching nurtures an environment where leaders are able to authentically embed sustainability by aligning organizational change with personal development and well-being. By facilitating a space where leaders are not just managers but also empathetic change-makers, coaching empowers organizations to move towards sustainability in a manner that is inclusive, authentic and, most importantly, sustainable in the long run.

Kristina Zumpolle, an experienced leadership consultant and author, shows how important coaching is for sustainable development, starting with personal change. She moved from a sales job to start her own leadership and coaching business, which was a big change for her both personally and professionally. Kristina believes that understanding yourself is key to building strong relationships with others and the environment. Her book *Finding Flow*, co-authored with Hanna Kiebert, talks about connecting with yourself, others and the planet. It suggests that real change comes from personal growth and encourages readers to think about how they can make a positive difference.[18]

Kristina uses various coaching methods, from individual sessions to large leadership programmes, to help people and groups find their purpose and reach their potential in line with sustainable development. When coaching someone, a key role is to help them make the unconscious conscious. As a coach, having an open mind and a curious attitude allows the person being coached to explore various life issues from multiple perspectives. This approach opens up new ways of seeing things; life is not just black and white, but filled with various shades and alternatives. Just because something has always been done a certain way, doesn't mean it must continue in that manner.

At times, one might feel that something is off, but without understanding why or what can be done about it. The distance between the mind and the body is short but can be challenging to navigate. Coaching helps bridge this gap, bringing clarity and new possibilities for change and growth. Kristina and her experience shows that coaching can be a powerful way to start changes and support sustainability from within. Her main advice is to focus on personal growth and think carefully about how to contribute positively to the world, making sure that personal development and caring for the planet go hand in hand.[19]

Growing and developing in your sustainability role

Regardless of your starting point, there's always room for improvement and continued growth in learning and development. The points below have been useful to us, and we believe they can be universally applicable and valuable, no matter your current position or future aspirations. Each of these points provides a stepping stone towards a more profound and impactful engagement in sustainability. By integrating these strategies into your approach, you position yourself not just as a participant in the sustainability movement, but as a driving force for change and innovation:

- **Continuous learning and education:** Immerse yourself in the study and research of social and environmental issues. Stay inquisitively engaged, constantly seeking new knowledge and understanding how you can contribute meaningfully. This continuous learning keeps you at the forefront of sustainability trends and solutions.
- **Sharing knowledge and collaboration:** Generously share your learnings and help others. In the field of sustainability, collaboration and knowledge sharing are more valuable than competition. By helping others, you contribute to a broader culture of sustainability.
- **Strategic networking:** Building a diverse network is vital. Connect with individuals from various fields and types of expertise relevant to sustainability. Start by pinpointing key people who can influence your work positively. Leverage your existing network to reach these individuals and groups, and make sure you're active on both physical and digital platforms where these conversations happen. Remember, it's often about giving support before expecting it in return.
- **Forming partnerships and alliances:** Recognize the power of collaboration. Sustainable change is seldom a solo endeavour; it involves collective effort and strong partnerships to effect system-wide changes.
- **Balanced ambition:** Be driven and authentic, yet pragmatic in your approach. It's crucial to understand that achieving perfection in sustainability initiatives isn't always immediate. It requires a blend of strong motivation and patience.
- **Opportunity-focused mindset:** While acknowledging the challenges, focus primarily on opportunities and progress.

- **Developing your skills:** Every skill set has a place in the sustainability transition. Focus on honing your skills to excel in your area of expertise. It is also beneficial to develop new skills in a completely different area. Learning a new language or instrument enhances cognitive functions, improves problem solving and multitasking abilities, and boosts memory, stress reduction and self-confidence.[20]
- **Resilience and patience:** Understand that change is often gradual. You might notice a 'ketchup effect', where numerous small actions accumulate to create substantial impact. Remember the discussions about exponential growth and movements from earlier chapters.

Summary and key take-aways

As a CSO, you are not just leading a company's sustainability transformation; you are influencing an entire ecosystem of stakeholders and shaping the future. The role of the CSO is a multifaceted role – a position we've identified as one of the most rewarding and crucial jobs of our era. From navigating all the internal and external challenges that come with the role to the deeply personal journey of finding purpose within this role, the CSO's path is as demanding as it is fulfilling. To maintain one's sanity amid such complexities, it's important to stay anchored to one's core values, to remain patient yet persistent and to celebrate the small victories along the way. It's also about the continual pursuit of growth, both personal and professional. In short, we hope that this chapter, and essentially this book, has shown you the following:

1. The challenge of sustainability is vast and not limited to any single function or organization. It requires a collective and interdisciplinary approach.
2. Embedding sustainability is everyone's responsibility. All individuals can contribute through their unique functions, roles and skills. Embedding sustainability in an organization requires a dual approach: both bottom-up through employee engagement, enabling individual initiative, and top-down through structural integration, ensuring sustainability is woven into the operating model, decision-making forums, role descriptions and budget processes.
3. The process of embedding sustainability, as outlined in this book, involves assessing the organization's current state; setting a strategic direction; organizing and structuring for sustainability; engaging with stakeholders

and managing change; focusing on reporting, learning and continuous improvement; and effective communication. This needs to be maintained as a continuous learning loop for lasting impact.

4. Leaders must also prioritize their personal leadership and well-being, recognizing that achieving sustainability is a long-term commitment, not a short-term race.
5. It is important to maintain a learning approach and an optimistic view of the future.

For those who hold this position, or aspire to, know that you stand at the confluence of passion, profession and purpose. You have the opportunity to make a difference not just in your company, but in the world. And while the road ahead is filled with uncertainty, it is also ripe with potential. So carry on with resolve and hope. Let the challenges invigorate you and the opportunities inspire you. In the story of our time, let the legacy of your leadership in sustainability be one of the chapters that future generations will look back on with gratitude, for you didn't just witness the change – you were the change.

Endnotes

1. Story found in Torgny Wirén (2019) *Djupare under ytan*, Verbum Förlag, Oslo
2. Ayse Yemiscigil, Melis Sena Yılmaz and Matthew T Lee. How to find your purpose, Harvard Business Review, 15 September 2023. hbr.org/2023/09/how-to-find-your-purpose (archived at https://perma.cc/53T8-GCBE)
3. Simon Sinek (2011) *Start With Why: How great leaders inspire everyone to take action*, Penguin, London
4. Hector Garcia and Francesc Miralles (2019) *Ikigai: den japanska livskonsten till ett långt och lyckligt liv*, Norstedts, Stockholm
5. See www.innerdevelopmentgoals.org (archived at https://perma.cc/7HC6-2FQT)
6. Catherine Bailey and Adrian Madden. What makes work meaningful – or meaningless, MIT Sloan Management Review, 1 June 2016. sloanreview.mit.edu/article/what-makes-work-meaningful-or-meaningless/#ref2 (archived at https://perma.cc/YK7Q-Q7W5)
7. Björn Lindeblad Natthiko (2023) *I May Be Wrong*, Bloomsbury, London
8. Chrissa Pagitsas (2022) *Chief Sustainability Officers at Work: How CSOs build successful sustainability and ESG strategies*, APress, New York
9. 4th Annual CSR Insights Survey, Association of Corporate Citizenship Professionals (ACCP), Summer 2023. accp.org/resources/csr-resources/4th-annual-csr-insights-survey/ (archived at https://perma.cc/LS46-MGQA)

10 Mark Segal. Over 90% of companies planning to increase environmental sustainability budget over next year: Honeywell, ESG Today, 1 November 2022. www.esgtoday.com/over-90-of-companies-planning-to-increase-environmental-sustainability-budget-over-next-year-honeywell/ (archived at https://perma.cc/9QXS-GUWE)

11 Dennis Farcinsen Leth. Review of Manifesto for a moral revolution, LinkedIn, 27 March 2021. www.linkedin.com/pulse/review-manifesto-moral-revolution-dennis-farcinsen-leth/ (archived at https://perma.cc/MD3M-SEHK)

12 Alexa Mikhail. Neuroscientist Andrew Huberman says these 5 daily habits are key to optimal mental and physical health, Fortune, 5 September 2023. fortune.com/well/2023/09/05/andrew-huberman-daily-habits-optimal-mental-physical-health/ (archived at https://perma.cc/8YUG-TRW4)

13 Erin Urban. Seven self-care strategies of successful leaders, *Forbes*, 21 February 2020. www.forbes.com/sites/forbescoachescouncil/2020/02/21/seven-self-care-strategies-of-successful-leaders/ (archived at https://perma.cc/P8QB-VJLJ); Dana Berri. How can you integrate self-care practices into your leadership routine? LinkedIn, 10 November 2023. www.linkedin.com/advice/0/how-can-you-integrate-self-care-practices-your-leadership-gglie (archived at https://perma.cc/9G7R-FGXU)

14 Björn Lindeblad Natthiko (2023) *I May Be Wrong*, Bloomsbury, London

15 Ron McIntyre. History of the 'mean world syndrome' and ways to cope, Medium, 21 September 2023. ronmci.medium.com/history-of-the-mean-world-syndrome-and-ways-to-cope-278dd0df27a7 (archived at https://perma.cc/JR5C-55YA)

16 Zaria Gorvett. How the news changes the way we think and behave, BBC News, 12 May 2020. www.bbc.com/future/article/20200512-how-the-news-changes-the-way-we-think-and-behave (archived at https://perma.cc/E3RD-6NH9)

17 Paul Hawken (2018) *Drawdown: The most comprehensive plan ever proposed to reverse global warming*, Penguin, London

18 Kristina Zumpolle and Hanna Kiebert (2020) *Finding Flow: Vind verbinding met jezelf, anderen en de planeet*, Zumflow, Blaricum

19 Interview conducted December 2021

20 Baycrest Centre for Geriatric Care. Learning music or speaking another language leads to more efficient brains, Science Daily, 17 May 2018. www.sciencedaily.com/releases/2018/05/180517123254.htm (archived at https://perma.cc/B3PG-G3H2)

Key principles of effective sustainability leadership

11

This final chapter outlines 12 key principles that form the bedrock of effective sustainability leadership. They are not complete, and others might find other principles helpful; however, they are a summary of key learnings that we have both taken from our work with embedding sustainability in large organizations, and they thus summarize this book. Some of these principles might feel familiar, echoing the values we've threaded throughout our discussions in the earlier chapters. Others might be new ideas that can spark fresh insights.

Principles are those core beliefs and values that help a leader make choices and take actions that are not just effective, but also right and good. These principles shape how leaders interact with their teams, make important decisions and handle the responsibilities that come with their role. Our hope is that these principles will be like helpful signposts for you, guiding you towards successful and sustainable leadership.

Use a human-centric and positive view on people and the future

In this book, we have adopted a human-centred approach, placing people at the heart of our sustainability efforts and the integration of sustainability within organizations. Additionally, we wish to highlight that although the world can sometimes be malevolent and people may act harmfully, we firmly believe that, at their core, *humans are inherently good and strive to do good.*

This sentiment is echoed in Rutger Bregman's book *Humankind: A Hopeful History*, discussed in Part 2, and it is a key message we hope you, as the reader, will take to heart.[1]

It's crucial in leadership to adopt a positive outlook, to see people in a favourable light and to interpret their actions in a broader context. Ask yourself: what lies behind their actions? What can be done to create optimal conditions?

Our fundamental belief is unwavering: when given the opportunity, people will choose to act virtuously. Our worldview is tinged with optimism, recognizing the innate goodness in humanity despite the obvious presence of hatred and malevolence.

We must openly acknowledge that much of the world's hostility and violence arise from injustice and unequal conditions. It's no accident that terrorist organizations often emerge in areas plagued by poverty and a lack of alternatives. When presented with better opportunities, the majority of people will undoubtedly choose such opportunities. Applying this understanding to various situations reveals that many are unwittingly constrained by systems that inadvertently limit our capacity to make ethical decisions. This is due to a range of factors, such as restrictive job roles, reward systems and reporting mechanisms, which may unintentionally steer individuals towards less virtuous paths.

Social and environmental sustainability goes hand in hand

One cannot care about children, and not about nature. Or about health, and not about climate. Or poverty and not biodiversity. These topics are all interconnected. Sustainability is equally about people; it is as much about diversity, gender and inclusion as it is about the environment. In other words, we cannot achieve sustainability if we fail to recognize the interconnectedness of environmental and social issues, and sustainability's dependence on economic responsibility. By taking a holistic approach, we can work towards creating a more sustainable world that benefits both people and the planet, for a fair, just and liveable planet and society. That is why there are 17 SDGs, covering a wide spectrum of sustainability topics.

The interconnectedness of social and environmental sustainability is a truth that remains undeniable in today's global context. Caring about our children's future inevitably requires us to extend the same care to our natural world, as the health and vitality of both are intertwined. Similarly, taking measures to improve public health without addressing climate change is a futile endeavour, as climate-related hazards pose significant risks to our collective well-being. Likewise, striving to alleviate poverty while ignoring biodiversity loss would be a misguided approach, considering that biodiversity underpins our global food system and serves as a lifeline for billions of people, particularly those living in poverty.

Sustainability, therefore, cannot be a fragmented or siloed effort. It must be holistic, including people in all their diversity and the environmental ecosystems they inhabit. As such, the path to sustainability does not involve only 'going green' or promoting economic growth. It also entails advocating gender equality, enhancing diversity, fostering inclusion and upholding social justice, all of which are integral components of a truly sustainable society.

Our efforts to mitigate climate change, protect biodiversity and transition to a low-carbon economy will be significantly bolstered when paired with strategies to eradicate poverty, promote health and education and enhance social equity. By acknowledging and acting upon this interdependence, we can develop comprehensive solutions that reflect the multifaceted reality of sustainability.

In essence, sustainability is a shared endeavour that requires us to consider not only the well-being of the planet but also the welfare of all people. This comprehensive, integrated approach has the potential to create transformative change. It gives us an opportunity to reshape our world in a way that ensures a prosperous and sustainable future for all. By working collectively and collaboratively, we can bring about a world where both people and the planet thrive.

EXAMPLE Social and environmental interdependency

Let's take the example of deforestation in Indonesia, which presents critical challenges. Smallholder farmers often resort to tree clearing to sustain livelihoods, but this leads to habitat destruction for various species, the cultivation of monocultures and environmental degradation. This cycle negatively affects communities and prompts youth migration from rural areas. Kulaku, an Indonesian social enterprise, confronts these issues by enhancing coconut farmers' income. They assist farmers in transforming raw coconuts into high-value products, simultaneously offering educational scholarships to farmers' children. This approach helps counteract the necessity for deforestation by providing sustainable, economically viable alternatives, illustrating how interconnected social and environmental solutions can be.[2]

Now imagine a wildlife reserve that is located near impoverished communities. The local residents might resort to poaching as a means of survival. These communities often face limited economic opportunities, and the immediate financial gain from poaching can be seen as a necessary means to provide for their families. In such cases, even though poaching is illegal and harmful to wildlife, the local residents' pressing need to survive can outweigh these concerns. Now, imagine an alternative approach where conservation efforts are combined with community development. In this model, the wildlife reserve works closely with the surrounding communities, providing them with sustainable livelihood opportunities related to conservation. This could include jobs in ecotourism, wildlife monitoring and conservation education. By being directly involved in and benefiting from the conservation efforts, the local residents would develop a sense of ownership and pride in protecting wildlife. With their basic needs met through sustainable means, the incentive to engage in poaching would diminish significantly.

In both scenarios, the fundamental needs and capabilities of the local communities are the same. However, the approach to conservation and community involvement dramatically alters their behaviour. When provided with viable economic alternatives and a sense of being part of the conservation solution, communities are more likely to engage in protecting wildlife. Conversely, in the absence of such opportunities and facing dire economic challenges, they may resort to poaching as a means of survival.

Everyone is welcome

Sustainability is not only for the people who seem to be doing everything right already. Embedding sustainability into everything we do is a universal challenge, not an exclusive club for the 'scouts' or the 'dark greens'. The fabric of a truly sustainable world is woven from the threads of everyone's efforts, big and small, expert or novice. The task of fostering sustainability, therefore, doesn't rest solely upon the shoulders of dedicated sustainability teams or those with specialized knowledge in this arena. No matter where you are in your personal or professional journey, your participation is not just wanted – it's crucial. We need everyone to be involved and engaged. Inclusive and welcoming approaches are vital in driving forward the sustainability agenda for other reasons too. The ripple effect of positive reinforcement has immense potential. It not only encourages individuals to embrace sustainable practices but also fosters an environment of continual improvement, innovation and collective growth. By building upon this momentum, we create a resonant energy that propels our journey towards a greener, healthier and more harmonious world.

On an organizational level, it's important for companies and innovators to actively collaborate and extend a hand to others. This means inviting diverse partners to contribute to solutions, sharing knowledge and breakthroughs openly. Such collaboration accelerates the journey towards a just and equitable transition. By working together and pooling resources and ideas, we can make significant strides in sustainability more efficiently and effectively.

Let's remember, it's the consistent and cumulative impact of small actions that make a colossal difference. So, no matter your background, experience or expertise, your contribution is valuable. You are needed in this universal mission towards sustainability. Together, we can, and we will, shape a more sustainable world – a testament to the power of collective action.

Stay optimistic

Creating a sustainable world is no small feat. It is, without a doubt, a serious commitment that involves global collaboration, perseverance and forward-thinking strategies. The vitality of our planet, the health and well-being of all species and the future of our children hinge on our actions today. Indeed, the stakes are high. Sustainability is serious business. It's about life and death. It's about the future of our children.

However, the journey towards sustainability doesn't have to be a sombre one. To be able to work with it on a daily basis, one must also laugh and make it fun. Otherwise, we will not last as leaders. And we will not bring people along. Thus, the importance of this journey does not preclude a space for laughter, joy and inspiration. It's critical to remember that the human spirit thrives on positivity, and this is especially true when we face challenges. Therefore, integrating joy and fun into our sustainable initiatives is not just an option; it's a necessity.

As leaders in sustainability, we need to remain resilient, and a positive mindset can help us immensely. If we approach this work with a sense of doom and gloom, we risk falling into despair and discouragement. Moreover, we may unintentionally deter people from joining the cause if we paint an overly bleak picture. Doomism – and a feeling that it is too late to act – is as dangerous as denial.

So, let's bring humour, creativity and optimism into our everyday work. By making our mission engaging and uplifting, we can create a more inviting space for people to contribute their ideas and energy. This is where fun and engaging methods like workshops, idea generation tools and gamification can play a pivotal role. They help to break down complex concepts into more digestible and accessible ideas. It's essential to strike a balance between conveying the gravity of our situation and inspiring hope for the future. When we nurture this balance, we counteract the dangers of both doomism and denial. We acknowledge the reality of our situation while also affirming our capacity to address it.

EXAMPLE Solution-based and optimistic approach

Books like *Factfulness* by Hans Rosling and *Drawdown* by Paul Hawken offer optimistic perspectives on development and focus on solution-based approaches, which can be essential in maintaining a positive outlook.[3]

Christiana Figueres, in her podcast *Outrage and Optimism*, underscores the importance of balancing outrage with optimism. Despite challenges like inadequate policies and the fossil fuel industry's focus on profits over renewable investments, she emphasizes reasons for hope, such as advancements in renewable energy and electric vehicles.[4]

Solitaire Townsend serves as yet another example of a business leader advocating for an optimistic approach to sustainability. As the co-founder of Futerra, a leading sustainability agency, she has been instrumental in shaping influential sustainability strategies for global organizations. Her advocacy emphasizes the power of human creativity in addressing environmental and social challenges. Townsend's optimistic perspective on sustainability underscores the potential for positive change, inspiring others in the business community to adopt a similarly hopeful and proactive mindset in tackling climate issues.[5]

Celebrate successes

Sustainability is about holistic and systemic change. Indeed, high ambition is vital in sustainability, and we should always aim high. However, we need to remember that big change comes from taking that very first step in the right direction. We need to value incremental progress and small victories, as they are the building blocks of the larger transformation we seek. While our instincts often compel us to aim for drastic transformations, we must not lose sight of the profound potential of smaller, incremental changes, especially when they occur on a large scale. Each step taken, each initiative implemented and each percentage point improved is a stride towards a more sustainable world. And each deserves to be celebrated.

Progress, no matter how small it may seem, is movement in the right direction, and it's always a better alternative to perfectionism, which may result in inaction and paralysis. When we highlight and celebrate the progress we have made, we are not only motivating ourselves to become and do *even better*, but also stirring a wave of inspiration that could spur others to follow suit.

Thus, celebrating progress, rather than shaming or judging, is key. Movement is better than perfection. By recognizing and applauding progress, we can build momentum and inspire others to take action towards creating a more sustainable world. At our core, we believe in celebrating every step taken towards this shared goal, not criticizing the size or pace of the stride. There's no room for blame, shame or judgement in the path towards a sustainable future – only for recognition, support and encouragement.

Make sustainability the easy choice

To make sustainable behaviour mainstream, we need to make sustainability the easy and obvious choice for individuals and organizations alike. By making sustainable choices more accessible and appealing, we can create a culture where sustainability is the norm rather than the exception. This can be accomplished through various methods, including offering superior sustainable products, the use of strategic nudging, the systematic removal of barriers to sustainable behaviour and the provision of incentives that reward such actions. Think of a carrot rather than a stick.

A pivotal aspect of this approach is to ensure that the sustainable products and solutions we develop outshine their less eco-friendly alternatives. They should not just be marginally better; they need to be significantly superior in terms of simplicity, efficiency and intelligence. These products and solutions should be meticulously designed for mass adoption, with ease of integration into everyday life and standard business practices at their core. They should be designed with mainstream adoption in mind, so that individuals and organizations can easily integrate them into their daily routines. This makes it easier for individuals and organizations to seamlessly incorporate them into their daily routines, thus transforming sustainability from a daunting challenge into an effortless habit.

To foster a widespread culture of sustainable living and working practices, it is crucial to make sustainability not just a viable option, but the most convenient and beneficial choice for both individuals and organizations. This goes beyond merely providing these options; it involves strategically presenting them in such a way that their benefits are clearly understood and appreciated, fostering a desire among people to choose them over less sustainable alternatives. In striving for these goals, we need to work towards enhancing the accessibility and attractiveness of sustainable choices. With the right mix of convenience, benefit and appeal, we can foster a cultural shift towards sustainability. The objective is to create a society in which sustainability is not just an alternative or an aspiration, but the universally accepted norm.

EXAMPLE Make sustainability the easy choice

Take a seemingly straightforward example regarding waste management practices, where we uncovered significant shortcomings. Plastics, cardboard and even spare parts were frequently discarded into residual waste, which is not only detrimental to the environment but also incurs heightened costs for the company. What was the cause of this? Despite being knowledgeable about waste sorting, employees were not adhering to the guidelines. The reason, as we discovered, was remarkably simple: the residual waste container was positioned closest to the entrance, leading busy co-workers to dispose of items in the most conveniently located container. Our solution was straightforward yet effective: we rearranged the order of the containers, positioning receptacles for plastics and cardboard more accessibly for co-workers and placing the container for residual waste further away. Additionally, we implemented clear communication strategies, reminding co-workers why we sort waste. We used green signs to indicate waste fractions providing income, and red for those incurring costs. This minimal adjustment significantly reduced waste contamination and amplified our recycling levels. Making it straightforward for people to act rightly is imperative.

Speak your stakeholder's language

Understanding the perspective of your stakeholders is the first key step in communicating the importance of sustainability in a meaningful way. Recognizing these concerns, and finding a way to make sustainability an engaging, relevant and uncomplicated topic is our central task. Tailor your communications to resonate with the stakeholders' existing concerns and aspirations.

There might be myriad concerns clouding stakeholders' minds – unfamiliarity with the concept, perceived high costs or a plethora of other tasks in their busy schedules – and sustainability may not be at the top of their list. This doesn't mean they don't care about it; it simply implies that they have not yet realized the direct connection between sustainability and their own goals.

Take the time to understand their objectives, aspirations and needs, and then look for intersections. By delving deeper, you'll likely discover points of interest that resonate with you. From there, build arguments to bridge the divide and come to a common understanding. To bring them on board, connect sustainability to what they already care about. For instance, financial benefits might be realized from investing in solar energy; introducing a circular repair model might result in job creation and greater commitment to work, as well as an improvement in health and well-being figures. Whether the stakeholders' aims are to attract top talent, reduce costs, boost sales or enhance their brand, demonstrate how sustainability can help them achieve these objectives.

To make sustainability truly matter to your stakeholders, it's important to link it to their core values. Show them that by embracing sustainable practices, they're not just doing good for the environment, but also living up to their values and enhancing their reputations. This way, you're not asking them to prioritize something new, but reinforcing their commitment to what they already believe in. Show how it connects to their values and who they are. Remember, the goal is not to convince stakeholders that sustainability is an essential component they should care about, but to illuminate how it is already intertwined with their existing priorities, their values and the very essence of their business. Making sustainability a priority shouldn't be an added burden; instead, it should be seen as a strategic initiative that can propel stakeholders towards their own goals in a more resourceful, resilient and responsible way.

Be creative

Sustainability, much like digitalization, is a powerful disruptor, with the potential to reshape businesses, communities and societies. It is an arena where the boundaries of creativity are expanded, where old systems are challenged and where novel ideas are born. More than just a business strategy, sustainability embodies a new way of thinking – a mindset that encourages continuous evolution and improvement. Sustainability can be an exciting innovation process. The pathway towards this objective might differ from traditional product or service development approaches. However, it's the distinctive framework that renders it a catalyst for out-of-the-box thinking, inciting us to look beyond the conventional and the familiar. Done right, it helps the organization to take big leaps forward.

By integrating sustainability into our organizational DNA, we unlock an array of possibilities. We stand on the precipice of creating better products, establishing more efficient services and shaping more resilient business models. Sustainability fosters a culture of curiosity, exploration and creativity that not only enables us to navigate today's complex landscape but also gear us up for the unknown future. Imagine a clothing company that initiates zero-waste designs, utilizing every inch of fabric to reduce waste. The company sources sustainable materials, like fabrics from recycled plastics, adding uniqueness to its products. They implement a circular fashion model, encouraging customers to return used items for refurbishment or recycling. Thus, rather than getting inspiration from the latest catwalks, the inspiration comes from waste.

Sustainability provides an unparalleled opportunity for organizations to reinvent themselves and take significant strides towards their envisioned future. Let's embrace the challenge. Let's reimagine our limits and harness the disruptive power of sustainability to catalyse our journey towards achieving monumental milestones.

EXAMPLE Think outside the box

Everlane's marketing campaign creatively addressed the issue of plastic waste in the fashion industry. They juxtaposed an image of a discarded plastic bottle in the sea with a photo of someone donning a jacket made from recycled polyester. The accompanying text cleverly contrasted 'warming the planet' with 'warming you', highlighting the environmental benefits of using recycled materials in clothing. This campaign not only raised awareness about sustainability in fashion but also showcased how recycled materials can be transformed into stylish and functional apparel.

Expanding on the concept of creativity, Chapter 3 discussed the idea of striving for symbiosis within ecosystems. This approach involves identifying opportunities where waste or by-products in one part of a system can be repurposed as resources or inputs in another. Such symbiotic relationships are key to creating circular economies, where the life cycle of materials is extended and waste is minimized. By reimagining waste as a valuable resource, businesses can innovate sustainable solutions that benefit both the environment and the economy, fostering a more balanced and efficient use of resources.

Show your flaws

It's often said that honesty is the best policy, and this holds true in the professional world as much as anywhere else. However, transparency and openness about sustainability challenges can often seem counter-intuitive to businesses. The fear is that admitting shortcomings might undermine their green credentials in the eyes of their consumers. However, not being open and transparent carries its own set of risks. Instead of concealing your flaws, have the courage to expose them. Dare to be open and transparent. Dare to be vulnerable. Being open about your imperfections doesn't mean you're incapable; on the contrary, it shows your willingness to learn, grow and improve. It's okay if you haven't reached your desired level of proficiency yet – after all, progress is a journey, not a destination. Embrace these imperfections and allow them to become a testament to your authenticity.

Perhaps you are not there yet. Admit that and invite others (individuals, teams or organizations) to join and help you on the journey. Proactively share your development plans, discuss your challenges openly and welcome constructive feedback. This will not only strengthen the bonds of trust within your team, but also build your reputation as an organization that values honesty and continuous learning. Remember, the path to success is not about being perfect; it's about being real, being open and being ready to grow. Your willingness to show your flaws can be your greatest strength.

In conclusion, while it's understandable that businesses might be hesitant to be open about their sustainability challenges, the risks of not doing so can far outweigh the benefits. Transparency fosters trust, encourages collaboration, enhances regulatory compliance and drives innovation. In the long run, businesses that embrace openness and transparency about their sustainability challenges are likely to be more successful in their journey towards true sustainability.

Collaborate with others

Expanding the journey towards a sustainable future is not a solo expedition, but a group endeavour. The essence of collaboration lies in the belief that no one individual or entity has all the solutions. It is collective wisdom and joint effort that propel us towards innovation and transformation. Thus, by fostering a sense of community and interconnectedness, we create a foundation for sustainable progress. By inviting collaborators, critics and various other stakeholders into the conversation, we encourage a constructive dialogue that can help us shape a brighter future. Such collaboration also underlines the importance of understanding your role in a broader ecosystem and societal system, where the actions of one organization are interconnected with the others.

Communication is key. Create platforms where employees and other relevant stakeholders can share ideas, feedback and concerns. Encourage friendly competition and criticism to spur innovative thinking and foster an environment that rewards sustainability-focused initiatives. An inclusive, participatory culture where everyone feels seen and heard boosts morale and cultivates a shared sense of purpose. Education is another cornerstone in this collaborative effort. Equip your teams with the knowledge and tools they need to contribute effectively. Tailor your educational approach to meet individuals at their level of understanding and involvement. This ensures that everyone, regardless of their role or department, can actively participate and contribute their unique insights.

By recognizing that sustainability is a shared responsibility, we can foster a sense of community and work towards a more sustainable future together. It is only through collaboration and a collective effort that we can achieve lasting change. By creating an inclusive, engaging and educated community, we are not just working towards sustainability – we are building a resilient, future-focused organization. It is this unity and shared dedication that will drive us towards a more sustainable, prosperous and brighter future.

Give it all you've got

Sustainability isn't a journey of small, incremental steps – it's about transformative, substantial change. Working with sustainability is, therefore, not about cheese slicing. It will only cause confusion. And besides that, we simply don't have the time. So go all in. Set the bar high and strive for excellence. Set clear and ambitious targets. Thus, don't hesitate to fully commit, to dive in headfirst. Shift your gaze towards the horizon of possibilities. Envision the sustainable future we aspire to create, and let this image serve as your guiding star.

Having a lofty goal, and a North Star, isn't enough. We need to pair this vision with a detailed road map, clearly marking our short-term and long-term milestones. This way, we have a concrete plan of action for tomorrow, next week and the years to come. The road map will keep us grounded, ensuring that we not only dream of a greener future in 10 years, but also take the right steps each day to make that future a reality.

However, bear in mind that meaningful change doesn't happen overnight. It's okay if the solutions aren't immediately apparent. Remember that the essence of innovation lies in exploration and learning, not in having all the answers upfront. So, it is acceptable to let change take (some) time, and to not have all the answers at once. Focus on where and what we want and dream of, rather than what we want to avoid. It's all about balancing audacity with practicality, and commitment with patience. As we journey towards a more sustainable future, let's do so with purpose, passion and determination. After all, we're in it for the long run.

EXAMPLE Go all in!

Kresse Wesling and James Henrit, the driving forces behind the social enterprise Elvis & Kresse, embody the spirit of 'giving it all you've got' in sustainability and social impact. They've taken a bold stance, through not just working with waste but actively eradicating fire hose waste in the UK. Their commitment extends to providing employment opportunities for individuals who face challenges entering the workforce.

In tackling leather waste, they're setting their sights on another ambitious goal: waste elimination. This luxury bag brand isn't just about fashion; it's a beacon of holistic sustainability. By turning discarded fire hoses into high-end products and partnering with brands like Burberry to rescue leather, they're redefining luxury. Their ventures into regenerative agriculture and sustainable living are further proof of their all-encompassing approach. Elvis & Kresse's journey is a testament to the power of integrating sustainability into every facet of a business, serving as a trailblazing model for environmental solutions and sustainable innovation.

Cover the basics while finding new ways forward

Sustainability is as much about management – for example securing set goals, following up on their performance and complying with legislation – as it is about leadership in the form of setting ambitious road maps that inspire people to join the movement and enabling your organization to contribute to the SDGs. Maintaining a strong foundation in reporting and compliance may not seem like the most thrilling prospect, yet these components play a fundamental role in shaping a responsible and sustainable business model, as they provide transparency and set a minimum base.

From reading this book, you'll have gleaned that sustainability should be deeply embedded in the business model, decision-making processes, values and core mission statement of an organization. However, embracing sustainability is fundamentally a transformative journey. To maintain momentum and energy within the organization, this approach is essential. Thus, sustainability can be much more than just satisfying the regulatory benchmarks; it can become an inspirational instrument for fostering employee engagement, sparking innovation and fueling business development. Consider the integration of sustainability as an exciting journey rather than merely a compliance checkbox. Imagine initiatives and projects that are not only beneficial for the environment but that also enthuse team members and stakeholders. Furthermore, such initiatives generate meaningful stories to share with your community and customers, further strengthening your brand's connection with sustainability.

Endnotes

1 Rutger Bregman (2021) *Humankind: A hopeful history*, Bloomsbury, London

2 Kulaku Indonesia, Instagram. www.instagram.com/kulaku.indonesia/ (archived at https://perma.cc/N42P-GPZN)

3 Hans Rosling (2019) *Factfulness: Ten reasons we are wrong about the world and why things are better than you think*, Hodder Stoughton, London; Paul Hawken (2018) *Drawdown: The most comprehensive plan ever proposed to reverse global warming*, Penguin, London

4 Vikas Shah. A conversation with Christiana Figueres, one of the architects of the Paris Agreement & co-founder of Global Optimism, Thought Economics, 19 October 2023. thoughteconomics.com/christiana-figueres/ (archived at https://perma.cc/U5ND-ZF4M)

5 Solitaire Townsend's Ted Talk, Futerra. www.wearefuterra.com/thinks/solitaire-townsend-ted-talk (archived at https://perma.cc/QK7S-BX2X)

Closing remarks

12

Sustainability is essentially about building a better world for today and tomorrow. It emphasizes the importance of maintaining optimism and collective action during difficult periods to drive positive change towards a more sustainable and equitable world. The focus is on harnessing challenging moments as opportunities for collaboration and progress in achieving sustainability goals. We strive to ensure that the joys of skiing down a snow-laden mountain, snorkeling amidst vibrant coral reefs and witnessing the marvel of diverse species continue to exist for future generations. And we aspire to preserve a liveable environment, where we can keep working outdoors as temperatures remain at a manageable level and where the negative health impacts of climate change do not get out of control. The goal is to hand over a thriving planet, not one that is merely surviving. Broadening our scope, we aspire towards a world that upholds justice and equality. Sustainability isn't restricted to our physical environment; it's about nurturing humanity, eradicating poverty and starvation, promoting peace and driving equality.

Hopefully we are clear throughout this book: continuing with our old ways is no longer viable. We must adopt new ways of thinking and acting, with a focus on the interconnectedness of our actions and their impacts. This involves greater care for our planet, improving our relationships with each other and thinking beyond our immediate needs. Individual efforts, no matter how small, contribute to this change. We've witnessed incredible acts of kindness, collaboration and innovation, especially in difficult times, demonstrating people's capacity for positive change.

Sustainability is not a project, or a strategic objective; it's a long-term commitment rooted in the love for our planet and its inhabitants, including those yet unborn. This work is not solely about us, but about the legacy we leave behind for our children, our grandchildren and subsequent generations. We are crafting a sustainable future where they have the opportunity to breathe clean air, drink pure water and partake in a food system that provides healthy, affordable food for all. Our collective ambition is encapsulated in the UN's SDGs, the realization of which would signify a future that's better for both people and the planet. As depicted in the documentary *Decade of Action*, leaders are articulating their commitments to future generations by writing letters to their grandchildren. One such quote resonates deeply: 'We are crafting the future not as an obligation, but as a love letter to you. Every step towards sustainability is a pledge, a promise that you will inherit a world where you can not only survive but thrive and live in harmony with nature.'[1]

As we wrap up our exploration of embedding sustainability, we remain optimistic. The solutions are not just on the horizon; they're here, awaiting widespread and fast adoption. The momentum we witness today is palpable, with many entities making notable strides in sustainability. This momentum has been amplified by investors, the financial industry and evolving legal frameworks, all of which have sustainability high on their agendas. Drawing inspiration from Paul Hawken's words, we firmly believe that businesses stand as unique entities capable of driving monumental change.[2] The potential is vast, and the opportunity is golden.

As a reader and leader, you have the power to initiate and drive change: by making sustainability and social impact the job of everyone, everywhere. By truly embedding sustainability at the heart of your organization, you're not just driving business growth; you're contributing significantly to a more resilient and sustainable society. The future beckons, and it's a journey we must undertake together.

In essence, our pursuit of sustainability is a testament to our faith in humanity's capacity to evolve and create a world that isn't just sustainable, but flourishing. Through our actions, we are ensuring this vision becomes reality, passing on a healthier, more equitable and more beautiful world to future generations. Yet, our optimism is tempered with concern. The urgent question remains: can we accelerate our efforts to match the pressing timeline that our planet demands? The challenges of social unrest, global conflicts and an increasingly polarized world further amplify the urgency. As Winston Churchill said on 10 November 1942, 'Now this is not the end. It is not even the beginning of the end. But it is, perhaps, the end of the beginning.'

Thank you so much for taking the time to read this book. We genuinely hope that you have gotten some new insights, inspiration and encouragement to continue your path of contributing to sustainability through your work.

Although it does not always seem that way, we truly believe we are gearing up for a more sustainable and inclusive world. It will not happen without effort. But it will happen because of people and change-makers like you. It will happen in our workplaces. And we should remember that even small changes can have an impact. It starts with one person, one action, which can lead to systems change.

Please do not hesitate to reach out or ask questions.

Good luck with your journey!

Endnotes

1 Wim Vermeulen and Bart Lombaerts. *Decade of Action*, documentary, 2020. www.youtube.com/watch?v=yCuheTKZA88 (archived at https://perma.cc/2NBS-TS2J)

2 Paul Hawken (2018) *Drawdown: The most comprehensive plan ever proposed to reverse global warming*, Penguin, London

INDEX

Note: Page numbers in *italics* refer to tables or figures.

Also from Kogan Page

ISBN: 9781398602748

ISBN: 9781398604049

ISBN: 9781398612242

ISBN: 9781398614246

www.koganpage.com

KoganPage

EU Representative (GPSR)

Authorised Rep Compliance Ltd, Ground Floor, 71 Lower Baggot Street, Dublin, D02 P593, Ireland

www.arccompliance.com

www.ingramcontent.com/pod-product-compliance
Lightning Source LLC
Chambersburg PA
CBHW062022110925
32450CB00041B/277
* 9 7 8 1 3 9 8 6 1 5 8 0 9 *